Rick Steves

BARCELONA

D0126542

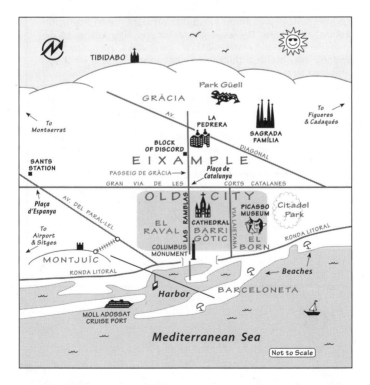

Welcome to Rick Steves' Europe

Travel is intensified living—maximum thrills per minute and one of the last great sources of legal adventure. Travel is freedom. It's recess, and we need it.

I discovered a passion for European travel as a teen and have been sharing it ever since—through my tours, public television and radio shows, and travel guidebooks. Over the years, I've taught thousands of travelers how to best enjoy Europe's blockbuster sights—and experience "Back Door" discoveries that most tourists miss.

This book offers you a balanced mix of Barcelona's blockbuster sights and lesser-known gems. It's selective: Rather than listing dozens of tapas bars, I recommend only the best ones. And it's in-depth: My self-guided sight tours and city walks provide insight into the city's vibrant history and today's living, breathing culture.

I advocate traveling simply and smartly. Take advantage of my money- and time-saving tips on sightseeing, transportation, and more. Try local, characteristic alternatives to expensive hotels and restaurants. In many ways, spending more money only builds a thicker wall between you and what you traveled so far to see.

We visit Barcelona to experience it—to become temporary locals. Thoughtful travel engages us with the world, as we learn to appreciate other cultures and new ways to measure quality of life.

Judging by the positive feedback I receive from readers, this book will help you enjoy a fun, affordable, and rewarding vacation—whether it's your first trip or your tenth.

Bon viatge! Happy travels!

Rick Steves

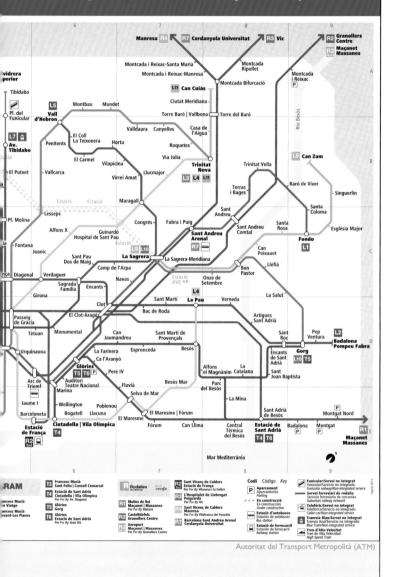

ed Ferroviaria Integrada Central *Central Integrated Railway Network*

Manresa **R4** ← **R7** Cerdanyola Universitat → **R3** Vic → **R2** Granollers Centre
R2 Maçanet Massanes

vidrera perior

Tibidabo
Pl. del Funicular

L7 **Av. Tibidabo**

El Putxet

Vallcarca

Pl. Molina

Fontana

ça | Diagonal

Passeig de Gràcia

Tetuan

Urquinaona

Arc de Triomf

Jaume I

Barceloneta

Estació de França
R2

Montbau | Mundet
L5 **Vall d'Hebron**

El Coll La Teixonera | Horta
Penitents
El Carmel | Vilapicina
Virrei Amat
Llucmajor

Lesseps | Estació | Estació
Alfons X
Joanic | Guinardó Hospital de Sant Pau | Estació
L9 **L10** Sant Pau Dos de Maig
La Sagrera
Verdaguer | Camp de l'Arpa
Sagrada Família | Encants | Navas
Girona | Clot
El Clot-Aragó
Monumental | Can Jaumandreu
La Farinera
Ca l'Aranyó
T5 **T6** **P**
Glòries | Pere IV
Auditori Teatre Nacional | Fluvià
Marina
Wellington | Poblenou
Bogatell | Llacuna
El Maresme
Ciutadella | Vila Olímpica
T4 | Fòrum | Can Llima

Montcada i Reixac-Santa Maria
Montcada i Reixac-Manresa
Montcada Ripollet
Montcada Bifurcació
L11 **Can Cuiàs**
Ciutat Meridiana
Torre Baró | Vallbona ← Torre del Baró
Valldaura | Canyelles
Casa de l'Aigua
Roquetes
Via Júlia
Trinitat Nova
L3 **L4** **L11**
Congrés | Fabra i Puig | Sant Andreu
Sant Andreu Arenal
R7
La Sagrera-Meridiana
Sant Martí | **La Pau** | Verneda
Bac de Roda
Sant Martí de Provençals | Besòs
Espronceda
Alfons el Magnànim | La Catalana
Besòs Mar
Selva de Mar | Parc del Besòs
La Mina
El Maresme | Fòrum
Central Tèrmica del Besòs

Mar Mediterrània

Montcada i Reixac **P**

Riu Besòs

Trinitat Vella
Torras i Bages
L9 **Can Zam**
Baró de Viver | Singuerlin
Santa Coloma
Santa Rosa | Església Major
Can Peixauet
Llefià | **Fondo** **L1**
La Salut
Artigues Sant Adrià
Sant Roc | Pep Ventura | **L2** **Badalona Pompeu Fabra**
Gorg
Encants de Sant Adrià **L10** **T5**
Sant Joan Baptista
Sant Adrià de Besòs
Estació de Sant Adrià
T4 **T6** | Badalona **P** | Montgat **P** | Montgat Nord **P**
R1 Maçanet Massanes

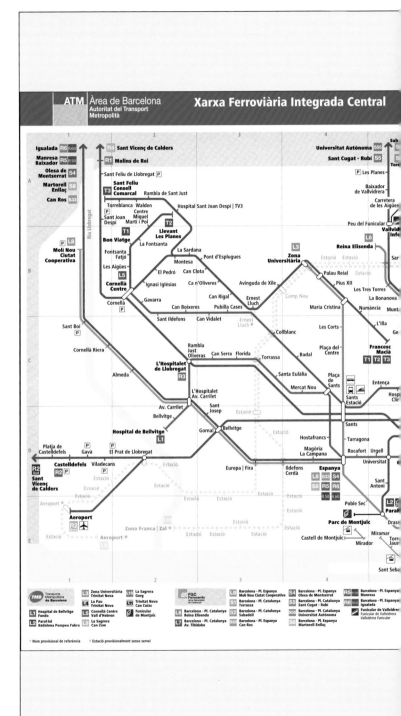

ATM | Àrea de Barcelona
Autoritat del Transport Metropolità
Xarxa Ferroviària Integrada Central

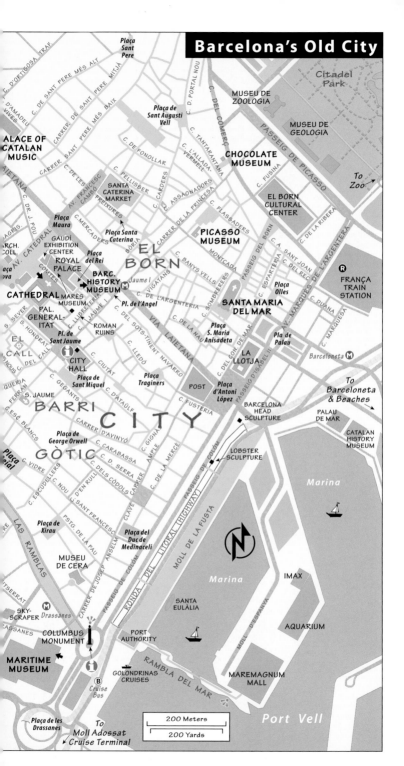

Barcelona's Old City

Plaça Sant Pere

C. D'ORTIGOSA TRAF.

C. DE SANT PERE MÉS ALT

DAMADEL
VIVES

C. DE SANT PERE MITJA

Plaça de Sant Augustí Vell

C. D. PORTAL NOU

Citadel Park

MUSEU DE ZOOLOGIA

CARRER SANT PERE MÉS BAIX

C. DEL COMERÇ

PASSEIG DE PICASSO

MUSEU DE GEOLOGIA

ALACE OF CATALAN MUSIC

C. DE FONOLLAR

CHOCOLATE MUSEUM

To Zoo

C. TANTARRANTANA

C. L'ALLADA VERMELL

C. FUSINA

AV. FRANCESC CAMBÓ

C. DE LES

C. PELLISSER

C. CARDERS

C. ASSAONADORS

C. CARDERS

EL BORN CULTURAL CENTER

IAIETANA
AV. DR. J. POU

C. DR. J. POU

Plaça Maura

C. MERCADERS

SANTA CATERINA MARKET

FREIXURES

Plaça Santa Caterina

BÒRIA

CARRER DE LA PRINCESA

PICASSO MUSEUM

C. FLASSADERS

C. DE LA RIBERA

ÀGROS

ARCH. COLL.

GAUDÍ EXHIBITION CENTER

Plaça del Rei

EL BORN

C. BANYS VELLS

PASSEIG DEL BORN

C. A. SANT JOAN

FRANÇA TRAIN STATION

aça
ova

AV. CATEDRAL

ROYAL PALACE

COMTES

BARC. HISTORY MUSEUM

MONTCADA

C. SOMBRERERS

Plaça Olles

C. DEL REC

C. PUANA

CATHEDRAL

MARÈS MUSEUM

Jaume I

C. DE L'ARGENTERIA

SANTA MARIA DEL MAR

C. MARQUESA

S. SEVER

PAL. GENERAL-ITAT

Pl. de l'Angel

Plaça S. Maria Anisadeta

Barceloneta

S. HONRAT

ROMAN RUINS

VIA LAIETANA

C. DE LA NAU

El
CALL

Pl. de Sant Jaume

C. DEL SOTS-TINENT NAVARRO

LA LLOTJA

Pla de Palau

To Barceloneta & Beaches

QUERIA

FERRAN

CITY HALL

C. CIUTAT

C. LLEDÓ

Plaça d'Antoni López

PALAU DE MAR

S. JAUME

Plaça de Sant Miquel

Plaça Traginers

POST

C. FUSTERIA

BARCELONA HEAD SCULPTURE

CATALAN HISTORY MUSEUM

BARRI

CARRER D'AVINYÓ

CITY

C. GIGNÀ

Marina

C.ESC. BLANCS

GÒTIC

Plaça de George Orwell

C. DATAÜLF

C. CARABASSA

C. D. SERRA

C. DE LA MERCÈ

PASSEIG DE COLÓM

LOBSTER SCULPTURE

aça
tal

C. VIDRE

C. DELS CÒDOLS

C. NOU

C. ESCUDELLERS

C. D'EN RULL

C. SANT FRANCESC

PSTG. DE LA PAU

CLAVE

PASSEIG DE COLÓM

RONDA DEL LITORAL (HIGHWAY)

MOLL DE LA FUSTA

Marina

LAS RAMBLAS

Plaça de Xirau

MUSEU DE CERA

CARRER DE JOSEP ANSELM

Plaça del Duc de Medinaceli

IMAX

TSERRAT

SKY-SCRAPER

Drassanes

SANTA EULÀLIA

MOLL D'ESPANYA

AQUARIUM

SSANES

COLUMBUS MONUMENT

PORT AUTHORITY

MARITIME MUSEUM

Cruise Bus

GOLONDRINAS CRUISES

RAMBLA DEL MAR

MAREMAGNUM MALL

Plaça de les Drassanes

To Moll Adossat Cruise Terminal

200 Meters

200 Yards

Port Vell

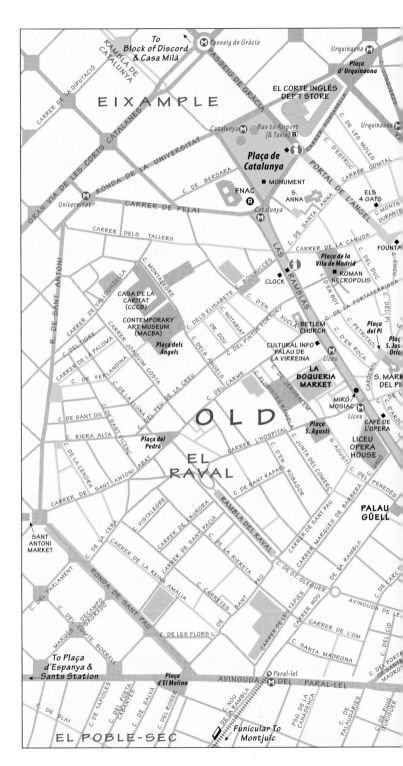

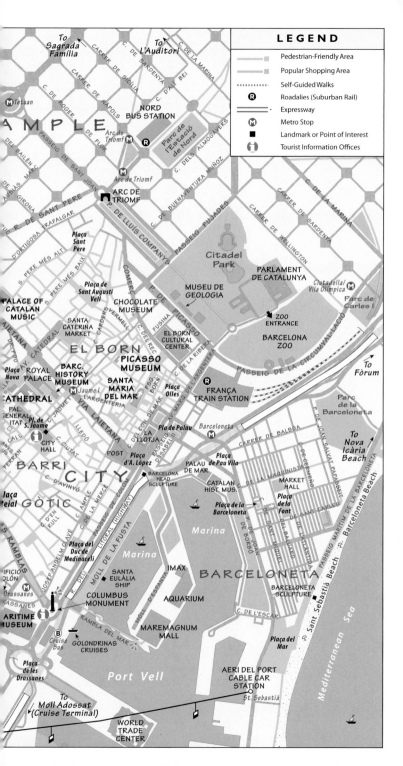

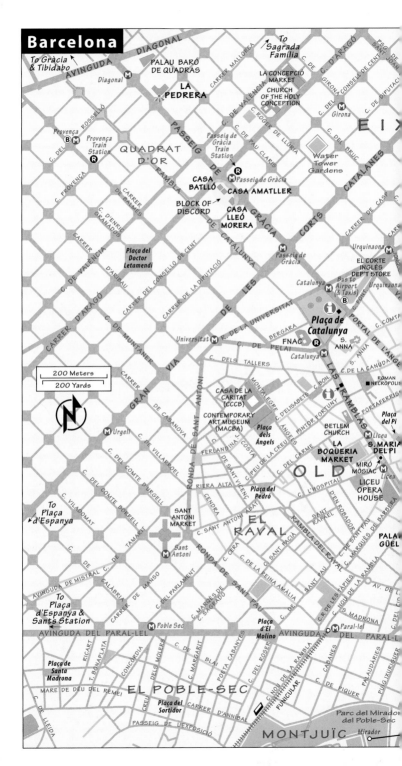

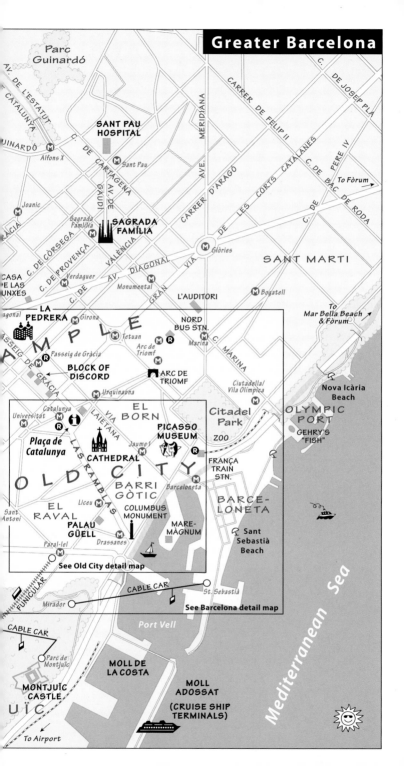

Greater Barcelona

Parc Guinardó

AV. DE L'ESTATUT

CATALUNYA

GUINARDÓ

Alfons X

Joanic

GRÀCIA

SANT PAU HOSPITAL

C. DE CARTAGENA

AV. DE GAUDÍ

Sant Pau

Sagrada Família

SAGRADA FAMÍLIA

CARRER DE FELIP II

MERIDIANA

AVE.

CARRER DE LES CORTS CATALANES

CARRER D'ARAGÓ

DE JOSEP PLA

PERE IV

C. DE BAC DE RODA

To Fòrum

CASA DE LAS PUNXES

C. DE CÒRSEGA

C. DE PROVENÇA

Verdaguer

Monumental

C. DE

VALÈNCIA

AV. DIAGONAL

GRAN

VIA

Glòries

DE

C. DE

C. MARINA

SANT MARTI

L'AUDITORI

Bogatell

LA PEDRERA

AMPLE

Girona

PASSEIG DE GRÀCIA

Tetuan

Passeig de Gràcia

Arc de Triomf

NORD. BUS STN.

Marina

To Mar Bella Beach & Fòrum

BLOCK OF DISCORD

Urquinaona

ARC DE TRIOMF

Ciutadella/ Vila Olímpica

Nova Icària Beach

Catalunya

Universitàt

EL BORN

VIA LAIETANA

LAS RAMBLAS

Plaça de Catalunya

CATHEDRAL

Jaume I

PICASSO MUSEUM

Citadel Park

ZOO

OLYMPIC PORT

GEHRY'S "FISH"

FRANÇA TRAIN STN.

Liceu

BARRI GÒTIC

Barceloneta

BARCE-LONETA

OLD CITY

EL RAVAL

Sant Antoni

PALAU GÜELL

COLUMBUS MONUMENT

MARE-MÀGNUM

Sant Sebastià Beach

Paral·lel

Drassanes

See Old City detail map

Mediterranean Sea

FUNICULAR

CABLE CAR

Mirador

St. Sebastià

See Barcelona detail map

Port Vell

CABLE CAR

Parc de Montjuïc

MONTJUÏC CASTLE

ÜIC

To Airport

MOLL DE LA COSTA

MOLL ADOSSAT

(CRUISE SHIP TERMINALS)

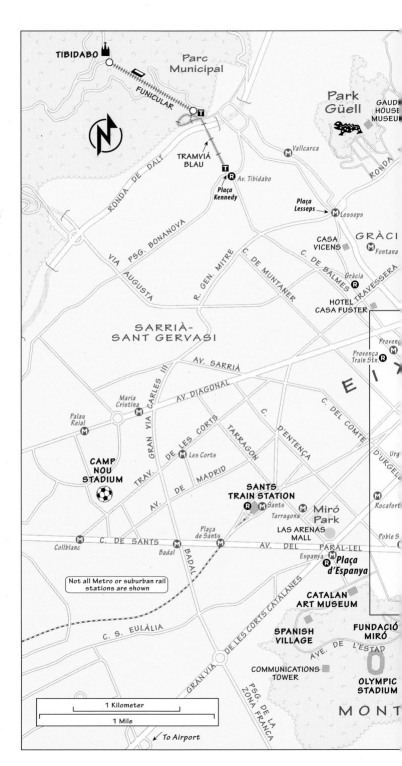

CONTENTS

INTRODUCTION

If you're in the mood to surrender to a city's charms, let it be in Barcelona. The capital of Catalunya and Spain's second city, Barcelona bubbles with life—in its narrow Barri Gòtic alleys, along the pedestrian boulevard called the Ramblas, in the funky bohemian quarter of El Born, along the bustling beach promenade, and throughout the chic, grid-planned part of town called the Eixample.

Barcelona's Old City is made for seeing on foot, full of winding lanes that emerge into secluded squares dotted with palm trees

and ringed with cafés and boutiques. The waterfront bristles with life, overlooked by the park-like setting of Montjuïc. Everywhere you go, you'll find the city's architecture to be colorful, playful, and unique. Rows of symmetrical ironwork balconies are punctuated with fanciful details: bay windows, turrets, painted tiles, hanging lanterns, flower boxes, and carved reliefs.

As the capital of the Catalan people, Barcelona is full of history. You'll see Roman ruins, a medieval cathedral, twisty Gothic lanes, and traces of Columbus and the sea trade. But by the late 19th century, the city had boomed into an industrial powerhouse and became the cradle of a new artistic style—Modernisme. Pablo Picasso lived in Barcelona as a teenager, just as he was on the verge of reinventing painting; his legacy is today's Picasso Museum. Catalan architects, including Antoni Gaudí, Lluís Domènech i Montaner, and Josep Puig i Cadafalch, forged the Modernista style and remade the city's skyline with curvy, playful fantasy buildings—culminating in Gaudí's over-the-top Sagrada Família, a church still under construction. Salvador Dalí and Joan

Miró join the long list of world-changing 20th-century artists with ties to this city.

Today's Barcelona is as vibrant as ever. Locals still join hands and dance the everyone's-welcome *sardana* in front of the cathedral every weekend. Neighborhood festivals jam the events calendar. The cafés are filled by day, and people crowd the streets at night, pausing to fortify themselves with a perfectly composed bite of seafood and a drink at a tapas bar. Barcelona's lively culture is on an unstoppable roll in Spain's most cosmopolitan and European corner.

Planning Your Trip

This section will help you get started planning your trip—with advice on trip costs, when to go, and what you should know before you take off. Design an itinerary that enables you to visit sights at the best possible times. Note holidays, specifics on sights, and days when sights are closed or most crowded.

TRIP COSTS

Five components make up your trip costs: airfare to Europe, transportation in Europe, room and board, sightseeing and entertainment, and shopping and miscellany.

Airfare to Europe: A basic round-trip flight from the US to Barcelona can cost, on average, about $1,000-2,000 total, depending on where you fly from and when (cheaper in winter). If Barcelona is part of a longer trip, consider saving time and money in Europe by flying into one city and out of another; for instance, into Barcelona and out of Paris. Overall, Kayak.com is the best place to start searching for flights on a combination of mainstream and budget carriers.

Transportation in Europe: A 10-ride Metro card costs about $12.50. For round-trip train rides to day-trip destinations, allow about $30 for Montserrat and $45 for Figueres. To travel between El Prat airport and Barcelona, figure (one-way) $5-7 by public transportation, or $40 by taxi.

Room and Board: You can manage comfortably in Barcelona on $130 a day per person for room and board. This allows $5 for breakfast, $15 for lunch, $25 for dinner, and $85 for lodging (based on two people splitting the cost of a $170 double room). Students and tightwads can enjoy Barcelona for as little as $80 a day ($45 for a bed, $35 for meals and snacks).

Sightseeing and Entertainment: It's worth considering the $33 Articket BCN sightseeing pass, which admits you to six museums, including the recommended Picasso Museum, Catalan Art Museum, and Fundació Joan Miró (for more information, see page

20). Otherwise, figure $15-25 per major sight, and $10 for others. An overall average of $40 a day works for most people. Don't skimp here. After all, this category is the driving force behind your trip—you came to sightsee, enjoy, and experience Barcelona.

Shopping and Miscellany: Figure roughly $3 per coffee, ice-cream cone, or soft drink. Shopping can vary in cost from nearly nothing to a small fortune. Good budget travelers find that this category has little to do with assembling a trip full of lifelong memories.

WHEN TO GO

Sea breezes off the Mediterranean and a generally warm climate make Barcelona pleasant for much of the year. Late spring and early fall offer the best combination of good weather, somewhat lighter crowds, long days, and plenty of tourist and cultural activities. You'll encounter hot, humid weather and the biggest crowds in July and August, and some shops and restaurants close down in August. Winter temperatures are far from freezing, but rainfall is abundant.

Before You Go

You'll have a smoother trip if you tackle a few things ahead of time. For more information on these topics, see the Practicalities chapter (and www.ricksteves.com, which has helpful travel tips and talks).

Make sure your passport is valid. If it's due to expire within six months of your ticketed date of return, you need to renew it. Allow up to six weeks to renew or get a passport (www.travel.state. gov).

Arrange your transportation. Book your international flights.

You won't want a car in congested Barcelona, but if you'll be touring other parts of Spain or beyond, figure out your main form of transportation: You can buy train tickets as you go, get a rail pass, rent a car, take a long-distance bus, or book a cheap flight. (You can wing it in Europe, but it may cost more.) Drivers: Consider bringing an International Driving Permit along with your license (sold at AAA offices in the US, www.aaa.com).

If you're taking an **overnight train,** especially to international destinations, and need a sleeping berth *(litera)*—and you must leave on a certain day—consider booking it in advance through a US agent (such as www.ricksteves.com/rail), even though it may cost more than buying it in Spain. All high-speed trains in Spain require a seat reservation, but it's usually possible to make arrangements in Spain just a few days ahead unless it's a holiday weekend. (For more on train travel, see the Practicalities chapter.)

"You're Not in Spain, You're in Catalunya!"

This is a popular nationalistic refrain you might see on T-shirts or stickers around town. Catalunya is *not* the land of bullfighting and flamenco that many visitors envision when they think of Spain (visit Madrid or Sevilla for those).

The region of Catalunya, with Barcelona as its capital, has its own language, history, and culture. Its people—eight million strong—have a proud, independent spirit. Historically, Catalunya ("Cataluña" in Spanish, sometimes spelled "Catalonia" in English) has often been at odds with the central Spanish government in Madrid. Today, it still is, especially since the 2017 illegal referendum to separate was held, and Spain's prime minister dissolved the Catalan parliament.

The Catalan language and culture were discouraged or even outlawed at various times in history, as Catalunya often chose the wrong side in wars and rebellions against the kings in Madrid. In the Spanish Civil War (1936-1939), Catalunya was one of the last pockets of democratic resistance against the military coup of the fascist dictator Francisco Franco, who punished the region with four decades of repression. During that time, the Catalan flag was banned—but locals vented their national spirit by flying their football team's flag instead.

Three of Barcelona's monuments are reminders of royal and Franco-era suppression. Citadel Park was originally a much-despised military citadel, constructed in the 18th century to keep locals in line. The Castle of Montjuïc, built for similar reasons, has been the site of numerous political executions, including hundreds during the Franco era. The Sacred Heart Church atop Tibidabo, completed under Franco, was meant to atone for the sins of Barcelonans during the civil war—the main sin being opposition to Franco. Today, Catalunya is divided: Some favor independence, while others remain loyal to Spain (see the "Independence for Catalunya?" sidebar on page 122).

Book rooms well in advance, especially if your trip falls during peak season or any major holidays or festivals.

Make reservations or buy tickets ahead for major sights. Barcelona is extremely popular, and the work of its Modernista architects (Gaudí and company) and the city's Picasso Museum are trendy. It's the biggest cruise port in the Mediterranean (serving nearly a thousand ships and over three million cruisers a year).

To see real Catalan culture, look for the *sardana* dance or an exhibition of *castellers* (both described on page 42). The main symbol of Catalunya is the dragon, which was slain by St. George ("Jordi" in Catalan)—the region's patron saint. You'll find dragons all over Barcelona, along with the Catalan flag—called the Senyera—with four horizontal red stripes on a gold field. Nineteenth-century Catalan Romantics embraced a vivid (almost certainly false) story about the origins of their flag: In the ninth century, Wilfred the Hairy—a count of Barcelona and one of the founding fathers of Catalunya—was wounded in battle. A grateful neighboring king rewarded Wilfred's bravery with a copper shield and ran Wilfred's four bloody fingers across its surface, leaving four red stripes.

The Catalan language is irrevocably tied to the history and spirit of the people here. After the end of the Franco era in the mid-1970s, the language made a huge comeback. Schools are now required by law to conduct all classes in Catalan; most school-age children learn Catalan first and Spanish second. While all Barcelonans still speak Spanish, nearly all understand Catalan, three-quarters speak Catalan, and half can write it.

Most place names in this book are listed in Catalan. Here's how to pronounce some of the city's major landmarks:

Plaça de Catalunya	PLAH-sah duh kah-tah-LOON-yah
Eixample	eye-SHAM-plah
Passeig de Gràcia	PAH-sehj duh GRAH-see-ah
Catedral	KAH-tah-dral
Barri Gòtic	BAH-ree GOH-teek
Montjuïc	mohn-jew-EEK

When finding your way, these terms will be useful:

exit	*sortida* (sor-TEE-dah)
square	*plaça* (PLAH-sah)
street	*carrer* (kah-REHR)
boulevard	*passeig* (PAH-sehj)
avenue	*avinguda* (ah-veen-GOO-dah)

For more Catalan words, see the survival phrases in the appendix.

Every visitor wants to see the same sights—the Picasso Museum, La Pedrera (Casa Milà), Sagrada Família church, Casa Batlló, and Park Güell—so it's essential to book in advance. While technically you can try to buy tickets at the sight, in Barcelona I consider reservations essential.

Booking ahead is also a must if you'll visit the Dalí sights in Figueres and/or Cadaqués.

INTRODUCTION

🎧 Stick This Guidebook in Your Ear!

My free Rick Steves Audio Europe app makes it easy to download my audio tours of many of Europe's top attractions and listen to them offline during your travels. In this book, this in-

cludes my Barcelona City Walk (and my Eixample Walk audio tour, which will be available in 2019). Sights covered by audio tours are marked in this book with this symbol: 🎧. The app also offers insightful travel interviews from my public radio show with experts from Spain and around the globe. It's all free! You can download the app via Ap-

ple's App Store, Google Play, or Amazon's Appstore. For more info, see www.ricksteves.com/audioeurope.

Consider travel insurance. Compare the cost of the insurance to the cost of your potential loss. Check whether your existing insurance (health, homeowners, or renters) covers you and your possessions overseas.

Call your bank. Alert your bank that you'll be using your debit and credit cards in Europe. Ask about transaction fees, and get the PIN number for your credit card. You don't need to bring euros for your trip; you can withdraw euros from cash machines in Europe.

Use your smartphone smartly. Sign up for an international service plan to reduce your costs, or rely on Wi-Fi in Europe instead. Download any apps you'll want on the road, such as maps, translation, transit schedules, and Rick Steves Audio Europe (see the sidebar).

Pack light. You'll walk with your luggage more than you think. Bring a single carry-on bag and a daypack. Use the packing checklist in the appendix as a guide.

TRAVEL SMART

If you have a positive attitude, equip yourself with good information (this book), and expect to travel smart, you will.

Read—and reread—this book. To have an "A" trip, be an "A" student. Note opening hours of sights, closed days, crowd-beating tips, and whether reservations are required or advisable. Check the latest at www.ricksteves.com/update.

Be your own tour guide. As you travel, get up-to-date info on sights, reserve tickets and tours, reconfirm hotels and travel arrangements, and check transit connections. Visit local tourist information offices (TIs). Upon arrival in a new town, lay the groundwork for a smooth departure; confirm the train, bus, or road you'll take when you leave.

Barcelona Almanac

Population: 1.6 million.

Languages: Spanish and Catalan are the two official languages of Catalunya, but Catalan is the preferred language in schools and offices. Catalan is not a dialect of Spanish, but an independent language.

Currency: Euro (€)

City Layout: The tangled Gothic Quarter (Barri Gòtic) lies at the heart of the city, edged by the connected boulevards of the Ramblas. The more orderly Eixample district spreads north of the Old City, while unassuming Barceloneta spills along the seafront. Looking down over it all is the big Montjuïc hill.

Tourist Tracks: More than 23 million people visit Barcelona each year, and 8 million stay overnight. The Ramblas sees more than 150,000 people daily. Avinguda del Portal de l'Angel is Spain's most walked street, trod upon by 3,500 pairs of feet every hour.

Architecture: Barcelona is home to the Modernista style championed by Catalan architect Antoni Gaudí, whose most famous work is the Sagrada Família church. Nearly 30 of his buildings are scattered throughout the greater Barcelona area.

Fun in the Sun: Until 1992, when the city hosted the Olympic Games, Barcelona had only one small beachfront area, in Barceloneta. Other waterfront property was taken up by industrial purposes. For the Olympics, the seaside was reconstructed, and the city shoreline is now spanned by nine beaches along a three-mile stretch.

Soccer: Futbol Club (FC) Barcelona has the largest privately owned stadium in the world, with a seating capacity of 99,000. Every year, more than 1.5 million people visit its museum.

The Average Jordi: The average Barcelonan is 41 years old, will live to age 81, and is likely Catholic. The majority (62 percent) of Barcelona's residents were born in Catalunya.

Outsmart thieves. Pickpockets abound in crowded places where tourists congregate. Treat commotions as smokescreens for theft. Keep your cash, credit cards, and passport secure in a money belt tucked under your clothes; carry only a day's spending money in your front pocket. Don't set valuable items down on counters or café tabletops, where they can be quickly stolen or easily forgotten.

Minimize potential loss. Keep expensive gear to a minimum. Bring photocopies or take photos of important documents (passport and cards) to aid in replacement if they're lost or stolen. Back up photos and files frequently.

Beat the summer heat. If you wilt easily, choose a hotel with air-conditioning, start your day early, take a midday siesta at your hotel, and resume your sightseeing later. Churches offer a cool haven (though dress modestly—no bare shoulders, shorts, or skirts above the knee). Take frequent ice cream breaks.

Guard your time and energy. Taking a taxi can be a good value if it saves you a long wait for a cheap bus or an exhausting walk across town. To avoid long lines, follow my crowd-beating tips, such as making advance reservations, or sightseeing early or late (see the Nightlife in Barcelona chapter for a list of sights open late).

Be flexible. Even if you have a well-planned itinerary, expect changes, strikes, closures, sore feet, bad weather, and so on. Your Plan B could turn out to be even better.

Attempt the language. Many Catalans—especially in the tourist trade and in cities—speak English, but if you learn some Catalan or Spanish, even just a few phrases, you'll get more smiles and make more friends. Practice the survival phrases near the end of this book, and even better, bring a phrase book.

Connect with the culture. Interacting with locals carbonates your experience. Enjoy the friendliness of the Catalan people. Ask questions; most locals are happy to point you in their idea of the right direction. Set up your own quest for the best square, cloister, or tapas bar. When an opportunity pops up, make it a habit to say "yes."

Barcelona...here you come!

ORIENTATION TO BARCELONA

Bustling Barcelona is geographically big and culturally complex. Plan your time carefully, carving up the metropolis into manageable sightseeing neighborhoods. Use my day plans to help prioritize. Be sure to make advance reservations online for Barcelona's most popular sights—otherwise you might not get into them at all. For efficiency, learn how to navigate Barcelona by Metro, bus, and taxi. Armed with good information and a thoughtful game plan, you're ready to go. Then you can relax, enjoy, and let yourself be surprised by all that Barcelona has to offer.

BARCELONA: A VERBAL MAP

Like Los Angeles, Barcelona is a basically flat city, sloping gently from the foothills down to the sea. It's huge (1.6 million people, with about three times as many people in greater Barcelona), but travelers need only focus on four areas: the Old City, the harbor/Barceloneta, the Eixample, and Montjuïc.

A large square, **Plaça de Catalunya,** sits at the center of Barcelona, dividing the older and newer parts of town. Below Plaça de Catalunya is the Old City, with the boulevard called the Ramblas running down to the harbor. Above Plaça de Catalunya is the modern residential area called the Eixample. The Montjuïc hill overlooks the harbor. Outside the Old City, Barcelona's sights are widely scattered, but with a map and a willingness to figure out public transit (or take taxis), all is manageable.

Here are overviews of the major neighborhoods:

ORIENTATION

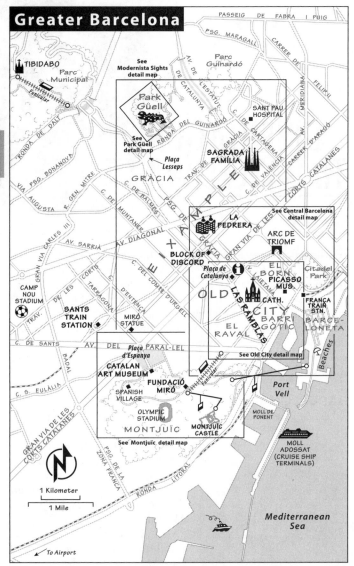

Greater Barcelona

PASSEIG DE FABRA I PUIG

PSG. MARAGALL

TIBIDABO

Parc Municipal

Funicular

See Modernista Sights detail map

Parc Guinardó

Park Güell

SANT PAU HOSPITAL

See Park Güell detail map

Plaça Lesseps

SAGRADA FAMÍLIA

GRÀCIA

EIXAMPLE

LA PEDRERA

See Central Barcelona detail map

ARC DE TRIOMF

BLOCK OF DISCORD

Plaça de Catalunya i

CAMP NOU STADIUM

SANTS TRAIN STATION

MIRÓ STATUE

EL BORN

PICASSO MUS.

Citadel Park

OLD CITY

CATH.

FRANÇA TRAIN STN.

LAS RAMBLAS

BARRI GÒTIC

BARCE-LONETA

EL RAVAL

See Old City detail map

Plaça d'Espanya

PARAL-LEL

Beaches

CATALAN ART MUSEUM

SPANISH VILLAGE

FUNDACIÓ MIRÓ

Funicular

Port Vell

OLYMPIC STADIUM

MONTJUÏC

MONTJUÏC CASTLE

MOLL DE PONENT

See Montjuïc detail map

MOLL ADOSSAT (CRUISE SHIP TERMINALS)

N

1 Kilometer

1 Mile

Mediterranean Sea

To Airport

Old City (Ciutat Vella): This is the compact core of Barcelona—ideal for strolling, shopping, and people-watching—where you'll probably spend most of your time. It's a labyrinth of narrow streets that once were confined by the medieval walls. The lively pedestrian drag called the **Ramblas** goes through the heart of the Old City from Plaça de Catalunya to the harbor. The Old City is divided into thirds by the Ramblas and Via Laietana, a vehicle-

Barcelona Neighborhood Overview

TIBIDABO

Park Güell

GRÀCIA

BEYOND THE EIXAMPLE

SAGRADA FAMÍLIA

LA PEDRERA

PASSEIG DE GRÀCIA

BLOCK OF DISCORD

CAMP NOU STADIUM

EIXAMPLE

EL BORN

Citadel Park

PICASSO MUSEUM

Plaça de Catalunya

CATHEDRAL

VIA LAIETANA

OLD CITY

BARRI GÒTIC

LAS RAMBLAS

SANTS STATION

EL RAVAL

BARCELONETA & BEACHES

AV. DEL PARAL·LEL

Port Vell

Not to Scale

Plaça d'Espanya

CATALAN ART MUSEUM

MONTJUÏC

To Airport

CRUISE PORT

Mediterranean Sea

heavy thoroughfare running roughly parallel to the Ramblas. Between the Ramblas and Via Laietana is the characteristic **Barri Gòtic** (BAH-ree GOH-teek, Gothic Quarter), with the cathedral as its navel. Locals call it "El Gòtic" for short. To the east of Via Laietana is the trendy **El Born** district (a.k.a. "La Ribera"), a shopping, dining, and nightlife mecca centered on the Picasso Museum and the Church of Santa Maria del Mar. To the west of the Ramblas is **El Raval** (rah-VAHL), enlivened by its university and modern-art museum. El Raval is of least interest to tourists and that's part of its charm. While rough-edged in places, it is the emerging lively, foodie zone.

Harborfront: The old harbor, **Port Vell,** gleams with landmark monuments and new developments. A pedestrian bridge links the Ramblas with the modern Maremagnum shopping/aquarium/entertainment complex. On the peninsula across the quaint sailboat harbor is **Barceloneta,** a traditional fishing neighborhood with gritty charm and some good seafood restaurants. Beyond Barceloneta, a gorgeous man-made **beach** several miles long leads east to the commercial and convention district called the **Fòrum.**

Eixample: Above the Old City, beyond the bustling hub of Plaça de Catalunya, is the elegant Eixample (eye-SHAM-plah) district, its grid plan softened by cutoff corners. Much of Barcelona's Modernista architecture is found here—especially along the swanky artery Passeig de Gràcia, an area called **Quadrat d'Or**

Barcelona: From Small to Sprawl

The city of Barcelona has grown with its history. The original Roman town from the time of Christ was contained inside the knot of streets clustered around today's cathedral and enclosed by an oval-shaped ring of Roman walls (stretching basically southeast from the square in front of the cathedral).

When Rome fell (around AD 476), the Christian Visigoths made the cathedral the center of town, and the populace remained huddled inside the Roman walls. During the Dark Ages, the city was ruled briefly by Moors (714-801) and Franks (ninth century). When the Counts of Barcelona unified Catalunya (10th century), the city began expanding. They built churches outside the Roman walls (or *extra muro*), each a magnet gathering a small community. By 1250, they needed to build a larger wall to contain these new settlers. This medieval wall stretched from Plaça de Catalunya to the sea, embracing the whole Old Town. The hilltop of Montjuïc—outside the residential area—was topped with a harbor-guarding fortress.

Barcelona is a good example of how a city's architectural heritage rises and falls with economic times. In the 14th century, when the Mediterranean was the epicenter of trade, Barcelona thrived. That's why there are a lot of Gothic buildings here. After 1492, when the Age of Discovery opened up new sea routes, trade shifted to the Atlantic and away from Mediterranean ports. The following centuries saw little grand building in Barcelona.

Then, in the 19th century, Barcelona bounced back, powered by the Industrial Revolution. By 1850, the city was bursting at the seams. The outer wall was torn down and replaced by circular boulevards (named Rondas, meaning "to go around"). The city expanded in a regimented grid of modern boulevards—an urban waffle known as the Eixample. With affluence came big shots with big egos and plenty of money to finance the Modernista architectural wonders that now grace the city.

In 1992, Barcelona hosted the Summer Olympics, which quickly accelerated modernization and stoked Barcelona's economy. In a brilliant move, organizers of the games housed much of the one-time rush of visitors on huge cruise ships. It seems this helped jump-start a thriving cruise ship industry. In 1992, 70 cruise ships called here. Today Barcelona is the leading cruise port in Europe, and the city hosts about 900 cruise ships annually, most of them massive.

A big issue for the character of the city today is the end of rent control for landowners and their tenants in the city center. Now that the ceiling has been lifted, many of the charming shops that add so much character to the old quarter have been driven out of business, replaced by branches of much mightier corporate retailers. But the rising affluence and trendiness of the city have worked to keep the town vibrant and colorful.

Today, Barcelona's population sprawls beyond city maps, creating a greater metropolitan area of some 5 million people—more than half of all the people in Catalunya.

Don't Miss Out!
Book Key Sights in Advance

To ensure you'll see Barcelona's top (and very crowded) sights—the Picasso Museum, La Pedrera (Casa Milà), Sagrada Família, Casa Batlló, and Park Güell—book reserved-time tickets in advance. It's easy, it's cheaper, and it's for your own good. For these sights, I list prices and details for on-line advanced booking. Barcelona's Casa Amatller and Palace of Catalan Music, and Dalí's house in Cadaqués all require a guided tour, which also must be reserved in advance. If heading to Figueres for the Dalí Theater-Museum, you should buy advance tickets to that as well. Book as far in advance as possible for these sights (same-day tickets *may* be an option—but why risk it?).

Booking Process: Once you book a reservation, you'll receive your ticket by email. (If you don't get it, check your junk folder.) You can either print the ticket or show the bar code on your mobile phone as you enter.

("Golden Quarter"). Beyond that is the **Gràcia** district and Antoni Gaudí's **Park Güell.**

Montjuïc: The large hill overlooking the city to the southwest is Montjuïc (mohn-jew-EEK), home to a variety of attractions, including some excellent museums (Catalan Art, Joan Miró) and the Olympic Stadium. At the base of Montjuïc, stretching toward Plaça d'Espanya, are the former **1929 World Expo Fairgrounds,** with additional fine attractions (including the CaixaForum art gallery and the bullring-turned-mall, Las Arenas).

Apart from your geographical orientation, it's smart to orient yourself linguistically to a language distinct from Spanish. Although Spanish ("Castilian"/*castellano*) is widely spoken, the native tongue in this region is Catalan—nearly as different from Spanish as Italian (see the sidebar on page 4).

PLANNING YOUR TIME

Barcelona is easily worth two days, and no one would regret having a third day (or more). If you can spare only one full day for the city, it will be a scramble, but a day you'll never forget.

When planning your time, be aware that many top sights are closed on Monday—making them especially crowded on Tuesday and Sunday (for itinerary considerations on a day-by-day basis, see the "Daily Reminder" sidebar, later). Be careful on the first Sunday of the month; sights such as Palau Güell and the Catalan Art Museum are jammed because they're free. And I'll say it again—without buying tickets in advance, you won't even get in to the city's top sights.

Barcelona in One Day

For a relaxing day, stroll the Ramblas, see the Sagrada Família, add the Picasso Museum if you're a fan, and have dinner in the El Born district.

To fit in much more, try the following ambitious but doable plan. You'll have to rush through the big sights (cathedral, Picasso Museum, Sagrada Família), having just enough time to visit each one but not to linger.

9:00   From Plaça de Catalunya (with its handy TI), follow my Barri Gòtic Walk and Barcelona Cathedral Tour. (These sights are covered in my free ∩ Barcelona City Walk audio tour, which can also provide a relaxing introduction the night before—see page 6.)

11:00   Circle back to Plaça de Catalunya and follow my Ramblas Ramble to the harborfront.

12:30   Walk along the harborfront to El Born, grabbing an early lunch.

14:00   Take my Picasso Museum Tour.

16:00   Hop a taxi or the Metro to the Sagrada Família.

18:00   Follow my Eixample Walk (from Passeig de Gràcia to see the exteriors of Gaudí's La Pedrera and the Block of Discord, then back down to Plaça de Catalunya).

19:00   Wander back into the Barri Gòtic at prime paseo time. Enjoy an early tapas dinner along the way, or a restaurant dinner later in the Old City.

Barcelona in Two or More Days

With at least two days, divide and conquer the town geographically: Spend one day in the Old City (Ramblas, Barri Gòtic/cathedral area, Picasso Museum/El Born) and another on the Eixample and Gaudí sights (La Pedrera, Sagrada Família, Park Güell). If you have a third day, visit Montjuïc and/or side-trip to Montserrat.

With extra time on any day, consider taking a hop-on, hop-off bus tour for a sightseeing overview (for example, the Bus Turístic blue route links most Gaudí sights and could work well on Day 2).

Day 1: Old City

9:00   Follow my Barri Gòtic Walk and Barcelona Cathedral Tour.

11:00   Head to the Ramblas using the route described in my Barri Gòtic Shopping Walk, then follow my Ramblas Ramble down to the harborfront.

13:00   Grab lunch in El Born or the Barri Gòtic.

14:00   Tour the Palace of Catalan Music in El Born.

15:00   Follow my El Born Walk, including a visit to the

Picasso Museum. Afterwards shop to your heart's content.

Evening For an early dinner, sample tapas at several bars in El Born (or the Eixample or Barri Gòtic); to dine at a restaurant, go when locals do, around 21:00. Evening activities include sightseeing; performances of Spanish guitar, flamenco, or jazz; concerts at La Pedrera or the Palace of Catalan Music; or hanging out at a *chiringuito* beach bar in Barceloneta.

Another fun evening activity is to zip up to Montjuïc for the sunset and a drink on the Catalan Art Museum's terrace, then head down to the Magic Fountains (see page 70 for show schedule) For more ideas, and a list of sights open late, see the Nightlife in Barcelona chapter.

Day 2: Modernisme

9:00 Take my Eixample Walk, touring La Pedrera and/or one of the Block of Discord houses—Casa Batlló, or Casa Amatller.

12:00 Eat an early lunch in the Eixample, then tour the Sagrada Família.

15:00 Choose among these options: Taxi to Park Güell for more Gaudí. Or take the bus to Montjuïc (if you're not going to Montjuïc on Day 3) to enjoy the city view and your pick of sights. Or explore the harborfront La Rambla de Mar and Old Port.

Evening Choose among the evening activities listed earlier.

Day 3: Montjuïc and Barceloneta

Tour Montjuïc from top to bottom (both physically and in order of importance), stopping at these sights: Fundació Joan Miró, Catalan Art Museum, and CaixaForum. If the weather is good, take the scenic cable-car ride down from Montjuïc to the port, and spend the rest of the day at Barceloneta—stroll the promenade, hit the beach, and find your favorite *chiringuito* (beach bar) for dinner.

Day 4

Consider these options: Visit the markets (La Boqueria and Santa Caterina—both closed Sun). Tour more sights (Palau Güell's Modernista interior, Barcelona History Museum, Frederic Marès Museum, Chocolate Museum, and more). Take a walking or bike tour. Relax or rent a rowboat in Citadel Park.

Days 5-7

With more time, choose among several day trips, including the mountaintop monastery of Montserrat, the beach resort town of

Sitges, and the Salvador Dalí sights at Figueres and Cadaqués (re-serve both in advance, see the Day Trips from Barcelona chapter).

Connecting with the Rest of Spain

Located in the far northeast corner of Spain, Barcelona makes a good first or last stop for your trip. With the high-speed AVE train, Barcelona is three hours away from Madrid—faster and more comfortable than flying. Or you could sandwich Barcelona between flights. From the US, it's as easy to fly into Barcelona as it is to land in Madrid, Lisbon, or Paris. Those who plan on renting a car later in their trip can start here, take the train or fly to Madrid, and sightsee Madrid and Toledo, all before picking up a car—clever-ly saving on several days' worth of rental fees. For more on train travel and car rentals in Spain, see the Practicalities chapter.

Overview

TOURIST INFORMATION

Barcelona's TI has several branches (central tel. 932-853-834, www.barcelonaturisme.cat). The primary TI is beneath the main square, **Plaça de Catalunya** (daily 8:30-21:00, entrance just across from El Corte Inglés department store—look for red sign and take stairs down).

Other branches are scattered around the city and generally have the same hours (daily 8:30-20:30, some have shorter hours on Sun). Locations include near the top of the **Ramblas** (kiosk at #115, on **Plaça de Sant Jaume** just south of the cathedral (inside Barcelona City Hall at Ciutat 2), inside the base of the harborside **Columbus Monument,** at the **airport** (terminals 1 and 2B), and at the **Sants train station.**

Smaller info kiosks pop up in touristy locales: on **Plaça d'Espanya,** in the park across from the **Sagrada Família** entrance, near the **Columbus Monument** (where the shuttle bus from the cruise port arrives), at the **Nord bus station,** at the various **cruise terminals** along the port, and on **Plaça de Catalunya.** In addition, throughout the summer, young red-jacketed tourist-info helpers appear in the most touristy parts of town; although they work for the hop-on, hop-off Bus Turístic, they are happy to answer questions.

At any TI, pick up the monthly *Visit Barcelona* guidebook (with basic tips on sightseeing, shopping, events, and restaurants). Other publications that may be available in larger TIs include *Time Out BCN Guide* (concise but thorough day-by-day list of events, www.timeout.com/barcelona); *Barcelona Metropolitan* magazine (timely coverage of local topics and events, www.barcelona-metropolitan.com); and *Barcelona Prestige* (listings for more upscale dining and

Daily Reminder

Sunday: The Boqueria and Santa Caterina markets are closed. Some sights close early today, including the Olympic and Sports Museum and Camp Nou Stadium (14:30); and the Fundació Joan Miró, Palace of Catalan Music, and Catalan Art Museum (15:00). Informal performances of the *sardana* national dance take place in front of the cathedral at 11:15 (none in Aug).

Some museums are free at certain times: Catalan Art Museum, Palau Güell, and Picasso Museum (first Sun of month); Maritime Museum (after 15:00); Barcelona History Museum and Frederic Marès Museum (first Sun of month plus other Sun from 15:00).

The Magic Fountains come alive on summer evenings (June-Sept).

Monday: Many sights are closed, including the Picasso Museum, Catalan Art Museum, Palau Güell, Barcelona History Museum, *Santa Eulàlia* schooner (part of the Maritime Museum), Fundació Joan Miró, Frederic Marès Museum, El Born Cultural Center, and Olympic and Sports Museum. But most major Modernista sights are open today, including the Sagrada Família, La Pedrera, Park Güell, Casa Batlló, and Casa Amatller.

Tuesday: All major sights are open.

Wednesday: All major sights are open. The Magic Fountains spout on summer evenings. (June-Sept).

Thursday: All major sights are open. The Magic Fountains make a splash (March-Dec).

Friday: All major sights are open. The Magic Fountains light up Montjuïc (March-Dec).

Saturday: All major sights are open. Barcelonans sometimes dance the *sardana* on Saturdays at 18:00 in front of the cathedral. The Magic Fountains dance March-Dec. The Catalan Art Museum is free after 15:00.

Late-Hours Sightseeing: For a list of sights open late, see the sidebar on page 216.

shopping, www.bcn-guide.com). All are also available online and make good pretrip planning tools. The free El Corte Inglés map provided by most hotels is better than the TI's map.

TIs are handy places to buy the **Articket BCN** sightseeing pass, or tickets for the Bus Turístic or TI-run walking tours (all described later). They also sell tickets to FC Barcelona soccer games.

Modernisme Route: A handy map showing all 116 Modernista buildings is available online (www.barcelonabooks.com) or in person at the Institut Municipal del Paisatge Urbà, inside the Edificio Colón, the city's first skyscraper (Mon-Fri 9:00-14:00, closed Sat-Sun, Avinguda de les Drassanes 6, 21st floor, www.rutadelmodernisme.com). They also offer a sightseeing discount

ORIENTATION

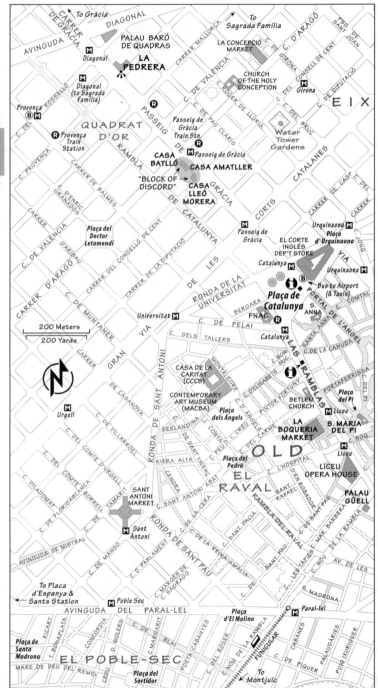

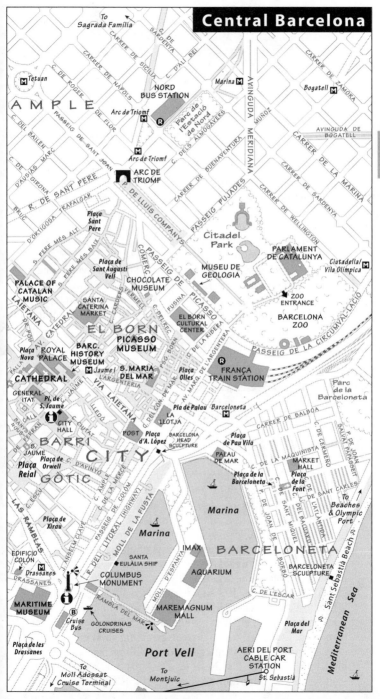

package (€12 for a great guidebook and 20-50-percent discounts at many Modernista sights—worthwhile if going beyond the biggies I cover in depth; for €18 you'll also get a guidebook to Modernista bars and restaurants).

Regional Catalunya TI: The all-Catalunya TI, inside a former palace, can help with travel and sightseeing tips for the entire region. They also have a relaxing café and a space for tasting regional treats (daily 10:00-21:00, Palau Moja, midway along the Ramblas at #118, Portaferrisa 1, tel. 933-162-740, www.palaumoja.com).

Sightseeing Passes: The **Articket BCN** pass covers admission to six art museums and their temporary exhibits, letting you skip the ticket-buying lines. Sights include the recommended Picasso Museum, Catalan Art Museum, and Fundació Joan Miró (€30, valid 12 months; sold online or at participating museums and the TIs at the airport, Plaça de Catalunya, Plaça de Sant Jaume, and Sants train station; www.articketbcn.org). If you're planning to go to three or more covered museums, this ticket can save you money and time. Just show your Articket BCN (to the ticket taker, at the info desk, or at a special Articket window), and you'll get your ticket, which you can use to enter at any time (especially useful for Picasso Museum).

For most travelers, the **Barcelona Card** and the **Barcelona Card Express** are not worth the trouble.

ARRIVAL IN BARCELONA

For more information on getting to or from Barcelona by train, plane, bus, or cruise ship, see the Barcelona Connections chapter.

HELPFUL HINTS

Theft and Scam Alert: You're more likely to be pickpocketed here—especially on the Ramblas—than about anywhere else in Europe. The Sagrada Família (both inside and out), with its hordes of tourists gawking skyward, is also a popular pickpocketing place. Most crime is nonviolent, but muggings do occur. Leave valuables in your hotel and wear a money belt. Whenever you pay with cash, count your change carefully.

Street scams are easy to avoid if you recognize them. Most common is the too-friendly local who tries to engage you in conversation. If a super-friendly man acts drunk and wants to dance because his soccer team just won, he's a pickpocket. Beware of thieves posing as lost tourists who ask for your help. Don't fall for any street-gambling shell games. Beware of groups of women aggressively selling flowers, people offering to clean off a stain from your shirt, and so on. If you stop for any commotion or show on the Ramblas, put your hands in your pockets before someone else does. Assume any scuffle is simply a distraction by a team of thieves. Note that in pedestrian streets, thieves on bikes are adept at swooping by and grabbing a purse or day bag left on the ground at your feet. Don't be intimidated...just be smart.

Personal Safety: Some areas feel seedy and can be unsafe after dark. Certain parts of the Barri Gòtic (basically the two or three blocks directly south and east of Plaça Reial) and El Raval (just west of the Ramblas) can be dicey. One block can separate a comfy tourist zone from the junkies and prostitutes. If you use common sense in avoiding dark and lonely lanes, you should be fine.

Language Barrier: In posted information throughout the city (such as museum descriptions), you'll see Catalan first, followed by Spanish (Castellano), and English. Young people, the well-educated, and people in tourism generally speak English in this very touristy city. You will notice a little political tension showing itself in a tendency to favor English over Castellano.

Wi-Fi: The free city network, Barcelona WiFi, has hundreds of hotspots; look for the blue diamond-shaped sign with a big "W" (www.bcn.cat/barcelonawifi).

Baggage Storage: Locker Barcelona is located near the recommended Hotel Denit. You can pay for the day and access your locker as many times as you want, and can even leave bags overnight (daily 8:30-22:00, slightly shorter hours in winter, Carrer Estruc 36, tel. 933-028-796, www.lockerbarcelona. com).

Pharmacy: Pharmacies are sprinkled throughout the Barri Gòtic and Eixample: Look for a bright green illuminated cross. A 24-hour pharmacy is across from La Boqueria Market at #98 on the Ramblas.

Laundry: Several self-service launderettes are located around the Old City. The clean-as-a-whistle **LavaXpres** is centrally located near recommended Plaça de Catalunya and Ramblas hotels (self-service, instructions in English, daily 8:00-22:00, Passatge d'Elisabets 3, www.lavaxpres.com). **Wash 'n Dry,** just off the Ramblas, is in a seedier neighborhood just down the street past Palau Güell (self-service and full service, daily 9:00-22:00, Carrer Nou de la Rambla 19, tel. 934-121-953). For both locations, see the map on page 175.

Bike Rental: Biking is a joy in Citadel Park, the Eixample, and along the beach (suggested route on page 73), but it's stressful in the city center. There are bike-rental places in just about every part of the city; I've listed just a few (all prices include helmets and locks). Handy **Bike Tours Barcelona,** near the Church of Santa Maria del Mar (50 yards behind the flame memorial, near the bike-friendly harborfront), rents bikes and gives out maps and suggested routes (€5/hour, €10/4 hours, €15/24 hours, daily 10:00-19:00, leave €250 or photo ID as deposit, Carrer de l'Esparteria 3—see map on page 175, tel. 932-682-105, www.biketoursbarcelona.com); they also lead bike tours (see "Tours in Barcelona," later).

Barcelona Rent-A-Bike rents bicycles from three locations (€6/2 hours, €10/4 hours, €15/24 hours, all are open daily until 20:00, shorter hours in winter, www.barcelonarentabike. com). You'll find branches in Barceloneta (about four blocks from the Barceloneta Metro stop at Passeig de Joan de Borbó 35—see map on page 74, tel. 932-212-790); near Plaça de Catalunya (inside the courtyard at Carrer dels Tallers 45—see map on page 175, tel. 933-171-970); and at the top of Citadel Park near the Triumphal Arch (Passeig de Lluís Companys 175).

You'll see racks of government-subsidized "Bicing" **borrow-a-bikes** around town, but these are only for locals, not tourists.

GETTING AROUND BARCELONA

Barcelona's Metro and bus system is run by **TMB**—Transports Metropolitans de Barcelona (tel. 902-075-027, www.tmb.cat). It's worth asking for TMB's excellent Metro/bus map at the TI, larger stations, or the TMB information counter in the Sants train station (not always available).

Helpful Apps: The **Barcelona Metro** app provides step-by-step route planning for Metro riders, includes an official TMB Metro map, finds your closest station, and can be used offline. The Barcelona **Citymapper** app covers all public transit. **CityMaps-2Go** lets you download searchable offline Barcelona maps.

By Metro

The city's Metro, among Europe's best, connects just about every place you'll visit. A single-ride ticket *(bitllet senzill)* costs €2.20. The T10 Card—€10.20 for 10 rides—is a great deal (cutting the per-ride cost by more than half). The card is shareable, even by companions (insert the card in the machine per passenger). The back of your T10 card will show how many trips were taken, with the time and date of each ride. One "ride" covers

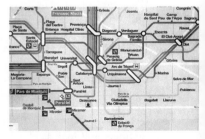

you for 1.25 hours of unlimited use on all Metro and local bus lines, as well as local rides on the Renfe and Rodalies de Catalunya train lines (including the ride to the train station) and the suburban FGC trains. Transfers made within your 1.25-hour limit are not counted as a new ride, but you still must revalidate your T10 Card whenever you transfer.

Multiday "Hola BCN!" travel cards are also available (€15/2 days, €22/3 days, €28.50/4 days, €35/5 days).

Buy tickets from ticket machines in the Metro station. They're easy—just press "English" to start. They'll give you the whole array of tickets you can buy, from individual to T10. Most machines accept coins, bills, and credit/debit cards.

Whatever type of ticket you use, insert it in the turnstile, retrieve it, and walk through. To exit, you don't need to insert it into the turnstile, but keep it until you have exited in case an inspector asks to see it.

Barcelona has several color-coded Metro lines. Most useful for tourists is the **L3 (green)** line. Handy city-center stops on this line include (in order):

Sants Estació: Main train station

Espanya: Plaça d'Espanya, with access to the lower part of Montjuïc and trains to Montserrat

Paral-lel: Funicular to the top of Montjuïc

Drassanes: Bottom of the Ramblas, near Maritime Museum and Maremagnum mall

Liceu: Middle of the Ramblas, near the heart of the Barri Gòtic and cathedral

Plaça de Catalunya: Top of the Ramblas and main square with TI, airport bus, and lots of transportation connections

Passeig de Gràcia: Classy Eixample street at the Block of Discord; also connection to L2 (purple) line to Sagrada Família and L4 (yellow) line (described below)

Diagonal: Gaudí's La Pedrera

The **L4 (yellow)** line, which crosses the L3 (green) line at Passeig de Gràcia, has a few helpful stops, including **Joanic** (bus #116 to Park Güell), **Jaume I** (between the Barri Gòtic/cathedral and El Born/Picasso Museum), and **Barceloneta** (at the south end of El Born, near the harbor action).

Before riding the Metro, study a map (available at TIs, posted at entrances, and printed on some tourist city maps and in the front of this book) to get familiar with the system. Look for your line number and color, and find the end stop for your direction of travel. Enter the Metro by inserting your ticket into the turnstile (with the arrow pointing in), then reclaim it. Follow signs for your line and direction. On board, most trains have handy lighted displays that indicate upcoming stops. Because the lines cross one another multiple times, there can be several ways to make any one journey. (It's

ORIENTATION

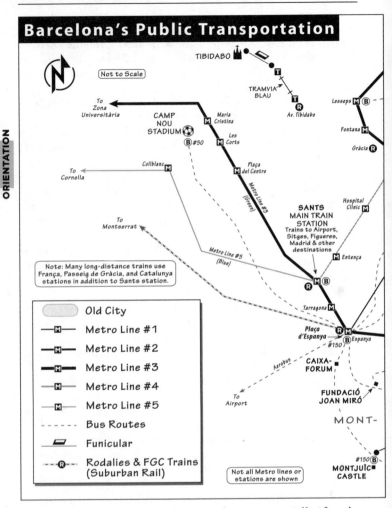

Barcelona's Public Transportation

a good idea to keep a general map with you—especially if you're transferring.)

Watch your valuables. If I were a pickpocket, I'd set up shop along the made-for-tourists L3 (green) line.

By Bus

Given the excellent Metro service, it's unlikely you'll spend much time on **local buses** (also €2.20, covered by T10 Card, insert ticket in machine behind driver). However, buses are useful for reaching Park Güell, connecting the sights on Montjuïc, and getting to the beach. For information on **hop-on, hop-off bus tours,** see "Tours in Barcelona," later.

By Taxi

Barcelona is one of Europe's best taxi towns. Taxis are plentiful and honest, and cab rates are reasonable (€2.10 drop charge, about €1/kilometer, slightly more expensive *"Tarif 2"* rates are in effect weekdays 20:00-8:00 as well as holidays, *"Tarif 3"* rates apply on weekend evenings 20:00-6:00, €1 surcharge per large suitcase, €2.10 surcharge to/from Sants train station, €3.10 surcharge for airport or cruise port, other fees posted in window). Save time by catching a cab (figure €10 from Ramblas to Sants station).

City of Festivals

Barcelona celebrates more festivals, markets, and street fairs than your average city. They dance the *sardana* (a circle dance), build human pyramids, parade colorful *gegants* (giant puppets), and light up the night with fireworks displays called *correfoc* (fire run). Here's a rundown of Barcelona's most lively festivals, listed roughly in chronological order.

Les Festes de Santa Eulàlia: Celebrating the patron saint of the city, this four-day festival features parades, dancing, *correfocs*, and many kid-friendly activities (mid-Feb, www.bcn.cat/santaeulalia).

El Día de Sant Jordi: This celebration of St. George, the patron saint of Catalunya, is also Barcelona's version of Valentine's Day, when lovers and friends exchange books and flowers, and the streets are draped with the red-and-gold Catalan flag (April 23).

Corpus Christi: This festival, dating to 1320, contains traditional elements such as processions, music, and "dancing" eggs. The eggs, placed in flower-decorated fountains, spin ("dance") atop jets of water (late May/early June, http://barcelonacultura.bcn.cat, click on "Festivals and Traditions").

Grec Festival de Barcelona: The city's premier summer arts festival has dance, theater, and music, with several events at Teatre Grec—a Greek-style amphitheater (usually July, http://grec.bcn.cat).

Música als Parcs: Jazz and classical music fill the air in this popular series of evening concerts at city parks (June-Aug).

La Festa Catalana: The city hosts a little spectacle of local folk traditions—human towers *(castells)*, giant puppets *(gegants)*, folk music and dancing—in spring and summer on the square in front of the cathedral (Saturdays at 19:30, May-Sept).

Festes de Sant Roc: The Barri Gòtic's biggest street party is filled with *gegants*, *sardana* dancing, street games, and fireworks (mid-Aug).

Festa Major de Gràcia: For eight days and nights, this festival features live music, *sardana* dancing, human pyramids, and traditional food and drinks (mid-Aug, www.festamajordegracia.cat).

La Mercè: Barcelona's main street festival is named after the city's patron saint, the Virgen de la Mercè. During the five-day festival the city is filled with fireworks, music, an air show, human pyramids, a parade, and much more (late Sept, http://lameva.barcelona.cat/merce/en).

Tours in Barcelona

ON FOOT

🎧 To sightsee on your own, download my free Barcelona City Walk audio tour, which illuminates some of the city's top sights and neighborhoods. My Eixample Walk audio tour will be available in 2019. See the sidebar on page 6 for details.

TI Walking Tours

The TI at Plaça de Sant Jaume offers great guided walks through the **Barri Gòtic.** You'll learn the medieval story of the city as you walk from Plaça de Sant Jaume through the cathedral neighborhood (€16, daily at 9:30, 2 hours, groups limited to 35, buy online in advance—especially in summer, otherwise buy ticket 15 minutes early at the TI desk—not from the guide, tel. 932-853-832, www.barcelonaturisme.cat). The TI at Plaça de Sant Jaume also offers walks for **gourmets** (€22, Mon-Fri at 10:30, 2 hours) and fans of **Modernisme** (€16, April-Oct Wed and Fri at 18:00, off-season at 15:30, 2 hours).

The TI at Plaça de Catalunya offers a **Picasso** walk, taking you through the streets of his youth and early career and finishing in the Picasso Museum (€22, includes museum entry, runs Tue-Sat at 15:00, 2 hours including museum visit). It's always smart to reserve in advance and double-check departure times with the TI.

Discover Walks

Discover Walks offers good walking tours in under two hours for €19-22. These include **Gaudí** (daily at 10:30, meet in front of KFC at Avinguda de Gaudí 2) and the **Ramblas and Barri Gòtic** (Tue, Thu, and Sat at 15:00, meet in front of Liceu Opera House on the Ramblas). They also have a daily Gaudí tour for €59, which includes entry to Casa Batlló (skipping the line). The company uses exclusively native-born guides—no expats (tel. 931-816-810, www.discoverwalks.com).

"Free" Walking Tours

A dozen or so companies offer "free" walks that rely on—and expect—tips to stay in business. Though led by young people who've basically memorized a clever script (rather than trained historians), these walks can be a fun, casual way to get your bearings. If you see a "free tour" gathering, and it seems like it may be fun and interesting, you're welcome to just join in. **Runner Bean Tours,** run by Gorka, Ann-Marie, and a handful of local guides, is reliable and well established. They offer two 2.5-hour, English-only walks, one on the Old City and the other covering Gaudí (both tours depart from Plaça Reial daily at 11:00, also at 16:30 March-Sept and 15:00 Oct-Dec, mobile 636-108-776, www.runnerbeantours.

com). They also do night tours (€16), family walks (€15), and more. Groups can range from just a couple of people up to 30.

Local Guides

The **Barcelona Guide Bureau** is a co-op with about 35 local guides who give themed group tours as well as private, customized tours (check website for prices of group walks; private tours start at about €180/2 hours and can go up to €500/4 hours with tickets included; Via Laietana 50, tel. 932-682-422, www.barcelonaguidebureau. com). I've enjoyed working with Sonia Crespo, Mariona Prats, and Monica Sanchez.

José Soler is a great and fun-to-be-with local guide who enjoys tailoring a walk through his hometown to your interests (€250/half-day per group, mobile 615-059-326, see his program details at www.pepitotours.com, info@pepitotours.com). He and his driver can take small groups by car, van, or minibus on a four-hour Barcelona Highlights tour or even a tour outside the city (from €475); they can meet you at your hotel, the cruise port, or airport.

Live Barcelona is a team of guides led by Cristina Sanjuán. They are professional, enthusiastic, lead several different walking or chauffered tours, and can also arrange cruise excursions (from €195/3 hours, tel. 936-327-259, mobile 609-205-844, www. livebarcelona.com, info@livebarcelona.com).

ON WHEELS

Guided Bus Tours

The **Barcelona Guide Bureau** offers several sightseeing tours leaving from Plaça de Catalunya. Tours include most sight admissions and are designed to end at a major sight in case you'd like to spend more time there. The Gaudí tour visits Casa Batlló and Sagrada Família, as well as the facade of La Pedrera (€74, daily at 9:00, 3.5 hours). Other tours offered year-round include Montjuïc (€35, daily at 12:30, 2.5 hours); Barcelona Highlights (€70, daily at 10:00, also Mon-Sat at 12:30, 5 hours); and Montserrat (€52, Mon-Sat at 15:00, 4 hours—a convenient way to get to this mountaintop monastery if you don't want to deal with public transportation). During high season, there are additional itineraries. You can get details and book tickets at a TI, on their website, or simply by showing up at their departure point on Plaça de Catalunya in front of the Deutsche Bank (next to Hard Rock Café—look for guides holding orange umbrellas; tel. 933-152-261, www.barcelonaguidebureau. com).

Catalunya Bus Turístic runs excursions to nearby destinations, including some that are difficult to reach by public transportation. Trips run April-October and include **Montserrat & Gaudí** (€71, Mon-Sat at 8:30, Mon and Fri only in winter,

8 hours, includes Gaudí's unfinished Colònia Güell development); **Easy Montserrat** (€49, Sun-Fri at 10:00, 6 hours, includes the rack railway); and **Salvador Dalí sights** in Figueres and Girona (€79, Tue-Sun at 8:30, 11 hours). All itineraries depart from Plaça de Catalunya in front of El Corte Inglés (live trilingual commentary in Catalan, Spanish, and English; €5 extra for a more in-depth English audioguide; book at TIs, by phone, or online—10 percent web discount; tel. 932-853-832, www.catalunyabusturistic.com).

Hop-On, Hop-Off Buses

The handy hop-on, hop-off **Bus Turístic** offers three multistop circuits in colorful double-decker buses that go topless in sunny weather and are useful as a once-over-lightly tour or simply to get around. The two-hour blue route covers north Barcelona (most Gaudí sights); the two-hour red route covers south Barcelona (Barri Gòtic and Montjuïc); and the 40-minute green route covers the beaches and modern Fòrum complex (this route runs April-Oct only). All have headphone commentary and free Wi-Fi (daily 9:00-

20:00 in summer, off-season until 19:00, buses run every 10-25 minutes, most frequent in summer, www.barcelonabusturistic.cat). One-day (€30) and two-day (€40) tickets, which you can buy on the bus, at the TI, or cheaper online, offer discounts on the city's major sights and walking tours. From Plaça de Catalunya, the blue northern route leaves from El Corte Inglés; the red southern route leaves from the west—Ramblas—side of the square. A different company, **Barcelona City Tour,** offers a nearly identical service (same price and discounts, two loops instead of three, www.barcelona.city-tour.com).

Bike Tours

Bike Tours Barcelona offers three-hour English-only bike tours, during which you'll ride from sight to sight, mostly on bike paths and through parks, with stop-and-go commentary (€25, daily at 11:00, also Fri-Mon at 16:30 in April-mid-Sept, no reservations needed, includes one drink, tours meet just outside TI on Plaça Sant Jaume in Barri Gòtic—or, 15 minutes later, at their bike shop in El Born near the Church of Santa Maria del Mar; for contact info see their bike-rental listing earlier, under "Helpful Hints").

SPECIALTY TOURS AND ACTIVITIES
Spanish Civil War Tours

Nick Lloyd is the author of *Forgotten Places: Barcelona and the Spanish Civil War.* Both he and his partner, Catherine Howley, are passionate teachers, taking small groups on highly regarded walks through the Old Town to explain the social context and significance of the Spanish Civil War (1936-1939) in Barcelona. History buffs absolutely love this tour (€30/person, Mon-Tue and Thu-Sat mornings, fewer in winter, 5 hours with a pair of hour-long stops in cafés for sit-down talks, English only, www.iberianature.com, nick.iberianature@gmail.com).

Cooking Classes and Food Tours

Cook & Taste offers private and group cooking classes in which you'll make and eat four traditional dishes paired with local wines (group classes daily at 11:00 and 17:00, €65/person, €13 extra for guided La Boqueria or Santa Caterina visit offered Tue-Sat morning or Fri afternoon before the cooking class; private class for 2 people-€215/person, less per person for larger groups, includes market visit, meal, and wine; Carrer Paradís 3, tel. 933-021-320, www.cookandtaste.net, info@cookandtaste.net). They also offer a gastronomic tour guided by a chef who shows you gourmet food and wine shops and takes you to La Boqueria.

At **The Barcelona Taste,** Jo Marvel and Joe Littenberg, American ex-pat foodie guides and long-time Barcelona residents, take small groups on guided walks, making three or four stops in roughly three hours. They enthusiastically introduce you to lots of local taste treats and drinks. You can choose from a tour of the Barri Gòtic or the Poble Sec neighborhood at the foot of Montjuïc (€95/person, Tue-Sat at 19:00, reserve early in season, www.thebarcelonataste.com, contact@thebarcelonataste.com).

The team of locals at **Food Lovers Company** carefully select traditional and atmospheric spots where you can sample high-quality seasonal specialties as they share personal insights on Barcelona and its cuisine. You get it all: a tour of the city, learning about and tasting delicious food, and great conversation (€95/person morning tapas tour over 3 hours, €140/person afternoon food tour over 4 hours, maximum 6 people, mobile 617-710-624, www.foodloverscompany.com, hello@foodloverscompany.com).

TOUR PACKAGES FOR STUDENTS

Andy Steves (Rick's son) runs **Weekend Student Adventures** (WSA Europe), offering three-day and 10-day budget travel packages across Europe including accommodations, skip-the-line sightseeing, and unique local experiences. Locally guided and DIY options are available for student and budget travelers in 13 of Europe's most popular cities, including Barcelona (guided trips from €199, see www.wsaeurope.com for details). Check out Andy's tips, resources, and podcast at www.andysteves.com.

ORIENTATION

SIGHTS IN BARCELONA

The sights listed in this chapter are primarily arranged by neighborhood for handy sightseeing. When you see a 📖 in a listing, it means the sight is covered in much more depth in one of my walks or self-guided tours. A 🎧 means the neighborhood is also covered by my free Barcelona audio tours (via my Rick Steves Audio Europe app—see page 6). This is why some of Barcelona's greatest sights get less coverage in this chapter—we'll explore them later in the book, where you'll also find info on avoiding lines, saving money, and finding a decent bite to eat nearby.

For the most popular sights (the Picasso Museum and the big Modernista sights—Sagrada Família, Park Güell, Casa Batlló, and La Pedrera), make online reservations well in advance. For more tips, see the "Sightseeing" section in the Practicalities chapter.

ON OR NEAR THE RAMBLAS

For a self-guided walk down this pedestrian boulevard, see the 📖 Ramblas Ramble chapter. For food and drink recommendations nearby, see the Eating in Barcelona chapter.

▲▲The Ramblas

Meandering through the heart of the Old City is the Ramblas, Barcelona's most famous boulevard. Named for the long-gone stream *(rambla)* whose course it followed, the Ramblas flows from Plaça de Catalunya, past the core of the Barri Gòtic, to the harborfront Columbus Monument. Boasting a generous pedestrian strip down the middle,

the Ramblas feels like a long street festival packed with people—mostly tourists—out browsing. Though it was once vibrant with flowers, a bird market, and newspaper stands, today it's mostly just a big, fun, international promenade with a fabled history. Halfway down is the booming La Boqueria Market.

▲La Boqueria Market

Barcelona has many characteristic market halls, but this is the most central—and the most crowded. Housed in a cool glass-and-steel structure, La Boqueria features a wide variety of produce and Catalan edibles that you'll pay a premium for. Still, La Boqueria's handy location right in the heart of the Old City makes it well worth a visit. For less touristy markets, consider Santa Caterina in El Born (with avant-garde architecture; see page 118), La Concepció in the Eixample (with a neighborhood vibe; see page 151), or Sant Antoni in El Raval.

Cost and Hours: Free, Mon-Sat 8:00-20:00, best mornings after 9:00, closed Sun and many stalls shut down early on Mon, Rambla 91, tel. 933-192-584, www.boqueria.info.

▲Palau Güell

Just as the Picasso Museum reveals a young genius on the verge of a breakthrough, this early building by Antoni Gaudí (completed in 1890) shows the architect taking his first tentative steps toward what would become his trademark curvy style. Dark and masculine, with castle-like rooms, Palau Güell (pronounced "gway") was custom built to house the Güell clan and gives an insight into Gaudí's artistic genius. The rooftop has his signature colorful tile mosaic chimneys and offers a panorama of the city. While some people will find this redundant if also visiting La Pedrera, others will appreciate this exquisite building for its delightfully loopy rooftop and far fewer crowds.

Cost and Hours: €12 timed-entry ticket includes good audioguide—buy in advance online, free first Sun of the month; open Tue-Sun 10:00-20:00, Nov-March until 17:30, closed Mon year-round; last entry one hour before closing, rooftop closes when raining; a half-block off the Ramblas at Carrer Nou de la Rambla 3, Metro: Liceu or Drassanes, tel. 934-725-775, www.palauguell.cat.

Visiting the House: The parabolic-arch **entryways,** viewable from the outside, are the first clue that this is not a typical townhouse. For inspiration, Gaudí hung a chain to create a U-shape,

Barcelona at a Glance

▲▲▲**Picasso Museum** Extensive collection offering insight into the brilliant Spanish artist's early years. **Hours:** Tue-Sun 9:00-19:00, Thu until 21:30, closed Mon. See page 45.

▲▲▲**Sagrada Família** Gaudí's remarkable, unfinished church—a masterpiece in progress. **Hours:** Mon-Sat 9:00-20:00, Sun 10:30-20:00, March and Oct until 19:00, Nov-Feb until 18:00. See page 55.

▲▲**The Ramblas** Barcelona's colorful, gritty, tourist-filled pedestrian thoroughfare. See page 32.

▲▲**Palace of Catalan Music** Best Modernista interior in Barcelona. **Hours:** One-hour English tours daily every hour 10:00-15:00, plus frequent concerts. See page 45.

▲▲**La Pedrera (Casa Milà)** Barcelona's quintessential Modernista building and Gaudí creation. **Hours:** Daily 9:00-20:00, Nov-Feb until 18:30. See page 53.

▲▲**Park Güell** Colorful Gaudí-designed park overlooking the city. **Hours:** Monumental Zone open daily 8:00-20:30 (May-Aug until 21:30), Nov-March 8:30-18:15. See page 56.

▲▲**Catalan Art Museum** World-class showcase of this region's art, including a substantial Romanesque collection. **Hours:** Tue-Sat 10:00-20:00 (Oct-April until 18:00), Sun 10:00-15:00, closed Mon year-round. See page 66.

▲**La Boqueria Market** Colorful but touristy produce market, just off the Ramblas. **Hours:** Mon-Sat 8:00-20:00, best mornings after 9:00, closed Sun, many stalls shut down early on Mon. See page 33.

▲**Palau Güell** Exquisitely curvy Gaudí interior and fantasy rooftop. **Hours:** Tue-Sun 10:00-20:00, Nov-March until 17:30, closed Mon year-round. See page 33.

▲**Maritime Museum** A sailor's delight, housed in a medieval shipyard. **Hours:** Daily 10:00-20:00. See page 37.

▲**Barcelona Cathedral** Colossal Gothic cathedral ringed by distinctive chapels. **Hours:** Generally open to visitors Mon-Fri 8:30-19:30, Sat-Sun until 20:00. See page 41.

SIGHTS

▲*Sardana* **Dances** Patriotic dance in which proud Catalans join hands in a circle. **Hours:** Every Sun at 11:15, sometimes also Sat at 18:00, no dances in Aug. See page 41.

▲**Gaudí Exhibition Center** Fine exhibit about the man who made Barcelona what it is today. **Hours:** Daily 10:00-20:00, Nov-Feb until 18:00. See page 41.

▲**Frederic Marès Museum** Quirky museum highlighted by Marès' collection of bric-a-brac from 19th-century Barcelona. **Hours:** Tue-Sat 10:00-19:00, Sun until 20:00, closed Mon. See page 43.

▲**Barcelona History Museum** One-stop trip through town history, from Roman times to today. **Hours:** Tue-Sat 10:00-19:00, Sun until 20:00, closed Mon. See page 44.

▲**Santa Caterina Market** Fine market hall built on the site of an old monastery and updated with a wavy Gaudí-inspired roof. **Hours:** Mon-Sat 7:30-15:30, open until 20:30 on Tue and Thu-Fri, closed Sun. See page 47.

▲**Church of Santa Maria del Mar** Catalan Gothic church, built by wealthy medieval shippers. **Hours:** Generally open to visitors Mon-Sat 9:00-20:30, Sun from 10:00. See page 48.

▲**Casa Batlló** Gaudí-designed home topped with fanciful dragon-inspired roof. **Hours:** Daily 9:00-21:00. See page 52.

▲**Fundació Joan Miró** World's best collection of works by Catalan modern artist Joan Miró and his contemporaries. **Hours:** Tue-Sat 10:00-20:00 (Thu until 21:00), Sun 10:00-15:00, shorter hours in winter, closed Mon year-round. See page 62.

▲**Magic Fountains** Lively fountain spectacle near Plaça d'Espanya. **Hours:** June-Sept Wed-Sun 21:30-22:30, April-May and Oct Thu-Sat 21:00-22:00, winter Thu-Sat 20:00-21:00 (no shows Jan-Feb). See page 70.

▲**CaixaForum** Modernista brick factory, now occupied by cutting-edge cultural center featuring good temporary art exhibits. **Hours:** Daily 10:00-20:00. See page 71.

▲**Barcelona's Beaches** Fun-filled, man-made beaches reaching from the harbor to the Fòrum. See page 73.

SIGHTS

then flipped it upside-down. The wrought-iron doors were cleverly designed so that those inside could see out, and light from the outside could get in—but not vice versa.

The Neo-Gothic **cellar,** with its mushroom pillars, was used as a stable—notice the rings on some of the posts used to tie up the horses (WCs are in the far corner).

A grand staircase leads to the **living space,** including a family room, dining room, and so on. Photos show how the Güell fam-

ily—with their textile wealth—originally furnished the place. The intricacy of Gaudí's design work evokes the impossibly complex patterns that decorate great Moorish palaces. Step onto the terrace out back, and take a look at the bay window, elaborately decorated in a sort of industrial fantasy.

The tall, skinny, atrium-like **central hall** fills several floors under a parabolic dome. Behind the grand, gilded doors is a personal chapel, which made it easy to instantly convert the hall from a secular space to a religious one.

Upstairs are Isabel Güell's bedrooms, rooms with period furniture, and a film telling the story of the two men behind this building: Gaudí and his patron, the building's resident and namesake, Eusebi Güell. At a time when most wealthy urbanites were moving to the Eixample, Güell decided to stay in the Old City.

The most dramatic space is the **rooftop;** Gaudí slathered the 20 chimneys and ventilation towers with bits of stained glass, ceramic tile, and marble to create a forest of giant upside-down ice-cream cones. Move around the rooftop, which follows the form of the parabolic dome you

just saw inside, and admire the view of Barcelona from this high perch.

Plaça Reial

This genteel-feeling square, with palm trees and a pair of Gaudí-designed lampposts, is a welcoming open space in the otherwise claustrophobic Old City. You can sit down for a drink at one of the touristy bars, or just lean up against the fountain and take it all in.

LOWER RAMBLAS AND HARBORFRONT
▲Maritime Museum (Museu Marítim)

Barcelona's medieval shipyard, the best preserved in the entire Mediterranean, is home to an excellent museum near the bottom of the Ramblas. The museum's permanent collection covers the salty history of ships and navigation from the 13th to the 18th century (restoration projects on their permanent collection will eventually reveal pieces from the 18th to the 20th century). Even if you choose not to pay for a full visit, the building is worth a look; interesting free exhibits are in the lobby (inside the main entrance facing the water), where you can get a glimpse of the building's interior.

Cost and Hours: €10, free Sun from 15:00 and for kids 16 and under, ticket includes audioguide and visit to *Santa Eulàlia* boat; open daily 10:00-20:00, nice café with seating inside or out on the museum courtyard (free to enter), Avinguda de les Drassanes, Metro: Drassanes, tel. 933-429-920, www. mmb.cat.

Visiting the Museum: The building's cavernous halls evoke the 14th-century days when Catalunya was a naval and shipbuilding power, cranking out 30 huge galleys each winter. As in the US today, military and commercial ventures mingled as Catalunya built its trading empire.

Start your visit in the video room for a six-minute introduction to the building and its history. Then head to the highlight: the impressively huge and richly decorated replica of the royal galley *Juan de Austria,* which fought in the 1571 Battle of Lepanto. Displays describe its history and daily life on a galley. At the stern of the boat, a screening room shows a five-minute first-person dramatized video about galley life. To get a seagulls' eye view, go up the stairs to a raised platform at either end of the ship.

Several other less interesting boats are scattered around the halls. Return your audioguide system before entering the exhibit *7Vaixells, 7Histories* (7 Boats, 7 Stories), which delves into the boats' experiences with conflict, leisure, discoveries, cargo transport, pirating, travel, and technological advances.

Nearby: Your museum ticket includes entrance to the *Santa Eulàlia,* an early 20th-century schooner docked a short walk from the Columbus Monument (otherwise €3, Tue-Sun 10:00-20:30, Nov-March until 17:30, closed Mon year-round). On Saturday mornings, you can sail around the harbor on the schooner for three

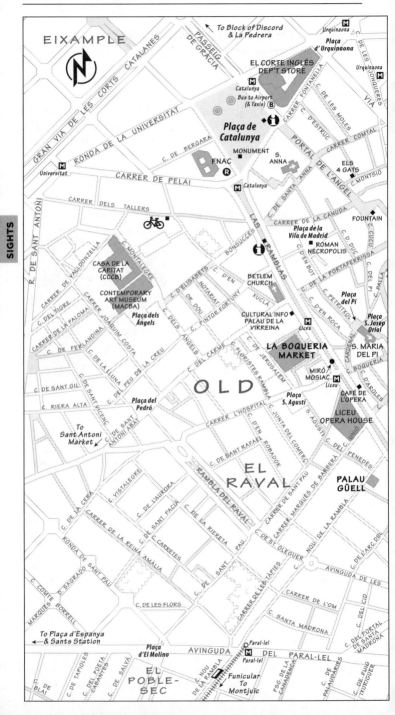

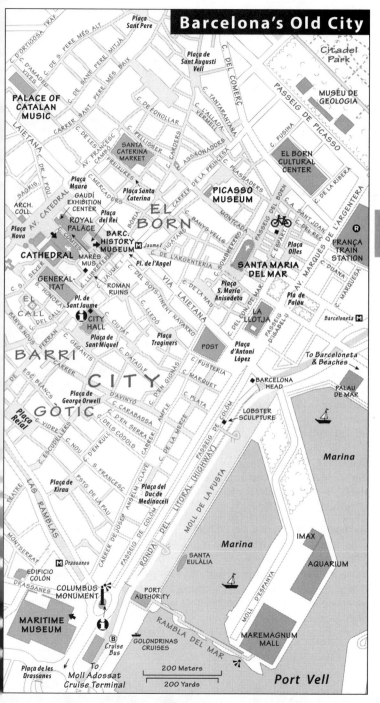

Barcelona's Old City

hours—reserve well in advance (Sat 10:00-13:00, €12 for adults, €6 for kids 6-14, tel. 933-429-920, reserves.mmaritim@diba.cat).

Columbus Monument (Monument a Colóm)

Located where the Ramblas hits the harbor, this 200-foot-tall monument was built for the 1888 world's fair and commemorates Columbus' visit to Barcelona following his first trip to America. A tight four-person elevator takes you to a glassed-in observation area at the top for congested and average views (for better options, see the "Barcelona's Best Views" sidebar, later). There is a small and usually uncrowded TI inside the base of the monument.

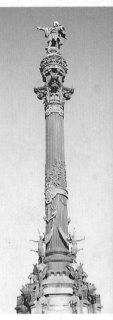

Cost and Hours: Elevator-€6, daily 8:30-19:30, when crowded line may close up to an hour early, Plaça del Portal de la Pau.

Golondrinas Cruises

At the harbor near the Columbus Monument, tourist boats called *golondrinas* offer two different unguided trips, giving you a view of Barcelona's (unimpressive) skyline from the water. The shorter version goes around the harbor in 40 minutes (€7.70, daily about 11:30-19:00, more in summer, fewer in winter, tel. 934-423-106, www.lasgolondrinas.com). The 1.5-hour trip goes up the coast to the Fòrum complex and back (€15.20, can disembark at Fòrum in summer only, daily 11:30-19:30, shorter hours off-season).

BARRI GÒTIC

For more details on this area and several of the following sights, see the 📖 Barri Gòtic Walk chapter or download my free 🎧 Barcelona City Walk audio tour.

Avinguda del Portal de l'Angel

This broad, traffic-free boulevard, which connects the modern Plaça de Catalunya to its historic cathedral district, is Barcelona's most well-trodden street. Although overrun with Spanish and international chain stores, its circa-1888 remodel has left it with a certain dignified air. Just off this drag, you'll discover humble old churches and the famous bar called Els Quatre Gats, where a young Picasso got his start. For tips on shopping along this street, see page 212.

▲Barcelona Cathedral (Catedral de Barcelona)

The city's 14th-century, Gothic-style cathedral (with a Neo-Gothic facade) has played a significant role in Barcelona's history—but as far as grand cathedrals go, this one is relatively unexciting. Still, it's worth a visit to see its richly decorated chapels, finely carved choir, tomb of Santa Eulàlia, and restful cloister with gurgling fountains and resident geese.

Cost: Free to enter Mon-Sat before 12:30, Sun before 13:45, and daily after 17:45, but during those times you must pay €3 each to visit the choir or the terrace (the museum is closed during these hours, and church access may be limited during services). The church is open to tourists for several hours each afternoon (Mon-Sat 12:30-17:30, Sun 14:00-17:15), but you must pay €7 (covers admission to choir, terrace, and museum).

Hours: Cathedral generally open to visitors Mon-Fri 8:30-19:30, Sat-Sun until 20:00. The cathedral's three minor sights are open Mon-Sat (with different hours) and closed Sun: choir—9:00-19:00, terrace—9:00-18:00, museum—12:30-17:15. Both the choir and terrace may close earlier on slow days.

Information: Tel. 933-151-554, www.catedralbcn.org.

□ See the Barcelona Cathedral Tour chapter.

▲*Sardana* Dances

If you're in town on a weekend, you can see the *sardana*, a patriotic dance in which Barcelonans link hands and dance in a circle (Sun at 11:15, many Sat at 18:00, no dances in Aug, event lasts 1-2 hours, in the square in front of the cathedral; for details, see the sidebar).

▲Gaudí Exhibition Center

This center fills the stony complex of ancient and medieval buildings immediately to the left of the cathedral with a beautifully lit, thoughtful, and well-described exhibit. With plenty of historic artifacts, it provides the best introduction to Antoni Gaudí—the man and the architect. You'll spend about an hour following the included audioguide through six rooms on three floors.

Cost and Hours: €15; daily 10:00-20:00, Nov-Feb until 18:00, last entry one hour before closing; Pla de la Seu 7, Metro: Jaume I, tel. 932-687-582, www.gaudiexhibitioncenter.com. While a combo-ticket sold here includes entrance to the great Modernista sights, it's impractical considering the necessity of booking those sights in advance.

SIGHTS

SIGHTS

Circle Dances in Squares and Castles in the Air

From group circle dancing to human towers, Catalans have some interesting and unique traditions. A memorable Barcelona experience is watching (or participating in) the patriotic **sardana** dances. Locals of all ages seem to spontaneously appear. For some it's a highly symbolic, politically charged action representing Catalan unity—but for most it's just a fun chance to kick up their heels. All are welcome, even tourists cursed with two left feet. The dances are held in the square in front of the cathedral on Sundays at 11:15 (and many Saturdays at 18:00).

Participants gather in circles after putting their things in the center—symbolic of community and sharing (and the ever-present risk of theft). Holding hands, dancers raise their arms—slow-motion, *Zorba the Greek*-style—as they hop and sway gracefully to the music. The band *(cobla)* consists of a long flute, tenor and soprano oboes, strange-looking brass instruments, and a tiny bongo-like drum *(tambori)*. The rest of Spain mocks this lazy circle dance, but considering what it takes for a culture to survive within another culture's country, it is a stirring display of local pride and patriotism. During the 36 years of Franco's dictatorship, the *sardana* was forbidden.

Another Catalan tradition is the **castell,** a tower erected solely of people. *Castells* pop up on special occasions, such as the Festa Major de Gràcia in mid-August and La Mercè festival in late September. Towers can be up to 10 humans high. Imagine balancing 50 or 60 feet in the air, with nothing but a pile of flesh and bone between you and the ground. The base is formed by burly supports called *baixos;* above them are the *manilles* ("handles"), which help haul up the people to the top. The *castell* is capped with a human steeple—usually a child—who extends four fingers into the air, representing the four red stripes of the Catalan flag. A scrum of spotters (called *pinyas*) cluster around the base in case anyone falls. *Castelleres* are judged both on how quickly they erect their human towers and how fast they can take them down. Besides during festivals, you can usually see *castells* in front of the cathedral on spring and summer Saturdays at 19:30 (as part of La Festa Catalana; see page 26). If you've never seen this, it's worth searching for the spectacle on YouTube.

One thing that these two traditions have in common is their communal nature. Perhaps it's no coincidence, as Catalunya is known for its community spirit, team building, and socialistic bent.

▲Frederic Marès Museum (Museu Frederic Marès)

This delightful museum, adjacent to the cathedral, features the eclectic collection of Frederic Marès (1893-1991), a local sculptor and packrat. The museum sprawls through several old Barri Gòtic buildings around a peaceful courtyard. It offers a fascinating look at ancient Roman statues from this region and is an exquisite warehouse of Romanesque and Gothic Christian art from Catalunya.

Cost and Hours: €4.20, free first Sun of the month and all other Sun from 15:00; open Tue-Sat 10:00-19:00, Sun until 20:00, closed Mon; audioguide-€1, Plaça de Sant Iu 5, Metro: Jaume I, tel. 932-563-500, www.museumares.bcn.cat.

Visiting the Museum: The entire museum is well described with the essential audioguide. Think of the first two floors as private inspiration for Marès, whose own art can be found in his former library/studio on floor 3.

The top floor offers a glimpse at life in 19th-century Barcelona through Marès' fascinating "Collector's Cabinet"—an entire attic stacked with curiosities. This quirky and intimate collection features a dozen rooms of scissors, keys, irons, fans, nutcrackers, stamps, pipes, snuffboxes, opera glasses, pocket watches, bicycles, toy soldiers, dolls, and other bric-a-brac.

Eating: The tranquil courtyard café offers a pleasant break, even when the museum is closed (café open in spring and summer only, until 22:00).

Plaça de Sant Jaume

This open-feeling square (a rarity in the tight Barri Gòtic) is flanked by the two most important administrative buildings in Catalunya: the Palau de la Generalitat (home of the autonomous Catalan government) and the Barcelona City Hall.

Roman Temple of Augustus (Temple Roma d'August)

Tucked inside a small medieval courtyard, four columns from an ancient temple of Augustus are a reminder of Barcelona's Roman origins. The temple, dating from the late first century BC, stood at one corner of the ancient forum quarter.

Cost and Hours: Free, Tue-Sat 10:00-19:00, Sun until 20:00, Mon until 14:00, Carrer del Paradís 10, tel. 933-152-311.

Plaça del Rei

Perhaps the best place in town to get a feel for Barcelona's faint connection to Old World royalty, this "Square of the Monarch" offers a good view of the Royal Palace, where both Spanish kings and Catalan counts once resided. Although the palace complex is mostly closed to tourists, parts of the building are used for exhibits for the Barcelona History Museum.

▲Barcelona History Museum
(Museu d'Història de Barcelona)

At this main branch of the city history museum (MUHBA for short), you can literally walk through the history of Barcelona, including an underground labyrinth of excavated Roman ruins.

Cost and Hours: €7; includes audioguide and other MUHBA branches; free all day first Sun of month and other Sun from 15:00—but no audioguide during free times; open Tue-Sat 10:00-19:00, Sun until 20:00, closed Mon; Plaça del Rei, enter on Carrer del Veguer, Metro: Jaume I, tel. 932-562-122.

Visiting the Museum: Though the museum is housed in part of the former Royal Palace complex, you'll see only a bit of that grand space. Instead, the focus is on the exhibits on the basement level. The included audioguide provides informative, if dry, descriptions of the exhibits; you'll also find abundant English handouts and a handful of video screens showing what this site must have once looked like.

Start with the 10-minute introductory video in the theater (at the end of the ground floor). Then take an elevator down 65 feet (and 2,000 years—see the date spin back as you descend) to stroll the streets of Roman Barcino—founded by Emperor Augustus around 10 BC.

The history is so strong here, you can smell it as you stroll across walkways over the excavated ruins of Roman Barcelona. This was a working-class part of town. The route leads through areas used for laundering clothes and dyeing garments, the remains of a factory that salted fish and produced *garum* (a fish-derived sauce used extensively in ancient Roman cooking), and facilities for winemaking. Next, wander through bits of a seventh-century early Christian church and an 11th-century bishop's palace that shows Barcelona through its glory days in the Middle Ages. The final section downstairs takes you through Visigothic remains, including the octagonal font where Christians were baptized.

Finally, head upstairs (or ride the elevator to floor 0) to see a model of the city from the early 16th century. From here, you can enter **Tinell Hall** (part of the Royal Palace), with its long, graceful, rounded vaults and displays on local medieval history in a Mediterranean context. The nearby 14th-century **Chapel of St. Agatha** sometimes hosts free temporary exhibits.

EL BORN

El Born (Metro: Jaume I) is home to the Picasso Museum, with narrow lanes sprouting from the neighborhood's main artery, Passeig del Born. For a tour of this neighborhood, see the ⏢ El Born Walk.

▲▲▲Picasso Museum (Museu Picasso)

Pablo Picasso may have made his career in Paris, but the years he spent in Barcelona—from age 14 through 23—were among the most formative of his life.

It was here that young Pablo mastered the realistic painting style of his artistic forebears—and it was also here that he first felt the freedom that allowed him to leave that all behind and give in to his creative, experimental urges. When he left Barcelona, Picasso headed for Paris...and revolutionized art forever.

The pieces in this excellent museum capture that priceless moment just before this bold young thinker changed the world. While you won't find Picasso's famous later Cubist works here, you will enjoy a representative sweep of his early years, from the careful crafting of art-school pieces to the gloomy hues of his Blue Period. You'll also see works from his twilight years, including dozens of wild improvisations inspired by Diego Velázquez's seminal *Las Meninas,* as well as a roomful of works that reflect the childlike exuberance of an old man playing like a young kid on the French Riviera. It's the top collection of Picassos here in his native country and the best anywhere of his early years.

Cost and Hours: €12 for timed-entry ticket to permanent collection, free Thu evening from 18:00 and all day first Sun of month, note you must also reserve free hours (up to four days in advance); open Tue-Sun 9:00-19:00, Thu until 21:30, closed Mon; audioguide-€5, Carrer de Montcada 15, tel. 932-563-000, www.museupicasso.bcn.cat.

Advance Tickets: While you can show up and try to buy a ticket or skip the line with an Articket BCN (which you can purchase around town or on-site), your best plan is to consider an advance timed-entry ticket booked online as obligatory.

⏢ See the Picasso Museum Tour chapter.

▲▲Palace of Catalan Music (Palau de la Música Catalana)

This concert hall, built in just three years, was finished in 1908. Its tall facade has many beautiful decorations, but its location—on a narrow street that offers little perspective—makes it hard to appreciate. Still, the building boasts my favorite Modernista interior in town (by Lluís Domènech i Montaner). Its inviting arches lead you

Barcelona's Best Views

Barcelona's delightful architecture is best seen up close, but to fully appreciate the city's scenic beauty, take advantage of one of many panoramic viewpoints. Many require an admission fee, but some are free, such as the castle at Montjuïc. When deciding between viewpoints, target the ones that are already on your sightseeing route.

Cable Car: Although it's pricey and slow to load, the Aeri del Port cable car between Montjuïc and Barceloneta (in either direction) offers a dramatic moving panorama of the city. See page 60.

Park Güell: Inviting, curvy benches along a spectacular terrace offer sweeping views of Barcelona from this foothills park (ticket required). Climb even higher to the Calvary for a free, bird's-eye view of the park and city below. See the Park Güell Tour chapter.

Sagrada Família Towers: Elevators take you up either the Nativity or Passion facade for a good view of the city and a unique angle on this fascinating church (tickets required). See the Sagrada Família Tour chapter.

Montjuïc: Overlooking the port, this hilltop affords free city views from its castle ramparts and Miramar viewpoint park, as well as from the Catalan Art Museum's terrace and stylish restaurant. See page 57.

El Corte Inglés: The gigantic department store on Plaça de Catalunya has a great view cafeteria on its ninth floor. See page 213.

La Pedrera: The rooftop of this Gaudí masterpiece offers up-close views of fairytale chimneys plus a vista of the Eixample and the distant spires of the Sagrada Família. See page 53.

Las Arenas: Take a pay glass elevator or escalate for free (from inside the building) to the restaurant-ringed roof terrace atop this former bullring—now a mall—for some of the best views of the World Expo Fairgrounds and Montjuïc.

Tibidabo: The city's highest peak offers almost limitless (but distant) city and Mediterranean views—if the weather and air quality cooperate. See page 56.

Barcelona Cathedral: A pay elevator takes you up to a view terrace for an expansive city view from the heart of the Barri Gòtic. See page 41.

into the 2,138-seat hall, which is accessible only with a tour (or by attending a concert). A kaleidoscopic skylight features a choir singing around the sun, while playful carvings and mosaics celebrate music and Catalan culture. If you're interested in Modernisme, taking this tour is one of the best experiences in town—and helps balance the hard-to-avoid focus on Gaudí as "Mr. Modernisme."

Cost and Hours: €20, daily one-hour tours in English run every hour 10:00-15:00, tour times may change based on performance schedule, about six blocks northeast of cathedral, Carrer Palau de la Música 4, Metro: Urquinaona, tel. 932-957-200, www.palaumusica.cat.

Advance Reservations Required: You must buy tickets in advance to get a spot on an English guided tour (tickets available up to four months in advance—purchase yours at least two days before, though they're sometimes available the same day or day before—especially Oct-March). You can buy tickets in person at the concert hall box office or at its Modernista ticket window to the left of the main concert hall entrance (box office open Mon-Sat 9:30-21:00, Sun 10:00-15:00, 10-minute walk from the cathedral or Picasso Museum). You can also purchase tickets over the phone (no extra charge, tel. 902-475-485) or on the concert hall website (€1 fee).

Concerts: An excellent way to see the hall is by attending a concert (300 per year, €20-150 tickets, see website for details and to buy tickets, box office tel. 902-442-882). Be aware that concerts advertised as "Palace of Catalan Music" can be performed in two separate concert halls. The Petit Palau hall is new, with none of the Modernisme you're hoping to see. The main concert hall (Sala de Concerts) is Modernista.

▲Santa Caterina Market (Mercat de Santa Caterina)

This eye-catching market hall was built on the ruins of an old Dominican monastery, then renovated in 2006 with a wildly colorful, swooping, Gaudí-inspired roof and shell built around its original white walls (a good exhibition at the rear entrance provides a view of the foundations and English explanations). The much-delayed construction took so long that locals began calling the site the "Hole of Shame."

Come for the outlandish architecture, but stay for the food and the local color (it lacks the tourist logjam of La Boqueria). It's one of my favorite lunch spots in town—either at the recommended **Cuines Santa Caterina** (with inviting restaurant seating inside and out) or at one of several tapas bars in the market. These tapas bars epitomize all that is good with this kind of eating in Spain.

Cost and Hours: Free, Mon-Sat 7:30-15:30, open until 20:30 on Tue and Thu-Fri, closed Sun, Avinguda de Francesc Cambó 16, www.mercatsantacaterina.cat.

▲Church of Santa Maria del Mar
(Basílica de Santa Maria del Mar)

This so-called "Cathedral of the Sea" was built entirely with local funds and labor, in the heart of the wealthy merchant El Born quarter. Proudly independent, the church features a purely Catalan Gothic interior that was forcibly uncluttered of its Baroque decor by civil war belligerents.

Cost and Hours: Entry is free Mon-Sat 9:00-13:00 & 17:00-20:30, Sun 10:00-14:00 & 17:00-20:30. Entry is €5 (when the interior is illuminated and you have access to the choir and the crypt) Mon-Sat 13:00-17:00, Sun from 14:00. They offer €8 guided rooftop tours more or less on the hour during paid entry times (45 minutes, check for English tours and sign up at the door); Plaça Santa Maria, Metro: Jaume I, tel. 933-102-390, www.santamariadelmarbarcelona.org.

El Born Cultural Center
(El Born Centre de Cultura i Memòria)

Occupying the cast-iron structure of a 19th-century market, El Born Cultural Center hosts an exhibition devoted to Barcelona in the 18th century, an active medieval archaeological site, temporary exhibits, and a café.

Cost and Hours: Center—free and open Tue-Sun 10:00-20:00, Oct-Feb until 19:00, closed Mon year-round; Barcelona 1700 exhibit—€4.40, free all day first Sun of month and other Sun from 15:00, includes audioguide, same hours; Plaça Comercial 12, http://elborncuturaimemoria.barcelona.cat.

Chocolate Museum (Museu de la Xocolata)

This museum—operated by the local confectioners' guild—tells the story of chocolate from Aztecs to Europeans via the port of Barcelona, where it was first unloaded and processed. It's a surprisingly serious museum, with good English information, some old chocolate-making equipment, and fancy audiovisual displays. But the history lesson is just an excuse to show off a series of remarkably ornate chocolate sculptures. These works of edible art—which change every year but often include such themes as Don Quixote or Gaudí's dragon from Park Güell—begin as store-window displays for Easter or Christmas. Once the holiday passes, the confectioners bring the sculptures here to be enjoyed.

Cost and Hours: €6, free for kids 6 and under; Mon-Sat 10:00-19:00, summer until 20:00, Sun 10:00-15:00 year-round; between Picasso Museum and Citadel Park at Carrer del Comerç 36, Metro: Jaume I, tel. 932-687-878, www.museuxocolata.cat.

EL RAVAL

El Raval is Barcelona's "new El Born"—a bohemian-chic magnet for the young and trendy and the foodie crowd. El Born, while still lots of fun, is well discovered, and higher rents are driving away small galleries and artisan shops (and opening the door to the big chain stores). Barcelona is restricting business licenses to rein in the congestion there.

Now El Raval is the new frontier for legit businesses. Drug pushers and prostitutes have been bullied out, and this formerly dark, dangerous, and foreboding "wrong" side of the Ramblas is booming. The new **Museum of Contemporary Art** and the massive **Sant Antoni market hall,** reopened after a major renovation, are gentrifying the area like the Picasso Museum and Santa Caterina Market did in El Born. Once congested streets are becoming pedestrian-only. And you can just feel the coming boom in creative and fun-loving shops, cafés, bars, and restaurants. Entrepreneurs, artists, and chefs with more vision than money are finding their future in El Raval.

El Raval was long "outside the walls," a place of abbeys and hospitals, where people with scary diseases could be quarantined safely away from the general populace. Today ancestors of these institutions, modern hospitals, the university, and the Museum of Contemporary Art are injecting energy and decency into the neighborhood.

Visiting El Raval: To explore the area, I'd follow this route (see the color "Barcelona" map at the front of this book). From the top of the Ramblas take a right on Carrer del Bonsuccés, which becomes Carrer d'Elisabets and leads to the Museum of Contemporary Art and Casa de la Caritat (a cultural center). Then turn left on Carrer dels Àngels to reach Carrer del Carme, where a right takes you to the community square at Plaça del Pedró. Continue down Carrer de Sant Antoni Abat to the Sant Antoni Market (a massive 19th-century hall—the heart of the neighborhood), then follow tree-lined Ronda de Sant Pau to Carrer del Parlament, which ends at the Poble Sec Metro stop on wide Avinguda del Paral-lel. Cross this busy street into the El Poble-Sec neighborhood at the base of the Monjuïc hill. Follow the pedestrian street Carrer de Blai (with cheap tapas bars—see next) and Carrer del Roser to Metro Paral-lel.

Eating and Drinking in El Raval: Try **La Masia Bar,** a very local, tight, and rough dive (cheap salads and tapas, Carrer d'Elisabets 16); **Muy Buenas Cocktail Bar,** with a charming 1928 interior (tapas from 20:00, Carrer del Carme 63); **Bar Lobo,** a modern, bright place for tapas (Carrer del Pintor Fortuny 3, tel. 934-815-346); **Els Sortidors del Parlament,** a rustic but high-end, trendy tapas bar with an inviting menu (Carrer del Parlament 53); **Horchatería Sirvent,** famous for its *horchata* (Carrer del Parlament 56); and the elegant **Sirvent Barcelona Ice Cream Shop** (also good for *horchata*, Ronda de Sant Pau 67). **Carrer de Blai** is a long stretch of thriving bars and youthful restaurants where €1 tapas are the norm—half what you'd pay in El Born.

THE EIXAMPLE

For many visitors, Modernista architecture is Barcelona's main draw. And one name tops them all: Antoni Gaudí (1852-1926). Barcelona is an architectural scrapbook of Gaudí's galloping gables and organic curves. A devoted Catalan and Catholic, he immersed himself in each project, often living on-site. At various times, he called Park Güell, La Pedrera (Casa Milà), and the Sagrada Família home. For more on Gaudí and some of his contemporaries, and to learn about Modernisme, see the Eixample Walk chapter.

At the heart of the Modernista movement was the Eixample, a carefully planned "new town," just beyond the Old City, with wide sidewalks, hardy shade trees, and a rigid grid plan cropped at the corners to create space and lightness at each intersection. Conveniently, all of this new construction provided a generation of Modernista architects with a blank canvas for creating boldly experimental designs. At the edge of the Eixample is Gaudí's greatest piece of work, the yet-to-be-finished Sagrada Família.

In this section, I've focused on the big Modernista sights in the Eixample, starting at the center of this neighborhood with the **Block of Discord,** where three colorful Modernista facades compete for your attention: Casa Batlló, Casa Amatller, and Casa Lleó Morera (all on Passeig de Gràcia—near the Metro stop of the same name—between Carrer del Consell de Cent and Carrer d'Aragó). All were built by well-known Modernista ar-chitects at the end of the 19th century. Because the mansions look as though they are trying to outdo each other in creative twists, locals nicknamed the noisy block the "Block of Discord." Of the

SIGHTS

three houses, two are open to visitors—Casa Batlló and the less-crowded Casa Amatller.

By the way, if you're tempted to snap photos from the middle of the street, be careful—Gaudí died after being struck by a street-car.

From the Block of Discord, you're four blocks from Gaudí's **La Pedrera,** and a quick subway ride from his **Sagrada Família.**

Even though Modernisme revolved around the Eixample, traces of this style can also be found elsewhere. Other Modernista highlights include Gaudí's **Park Güell,** where he put his colorful stamp on 30 acres of greenery, **Palau Güell,** just off the Ramblas, and **Casa Vicens** in the Gràcia district—the first house Gaudí designed. There's also Lluís Domènech i Montaner's **Palace of Catalan Music** in El Born and Josep Puig i Cadafalch's **CaixaForum,** at the base of Montjuïc. For information on more Modernista sights, you can visit the Plaça de Catalunya TI, where a special desk is set aside just for Modernisme seekers (see page 17) For a tour of the Eixample, including a route that connects some of these sights, see the 📖 Eixample Walk chapter, or download my free 🎧 audio tour (available in 2019).

▲Casa Batlló

While the highlight of this Gaudí-designed residence is the roof, the interior is also interesting—and much more over-the-top than La Pe-

drera's. The house features a funky mushroom-shaped fireplace nook on the main floor, a blue-and-white-ceramic-slathered atrium, and an attic with parabolic arches. There's barely a straight line in the house. You can also get a close-up look at the dragon-inspired rooftop. The ticket includes a good (if long-winded) videoguide that shows the rooms as they may have been.

Cost and Hours: €24.50 timed-entry includes videoguide—purchase in advance online; daily 9:00-21:00, check website for evening wine and music visits, Passeig de Gràcia 43, tel. 932-160-306, www.casabatllo.cat.

Casa Museu Amatller

The middle residence of the Block of Discord, Casa Amatller was designed by Josep Puig I Cadafalch in the late 19th century for the Amatller chocolate-making family. Only viewable via a group tour, it features mostly original furniture, placed just as the owners had it when they lived there.

Without a ticket, you can still admire the home's Neo-Catalan Gothic facade, with tiles and *esgrafiado* decoration, or step inside the foyer (free during open hours) to see the Modernista stained-glass door and ceiling, and an elaborate staircase. Past the foyer is a café and chocolate shop, where you can taste Amatller hot chocolate with toast.

Cost and Hours: €24 for one-hour English tour at 11:00, €19 for 40-minute videoguided group tour—generally on the hour and at :30 past the hour, admission includes treat from café; open daily 10:30-18:30, advance tickets available online, Passeig de Gràcia 41, tel. 934-617-460, www.amatller.org.

Casa Lleó Morera

This house was designed by Lluís Domènech i Montaner and finished in 1906. The architect demolished and rebuilt the facade, embellishing it with galleries and balconies. To create the sculptural ornamentation, he hired the city's best craftsmen. Look for the recurring references to mulberries in the decoration—an allusion to the family name, Morera (mulberry). The interior is closed to visitors.

SIGHTS

▲▲La Pedrera (Casa Milà)

One of Gaudí's trademark works, this house—built between 1906 and 1912—is an icon of Modernisme. The wealthy industrialist

Pere Milà i Camps commissioned it, and while some still call it Casa Milà, most call it La Pedrera (The Quarry) because of its jagged, rocky facade. While it's fun to ogle from the outside, it's also worth going inside, as it's arguably the purest Gaudí interior in Barcelona—executed at the height of his abilities (unlike his earlier Palau Güell)—and contains original furnishings. While Casa Batlló has a Gaudí facade and rooftop, these were appended to an existing building; La Pedrera, on the other hand, was built from the ground up according to Gaudí's plans. Your ticket includes entry to the interior (with the furnished apartment) and to the delightful rooftop, with its forest of tiled chimneys.

Cost and Hours: €22 timed-entry ticket includes good audioguide—purchase online in advance, €29 premium ticket allows you to skip all lines (see below); open daily 9:00-20:30, Nov-Feb until 18:30; roof may close when it rains; at the corner of Passeig de Gràcia and Provença (visitor entrance at Provença 261), Metro: Diagonal, info tel. 902-400-973, www.lapedrera.com.

Avoiding Lines: The pricey premium ticket makes you a VIP. It allows you to arrive whenever you wish (no entry time, valid 6

months from date of purchase) and skip all lines, including those for audioguides and the elevator to the apartment and roof (often up to a 30-minute wait).

Nighttime Visits: After-hour visits dubbed "Gaudí's Pedrera: The Origins" include a guided tour of the building (but not the apartment), with the lights turned down low and images projected onto the chimneys, along with a glass of *cava* (€34; daily mid-May-Oct from 21:00, Nov-mid-May from 19:00, details online). There's also the "La Pedrera Day and Night" ticket for €41, which combines a normal day visit with "The Origins" nighttime experience.

Concerts: On summer weekends, an evening rooftop concert series, "Summer Nights at La Pedrera," features live jazz and the chance to see the rooftop illuminated (€35, June-mid-Sept Fri-Sat at 20:15, book advance tickets online or by phone, tel. 902-101-212, www.lapedrera.com).

Visiting the House: A visit covers three sections—the rooftop, the attic, and the apartment.

Enter and head up the elevator to the jaw-dropping **rooftop,** where 30 chimneys and ventilation towers play volleyball with the

clouds. (It could be that George Lucas got his inspiration for his Darth Vader helmet from the chimneys.) Look for the archway that frames the Sagrada Família in the distance, and grasp the layout of the city from mountain to sea. For a great view of Eixample city planning, look over into this block's central area, filled with gardens.

Follow the signs to go down to the **attic,** which houses a sprawling multimedia exhibit tracing the history of the architect's career, with models, photos, and videos of his work. It's all displayed under distinctive parabola-shaped arches. While evocative

of Gaudí's style in themselves, the arches are formed this way partly to support the multilevel roof above. This area was also used for ventilation, helping to keep things cool in summer and warm in winter. Tenants had storage spaces and did their laundry up here. In the 1940s there were actually 13 apartment units in this attic space.

Continue the visit by going downstairs to the typical bourgeois **apartment,** decorated as it might have been when the building was first occupied by middle-class urbanites (a seven-minute video explains Barcelona society at the time). Notice Gaudí's clever use of the atrium to maximize daylight in all the apartments.

Back at the **ground level** of La Pedrera, poke into the dreamily painted original entrance courtyard.

▲▲▲Sagrada Família (Holy Family Church)

Gaudí's grand masterpiece sits unfinished in a residential Eixample neighborhood 1.5 miles north of Plaça de Catalunya. An icon of the city, the Sagrada Família boasts bold, wildly creative, unmistakably organic architecture and decor inside and out—from its melting Glory Facade to its skull-like Passion Facade to its rainforest-esque interior. Gaudí took over this project in 1883. It experienced some setbacks in the mid-20th century, but recent progress has been remarkable. The city has set a goal of finishing by 2026, the centennial of Gaudí's death. Visitors get a close-up view of the dramatic exterior flourishes, the chance to walk through the otherworldly interior, and access to a fine museum detailing the design and engineering behind this one-of-a-kind architectural marvel.

SIGHTS

Cost: Purchase timed-entry tickets online in advance; Basic ticket-€15 (church only), Guided Experience ticket-€24 (church and live guide), Audio Tour ticket-€22 (church and audioguide), Top Views ticket-€29 (church, audioguide, and tower elevator).

Hours: Mon-Sat 9:00-20:00, Sun 10:30-20:00, March and Oct until 19:00, Nov-Feb until 18:00, Metro: Sagrada Família, tel. 932-073-031, www.sagradafamilia.org.

Advance Tickets Recommended: Don't show up expecting to buy a ticket. Buying a timed-entry ticket in advance will save you time, money, and possibly the frustration of not getting in at all.

📖 See the Sagrada Família Tour chapter.

Hospital de la Santa Creu i Sant Pau

This distinctive Modernista-style hospital complex was designed by Lluís Domènech i Montaner. A short walk from the Sagrada Família and on the bus line to Park Güell, the hospital's interior and courtyards are well worth a look if you're in the area...and a Modernista fan.

Cost and Hours: €14, €17 with audioguide, €19 guided tour; Mon-Sat 10:00-18:30 (Nov-March until 16:30), Sun 10:00-14:30

year-round; English tours generally daily at 10:30, but times may vary; tel. 935-537-801, www.santpaubarcelona.org.

BEYOND THE EIXAMPLE
▲▲Park Güell

Gaudí fans enjoy the artist's magic in this colorful park, located on the outskirts of town. While it takes a bit of effort to get here, Park Güell (Catalans pronounce it "gway") offers a unique look at Gaudí's style in a natural rather than urban context. Designed as an upscale housing development for early 20th-century urbanites, the park is home to some of Barcelona's most famous symbols, including a dragon guarding a whimsical staircase and a wavy bench bordering a panoramic view terrace supported by a forest of columns. Gaudí used vivid tile fragments to decorate much of his work, creating a playful, pleasing effect.

Much of the park is free, but the part visitors want to see, the **Monumental Zone**—with all the iconic Gaudí features—has an admission fee and timed-entry ticket. Also in the park is the **Gaudí House Museum,** where Gaudí lived for a time—but it's not worth the entry fee for most travelers. Even without its Gaudí connection, Park Güell is simply a fine place to enjoy a break from a busy city, where green space is relatively rare.

Cost and Hours: €7.50 for timed-entry Monumental Zone ticket—purchase in advance online; daily 8:00-20:30 (May-Aug until 21:30), Nov-March 8:30-18:15; tel. 934-091-831, www.parkguell.cat.

Getting There: To reach Park Güell—about 2.5 miles from Plaça de Catalunya—it's easiest to take a taxi, though you can also get there by bus or a Metro plus bus combo. For details, see page 165. For instructions on linking the Sagrada Família to Park Güell, see page 164.

📖 See the Park Güell Tour chapter.

Tibidabo

Tibidabo comes from the Latin for "to thee I shall give," the words the devil used when he was tempting Christ. It's still an enticing offer: At the top of Barcelona's highest peak, you're offered the city's oldest fun-fair, a great spot for kids, and—if the weather and air quality are good—an almost limitless view of the city and the Mediterranean. If you go mostly for the views, a cheaper "Panoramic View" ticket allows access to several classic rides (such as the carousel and airplane ride) at the entrance of the park.

Cost and Hours: Amusement park—€28.50, free for kids under 3 feet tall, €10.30 for kids 3-4 feet tall; Panoramic View zone—€12.70, €7.80 kids under 3 feet tall; hours depend on season—generally July-Aug Wed-Sun 12:00-23:00, closed Mon-Tue, weekends only in off-season, lockers, café, tel. 932-117-942, www.tibidabo.cat.

Getting There: The direct "Tibibus" (#T2A) runs from Plaça de Catalunya to the park about every 20 minutes starting at 10:00 on days the park is open (€3, board on the corner of Plaça Catalunya and Rambla de Catalunya). While public transit gets you there too, if your time is worth much, the Tibibus or a taxi is a better value. Get off at Plaça Dr. Andreu, where you'll see a handful of bars and restaurants (see page 223). From there, take the funicular to the top (€7.70 round-trip, €4.10 if paying park admission, tel. 906-427-017).

Camp Nou Stadium

The home turf of FC Barcelona is a mecca for soccer fans. A tour takes you into the press room, by the box seats, through the trophy room, and past the warm-up bench, ending in a ground-level view of the field and, of course, a big shop to buy official "Barça" gear. You'll also tour a museum tracing the highlights of Barça history, with interactive touch screens and the six championship cups that the team won in a single season ("the sextuple," 2009-2010)—a feat, they say, that will never be repeated. For more on this team and its significance to Barcelona and Catalunya, see page 81.

Cost and Hours: €25 for Camp Nou Experience (includes tour and museum), free for kids 5 and under, €20 for kids 6-13; Mon-Sat 9:30-19:30 (off-season until 18:30), Sun 10:00-14:30 year-round, shorter hours on game days and sometimes the day before, Metro: Maria Cristina or Collblanc, tel. 902-189-900, www.fcbarcelona.cat.

Soccer Games: Buy tickets at the stadium, from Barça's official website, or at the TI. Popular matches (such as those with Real Madrid or A.C. Milan) sell out quickly, in which case you could try online resellers Entradas.com or SportsEvents365.

MONTJUÏC

Montjuïc (mohn-jew-EEK, "Mount of the Jews"), overlooking Barcelona's hazy port, has always been a show-off. Ages ago, it was capped by an impressive castle. When the Spanish enforced their rule, they built the imposing fortress that you'll see the shell of today. The hill has also played an integral role in the construction of Barcelona's great structures—significant parts of the historic city,

SIGHTS

SIGHTS

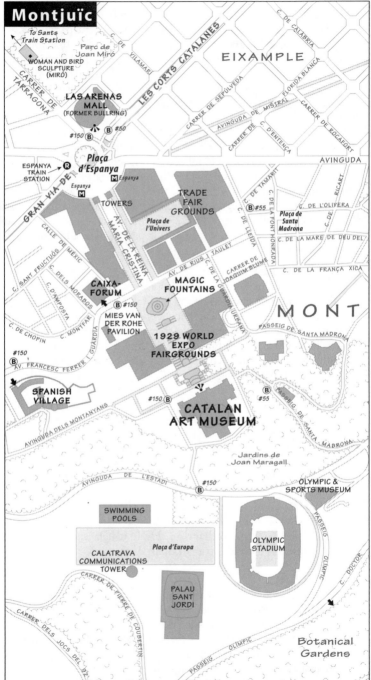

Montjuïc

To Sants Train Station

Parc de Joan Miró

WOMAN AND BIRD SCULPTURE (MIRÓ)

EIXAMPLE

CARRER DE TARRAGONA

C. DE VILAMARI

LES CORTS CATALANES

C. DE CALABRIA

LAS ARENAS MALL (FORMER BULLRING)

CARRER DE SEPULVEDA

FLORIDA BLANCA

AVINGUDA DE MISTRAL

CARRER DE ROCAFORT

CARRER DE LA REINA MARIA CRISTINA

C. D'ENTENÇA

#150 (B)   (B) #50

AVINGUDA

Plaça d'Espanya

ESPANYA TRAIN STATION (R)

GRAN VIA DE

(M) Espanya

Espanya (M)

TOWERS

TRADE FAIR GROUNDS

Plaça de l'Univers

C. DE TAMARIT

(B) #55

C. DE L'OLIVERA

G. DE RICART

Plaça de Santa Madrona

CALLE DE MEXIC

C. SANT FRUCTUOS

C. DELS MORABOS

C. D'AMPOSTA

AV. DE RIUS I TAULET

CAIXA-FORUM

C. DE LLEIDA

C. DE LA FONT HONRADA

C. DE LA MARE DE DEU DEL

MAGIC FOUNTAINS

CARRER DE JOAQUIM BLUME

C. DE LA FRANÇA XICA

C. DE CHOPIN

C. MONTFAR

MIES VAN DER ROHE PAVILION

(B) #150

CARRER DE LA GUARDIA URBANA

M O N T

PASSEIG DE SANTA MADRONA

1929 WORLD EXPO FAIRGROUNDS

#150 (B)

AV. FRANCESC FERRER I GUÀRDIA

SPANISH VILLAGE

AVINGUDA DELS MONTANYANS

#150 (B)

CATALAN ART MUSEUM

(B) #55

PASSEIG DE SANTA MADRONA

Jardins de Joan Maragall

AVINGUDA DE L'ESTADI

#150 (B)

OLYMPIC & SPORTS MUSEUM

SWIMMING POOLS

Plaça d'Europa

CALATRAVA COMMUNICATIONS TOWER

CARRER DE PIERRE DE COUBERTIN

CARRER DELS JOCS DEL 92

PALAU SANT JORDI

OLYMPIC STADIUM

PASSEIG OLIMPIC

C. DOCTOR

Botanical Gardens

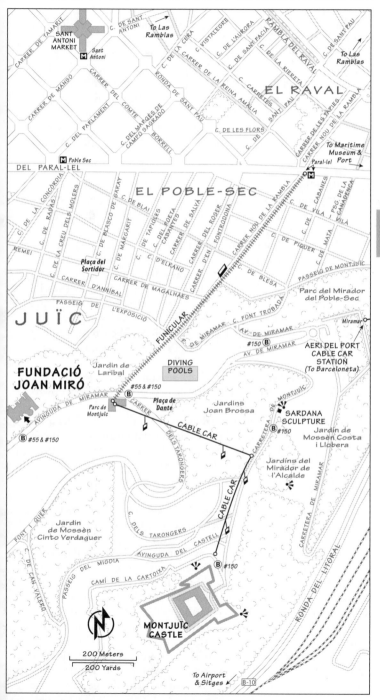

the cathedral, the Sagrada Família, and much more were all built with stones quarried from Montjuïc.

Montjuïc has also been prominent during the last century. In 1929, it hosted an international fair, from which many of today's sights originated. And in 1992, the Summer Olympics directed the world's attention to this pincushion of attractions once again. While Montjuïc lacks one knockout, must-see attraction, it is home to a variety of good sights. For art lovers, the most worthwhile destinations are the Fundació Joan Miró, Catalan Art Museum, and CaixaForum.

Sightseeing Strategies: I've listed these sights by altitude, from the hill-topping castle down to the 1929 World Expo Fairgrounds at the base of Montjuïc. If you're visiting them all, ride to the top by bus, funicular, or taxi, then visit them in this order so that most of your walking is downhill.

Here's one simple plan: From Metro Paral-lel, take the funicular up (included in your Metro ticket). Walk five minutes (left from exit) gradually downhill to the big white Fundació Joan Miró, five minutes more to the Olympic Stadium, and five more to the Catalan Art Museum. From there, descend the stairs to the Magic Fountains. Detour left (if interested) to the Mies Van der Rohe building, CaixaForum, and Spanish Village. Then return to the Magic Fountains and continue on to Plaça d'Espanya, Las Arenas mall, and a Metro stop to the rest of Barcelona.

Getting to Montjuïc: You have several choices. The simplest is to take a **taxi** directly to your destination (about €12 from downtown).

Buses also take you up to Montjuïc. From Plaça de Catalunya, bus #55 goes as far as Montjuïc's cable-car station/funicular. If you want to get higher (to the castle), ride the Metro or bus #50 from Plaça de Catalunya to Plaça d'Espanya, then make the easy transfer to bus #150 to ride all the way up the hill. Alternatively, the red Bus Turístic will get you to the Montjuïc sights.

Another option is by **funicular** (covered by Metro ticket, runs every 10 minutes 9:00-22:00). To reach it, take the Metro to the Paral-lel stop, then follow signs for *Parc Montjuïc* and the (mainly underground) funicular icon—you can enter the funicular without using another ticket. (If the funicular is closed, you'll find a shuttle bus.) From the top of the funicular, turn left and walk gently downhill for the Fundació Joan Miró, Olympic Stadium, and Catalan Art Museum. If you're heading all the way up to the Castle of Montjuïc, you can catch a bus or cable car from the top of the funicular (see castle listing, later).

For a scenic (if slow) approach to Montjuïc, you can ride the fun circa-1929 Aeri del Port **cable car** *(telefèric)* from the tip of the Barceloneta peninsula (across the harbor, near the beach) to the

Miramar viewpoint park in Montjuïc. (Another station, along the port near the Columbus Monument, is always closed.) The cable car is expensive, loads excruciatingly slowly (especially coming from the beach), and goes between

two relatively remote parts of town, so it's really not an efficient connection. It's only worthwhile for its sweeping views over town or to head back down to Barceloneta at the end of the day, as lines are shorter if you board in Montjuïc (€11 one-way, €16.50 round-trip, 3/hour, daily 11:00-17:30, June-Sept until 20:00, closed in high wind, tel. 934-414-820, www.telefericodebarcelona.com).

If you're only visiting the Catalan Art Museum and/or Caixa-Forum, you can take the Metro to Plaça d'Espanya and **walk** up (primarily riding handy escalators).

Getting Around Montjuïc: Up top, it's easy and fun to walk between the sights—especially downhill. You can also connect the sights using the red Bus Turístic or one of the public buses: Bus #150 does a loop around the hilltop and is the only bus that goes to the castle; on the way up, it stops at or passes near the Caixa-Forum, Mies van der Rohe Pavilion, Spanish Village, Catalan Art Museum, Olympic Stadium, Fundació Joan Miró, the lower castle cable-car station/top of the funicular, and finally, the castle. On the downhill run, it loops by Avinguda Miramar, the cable-car station for Barceloneta. Bus #55 connects only the funicular/cable-car stations, Fundació Joan Miró, and the Catalan Art Museum.

Castle of Montjuïc (Castell de Montjuïc)

The castle, which is pretty empty, is mostly worthwhile for the great city views from its ramparts. It was built in the 18th century with a Vauban-type star fortress design by the central Spanish government to keep an eye on Barcelona and stifle citizen revolt. Until the late 20th century, the place functioned more to repress the people of Barcelona than to defend them. Being "taken to Montjuïc" meant you likely wouldn't be seen again. When the 20th-century dictator Franco was in power, the castle was the site of hundreds of political executions. But in 2010, Spain's Prime Minister José Luis Rodríguez Zapatero, keeping a campaign promise, turned over control of the castle from Spain's national government to the city of Barcelona. These days it serves as a park, jogging destination, and host to a popular summer open-air cinema.

Beefy civil war-vintage cannons point visitors to grand Mediterranean vistas. Survey the boats in the harbor: Ships belonging to

Grimaldi Lines, an Italian company, sail off to Genoa, Rome, and Sardinia; Mallorca ferries make the eight-hour trip to Barcelonans' big party escape; and the cruise-ship terminal is the busiest in Europe (Barcelona is the biggest port of embarkation for Mediterranean cruises). The seafront stretching far to the left was part of an Olympic proj-

ect that turned a derelict industrial zone into a swanky stretch of promenades, beaches, and fancy condos. At the far right is Spain's leading port; you'll see containers stretching all the way to the airport.

Cost and Hours: €5, free Sun from 15:00; open daily 10:00-20:00, Nov-Feb until 18:00; €5 English tours daily at 11:30; www.bcn.cat/castelldemontjuic.

Getting There: To spare yourself the hike up, ride bus #150 to the base of the castle, catching it from Plaça d'Espanya, the top of the Montjuïc funicular, or various other points on Montjuïc. Or if the lines aren't too long, consider the much pricier **cable car** (Telefèric de Montjuïc), which departs from near the upper station of the Montjuïc funicular and offers excellent views (€8.40 one-way, €12.70 round-trip, runs daily June-Sept 10:00-21:00, shorter hours off-season).

▲Fundació Joan Miró

This museum has the best collection anywhere of works by Catalan artist Joan Miró (ZHOO-ahn mee-ROH, 1893-1983). Born in

Barcelona, Miró divided his time between Paris and Catalunya (including Barcelona and his favorite village, Mont-roig del Camp). This building—designed in 1975 by Josep Lluís Sert, a friend of Miró and a student of Le Corbusier—was purpose-built to show off Miró's art. The museum displays an overview of Miró's oeuvre (as well as generally excellent temporary exhibits of 20th- and 21st-century artists). Consider renting the wonderful videoguide, which is well worth the extra charge.

If you don't like abstract art, you'll leave here scratching your

Joan Miró: The Freedom of Simplicity

Miró believed that everything in the cosmos is linked—colors, sky, stars, love, time, music, dogs, men, women, dirt, and the

COPA DEL MUNDO DE FUTBOL ESPAÑA 82

void. He mixed simple symbols of these things creatively, as a poet uses words. It's as liberating for the visual artist to be abstract as it is for the poet: Both can use metaphors rather than being confined to concrete explanations. Miró would listen to music and paint. It's interactive, free interpretation. He said, "For me, simplicity is freedom."

Here are some tips to help you enjoy and appreciate Miró's art: First meditate on it, then read the title (for example, *The Smile of a Tear*), then meditate on it again. Repeat the process until you have an epiphany. There's no correct answer—it's pure poetry. Devotees of Miró say they fly with him and don't even need drugs. Psychoanalysts liken Miró's free-for-all canvases to Rorschach tests. Is that a cigar in that star's mouth?

SIGHTS

head. But those who love this place are not faking it...they understand the genius of Miró and the fun of abstraction. Children probably understand it the best. Eavesdrop on what they say about the art; you may learn something.

Cost and Hours: €12, 2-for-1 tickets Thu from 18:00; open Tue-Sat 10:00-20:00 (Thu until 21:00), Sun 10:00-15:00, shorter hours in winter, closed Mon year-round; great videoguide-€5; 200 yards from top of funicular, Parc de Montjuïc, tel. 934-439-470, www.fundaciomiro-bcn.org.

Services: The museum has a restaurant, café, and bookshop (all accessible without museum ticket).

Visiting the Museum: Follow the loosely chronological sequence of Miró works in Rooms 1-15. Temporary exhibits, featuring artists whose work connects to Miró's, are generally in Rooms 16-20 and Espai (Space) 13.

Room 1 (Sala Joan Prats): Young Miró is a sponge of different styles—Fauvism, Cubism, Catalan folk art, Impressionism (see the canvases of beaches and countryside), Orientalism *(Portrait of a Young Girl)*—and whatever else he is exposed to. In 1920, he goes to Paris, dabbles in Dada, and socializes with Surrealists. Is Miró himself a Surrealist? Sort of. They share the same goal: circumventing the viewer's preconceptions about art and reality by juxtaposing unlikely items in order to short-circuit the brain.

Miró's early work does resemble Dalí's. But as his own idiosyncratic style evolves, Miró adds more and more abstraction to the mix. In his Green Paintings series (1925-1927), instead of placing photorealistic items against an otherworldly background (as Dalí would have), Miró arranges highly abstract symbols against a flat background. By 1925, Miró has left the figurative world behind and leaps wholeheartedly into the abyss—pushing the boundaries of abstraction. He paints a completely uninterpretable canvas...and then, just to be cheeky, titles it *Painting*.

Rooms 2-10: In the 1920s, Miró, while attending literary groups in Paris, begins to merge poetry and painting. With the 1930s and the advent of the civil war, Miró temporarily becomes more figurative with his Wind Paintings. Recognizable monsters lurk threateningly. In the early 1940s, Miró flees the Nazi takeover of France and retreats to Spain. He becomes fixated on the heavens and produces his Constellations series—23 paintings of stars, moons, and other brightly colorful items cast against bright backgrounds.

By the late 1940s, Miró is becoming internationally appreciated and within a few years, begins to do more public commissions. But going corporate doesn't tame Miró, as his works from the 1960s and 1970s demonstrate. If anything, he continues to refine his trademark style and strip everything down to basics. Star. Moon. Bird. Woman. (For Miró, "woman" means his wife, Pilar Juncosa, to whom he was dedicated for all his life. His last words—on his deathbed—were put in writing to his wife: "I love you.") Increasingly, Miró's works are intended as something to meditate on. Some of his best-known and most appreciated works date from this period and can't be found in any museum, but are scattered around the streets of Barcelona: in the middle of the Ramblas (see page 87); in the park behind the nearby Las Arenas bullring mall (see page 73); and at the airport's old terminal (#2).

Room 11: The massive 400-square-foot *Tapestry of the Foundation,* which Miró designed for this space in 1979, has real texture—like a painting with thick brushstrokes. Notice Miró's trademark star and moon high above. (A different tapestry, which Miró custom-made for New York City's World Trade Center around this same period, was lost in the 9/11 terrorist attacks.)

In the hallway to the next room, look through the window to find the *Mercury Fountain,* by American sculptor Alexander Calder. This piece was created for the same 1937 exhibition at which Picasso premiered his seminal *Guernica.* Like Picasso's canvas, Calder's fountain was created to honor victims of the Spanish Civil War—in this case, the residents of Almadén, a mercury-mining town. Watch the liquid do its unpredictable thing as it drips and drops.

Room 12 (Sculpture Gallery): This gallery features several small bronze pieces by Miró. Ascend the ramp for a different angle. Nearby, find the stairs down to the Espai 13 installation space. Or continue to the end of the hall and downstairs to a room filled with pieces by other artists paying homage to Miró, plus a 15-minute film about Miró.

Second Floor: Return to earth with a visit to the terrace, where you'll find a modern sculpture gallery and views of the city. Inside there is a study center and good temporary exhibits (Rooms 16-20).

Olympic and Sports Museum (Museu Olímpic i de l'Esport)

This museum rides the coattails of the stadium across the street. You'll twist down a timeline-ramp that traces the history of the Olympic Games, interspersed with random exhibits about various sports. Downstairs you'll find exhibits designed to test your athleticism, a play-by-play rehash of the '92 Barcelona Olympiad, a commemoration of Juan Antonio Samaranch (the influential Catalan president of the IOC for two decades), a sports media exhibit, and a schmaltzy movie collage. High-tech but hokey, the museum is worth the time and money only for those nostalgic for the '92 Games.

Cost and Hours: €6, free for kids 14 and under; Tue-Sat 10:00-20:00 (Oct-March until 18:00), Sun 10:00-14:30, closed Mon year-round, unnecessary audioguide-€2, Avinguda de l'Estadi 60, tel. 932-925-379, www.museuolimpicbcn.cat.

Olympic Stadium (Estadi Olímpic)

Aside from the memories of the medals, Barcelona's Olympic Stadium offers little to see today. But if the doors are open, you're

welcome to step inside. History panels along the railings overlooking the playing field tell the stadium's dynamic story and show the place in happier times—filled with fans as Bon Jovi, the Rolling Stones, and Madonna pack the place.

The stadium was originally built for the 1929 World Expo, but soon thereafter, it played a big part in Barcelona's plan to host the "People's Olympiad." These were to take place in July 1936 as an alternative to Hitler's Fascist Olympics, which were scheduled for that same summer in Berlin (and which Spain had planned to boycott). But just days before the Barcelona games were to begin, civil war broke out in Spain, and the event was cancelled.

Fifty-something years later, the stadium was updated and expanded in preparation for the 1992 Summer Olympics. It was officially named for Catalan patriot Lluís Companys i Jover, the left-wing leader who was president when Spain's civil war began. Companys had pushed for the democratic alternative to Hitler's games; he was later arrested and executed by Franco.

The memorable XXV Olympiad kicked off here on July 25, 1992. At the opening ceremonies, an archer dramatically lit the Olympic torch—which still stands high at the end of the stadium overlooking the city skyline—with a flaming arrow. Over the next two weeks, Barcelona played host to the thrill of victory—most notably at the hands of Michael Jordan, Magic Johnson, Larry Bird, and the rest of the US basketball "Dream Team"—and the agony of defeat (i.e., the nightmares of the Dream Team's opponents). These Olympics also coincided with several turning points in global geopolitics. It was the first Olympiad after the fall of the Soviet Union (and the first since 1972 without boycotts). Twelve newly independent states sent their athletes as one big Unified Team. These were also the first Games in which the post-Apartheid South African team was invited to participate; the first Games after the breakup of Yugoslavia (with four teams from that region instead of one); and the first to feature a reunified German team.

Nearby: Hovering over the stadium is the futuristic **Montjuïc Communications Tower** (designed by prominent Spanish architect Santiago Calatrava), originally used to transmit Olympic highlights and lowlights around the world.

▲▲Catalan Art Museum
(Museu Nacional d'Art de Catalunya)

The mission of this wonderful museum is to showcase Catalan art from the 10th century through the mid-20th century. Often called

"the Prado of Romanesque art" (and "MNAC" for short), it holds Europe's best collection of Romanesque frescoes and offers a good sweep of modern Catalan art—fitting, given Catalunya's astonishing contribution to the Modern. It's all housed in the grand Palau Nacional (National Palace), an emblematic building from the 1929 World Expo, with magnificent views over Barcelona, especially from the building's rooftop terrace.

Cost and Hours: €12, €20 combo-ticket includes Spanish Village, free Sat from 15:00 and first Sun of month; open Tue-Sat 10:00-20:00 (Oct-April until 18:00), Sun 10:00-15:00, closed Mon year-round; worthwhile videoguide-€4; above Magic Fountains near Plaça d'Espanya—take escalators up; tel. 936-220-376, www. museunacional.cat.

Rooftop Terrace: You can visit the rooftop with your museum ticket; rooftop access is €2 without a ticket. To reach the terrace from the main entrance, walk past the bathrooms on the left and show your ticket to get on the elevator. You'll ride up nearly to the viewpoint, and from there hike up a couple of flights of stairs to the terrace. To take an elevator the whole way, go to the far end of the museum, through the huge dome room, to the far-right corner.

Visiting the Museum: As you enter, pick up a map. The left wing is Romanesque, and the right wing is Gothic, Renaissance, and Baroque. Upstairs is more Baroque, plus modern art, photography, coins, and more.

Romanesque: The MNAC's world-class collection of Romanesque (Romànic) art gives a rare glimpse into the medieval mind. Most pieces came from a handful of Catalan village churches clustered in a remote valley in the Pyrenees that thrived c. 1000-1300. These humble stone churches, passed over by the centuries, were rediscovered like time capsules in the 20th century. The art was moved to the museum (1920s) to save them from scavenging art dealers. A series of **videos** shows the process of extracting the frescoes from the walls and moving them here.

In **Room 1,** you're greeted by a fresco of Mary painted in a re-created apse of one of the churches.

Room 2 has the collection's most lively and colorful murals, painted in a straightforward literal style. In the evocative *Stoning of St. Stephen,* unbelievers throw baked-potato-size rocks at Stephen (kneeling at right), who's comforted by a heavenly beam of light. In the room's other scenes, do a Romanesque scavenger hunt to find a camel, roving minstrels, a falconer, a row of horned birds, and other fantastic beasts.

In **Room 4,** one apse features saints in halos (Peter with his keys alongside Mary with a flaming chalice) and the countess who paid for the painting (lower right). The other apse has winged angels (seraphim) who appear to the prophets Isaiah (lower left) and Ezekiel (right), alongside Ezekiel's vision of the four-wheeled flaming chariot.

Rooms 5-7 focus on one of the most popular images in the medieval world: Christ in Majesty (a.k.a. the Pantocrator, or Ruler of All). Jesus is depicted inside an almond-shaped halo, seated on a throne, with one hand raised in blessing, the other holding an open Bible (often with the words *Ego sum lux mundi*—"I am the light of the world"). He's surrounded by either seraphim or the four symbols of the Evangelists. Christ is always easy to identify—he's the only one with a cross in his halo. Room 7 puts all the Romanesque elements together for a great in situ experience—a replica church, with Christ in Majesty in the apse and other Romanesque themes. Become a 12th-century peasant and let these images speak to you.

Browse through **Rooms 8-16** seeing leafy column capitals, wooden crucifixes, and statues of Mary and the saints, until you spill back out into the main hall.

• *Cross the hall to the rooms of...*

Gothic Art: Picking up where Romanesque left off (c. 1300), fresco murals give way to vivid 14th-century wood-panel paintings of Bible stories. Make your way to **Room 26** (straight in, then to the left) and find the collection's highlight: a half-dozen paintings by the Catalan master Jaume Huguet (1412-1492), particularly his *Consagració de San Agustín (Consecration of Saint Augustine)*.

These paintings (impressive enough on their own) were once part of a huge altarpiece—an estimated 40 feet tall and 30 feet wide—with some 20 paintings, done for a church in El Born. Huguet labored on the project for more than 20 years. The theme was the life of St. Augustine. It started with the painting of young Augustine (in black robe and red cap) dropping his pagan books to the floor as he realizes the truth and converts to Christianity. In other scenes Augustine wears his golden robes and bishop's hat as he's shown preaching at a pulpit, or disputing a heretic (in green who tumbles to the ground before the power of Augie's words), or kneeling to wash the feet of a pilgrim (who turns out to be Christ in disguise), or greeting a boy (who turns out to be a vision of young Jesus).

Huguet's masterpiece was the *Consecration* scene, where Augustine becomes bishop and is crowned with the hat. The details are incredible: the bright colors and gold leaf, the sober expressive faces, the brocaded robe with pictures of saints, and the early attempt at 3-D created by the floor tiles. Notice that this isn't simply a "painting"—it has a raised surface, like a cameo. It's a sheet of wood topped with molded stucco, then covered with paints and gold leaf. Nearby is Huguet's *Last Supper,* which was also part of the Augustine altarpiece. The details and faces here are astonishing. There's even an attempt at realistic 3-D: There are saints in front and saints in back, and some disciples pose in profile, some face-out, some from behind. But the table looks slanted, and the food is about to slide off.

• *The Gothic collection leads into...*

Renaissance and Baroque: Browse several rooms, watching as Renaissance artists make altarpieces more balanced and serene, with distant realistic backgrounds. You'll see Spain's Golden Age (Zurbarán, heavy religious scenes, and Spanish royals with their endearing underbites) and examples of Romanticism (dewy-eyed Catalan landscapes). Room 32 has El Greco's *Christ Carrying the Cross* and José de Ribera's saints with wrinkled foreheads. In addition, you'll find minor works by major—if not necessarily Catalan—masters like Velázquez, Goya, Tintoretto, Rubens, and Titian.

Rest of the Museum: The Gothic/Renaissance/Baroque exit spills out by the room of the huge **dome,** which once housed an ice-skating rink and now has a cafeteria. This was the prime ceremony room and dance hall for the 1929 World Expo.

From here, you can ride the glass elevator upstairs to the **modern art** section, which takes you on an enjoyable walk from the late 1800s to about 1950. It's kind of a Catalan Musée d'Orsay, offering a big chronological clockwise circle from Room 1, covering Symbolism, Modernisme, fin de siècle fun, Art Deco, and more. Find the early 20th-century paintings by Catalan artists Santiago Rusiñol and Ramon Casas, both of whom had a profound impact on a young Picasso

(and, through him, on all of modern art). Casas was also one of the financiers of Els Quatre Gats, the hangout of Modernista artists; his fun Toulouse-Lautrec-esque works, including a whimsical self-portrait on a tandem bicycle, are crowd-pleasers. Also admire the central dome, which connects the modern art sections, and a mod 1978 tile panel that Miró created for the local headquarters of IBM.

Crossing over to the "Modern 2" section, you'll find more furniture (pieces that complement some of the empty spaces you may see if you visit Gaudí's buildings—including Gaudí-designed wooden chairs and a sofa), Impressionism, the shimmering landscapes of Joaquim Mir, and several distinctly-Picasso portraits of women.

The museum also has a coin collection, seductive sofas scattered about, the chic and pricey Oleum restaurant (with vast city views), and a comfy outdoor terrace café (serving snacks with more city views).

1929 WORLD EXPO FAIRGROUNDS AND NEARBY

With the World Expo in 1929, Montjuïc morphed into an extravagant center for fairs, museums, and festivals. Nearly every-

thing you see here dates from 1929 (the exceptions are CaixaForum and Las Arenas mall). The expo's theme was to demonstrate how electricity was about more than lightbulbs: Electricity powered the funicular, the glorious expo fountains, the many pavilion displays, and even the flame atop the fountain marking the center of Plaça d'Espanya (and celebrating the electric company that sponsored the show). If Barcelona is known for growing through big events, this certainly is a good example.

Standing at Plaça d'Espanya (or, better yet, on the rooftop terrace of the bullring mall—described later), look through the double-brick-tower gate, down the grand esplanade, and imagine it alive with fountains and lined by proud national pavilions showing off all that was modern in 1929. Today the site is home to the Fira de Barcelona convention center. The Neo-Baroque fountain provides a brilliant centerpiece for Plaça d'Espanya.

Getting There: The fairgrounds sprawl at the base of Montjuïc, from the Catalan Art Museum's doorstep to Plaça d'Espanya. It's easiest to see these sights on your way down from Montjuïc. Otherwise, ride the Metro to Espanya, then use the series of stairs and escalators to climb up through the heart of the fairgrounds (eventually reaching the Catalan Art Museum).

▲Magic Fountains (Font Màgica)

Music, colored lights, and huge amounts of water make an artistic and coordinated splash in the evening near Plaça d'Espanya.

Cost and Hours: Free, 20-minute shows start every half-hour; June-Sept Wed-Sun 21:30-22:30, April-May and Oct Thu-Sat 21:00-22:00, winter Thu-Sat 20:00-21:00 (no shows Jan-Feb);

from the Espanya Metro stop, walk toward the towering National Palace.

▲CaixaForum

The CaixaForum Social and Cultural Center is housed in one of Barcelona's most important Art Nouveau buildings. In 1911, Josep Puig i Cadafalch (a top architect often overshad-owed by Gaudí) designed the Casaramona textile factory, using Moderni-sta design in an industrial rather than a residential context. It functioned as a factory for less than a de-cade, then later served a long stint as a police station under Franco. Beautifully refurbished in 2002, the facility reopened as a great center for bringing culture and art to the people of Barcelona.

SIGHTS

Cost and Hours: Free entrance to building, exhibits-€4, daily 10:00-20:00, Avinguda de Francesc Ferrer i Guàrdia 6, tel. 934-768-600, www.caixaforum.es/barcelona.

Visiting the Center: From the lobby, signs point to *Sala 2, 3, 4,* and *5;* each typically hosts an outstanding temporary exhibition. Ride the escalator to the first floor, which features a modest but interesting exhibit about the history and renovation of the building, including a model and photos. Then head into the appealing red-brick courtyard to access the exhibition halls. The sight features some English descriptions.

Take the stairs or elevator up to the Modernista Terrace (*Planta 2,* or look for signs to *Aula 1*). This terrace, boasting a wavy floor and bristling with fanciful brick towers, offers views over the complex and to Montjuïc. Enjoy the genius of Puig i Cadafalch's Modernista design, which provided state-of-the-art working con-ditions—natural light, good ventilation, and even two trademark towers filled with water (which could be broken to put out any fac-tory fires). The various buildings (separated from each other to re-duce the risk of fire) were built on terraces to level out the Montjuïc slope. Notice that there's no smokestack. This was one of the first electric-powered factories in town.

Mies van der Rohe Pavilion (Pabellón Mies van der Rohe)

Architecture pilgrims enjoy the pavilion that Ludwig Mies van der Rohe designed for the German exhibits at the 1929 expo. Al-though it was dismantled at the end of the fair, the building was heralded as a seminal example of modern architecture, and in the 1980s, the city reconstructed it on the original site. It's small and stripped-down—a strictly functional "Modernist" (i.e., decidedly *not* Modernista) structure. Unless you're a huge fan, skip the entry fee and simply walk around the pavilion to get a peek inside (including views of the "Barcelona Chair," the tubular steel and leather-cushioned chair that's become an icon of 20th-century furniture design).

Cost and Hours: €6, daily 10:00-20:00, Nov-Feb until 18:00, Avinguda de Francesc Ferrer i Guàrdia 7, tel. 934-234-016, www. miesbcn.com.

Spanish Village (Poble Espanyol)

This five-acre model village was built as part of the 1929 expo to show off the cultural and architectural diversity in Spain. You'll see more than 100 building reproductions that show traditional architecture from all over Spain—all built in 1929. The village was mostly a shell to contain workshops and gift shops—and today it still serves the same purpose. While extremely touristy and a bit tacky, many find it enjoyable. Craftspeople do their traditional thing (making guitars, blowing glass, jewelers in action, and so on), and friendly shopkeepers offer plenty of tasty samples of traditional and local edibles. It's especially popular with hurried cruise groups eager to shop.

Cost and Hours: €12.60, €7 Tue-Sun from 20:00, €20 combo-ticket includes Catalan Art Museum, family ticket available; open Tue-Sun 9:00-24:00, Mon until 20:00, Jan-Feb closes earlier; €4.50 videoguide explains all the buildings, www.poble-espanyol. com.

Getting There: It's best to take bus #150, as it's a long hike up from the main World Expo esplanade.

Las Arenas (Bullring Mall)

What do you do with a big bullfighting arena that's been sitting empty for decades? Make a shopping mall. The grand Neo-Moorish Modernista *plaça de toros* functioned as an arena for bullfights from around 1900 to 1977, and then reopened in 2011 as a mall. It now hosts everything you'd expect in a modern shopping center: brand-name shops, a food-court basement, a 12-screen cinema complex, and a rock-and-roll museum.

The **rooftop terrace,** with stupendous views of Plaça d'Espanya and Montjuïc, is ringed with eateries (reachable by external glass elevator for €1 or from inside escalators/elevators for free). Besides getting a bird's-eye perspective of the fairgrounds, you can gaze down at Parc de Joan Miró, which includes the giant sculpture *Woman and Bird (Dona i Ocell)*. This was one of the works (along with the mosaic on the Ramblas) that the city commissioned from the artist to welcome visitors. Miró's sense of humor is evident—if the sculpture seems phallic, keep in mind that the Catalan word for "bird" is also slang for "penis."

Cost and Hours: Free, daily 10:00-22:00, outside elevator and restaurants open until 24:00, Gran Via de les Corts Catalanes 373, Metro: Espanya, exit following *Sortida Tarragona* signs, www. arenasdebarcelona.com.

THE BEACHES & NEARBY
▲Barcelona's Beaches

Barcelona has created a summer tourist trade by building a huge stretch of beaches east of the town center. From Barceloneta, an uninterrupted band of sand tumbles three miles northeast to the Fòrum. Before the 1992 Olympics, this area was an industrial wasteland nicknamed the "Catalan Manchester." Not anymore. The industrial zone was demolished and dumped into the sea, while sand was dredged from the seabed to make the pristine beaches locals enjoy today. Looking out to sea, you can't miss the W Hotel, shaped like a windblown sail, dominating a small peninsula.

The overall scene is great for sunbathing and for an evening paseo before dinner. It's like a resort island—complete with lounge chairs, volleyball, show-

ers, WCs, bike paths, and inviting beach bars called *chiringuitos*. Each beach segment has its own vibe: Sant Sebastià (closest, popular with older beach-goers and families), Barce-loneta (with many seafood restaurants), Nova Icària (pleasant family beach), and Mar Bella (attracts a younger crowd, clothing-optional).

Getting There: The Barceloneta Metro stop leaves you a long walk from the sand. To get to the beaches without a hike, take the bus. From the Ramblas, bus #59 will get you as far as Barceloneta Park; bus #D20 leaves from the Columbus Monument and follows a similar route. Bus #V15 runs from Plaça de Catalunya to the tip of Barceloneta (near the W Hotel).

Biking the Beach: For a break from the city, rent a bike (for rental shops, see page 21 and take the following little ride: Explore Citadel Park, filled with families enjoying a day out (described next). Then roll through Barceloneta. This artificial peninsula was

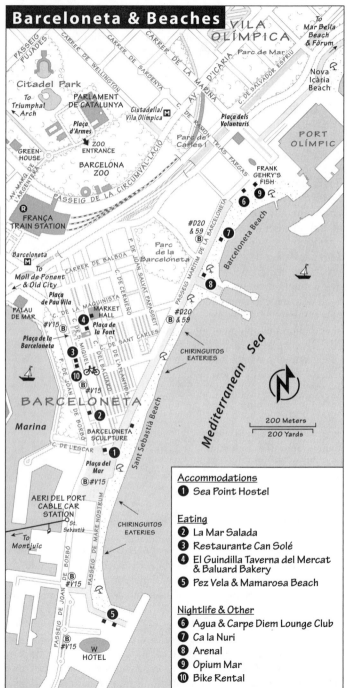

Barceloneta & Beaches

Accommodations
1 Sea Point Hostel

Eating
2 La Mar Salada
3 Restaurante Can Solé
4 El Guindilla Taverna del Mercat & Baluard Bakery
5 Pez Vela & Mamarosa Beach

Nightlife & Other
6 Agua & Carpe Diem Lounge Club
7 Ca la Nuri
8 Arenal
9 Opium Mar
10 Bike Rental

once the home of working-class sailors and shippers. From the Barceloneta beach, head up to the Olympic Village, where the former apartments for 13,000 visiting athletes now house permanent residents. The village's symbol, Frank Gehry's striking "fish," shines brightly in the sun. A bustling night scene keeps this stretch of harborfront busy until the wee hours. From here you'll come to a series of man-made crescent-shaped beaches, each with trendy bars and cafés. If you're careless or curious (down by Mar Bella), you might find yourself pedaling past people working on an all-over tan. In the distance is the huge solar panel marking the site of the Fòrum shopping and convention center.

Citadel Park (Parc de la Ciutadella)

In 1888, Barcelona's biggest, greenest park, originally the site of a much-hated military citadel, was transformed for a Universal Exhibition (world's fair). The stately Triumphal Arch at the top of the park, celebrating the removal of the citadel, was built as the main entrance. Inside you'll find wide pathways, plenty of trees and grass, a zoo, a museum of geology, and a castle-like former restaurant for the fair (closed to the public).

Barcelona, one of Europe's most densely populated cities, suffers from a lack of real green space. This park is a haven and is especially enjoyable on weekends, when it teems with happy families (for more on the zoo and kids' activities in Citadel Park, see the Barcelona with Children chapter). Enjoy the ornamental fountain that the young Antoni Gaudí helped design, and consider a jaunt in a rental rowboat on the lake in the center of the park. Check out the tropical Umbracle greenhouse and the Hivernacle winter garden, which has a pleasant café-bar (Mon-Sat 10:00-14:00 & 17:00-20:30, Sun 10:30-14:00, shorter hours off-season).

Cost and Hours: Park-free, daily 10:00 until dusk, north of França train station, Metro: Arc de Triomf, Barceloneta, or Ciutadella/Vila Olímpica.

The Fòrum

The original 1860 vision for Barcelona's enlargement would have extended the boulevard called Diagonal right to the sea. Developers finally realized this goal nearly a century and a half later, with the opening of the Fòrum neighborhood. Go here for a taste of today's Barcelona: nothing Gothic, nothing quaint, just big and modern—a mall, waterfront esplanade, and a convention center.

Among the modern structures here, you can't miss the triangular **Edifici Fòrum.** Built for a 2004 Universal Forum of Cultures conference and exhibition, the eccentric building was initially controversial, but it's since become a well-regarded landmark. Among other things, the Fòrum tries to be an inspiration for environmental engineering. Waste is burned to produce heat, and a giant solar panel creates perfectly clean and sustainable energy.

Getting There: You can get out to the Fòrum by bike, bus, or taxi via the long and impressive beach. Or the Metro zips you there in just a few minutes from the center (Metro: Fòrum).

RAMBLAS RAMBLE

From Plaça de Catalunya to the Waterfront

For more than a century, this walk down Barcelona's main boulevard has been a magnet for visitors. It's a one-hour stroll that goes from Plaça de Catalunya gently downhill to the waterfront, with an easy return by Metro.

Traditionally the Ramblas has been the place where locals flocked to buy flowers, lottery tickets, and a daily newspaper, or to enjoy a spot of shade while watching the world go by. But much of the local charm of the Ramblas has been taken over by hordes of sightseers, tacky trinkets, and lousy eateries. Unfortunately, the crush of tourists has driven up rents; shops now cater to visitors rather than locals, and the old neighborhood population has fled to more affordable places in the suburbs. Still, if you come to Barcelona...you've got to ramble the Ramblas. (And if you stroll first thing in the morning, you'll find it more charming.)

The word "Ramblas" is plural; the street is actually a succession of five separately named segments. But street signs and addresses treat it as a single long street—"La Rambla," singular. This walk will help you see beyond the tourist crowds to discover the essence of the area. On the wide central sidewalk, you'll raft the river of tourism as you pass plenty of historic bits and pieces of this great city.

Orientation

Length of This Walk: Allow an hour. If you have less time, focus on the stretch between the Fountain of Canaletes and the Miró mosaic at Liceu. With more time, dip into La Boqueria Market.

When to Go: The Ramblas is two different streets by day and by night. To fully experience its yin and yang, walk it once in the evening and again in the morning, grabbing breakfast on a stool in a market café. Note that the Ramblas can be rowdy and off-putting late at night or after the Barça soccer team wins a match. Saturday is the best time to see La Boqueria Market.

Getting There: This walk begins at the Plaça de Catalunya end of the Ramblas, across the square from El Corte Inglés department store (Metro: Plaça de Catalunya).

La Boqueria Market: Mon-Sat 8:00-20:00, best mornings after 9:00, closed Sun and many stalls shut down early on Mon.

Palau Güell: €12 timed-entry ticket, free first Sun of the month; open Tue-Sun 10:00-20:00, Nov-March until 17:30, closed Mon year-round.

Columbus Monument: Elevator-€6, daily 8:30-19:30.

Pickpockets: The Ramblas is prime hunting ground for pickpockets. Keep only today's spending money in your front pocket; secure your credit/debit cards, extra cash, and passport in your money belt.

Services: You'll find WCs at La Boqueria and the Maremagnum mall at the end of this walk.

Get Oriented: Along the Ramblas, odd street numbers are on your right; even numbers are on the left.

Eating: The eateries here are tourist traps: Avoid them. But just off the street you'll find a few handy lunch spots, and the stalls of La Boqueria Market invite grazing. For details, see page 183.

The Walk Begins

• *Start your ramble on Plaça de Catalunya, at the top of the Ramblas.*

❶ Plaça de Catalunya

Dotted with fountains, statues, and pigeons, and ringed by grand buildings, this plaza is Barcelona's center. Plaça de Catalunya is the hub for the Metro, bus, airport shuttle, and Bus Turístic. Of the region's 7.4 million Catalans, more than half live in greater Barcelona. Plaça de Catalunya is their Times Square.

Geographically, the 12-acre square links the narrow streets of old Barcelona with the broad boulevards of the newer city (the Eixample). Four great thoroughfares radiate from here: The Ramblas is the popular tourist promenade. Passeig de Gràcia, Barcelona's answer to Paris' Champs-Elysées, has fashionable shops and cafés

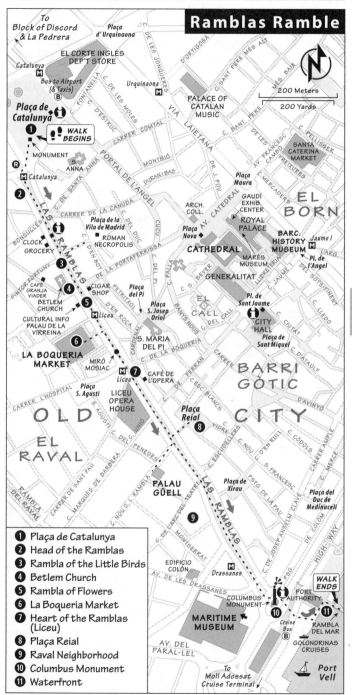

Ramblas Ramble

To Block of Discord & La Pedrera

Plaça d' Urquinaona

EL CORTE INGLÉS DEPT STORE

Catalunya

Bus to Airport (& Taxis)

Urquinaona

200 Meters
200 Yards

PALACE OF CATALAN MUSIC

Plaça de Catalunya

WALK BEGINS

MONUMENT

S. ANNA

Catalunya

SANTA CATERINA MARKET

Plaça Maura

LAS RAMBLAS

PORTAL DE L'ANGEL

BONSUCCES

Plaça de la Vila de Madrid

ROMAN NECROPOLIS

ARCH. COLL.

GAUDÍ EXHIB. CENTER

ROYAL PALACE

EL BORN

CLOCK GROCERY

Plaça Nova

CATHEDRAL

BARC. HISTORY MUSEUM

Jaume I

Pl. de l'Angel

CAFÉ GRANJA VIADER

CIGAR SHOP

Plaça del Pi

MARES MUSEUM

BETLEM CHURCH

GENERALITAT

EL CALL

CULTURAL INFO PALAU DE LA VIRREINA

Liceu

Plaça S. Josep Oriol

Pl. de Sant Jaume

CITY HALL

LA BOQUERIA MARKET

S. MARIA DEL PI

Plaça de Sant Miquel

BARRI GÒTIC

MIRÓ MOSAIC

Liceu

CAFÉ DE L'OPERA

Plaça S. Agusti

LICEU OPERA HOUSE

Plaça Reial

OLD EL RAVAL

CITY

PALAU GÜELL

Plaça de Xirau

Plaça del Duc de Medinaceli

RAMBLA DEL RAVAL

LAS RAMBLAS

EDIFICIO COLÓN

Drassanes

WALK ENDS

COLUMBUS MONUMENT

PORT AUTHORITY

MARITIME MUSEUM

Cruise Bus

RAMBLA DEL MAR

GOLONDRINAS CRUISES

AV. DEL PARAL·LEL

To Moll Adossat Cruise Terminal

Port Vell

1 Plaça de Catalunya
2 Head of the Ramblas
3 Rambla of the Little Birds
4 Betlem Church
5 Rambla of Flowers
6 La Boqueria Market
7 Heart of the Ramblas (Liceu)
8 Plaça Reial
9 Raval Neighborhood
10 Columbus Monument
11 Waterfront

RAMBLAS RAMBLE

(and noisy traffic). Rambla de Catalunya is equally fashionable but cozier and more pedestrian-friendly. Avinguda del Portal de l'Angel (shopper-friendly and traffic-free) leads to the Barri Gòtic.

Plaça de Catalunya links the modern city with its past. In the 1850s, Barcelona tore down its medieval walls to expand the city, and this square was one of the first places to be developed. It once boasted curvy and decorative Modernista buildings (which still predominate in the Eixample district, just above the plaza), but during the Franco years, they were replaced with structures with stern, straight lines.

While Plaça de Catalunya is the center of Barcelona, it's also the cultural heart of the entire Catalunya region. At the Ramblas end

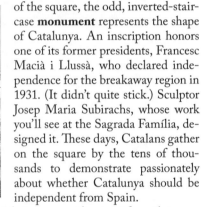

of the square, the odd, inverted-staircase **monument** represents the shape of Catalunya. An inscription honors one of its former presidents, Francesc Macià i Llussà, who declared independence for the breakaway region in 1931. (It didn't quite stick.) Sculptor Josep Maria Subirachs, whose work you'll see at the Sagrada Família, designed it. These days, Catalans gather on the square by the tens of thousands to demonstrate passionately about whether Catalunya should be independent from Spain.

The venerable Café Zürich, just across the street from the monument, was once a popular downtown rendezvous spot. Homesick Americans might prefer the nearby Hard Rock Café. And the giant El Corte Inglés department store towering above the square (on the northeast side) has just about anything you might need.

• *Cross the street, head down about 30 yards, and pause to take in the scene.*

❷ Head of the Ramblas

The street called the Ramblas stretches before you. It slopes gently downhill from here to the harbor. It's dotted with trees and ironwork lampposts, lined with fanciful buildings, paved with colorful mosaics, and trod upon by thousands of people both day and night.

Start with the ornate, black and gold lamppost on your right. The base is a water tap called the **Fountain of Canaletes,** which has been a local favorite for more than a century. When Barcelona tore down its medieval wall and created this elegant promenade, this fountain was one of its early attractions. Legend says that a drink from the fountain ensures that you'll come back to Barcelona one day. Watch the tourists—eager to guarantee a return trip—struggle with the awkwardly high water pressure. It's still a popular let's-meet-at-the-fountain rendezvous spot and a gathering place for celebrations and demonstrations. Fans of the Barcelona soccer team party here after winning a big match; the fountain has been toppled many times by happy revelers climbing it. It's also a good spot to fill up your water bottle.

As you survey the Ramblas action, get your bearings for our upcoming stroll. You'll see the following features here and all along the way:

Wavy Tile Work: The pavement decorations represent the stream that once flowed here. *Rambla* means "stream" in Arabic, and this used to be a drainage ditch along one of the medieval walls enclosing the Barri Gòtic (to the left). Many Catalan towns, established where rivers approach the sea, have streets called "Ramblas." Today Barcelona's "stream" has become a river of humanity.

Skinny Balconies: Look up to see the city's characteristic shallow balconies. They're functional as well as decorative, with windows opening from floor to ceiling to allow light and air into the tight, dark spaces of these cramped old buildings.

Hardy Plane Trees:  The deciduous trees lining the boulevard are known for their peeling bark and toughness in urban settings. They're ideal for the climate, letting in maximum sun in the winter and providing maximum shade in the summer.

Fixed Chairs: Nearby, notice the chairs fixed to the sidewalk at jaunty angles. It used to be that you'd pay to rent a chair here to look at the constant parade of passersby. Seats are now free, and it's still the best people-watching in town. Enjoy these chairs while you can—you'll find virtually no public benches or other seating farther down the Ramblas, only cafés that serve beer and sangria in just one (expensive) size: *gigante.*

ONCE Booths: Across from the fountain and a few steps down, notice the first of many booths along this walk that sell lottery tickets in support of ONCE, Spain's organization for the blind.

Soccer Souvenirs: You'll see soccer paraphernalia, especially the scarlet and blue of FC Barcelona—known as Barça. The team is owned by its more than 170,000 "members"—fans who buy season tickets, which come with a share of ownership. The team motto, "More than a club" *(Mes que un club)*, suggests that Barça represents not only athletic prowess but also Catalan cultural identity. This comes to a head during a match nicknamed "El Clásico," in which they face their bitter rivals, Real Madrid (whom many Barça fans view as stand-ins for Castilian cultural chauvinism).

• *Continue strolling.*

Walk 100 yards farther to #115, with an entrance flanked by two columns and a fine facade struggling to be noticed above the Ramblas ruckus. This marks the venerable **Royal Academy of Science and Arts building** (now home to a performing-arts theater). The building is emblematic of the city's striking architecture from the late 1900s—an industrial boom time that brought lots of construction. Look up: The clock high on the facade marks official Barcelona time—synchronize. The **Carrefour** supermarket next door has cheap groceries (at #113).

• *Remember that each of the Ramblas segments has its own name. You're now standing at what was the...*

❸ Rambla of the Little Birds (RIP)

A generation ago the Ramblas had a different kind of commerce. Locals came here for their newspapers, flowers, and even domestic pets. Traditionally, kids brought their parents here to buy birds, but also turtles and hamsters. But the clientele stopped coming and animal-rights groups lobbied to cut back on the stalls. Today, none of the traditional pet kiosks survive—and there's not a bird in sight. The commerce that remains is trinkets and drinks for hordes of tourists. Only the locals—and you—know the story behind the name for this stretch of the Ramblas, now lined with ice-cream and souvenir shops.

• *At #122 (the big, modern Citadines Hotel on the left), take a 100-yard detour through a modern passageway marked with the hotel's name to a restored...*

Roman Necropolis: Look down and imagine a 2,000-year-old road lined with tombs. Barcelona was founded about 10 BC by Romans, during the reign of Emperor Augustus, as the city of "Barcino," and this was the main road (Via Augusta) in and out of the walled town. (Today, the high-way from Barcelona to France still follows the route laid out by this Roman thoroughfare.) In Roman cities, tombs were generally placed along roads outside the city walls. Emperor Augustus spent a lot of time on the Iberian Peninsula conquer-

ing new land, so the Romans were sure to incorporate Hispania into the empire's infrastructure. Looking down at these ruins, you can see that Roman Barcino was about 10 feet lower than today's street level.

• *Return to the Ramblas and continue down 100 yards or so to the next cross street, Carrer de la Portaferrissa (on the left), to see the* **decorative tile** *over a fountain still in use by locals. The scene shows what this spot looked like three centuries ago: There's the original city wall with its gate, and merchants are busy selling flowers, bananas, and, I believe, Barça T-shirts. Now cross the boulevard to the front of the big church.*

❹ Betlem Church

This imposing church with diamond-shaped stonework is 17th-century Baroque: Check out the sloping roofline, ball-topped pin-

nacles, corkscrew columns, and scrolls above the entrance.

This Baroque style, so common elsewhere in Europe, is unusual in Barcelona. That's because during the Baroque and Renaissance eras (1500-1800), Barcelona was broke. The city enjoyed two heydays: in the 1300s as a medieval sea-trading power, and in the 1800s during the prosperous Industrial Age. In between, Barcelona languished as New World discoveries shifted lucrative trade to the Atlantic, and the Spanish crown kept unruly Catalunya on a short leash.

The church interior is stark, having been burned during Spain's civil war back in the 1930s. But the church is popular. It's dedicated to Bethlehem, and for centuries locals have flocked here at Christmastime to see nativity scenes.

For a sweet treat, head around to the narrow lane on the far side of the church (Carrer d'en Xucla) to the recommended **Café Granja Viader,** which has specialized in baked and dairy delights since 1870. Step inside to see Viader family photos and early posters advertising Cacaolat—the local chocolate milk Barcelonans love.

• *Continue down the boulevard, through the stretch called the...*

❺ Rambla of Flowers

Pause at this charming section of the Ramblas to admire the nice apartment facades. This colorful block of flower stands is (cleverly enough) called the Rambla of Flowers. Besides admiring the blossoms on display, gardeners will covet the seeds sold here for varieties of radishes, greens, peppers, and beans seldom seen in the US—including the iconic green Padrón pepper of tapas fame (if you buy seeds, you're obligated to declare them at US customs when returning home).

At #99 (on the right), the **cultural center** in Palau de la Virreina sells tickets to dance and musical concerts (easier to buy here than at the main TI).

At #97 (right), the **Casa Beethoven** shop is a cultural throwback to an earlier era, sedately selling music books, sheet music, and antiques like vinyl records.

On the left, at #100, **Tabacs Gimeno** has been selling cigars since the 1920s. Step inside and appreciate the dying art of cigar boxes and hand-crafted pipes. Go ahead, buy a Cuban (little singles for €1). As smoking has waned, shops like this have diversified. Tobacco shops sell stamps and phone cards, gifts for the man in your life, plus bongs and marijuana gear—the Spanish approach to pot is very casual. While people can't legally sell marijuana, they're allowed to grow it for personal use and consume it.

• *A little farther on, across the street (opposite the Erotic Museum) is the arcaded entrance to Barcelona's great covered market, La Boqueria.*

❻ La Boqueria Market

This lively market hall is an explosion of chicken legs, bags of live snails, stiff fish, delicious oranges, and odd odors.

Since as far back as 1200, Barcelonans have bought their animal parts here. Taxes made it more costly to trade within the city walls, so the market, as were many in medieval times, was originally located just outside the city. It later expanded into the colonnaded courtyard of a now-gone monastery before being covered with a colorful arcade in 1850.

While tourists are drawn to the area around the main entry, locals know that the stalls up front pay the highest rent—and therefore inflate their prices and cater to out-of-towners. Skip the tempting but more expensive juices sold here and head to a booth farther in or along the sides.

Stop in at the **Pinotxo Bar**—it's just inside the market, under the sign—and snap a photo of animated Juan. He and his family are always busy feeding shoppers. Getting Juan to crack a huge smile and a thumbs-up for your camera makes a great shot...and he loves it. The stools nearby are a fine perch for enjoying both your coffee and the people-watching.

The market and adjacent lanes are busy with tempting little eateries. Drop by a café for an *espresso con leche* or breakfast *tortilla española* (potato omelet). Once you get past the initial gauntlet, do some exploring. The small square on the north (uphill) side of the market hosts a farmers market in the mornings. Wander around—as local architect Antoni Gaudí used to—and gain inspiration. Go on a scavenger hunt for some of these items:

Fresh, Local Produce: Stands show off seasonal fruits and vegetables that you'll see on menus. ("Market cuisine" is big at

Barcelona restaurants—chefs come each morning to rustle up ingredients.) The focus here is on Spanish specialties like olives and saffron. The tubs of little green peppers that look like jalapeños are lightly fried for the dish called *pimientos de Padrón.* In a culinary form of Russian roulette, a few of these mild peppers sometimes turn out to be hot—greeting the eater with a fiery jolt. In the fall, you'll see lots of mushrooms; in the winter, artichokes.

Certain food items are associated with a particular town—for example, anchovies from L'Escala, shrimp from Palamós, and so on. Among Catalans, this is a sort of code designating quality (like "Idaho potatoes" or "Washington apples").

Ham: Full legs of *jamón* (ham) abound. The many varieties of *jamón serrano* are distinguished by the type of pig they come from and what that pig ate. Top quality are *ibérico* (Iberian type) and *bellota* (acorn eaters)—even by the slice these are very expensive, but gourmets pay €300 or more to go whole hock (see the "Sampling *Jamón*" sidebar on page 291).

Sausage: You'll see many types of the Catalan *botifarra* sausage. Some can be eaten as-is, while others must be cooked. *Chorizo* is the red Spanish sausage that's sometimes spicy (a rare bit of heat in an otherwise tame cuisine). A few meats are less common in American dishes, like rabbit and suckling pig. Beware: *Huevos de toro* means bull testicles—surprisingly inexpensive... and oh so good.

Seafood: The fishmonger stalls could double as a marine biology lab. In this Mediterranean city, people have come up with endless ways to harvest the sea. Fish is sold whole, not filleted—local shoppers like to look their dinner in the eye to be sure it's fresh. Count the many different types of shrimp *(gamba, langostino,* clawed *cigala).* Another popular treat is the tubular razor clam *(navaja).*

Cod: Some stalls specialize in dried salt cod *(bacalao).* Historically, codfish—preserved in salt and dried—provided desperately needed protein on long sea voyages as Catalan merchants ventured far from their homes. Before it can be eaten, salt cod must be rehydrated, so it's sold either covered in salt or already submerged in water, to hasten the time between market and plate.

Olives: These are a keystone of the Spanish diet. Take a look at the 25 kinds offered at the Graus Olives i Conserves shop (center, at the back).

• *After you've scoped out the market, head back to the street and continue down the Ramblas.*

On your left, you're skirting the old Barri Gòtic neighborhood. Glance left through a modern cutaway arch for a glimpse of the medieval church tower of **Santa Maria del Pi,** a popular venue for guitar concerts (see the Nightlife in Barcelona chapter). This marks the Plaça del Pi and a great shopping street, Carrer Petritxol, which runs parallel to the Ramblas. Also nearby is the **Taverna Basca Iratí,** one of many user-friendly, Basque-style tapas bars in town, perfect for a quick pick-me-up on this walk (for more on these types of bars, see page 182).

On the right side of the Ramblas (at #83), find the highly regarded **Escribà bakery,** with its appealing Modernista facade: Look for the *Antigua Casa Figueras* sign arching over the doorway, mosaics of twining plants, a stained-glass peacock displaying his tail feathers, and undulating woodwork. In the sidewalk in front of the door, a plaque dates the building to 1902 (plaques like this identify historic shops all over town). Step inside the fine interior and indulge in a unique edible treat before continuing your ramble.

• *After another block, you reach the Liceu Metro station, marking the...*

❼ Heart of the Ramblas

At the Liceu Metro station's elevators, the Ramblas widens a bit into a small, lively square (Plaça de la Boqueria). Liceu marks the midpoint of the Ramblas between Plaça de Catalunya and the waterfront.

Underfoot, find the much

trod-upon **Joan Miró mosaic** in red, white, yellow, and blue. Miró was born and grew up right here in the Gothic Quarter. The mosaic's black arrow represents an anchor, a reminder of the city's attachment to the ocean and a welcome to visitors arriving by sea (this is one of three Miró works welcoming visitors—there's also a mural at the airport and a sculpture at Sants train station). Miró's simple, colorful designs are found all over the city, from murals to mobiles to the La Caixa bank logo. The best place to see his work is in the Fundació Joan Miró at Montjuïc (see the listing in the Sights in Barcelona chapter).

The surrounding buildings have playful ornamentation typical of the city. The **Chinese dragon** holding a lantern (at #82) decorates a former umbrella shop (notice the fun umbrellas perched high up). While the dragon may seem purely decorative, it's actually an important symbol of Catalan pride for its connection to the local patron saint, St. George (Jordi).

A few steps down (on the right) is the **Liceu Opera House** (Gran Teatre del Liceu), which hosts world-class opera, dance, and theater (box office left of main entrance, open Mon-Fri 9:30-20:00). Opposite the opera house is **Café de l'Opera** (#74), an elegant stop for an expensive beverage. This bustling café, with Modernista decor and a historic atmosphere, boasts that it's been open since 1929, even during the Spanish Civil War.

• *We've seen the best stretch of the Ramblas; to cut this walk short, you could catch the Metro back to Plaça de Catalunya. Otherwise, let's continue to the port.*

Thirty yards along, pause and look left down a wide, straight street (Carrer de Ferran). Enjoy the view of elegant lamps, facades, and balconies as it leads to Plaça de Sant Jaume, the governmental center for both Barcelona and the region of Catalunya.

Head down the Ramblas another 50 yards (to #46), and turn left down an arcaded lane (Carrer de Colom) to the square called...

❽ Plaça Reial

Dotted with palm trees, surrounded by an arcade, and ringed by yellow buildings with white Neoclassical trim, this elegant square has a colonial ambience. It comes complete with old-fashioned taverns *(cervecerías),* modern bars with patio seating, and a Sunday coin-and-stamp market. Completing the picture are Gaudí's first public works (the two colorful helmeted lampposts).

This once-seedy part of town has been gentrified, making it more inviting and accessible. It's a lively hangout by day or by night (for after-dark options, see the Nightlife in Barcelona chapter). Big spaces like this (or the site of the Boqueria Market) often originated as monasteries. When these were dissolved in the 19th century, the government confiscated the land, turning the fine colonnaded squares into useful public spaces. To just relax over a drink and enjoy the scene, the **Ocaña cocktail bar** is a good bet.

• *Head back out to the Ramblas.*

Across the boulevard, a half-block detour down Carrer Nou de la Rambla brings you to **Palau Güell,** designed by Antoni Gaudí (on the left, at #3). Even from the outside, you get a sense of this innovative apartment, the first of Gaudí's Modernista buildings. As this is early Gaudí (built 1886-1890), it's darker and more Neo-Gothic than his more famous later work. The two parabolic-arch doorways and elaborate wrought-iron work signal his emerging nonlinear style. Completely restored in 2011, Palau Güell offers an informative look at a Gaudí interior (see the listing on page 33).

• *Return to the Ramblas and keep heading down.*

❾ Raval Neighborhood

The neighborhood on the right side of this stretch of the Ramblas was nicknamed the Barri Xinès—the world's only Chinatown with nothing even remotely Chinese in or near it. The name was a prejudiced term broadly applied to any foreigner—whether from abroad or another part of Spain. The neighborhood's actual inhabitants were poor Spanish, North African, and Roma (Gypsy) people. At night, the Barri Xinès was frequented by prostitutes, drug pushers, transvestites, and thieves, many of whom catered in one way or another to sailors wandering up from the port. Today, the Raval neighborhood is rapidly gentrifying (for a description of this area, see page 49).

At about this part of the Ramblas, you may see the first of the drag's surreal and goofy **human statues.** Such performers—with creative and elaborate costumes—were once everywhere along the

Ramblas, but now they must audition and register with the city government. These days, only 15 living statues (mainly experienced performance artists) are allowed, and they're limited to this part of the Ramblas. To enliven your ramble, drop coins into their cans (the money often kicks the statues into entertaining gear). Warning: Wherever people stop to gawk, pickpockets are at work.

All along the Ramblas you'll find *mantas,* sheets stretched out on the sidewalk with knock-offs of designer goods for sale. While police are supposed to run these vendors off and confiscate their merchandise, enforcement is lenient. It's almost a game: Police officers arrive, and vendors yank the strings attached to the four corners of their sheets, bundling their wares as they scatter. The police leave, and the vendors return.

The skyscraper to the right of the Ramblas is the Edificio Colón. When built in 1970, the 28-story structure was Barcelona's first high-rise. Near the skyscraper is the Maritime Museum, housed in what were the city's giant medieval shipyards.

• *Near the bottom of the Ramblas, take note of the Drassanes Metro stop, which can take you back to Plaça de Catalunya when you're ready. Up ahead is the...*

RAMBLAS RAMBLE

❿ Columbus Monument

The 200-foot column honors Christopher Columbus, who came to Barcelona in 1493 after journeying to America. This Catalan answer to Nelson's Column on London's Trafalgar Square (right down to the lions, perfect for posing with at the base) was erected for the 1888 Universal Exposition, an international fair that helped vault a surging Barcelona onto the world stage.

The base of the monument, ringed with four winged victories (taking flight to the four corners of the earth), is loaded with symbolism: statues and reliefs of map-makers, navigators, early explorers preaching to subservient Native Americans, and (enthroned just below the winged victories) the four regions of Spain. The reliefs near the bottom illustrate scenes from Columbus' fateful voyage. A tiny elevator ascends to the top of the column, lifting visitors to a covered observation area for fine panoramas over the city (the entrance/ticket desk is in the TI, inside the base of the monument; for details, see page 16).

It's ironic that Barcelona celebrates this explorer; the discoveries of Columbus started 300 years of decline for the city, as Europe began to face west, toward the Atlantic and the New World, rather than east, to the Mediterranean and the Orient. Within a few decades of Columbus, Barcelona had become a depressed backwater, and didn't rebound until events like the 1888 Expo cemented its status as a comeback city.

• *Scoot across the busy traffic circle and continue straight ahead to the water's edge. Turn left, walk 50 yards, and find a pedestrian bridge that juts out over the harbor (with a wavy design and a wooden floor). Walk onto the bridge, then turn back and face the Columbus statue. This is a good place from which to check out the...*

⓫ Waterfront

Survey Barcelona's bustling maritime zone. For more than 2,000 years, this harbor with its bustling sea trade has been the reason

Barcelona is on the world map. Even today, the city is one of Europe's top 10 ports, with many busy industrial harbors and several cruise terminals. (It's the busiest cruise port in the Mediterranean.) Despite the industrial activity, this low-impact stretch of seafront is clean, fresh, and people-friendly.

The wooden pedestrian **bridge** you're standing on is a modern extension of the Ramblas, called La Rambla de Mar ("Rambla of the Sea"). The bridge can swing out to allow boat traffic into the marina.

As you face Columbus, take in the sights. At the foot of the Ramblas are the docks with the *golondrinas* harbor-cruise boats (for details, see page 40). To the left of Columbus is the big Maritime Museum (see page 37). Farther left, in the distance, is the majestic, 570-foot bluff of parklike **Montjuïc,** with a number of sights and museums reachable by cable car (as you can see). To the right of the Columbus statue, the frilly yellow building is the fanciful Modernista-style port-authority building. Stretching to the right of that is a delightful promenade along the seawall of Barcelona's Old Port (Port Vell); it's worth a stroll. Along the promenade is a permanently moored historic schooner, the **Santa Eulàlia** (part of the Maritime Museum). Finally, over your right shoulder is Maremagnum, a modern shopping mall and entertainment complex with an IMAX cinema, a huge aquarium, restaurants, and piles of people. Late at night, it's a rollicking youth hangout.

Imagine: A little more than two decades ago, this was a gloomy, depressed warehouse zone. But for the 1992 Olympics, city leaders refurbished the port area and rerouted a busy highway underground. Now this timeless harbor is a fine space sprinkled with palm trees, restaurants, and eye-pleasing public art—a fitting gateway to the cosmopolitan city of Barcelona.

• *Your ramble is over. To get to other points in town, your best bet is to backtrack to the Drassanes Metro stop. Alternatively, you can catch bus #59 from the waterfront on Avenue Passeig de Colom back to Plaça de Catalunya, or hop in a cab.*

If you want to extend this walk, it's fun to stroll the length of the promenade to the iconic Barcelona Head *sculpture (by American Pop artist Roy Lichtenstein). This puts you right at the edge of El Born's shopping and restaurant area (◻ see the El Born Walk chapter). Or, from the* Barcelona Head, *circle back through Maremagnum to the spot you're standing on, making a nice pedestrian loop around the marina.*

BARRI GÒTIC WALK

From Plaça de Catalunya to Plaça del Rei

Barcelona's Barri Gòtic (Gothic Quarter) is a bustling world of shops, bars, and nightlife packed into narrow, winding lanes and undiscovered courtyards. This is Barcelona's birthplace—where the ancient Romans built a city, where medieval Christians built their cathedral, where Jews gathered together, and where Barcelonans lived within a ring of protective walls until the 1850s, when the city expanded.

Today, this area of atmospheric tight lanes—nicknamed simply "El Gòtic"—is Barcelona's most historic neighborhood. It's a tangled yet inviting grab bag of grand squares, schoolyards, Art Nouveau storefronts, classy antique shops (especially along Carrer de la Palla), and musty junk stores. You'll encounter street musicians strumming Catalan folk songs, and stroll among the lived-in balconies of the residents who make this a neighborhood.

Treat this self-guided walk from Plaça de Catalunya to Plaça del Rei as a historical scavenger hunt. You'll focus on the earliest chunk of Roman Barcelona, right around the cathedral, and explore some legacy sights from the city's medieval era.

Orientation

Length of This Walk: Figure 1.5 hours, not including entering sights.

When to Go: To visit the cathedral when admission is free, take this walk in the morning or late afternoon. If you plan to enter the museums mentioned on this walk, avoid Monday, when some sights are closed.

Getting There: Start at the southeast corner of the Plaça de Catalunya (Metro: Plaça de Catalunya).

Church of Santa Anna: €2, usually Mon-Sat 11:00-19:00, until 14:00 in Aug, Plazoleta de Santa Anna.

Barcelona Cathedral: Generally free except in afternoon (€7 to enter Mon-Sat 12:30-17:30, Sun 14:00-17:15), open Mon-Fri 8:30-19:30, Sat-Sun until 20:00. (For details, see the Barcelona Cathedral Tour chapter.)

Old Main Synagogue (Antigua Sinagoga Mayor): €2.50, Mon-Fri 10:30-18:30, Sat-Sun until 15:00, shorter hours off-season, Carrer Marlet 5, tel. 933-170-790, www.sinagogamayor.com.

Roman Temple of Augustus: Free, Tue-Sat 10:00-19:00, Sun until 20:00, Mon until 14:00, Carrer del Paradís 10.

Barcelona History Museum: €7, Tue-Sat 10:00-19:00, Sun until 20:00, closed Mon.

Eating: For restaurants and tapas bars along the way, see page 188.

The Walk Begins

• *Start on Barcelona's grand main square, **Plaça de Catalunya**. From the northeast corner (between the giant El Corte Inglés department store and the Banco de España), head down the broad pedestrian boulevard called...*

❶ Avinguda del Portal de l'Angel

For much of Barcelona's history, this was a major city gate. A medieval wall enclosed the city, and the entrance here—the "Gate of the Angel"—gave the street its name. An angel statue atop the gate purportedly kept Barcelonans safe from plagues and bid voyagers safe journey as they left the security of the city. Imagine the fascinating scene here at the Gate of the Angel, where Barcelona stopped and the Iberian wilds began.

Much later, this same boulevard (and much of the city) got a facelift in preparation for the 1888 Universal Exposition, the first international fair held in Spain. (The same event prompted construction of the Columbus Monument at the bottom of the Ramblas.) The improvements to the Gate of the Angel are a good example of Barcelona's habit of spiffing itself up for big events. The city dressed up for another exposition in 1929 (Plaça d'Espanya fairgrounds) and again for the 1992 Olympic Games (sports facilities on Montjuïc and rejuvenated waterfront).

Picture the traffic congestion here in the 1980s, before this street was closed to most motorized vehicles (if you visit in the morning you'll still dodge delivery trucks supplying this street's stores). Today, you're elbow to elbow with shoppers cruising through some of the most expensive retail space in town. You'll notice branches of Zara, Oysho, Bershka, and Massimo Dutti, all owned by the same man (Amancio Ortega, the third-richest per-

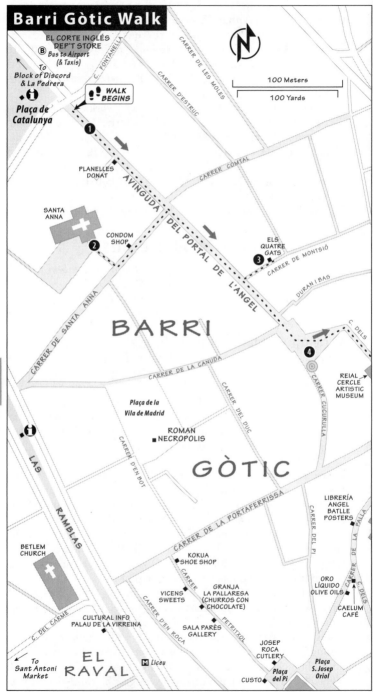

Barri Gòtic Walk

EL CORTE INGLÉS
DEP'T STORE
Ⓑ Bus to Airport
(& Taxis)

To
Block of Discord
& La Pedrera
ⓘ

Plaça de
Catalunya

C. FONTANELLA

CARRER DE LES MOLES

CARRER D'ESTRUC

👣 WALK
BEGINS

100 Meters

100 Yards

❶

AVINGUDA DEL PORTAL DE L'ANGEL

PLANELLES
DONAT

CARRER COMTAL

SANTA
ANNA ✚

CONDOM
SHOP

❷

ELS
QUATRE
GATS

❸

CARRER DE MONTSIÓ

DURAN I BAS

CARRER DE SANTA ANNA

BARRI

C. DELS

❹

CARRER DE LA CANUDA

CARRER CUCURULLA

REIAL
CERCLE
ARTISTIC
MUSEUM

ⓘ

Plaça de la
Vila de Madrid

ROMAN
NECROPOLIS

CARRER D'EN BOT

CARRER DEL DUC

GÒTIC

BARRI GÒTIC WALK

LAS
RAMBLAS

BETLEM
CHURCH ✚

CARRER DE LA PORTAFERRISSA

CARRER DEL PI

LIBRERÍA
ANGEL
BATLLE
POSTERS

CARRER DE LA PALLA

KOKUA
SHOE SHOP

VICENS
SWEETS

GRANJA
LA PALLARESA
(CHURROS CON
CHOCOLATE)

CARRER D'EN ROCA

SALA PARÉS
GALLERY

PETRITXOL

ORO
LÍQUIDO
OLIVE OILS

C. DELS

CAELUM
CAFÉ

CULTURAL INFO
PALAU DE LA VIRREINA

C. DEL CARME

To
Sant Antoni
Market

EL
RAVAL

Ⓜ Liceu

JOSEP
ROCA
CUTLERY

CUSTO

Plaça
del Pi

Plaça
S. Josep
Oriol

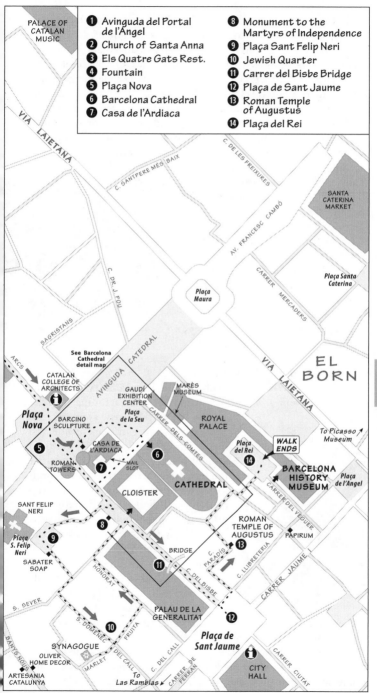

1. Avinguda del Portal de l'Angel
2. Church of Santa Anna
3. Els Quatre Gats Rest.
4. Fountain
5. Plaça Nova
6. Barcelona Cathedral
7. Casa de l'Ardiaca
8. Monument to the Martyrs of Independence
9. Plaça Sant Felip Neri
10. Jewish Quarter
11. Carrer del Bisbe Bridge
12. Plaça de Sant Jaume
13. Roman Temple of Augustus
14. Plaça del Rei

BARRI GÒTIC WALK

son in the world, according to locals). He gets the best locations for his shops, each targeted to a different market segment.

Although today this street has been globalized and sanitized, a handful of businesses with local roots survive. On the right at the first corner (at #25), a green sign and particularly appetizing display window mark **Planelles Donat**—long appreciated for its ice cream, sweet *turró* (or *turrón*, almond-and-honey candy), refreshing *orxata* (or *horchata*, almond-flavored drink), and *granissat* (or *granizado*, ice slush). Imagine how historic shops like this one started, with artisans from villages camping out here in a vestibule of some big building, selling baskets of their homemade goodies—and even-

tually evolving into real shops. Planelles Donat's *turrón* originated in the town of Xixona, in the coastal Alicante province.

• *A block farther down, pause at Carrer de Santa Anna to admire the Art Nouveau awning at another* **El Corte Inglés** *department store. From here, take a half-block detour to the right on Carrer de Santa Anna. At #32 go through a large entryway to the pleasant, flower-fragrant courtyard of the...*

❷ Church of Santa Anna

This austere Catalan Gothic church—a 12th-century gem—was part of a convent and still has its marker cross standing outside.

To the left of the cross, approach the gate, where you can peek inside the fine cloister—an arcaded walkway around a leafy courtyard. Climb the modern stairs across from the church for views of the bell tower. Inside the church you'll find a bare Romanesque interior, topped with an octagonal wooden roof. At the back of the nave, the recumbent-knight tomb is of Miguel de Boera, renowned admiral of Charles V. (Let's hope his hands were not that large.) To reach the cloister, enter the door at the far end

of the nave. Spanish-guitar concerts are often performed here (see www.spanishguitarbarcelona.es).

As you head back to the main drag, you'll pass—a few doors down—a **condom shop** on your left. It advertises (to men with ample self-esteem): *Para los pequeños placeres de la vida* ("For the little pleasures in life"). Spain is surprisingly liberal, considering that it was kept in a moralistic time-warp under the extremely conservative dictator Francisco Franco, who ruled from 1939 to 1975. In the generations since Franco, the major Catholic issues (contraception, abortion, divorce, cohabitation, and so on) have swung to the liberal side. (Catalans, however, are frustrated by the more conservative national government in Madrid, which constantly repeals more progressive laws passed by the people of this region.)

Take a moment here on Carrer de Santa Anna to look around and notice little details. Look up at pulleys (handy in buildings with no elevators). Take in the ironwork buildings with fine old entrances and cheaper facades (with plasterwork fashioned into fake columns). Note how all of the buildings maxed out their late-19th-century height limits. Here (and around town), you may see the *estelada* flag—red and gold with a blue triangle and white star—a symbol of Catalan separatists.

• *Backtrack to Avinguda del Portal de l'Angel. At Carrer de Montsió (on the left), just past the H&M store, side-trip a half-block to...*

❸ Els Quatre Gats

This restaurant (at #3) is a historic monument, tourist attraction, nightspot, and recommended eatery. It's famous for being the

circa 1900 bohemian-artist hangout where Picasso nursed drinks with friends and had his first one-man show. The building itself, by prominent architect Josep Puig i Cadafalch, represents Neo-Gothic Modernisme. Take a look around the corner from the entrance—it looks more like a medieval church or a castle, with pointed arches, windows with stone tracery, and gargoyles peeking from the stonework.

Stepping inside, you feel the turn-of-the-century vibe. Even if you don't eat or drink here, you can check out the circa-1900 photos on the wall, and take a quick look around (ask *"Solo mirar, por favor?"*). Rich Barcelona elites and would-be avant-garde artists looked to Paris (not Madrid) for cultural inspiration. This place was clearly influenced by Paris' Le Chat Noir, a cabaret/café and the hangout of Montmartre intellectuals. Like Le Chat Noir, Els Quatre Gats even published its own artsy magazine for a while. The story of the name? When the proprietor told his friends that he'd stay open 24 hours a day, they said, "No one will come." Using a popular Catalan phrase, they told him, "It'll just be you and four cats."

• *Return to and continue down Avinguda del Portal de l'Angel. You'll soon reach a fork in the road and a building with a...*

❹ Fountain

The blue and yellow tilework, a circa-1918 addition to this even older fountain, depicts ladies with big jugs of water. Picture the scene here back in the 17th cen-

tury. No one had indoor plumbing back then, and the neighborhood ladies would gather to fill their big crocks and take them home. This particular fountain was especially important as the last watering stop for horses before leaving town. As recently as 1940, about 10 percent of Barcelonans still got their water from fountains like this.

• *Shoppers will feel the pull of wonderful little shops down the street to the right. But be strong and take the left fork, down Carrer dels Arcs.*

Just past the corner, you'll pass the **Reial Cercle Artistic Museum,** a private collection of Dalí's work—sculptures, prints, and several hundred lithographs—that'll curl the moustaches of Surrealism fans. Don't miss the additional artwork in smaller rooms behind the red curtains (€10, daily 10:00-22:00).

• *Continue and enter the large square called...*

❺ Plaça Nova

As you enter the square, you can't miss the prickly steeple of the Barcelona Cathedral (which we'll see shortly). But first, take in a few other sights.

Two bold **Roman towers** flank a street leading off the square. These once guarded the entrance gate of the ancient Roman city

of Barcino. The big stones that make up the base of the (reconstructed) towers are actually Roman. Near the base of the left tower, **modern bronze letters** spell out "BARCINO." The city's name may have come from Barca, one of Hannibal's generals, who is said to have passed through during Hannibal's roundabout invasion of Italy. At Barcino's peak, the **Roman wall** (see the section stretching to the left of the towers) was 25 feet high and a mile around, with 74 towers. It enclosed a population of 4,000.

The Barri Gòtic Through History

As you tour the Old City, you'll see elements from every layer of Barcelona's 2,000-year history. There are ancient Roman ruins from when this was the important provincial capital of Barcino, enclosed within a circular wall. After Rome fell around the year 500, Barcelona remained vibrant while much of Europe floundered in darkness. Centered around the cathedral, a hive of merchants and artisans populated the twisty lanes of the Gothic Quarter, or "Barri Gòtic."

Barcelona thrived in the 1200s and 1300s as a cosmopolitan seaport. Later, that tradition of international trade made the city a natural port of call for none other than Christopher Columbus. (We'll see reminders of him along the walk.) By the late 1800s, the city had boomed into an industrial powerhouse. It became the cradle of a new artistic style—Modernisme—which produced fanciful Neo-Gothic buildings like El Quatre Gats restaurant and the cathedral facade. That energetic spirit is still alive today. It's obvious in the shops in this quarter, in the Catalan independence movement, and in the 24/7 energy of the Barri Gòtic's café culture.

One of the towers has a bit of reconstructed **Roman aqueduct** (notice the streambed on top). In ancient times, bridges of stone carried fresh water from the distant hillsides into the walled city.

Opposite the towers is the modern **Catalan College of Architects** building (Collegi d'Arquitectes de Barcelona, TI inside),

which is, ironically for a city with so much great architecture, quite ugly. The frieze was designed by Picasso (1962) in his distinctive simplified style. With just a few squiggly stick-figures, Picasso captured traditional Catalan activities. If you check out all three sides of the building, you'll see scenes suggesting music, bullfighting, sea trade, and the *sardana* dance. The branch-waving kings Picasso drew are the giant puppets *(gigantes)* paraded through the streets during local festivals. Picasso spent his formative years (1895-1904, age 14-23) here in the old town. He drank with fellow bohemians at Els Quatre Gats (which we just passed) and frequented brothels a few blocks from here on Carrer d'Avinyó ("Avignon")—which inspired his influential Cubist painting *Les Demoiselles d'Avignon*. Picasso's hunger to be on the cutting edge propelled him from the Barri Gòtic to Paris, where he eventually remade modern art.

• *Immediately to the left as you face the Picasso frieze,* **Carrer de la Palla** *is an inviting shopping street (described in the Shopping in Barcelona chapter). But let's head left through Plaça Nova to take in the mighty...*

❻ Barcelona Cathedral

The facade is a virtual catalog of Gothic motifs. There's the point-ed arch over the entrance and the stained-glass windows with elabo-rate stone tracery. Statues of robed saints stand in niches, and winged angels teeter on the octagonal bell towers. And the whole thing is topped with three tall steeples. These pointy spires are meant to give the impression of a church flickering with spiritual fires. This was the Gothic style called Flam-boyant—meaning "flame-like."

This has been Barcelona's holi-est spot for 2,000 years. The Romans built their temple of Jupiter right here. In AD 343, that pagan temple was replaced by a Chris-tian cathedral. Around the year 1000, that building was replaced again, this time by a Romanesque-style church. The current Gothic structure was started around 1300, during the medieval glory days of the Catalan nation, and finished in 1450. But the much newer facade, dating from the 1800s, is in the Neo-Gothic style of Mod-ernisme. That part of the construction was capped in 1913 with the central spire, 230 feet tall. So, in a way, the cathedral is evidence of Barcelona's two "golden ages"—its seaport heyday in the 1300s, and its 19th-century revival.

The area in front of the cathedral is where Barcelonans dance the *sardana* on weekends (see page 42).

The cathedral's interior—with its vast space, peaceful cloister, and many ornate chapels—is worth a visit (📖 see the Barcelona Cathedral Tour chapter). If you interrupt this tour to visit the ca-thedral now, you'll exit the cloister a block down Carrer del Bisbe. From there you can circle back to the right, following the wall of the cathedral to visit stop #7—or skip #7 and step directly into stop #8.

As you stand in the square facing the cathedral, look far to your left to see the multicolored, wavy canopy marking the roofli-ne of the **Santa Caterina Market.** The busy street between here and the market—called Via Laietana—is the boundary between the Barri Gòtic and the funkier, edgier **El Born** neighborhood.

BARRI GÒTIC WALK

• *For now, return to the Roman towers and pass between them to head up Carrer del Bisbe. Take an immediate left, up the ramp to the entrance of...*

❼ Casa de l'Ardiaca

It's free to enter this mansion, which was once the archdeacon's residence and now functions as the city archives. The elaborately carved doorway is Renaissance. To the right of the doorway is a carved mail slot by 19th-century Modernista architect Lluís Domènech i Montaner. Enter a small courtyard with a fountain. Notice how the century-old palm tree seems to be held captive by urban man. Next, step inside the air-conditioned lobby of the city archives, where—along the back of the ancient Roman wall—there are often free exhibits. At the left end of the lobby, go through the archway and look down into the stairwell for a peek at more impressive Roman stonework. Back in the courtyard, climb to the balcony for views of the cathedral steeple and gargoyles. From this vantage point, note the small Romanesque chapel on the right (the only surviving 13th-century bit of the cathedral) and how it's dwarfed by the towering cathedral.

• *Return to Carrer del Bisbe and turn left. After a few steps, you reach a small square with a bronze statue ensemble.*

❽ Monument to the Martyrs of Independence

Five Barcelona patriots—including two priests—calmly receive their last rites before being garroted (strangled) for resisting Napoleon's occupation of Spain in the early 19th century. They'd been

outraged by French atrocities in Madrid (depicted in Goya's famous *Third of May* painting in Madrid's Prado Museum). According to the plaque marking their mortal remains, these martyrs to independence gave their lives in 1809 *"por Dios, por la Patria, y por el Rey"*—for God, country, and king.

Tiles flanking the monument tell the story: On the far left, the patriots receive their last communion in prison. On the near left, they're escorted out of the citadel—that hated symbol of foreign occupation. On the near right is the execution scene. See the three doomed men huddled with their priests below the instruments of their coming execution: ropes and a ladder. Priests, considered privileged, were strangled, while the common people were hung. (Spain last used the garrote in 1974, and France last used the guillotine in 1977. Europe is generally appalled that the US still executes people.) After their execution, all the martyrs were buried across the way in the cathedral cloister.

The plaza offers interesting views of the cathedral's towers. Opposite the square is the "back door" entrance to the cathedral (through the cloister; relatively uncrowded and open during hours when the church is free).

• *Exit the square down tiny Carrer de Montjuïc del Bisbe (to the right as you face the martyrs). This leads to the cute...*

❾ Plaça Sant Felip Neri

This shaded square serves as the playground of an elementary school and is often bursting with energetic kids speaking Catalan (just a couple of generations ago, this would have been illegal and they would be speaking Spanish). The Church of Sant Felip Neri, which Gaudí attended, is still pocked with bomb damage from the Spanish Civil War. As a stronghold of democratic, anti-Franco forces, Barcelona saw a lot of fighting. The shrapnel that damaged this church was meant for the nearby Catalan government building (Palau de la Generalitat, which we'll see later on this walk).

Just as the Germans practiced their new air force technology in Guernica in the years leading up to World War II, the fascist friends of Franco (both German and Italian) also helped bomb Barcelona from the air. As was the fascist tactic, a second bombing followed the first as survivors combed the rubble for lost loved ones. A plaque on the wall (left of church door) honors the 42 killed—mostly children—in that 1938 aerial bombardment.

In the medieval tangle of the Barri Gòtic, people gathered densely within the city's protective walls, leaving very few open spaces—except for cemeteries clustering around churches. Many squares, like this one, started out as cemeteries. They later became open spaces when, with the Enlightenment (c. 1800) and modern concern for hygiene, graveyards were moved outside of town.

The buildings here were paid for by the guilds that powered the local economy. The shoemakers guild (to the right of the arch where you entered the square) is decorated above the windows with reliefs depicting boots.

• *Exit the square past the fun* **Sabater Hermanos** *artisanal soap shop, and head down Carrer de Sant Felip Neri. At the T-intersection, turn right onto Carrer de Sant Sever, then immediately left on Carrer de Sant Domènec del Call (look for the blue* El Call *sign). You've entered the...*

❿ Jewish Quarter (El Call)

In Catalan, a Jewish quarter goes by the name El Call—literally "narrow passage," for the tight lanes where medieval Jews were forced to live, under the watchful eye of the nearby cathedral. (Some believe El Call comes from the Hebrew *kahal*, which means congregation.) At the peak of Barcelona's El Call, some 4,000 Jews were crammed into just a few alleys in this neighborhood.

Walk down Carrer de Sant Domènec del Call, and pass through the charming little square (a gap in the dense tangle of medieval buildings cleared by another civil war bomb), where you will find a rust-colored sign displaying a map of the Jewish Quarter. Take the next lane to the right (Carrer de Marlet). On the right is the (literally) low-profile, four-foot-high entrance to what was likely Barcelona's **main synagogue** (Antigua Sinagoga Mayor) during the Middle Ages. The structure dates from the third century, but it was destroyed during a brutal pogrom in 1391. The city's remaining Jews were expelled in 1492, and artifacts of their culture—including this synagogue—were forgotten for centuries. In the 1980s, a historian tracked down the synagogue using old tax-collection records. Another clue that this was the main synagogue: In accordance with Jewish traditions, it stubbornly faces east (toward Jerusalem), putting it at an angle at odds with surrounding structures. You can visit the synagogue interior (admission includes a little tour by the attendant if you ask). The sparse interior includes access to two small subterranean rooms with Roman walls topped by a medieval Catalan vault. Look through the glass floor to see dyeing vats used for a later shop on this site run by former Jews who had been forcibly converted to Christianity.

• *From the synagogue, start back the way you came but then continue straight ahead, onto Carrer de la Fruita. Pause and look around. Imagine life here centuries ago. The place was filled with life, with people hauling water and selling goods from small carts, kids running around, and carriages banging against the stony corners. These tight lanes, like deep canyons, are in the shade for all but a few minutes a day.*

At the T-intersection, turn left, then right, to find your way back to the Martyrs *statue. From here, we'll turn right down Carrer del Bisbe to the...*

⓫ Carrer del Bisbe Bridge

This has been a main street since the days of ancient Barcino. The Romans built straight streets on a rectangular grid plan, and this one led to their town center.

Along Carrer del Bisbe today, you'll likely pass a street musician. The city strictly regulates buskers and gives permits only to quality performers at designated points like this one.

Arching across Carrer del Bisbe is a medieval-looking skybridge. This structure—reminiscent of Venice's Bridge of Sighs—connects the Catalan government building (on the right) with what was the Catalan president's ceremonial residence (on the left). Though the bridge appears to be centuries old, it was constructed in the 1920s by Catalan architect Joan Rubió (a follower of Gaudí), who also did the carved ornamentation on the buildings.

Check out the carved decor on the bridge and (even more) on the buildings. You'll see jutting angels, dragons, centaurs, skulls, goddesses, old men with beards, climbing vines, and coats of arms. The delicate facade a few steps farther down on the right is much older. It marks the 15th-century entry to the government palace.

• *Continue along Carrer del Bisbe to...*

⓬ Plaça de Sant Jaume

This stately central square of the Barri Gòtic takes its name from the Church of St. James (in Catalan: Jaume, JOW-mah) that once stood here. After the church was torn down in 1823, the square was fixed up and rechristened "Plaça de la Constitució" in honor of the then decade-old Spanish constitution. But the plucky Catalans never embraced the name, and after Franco, they went back to the original—even though the church is long gone.

Set at the intersection of ancient Barcino's main thoroughfares, this square was once a Roman forum. In that sense, it's been the seat of city government for 2,000 years. Today it's home to the two top governmental buildings in Catalunya: Palau de la Generalitat and, across from it, the Barcelona City Hall.

For more than six centuries, the **Palau de la Generalitat** (on the uphill side of the square) has housed the offices of the autonomous government of Catalunya. It always flies the Catalan flag next to the obligatory Spanish one. Above the building's doorway is Catalunya's patron saint—St. George (Jordi), slaying the dragon. The dragon (which you'll see all over town) is an important Catalan symbol. From these balconies, the nation's leaders (and soccer heroes) greet the people on momentous days. The square is often the site of festivals or demonstrations, from a single aggrieved citizen with a megaphone (the phone company billed me twice!) to riotous thousands (demanding independence from Spain, for instance).

Facing the Generalitat across the square is the **Barcelona City Hall** (Casa de la Ciutat). It sports a statue (in the niche to

the left of the door) of a different James—"Jaume el Conqueridor." The 13th-century King Jaume I is credited with freeing Barcelona from French control, granting self-government, and setting it on course to become a major city. He was the driving force behind construction of the Royal Palace (which we'll see shortly).

Locals treasure the independence these two government buildings represent. In the 20th century, when Barcelona opposed the dictator Franco, he retaliated by abolishing the regional government and (effectively) outlawing the Catalan language and customs. Two years after Franco's death in 1975, joyous citizens packed this square to celebrate the return of self-rule.

Look left and right down the main streets branching off the square; they're lined with ironwork streetlamps and balconies draped with plants. Carrer de Ferran, which leads to the Ramblas, is classic Barcelona.

In ancient Roman days, when Plaça de Sant Jaume was the town's central square, two main streets converged here—the Decumanus (Carrer del Bisbe—bishop's street) and the Cardus (Carrer de la Llibreteria/Carrer del Call). The forum's biggest building was a massive temple of Augustus, which we'll see next.

• *Facing the Generalitat, exit the square going up the second street to the right of the building, on tiny Carrer del Paradís. Follow this street as it turns right. When it swings left, pause at #10, the entrance to the...*

⓭ Roman Temple of Augustus (Temple Roma d'August)

You're standing at the summit of Mont Tàber, the Barri Gòtic's highest spot. A plaque on the wall by the entrance reads: "Mont Tàber, 16.9 meters" (elevation 55 feet). At your feet, a millstone inlaid in the pavement also marks a momentous spot. It was here that the ancient Romans founded the town of Barcino around 12 BC. They built a *castrum* (fort) on the hilltop, protecting the harbor, and this temple to honor their emperor, Augustus.

Go inside for a peek at the last vestiges of the imposing Roman

temple. All that's left are four columns and some fragments of the transept and its plinth (good English info on-site). The huge columns, dating from the late first century BC, are as old as Barcelona itself. They were part of the ancient town's biggest structure, dedicated to Augustus, who was worshipped as a god. These Corinthian columns (with deep fluting and topped with leafy capitals) were the back corner of a 120-foot-long temple that extended from here to Barcino's forum...Plaça de Sant Jaume, which you just visited.

• *Continue down Carrer del Paradís one block. When you bump into the back end of the cathedral, pause to notice how amazingly well-preserved the cityscape is here—under an assembly of gargoyles.*

Take a right, going down Carrer de la Pietat/Baixada de Santa Clara. (Is that a unicorn gargoyle on the side of the church? A unigoyle?) Go 100 yards until you emerge into a square called...

⓮ Plaça del Rei

This square is a great place to end our walk, as it calls up Barcelona's medieval Golden Age. The buildings enclosing the square sum up this period of Barcelona's history. The central section (topped by a five-story addition) was the core of the **Royal Palace** (Palau Reial Major). A vast hall on its ground floor once served as the throne room and reception room. From the 13th to the 15th century, the Royal Palace housed Barcelona's counts as well as the resident kings of Aragon. One of those kings of Aragon, Ferdinand, married Isabel, queen of Castile, creating the united country of Spain. In 1493, here in this Royal Palace, they hosted a triumphant Christopher Columbus, accompanied by six New World natives (whom he called *"indios"*) and several pure-gold statues. King Ferdinand and Queen Isabel welcomed him home and honored him with the title "Admiral of the Oceans."

To the right is the palace's church, the 14th-century **Chapel of Saint Agatha,** where royalty worshipped. The venerable church sits atop the foundations of a Roman wall (entrance included in Barcelona History Museum admission; see page 44.)

To the left is the **Viceroy's Palace** (Palau del Lloctinent). It was built in the 1500s for the right-hand man of the Spanish monarch, who was now located in far-off Castile. So, in a way, this building represents the rise of Spain and the decline of Aragon, Catalunya, and the city of Barcelona. Catalunya was swallowed up into greater Spain, the Royal Palace was demoted to a small regional residence, and Barcelona declined.

Step into the interior courtyard, a delightful Renaissance space with a fine staircase and coffered wood ceiling. Over the years, this building served as the local headquarters of the Spanish Inquisition. It currently houses the historical archives of the crown of Aragon. Among their treasures is the so-called **Santa Fe Capitulations**—the 1492 contract between Columbus and the Catholic Monarchs that set the terms for his upcoming sea voyage. (The document is rarely on display but there's often a poster of it on the courtyard wall.)

Ironically, Columbus' discoveries changed Barcelona forever. Spain shifted its focus to the New World, away from Barcelona and its Mediterranean trade routes. The political center moved to Madrid, and while Spain enjoyed its Golden Age, Barcelona spiraled downward. By the 1700s, it was a dirty, cramped city, crowded within the medieval walls of the Barri Gòtic. But Catalunya would rise again. In the 1800s, Barcelona became Spain's industrial engine; the city expanded and beautified itself. There was renewed interest in the Catalan language and culture. Today, Barcelona is a vibrant international metropolis. And, in the Barri Gòtic, the proud spirit of Catalunya lives on.

• *Our walk is over. While you're here, you could check out the **Barcelona History Museum**, starring some excavated Roman ruins. (For a peek at the Roman streets without going in, look through the low windows lining the street.)*

It's easy to get your bearings by backtracking to either Plaça de Sant Jaume or the cathedral (where you can follow my "Barri Gòtic Shopping Walk"—see page 209). The Jaume I Metro stop is two blocks away (leave the square on Carrer del Veguer and turn left). From here, you could head over to the Santa Caterina Market to browse for lunch before tackling my El Born Walk. Or simply wander through more of this area, enjoying Barcelona at its Gothic best.

BARCELONA CATHEDRAL TOUR

Although Barcelona's cathedral doesn't rank among Europe's finest (and frankly, barely cracks the Top 20), it's important, easy to visit, and—most of the time—free to see. This quick tour introduces you to the cathedral's highlights: its vast nave, rich chapels, tomb of Santa Eulàlia, and the oasis-like setting of the cloister. Other sights inside (which have admission fees) are the elaborately carved choir, the view terrace, and the altarpiece museum.

Orientation

Cost: The cathedral is free for worship and visits in both the morning (Mon-Sat before 12:30, Sun before 13:45) and evening (generally after 17:45), but during those times, you have to pay €3 each to visit the choir or terrace (the museum is closed during these hours). Access may be limited during church services.

The church is open for tourism for several hours in the afternoon (generally Mon-Sat 12:30-17:30, Sun 14:00-17:15), but you must pay €7 (which covers admission to the choir, terrace, and museum). Paying the afternoon admission can be worthwhile on a crowded day.

Hours: Cathedral generally open Mon-Fri 8:30-19:30, Sat-Sun until 20:00. The cathedral's three minor sights are open Mon-Sat (with different hours) and closed Sun: choir—9:00-19:00, terrace—9:00-18:00, museum—12:30-17:15. Both the choir and terrace may close earlier on slow days.

Information: Tel. 933-151-554, www.catedralbcn.org.

Dress Code: The dress code is strictly enforced; don't wear tank tops, shorts, or skirts above the knee.

Getting There: The huge, can't-miss-it cathedral is in the center of the Barri Gòtic on Plaça de la Seu (Metro: Jaume I). It's also easy to splice your cathedral visit into my Barri Gòtic Walk (see the previous chapter).

Getting In: The main, front door is open most of the time. While it can be crowded, the line generally moves fast. You can also enter directly into the cloister (through the door facing the *Martyrs* statue on the small square along Carrer del Bisbe) or through the side door (facing the Frederic Marès Museum along Carrer dels Comtes).

Tours: ∩ Download my free Barcelona City Walk audio tour, which includes a tour of the cathedral interior.

Length of This Tour: Allow 30 minutes, not counting the optional sights (choir, view terrace, museum).

Visitor Services: A tiny pay WC is in the center of the cloister.

BACKGROUND

This has been Barcelona's holiest spot for 2,000 years. The Romans built their Temple of Jupiter here. In AD 343, the pagan temple was replaced with a Christian cathedral. That building was supplanted by a Romanesque-style church (11th century). The current Gothic structure was started in 1298 and finished in 1450, during the medieval glory days of the Catalan nation. The facade was humble, so in the 19th century the proud local bourgeoisie (enjoying a second Golden Age) redid it in a more ornate, Neo-Gothic style. Construction was capped in 1913 with the central spire, 230 feet tall.

The Tour Begins

• *Enter the main door and look up. (If you're entering through another door, loop around to start at the rear of the nave.)*

❶ The Nave

The spacious church is 300 feet long and 130 feet wide. Tall pillars made of stone blocks support the crisscross vaults. Each round keystone where the arches cross features a different saint. Typical of many Spanish churches, there's a choir—an enclosed area of wooden seats in the middle of the nave, creating a more intimate space for worship, and isolating the selected elite who could actually get close to the altar and hear the sermons. The

BARCELONA CATHEDRAL

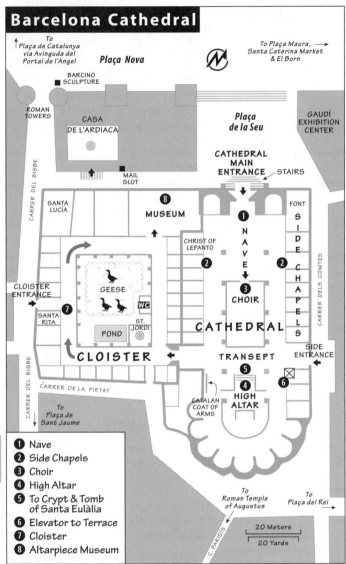

Barcelona Cathedral

To Plaça de Catalunya via Avinguda del Portal de l'Angel

Plaça Nova

To Plaça Maura, → Santa Caterina Market & El Born

BARCINO SCULPTURE

ROMAN TOWERS

CASA DE L'ARDIACA

GAUDÍ EXHIBITION CENTER

Plaça de la Seu

CATHEDRAL MAIN ENTRANCE — STAIRS

CARRER DEL BISBE

SANTA LUCÍA

MUSEUM ❽

MAIL SLOT

FONT

❶ N A V E

S I D E C H A P E L S

CHRIST OF LEPANTO

❷

❷

CARRER DELS COMTES

CLOISTER ENTRANCE

GEESE

WC

❸ CHOIR

SANTA RITA

❼

ST. JORDI

POND

CATHEDRAL

CARRER DEL BISBE

CLOISTER

TRANSEPT

SIDE ENTRANCE

CARRER DE LA PIETAT

❺

❻

To Plaça de Sant Jaume

CATALAN COAT OF ARMS

❹ HIGH ALTAR

To Roman Temple of Augustus

To Plaça del Rei

C. PARIDIS

20 Meters
20 Yards

❶ Nave
❷ Side Chapels
❸ Choir
❹ High Altar
❺ To Crypt & Tomb of Santa Eulàlia
❻ Elevator to Terrace
❼ Cloister
❽ Altarpiece Museum

BARCELONA CATHEDRAL

Gothic church also has fine stained glass, ironwork chandeliers, a 16th-century organ (left transept), tombstones in the pavement, and an "ambulatory" floor plan, allowing worshippers to amble around to the chapel of their choice.

❷ Side Chapels

The nave is ringed with 28 chapels. Besides creating worship spac-

es, the walls defining these chapels serve as interior buttresses supporting the roof (which is why the exterior walls are smooth, without the normal Gothic buttresses outside). Barcelona honors many of the homegrown saints found in these chapels with public holidays.

From the 13th to 15th century, these side chapels were simply moneymakers for the church. After the Black Death ravaged the population—and the economy—the church rented chapels to guilds to function as private offices, which came with the medieval equivalent of safety-deposit boxes and a notary public (documents signed here came with the force of God). Notice how the iron gates are more than decorative—they were protective. The rich ornamentation was sponsored by local guilds. Think of it: The church was the community's most high-profile space, and these chapels were a kind of advertising to illiterate worshippers.

The Church is still fundraising. Candles, which aren't free, power your prayers. As you visit the chapels, employ one or more electronic candles. Pop in a coin and you'll get a candle for every €0.10 you donate. Try it—€0.50 turns on five candles. Or save your coins to light a real candle in the cloister's chapels.

• *We'll walk past a few of these chapels, just to get a sense of them. Begin by heading to the back-left corner (over your left shoulder as you enter the main door).*

The chapel at the back corner of the nave has an old **baptismal font** that once stood in the original fourth-century church. The Native Americans that Columbus brought back to town were supposedly baptized here.

• *Work your way down the left aisle.*

The first chapel along the left wall is dedicated to **St. Severus,** the bishop here way back in AD 290.

The second chapel was by, for, and of the local **shoe guild.** Notice the two painted doors with shoes above them that lead to the back office. As the patron of shoemakers was St. Mark, there are plenty of winged lions in this chapel.

• *Cross the nave over to the large chapel in the back-right corner and work your way, one chapel at a time, down that side of the church.*

This chapel (reserved for worship) features the beloved **"Christ of Lepanto"** crucifix. They say the angular wooden figure of Christ, which swings to the left, leaned to dodge a cannonball during the history-changing Battle of Lepanto (1571), which stopped the Ottomans (and Islam) from advancing into Europe.

• *Now head down the right aisle.*

The next chapel has a statue of **St. Anthony** holding the Baby Jesus. His feast day (January 17) is one of many celebrated in the city with an appearance by the *gegants* (giant puppets), a street fair, horse races, and a blessing of pets.

The third chapel honors a 20th-century bishop, **San Josep Oriol,** who survived an assassination attempt in the cathedral cloister.

The golden fourth chapel is for **St. Roch** (at the top, pointing to his leg wound, above St. Pancraç), whose feast day is celebrated joyously in the Barri Gòtic in mid-August.

The fifth chapel has a black-and-white sideways statue of **St. Ramon (Raymond) of Penyafort** (1190-1275), the Dominican Bishop of Barcelona who heard Pope Gregory IX's sins and is the patron saint of lawyers (and, therefore, extremely busy). Ramon figures into the city's biggest festival, La Mercè, since he had a miraculous vision of the Virgin of Mercy.

The eighth chapel is worth a look for its over-the-top golden altarpiece decor nearly crowding out **Bishop Pacià**—considered one of the Church fathers (c. AD 310-391).

• *To visit the interior of the choir, pay the fee or show your ticket at the choir entrance (straight ahead from the church's main doors). Otherwise, you can circle around to the far end and peer through the barrier.*

❸ Choir

The 15th-century choir *(coro)* features ornately carved stalls. During the standing parts of the Mass, the chairs were folded up, but VIPs still had those little wooden ledges to lean on. Each was creatively carved and—since you couldn't sit on sacred things—the artists were free to enjoy some secular and naughty fun here. In 1518, the stalls were painted with the coats of arms of Europe's nobility. They gathered here as members of the Knights

of the Golden Fleece to honor Charles V, King of Spain, who was making his first trip to the country he ruled. Like a proto-United Nations, they also discussed how to work together to defend Europe from the Turkish threat. Check out the detail work on the impressive wood-carved pulpit near the altar, supported by flying angels.

• *At the front of the church stands the...*

❹ High Altar

Look behind the altar (beneath the crucifix) to find the bishop's chair, or cathedra. As a cathedral, this church is the bishop's seat—hence its Catalan nickname of *La Seu*. To the left of the altar is the organ and the elevator up to the terrace. To the right of the altar, the wall is decorated with Catalunya's yellow-and-red coat of arms. Under that, the two wooden coffins on the wall contain two powerful Counts of Barcelona (Ramon Berenguer I and his third wife, Almodis), who ordered the construction of the 11th-century Romanesque cathedral that preceded this structure.

• *Descend the steps beneath the altar, into the crypt, to see the...*

❺ Tomb of Santa Eulàlia

The marble-and-alabaster sarcophagus (1327-1339) contains the remains of Santa Eulàlia. The cathedral is dedicated to this saint.

Thirteen-year-old Eulàlia, daughter of a prominent Barcelona family, was martyred by the Romans for her faith in AD 304. Murky legends say she was subjected to 13 tortures. First she was stripped naked and had her head shaved, though a miraculous snowfall hid her nakedness. Then she was rolled down the street in a barrel full of sharp objects. After further torments failed to kill her, she was crucified on an X-shaped cross—a symbol you'll find carved into pews and seen throughout the church.

The relief on the coffin's side tells her story in three episodes: she preaches Christianity to the pagan Roman ruler; he orders her to die (while she pleads for mercy); and she's crucified on the X-shaped cross. As one of Barcelona's two patron saints, Eulàlia is honored with an annual festival (with *gegants*, fireworks, and human towers) in February.

• *The* ❻ *elevator in the left transept takes you up to the rooftop* **terrace** *(requires ticket), made of sturdy scaffolding pieces, for an expansive city view.*

Otherwise, exit through the right transept to enter the...

❼ Cloister

The cloister's arcaded walkway surrounds a lush circa-1450 courtyard. Ahhhh. It's a tropical atmosphere of palm, orange, and magnolia trees; a fish pond; trickling fountains; and squawking geese.

From within the cloister, look back at the **arch** you just came through, an impressive mix of Roman-

esque (arches with chevrons, from the earlier church) and Gothic (pointy top).

The nearby **fountain** has a tiny statue of St. Jordi (George) slaying the dragon. Jordi is one of the patron saints of Catalunya and by far the most popular boy's name here. During the Corpus Christi festival in June, kids come here to watch a hollow egg dance atop the fountain's spray.

As you wander the cloister (clockwise), check out the **coats of arms** as well as the **tombs** in the pavement. These were for rich merchants who paid good money to be buried as close to the altar as possible. A few pavement stones here and there have the symbols of their trades: scissors, shoes, bakers, and so on. The cloister had

a practical economic purpose. The church sold out its chapel space, and this opened up an entire new wing to donors. A second floor was planned (look up) but not finished.

The resident **geese** have been here for at least 500 years. There are always 13, in memory of Eulàlia's 13 years and 13 torments. Other legends say they're white as a symbol of her virginity. Before modern security systems, they acted as alarms. Any commotion would get them honking, alerting the monk in charge. Faithful to tradition, they honk to this very day.

Farther along the cloister, next to the door, the **Chapel of Santa Rita** (patron saint of impossible causes) usually has the most candles. In the next corner of the cloister is the barrel-vaulted **Chapel of Santa Lucía,** a small 13th-century remnant of the earlier Romanesque cathedral. It's quite dark, as churches were before the advent of Gothic style. People hoping for good eyesight (Santa Lucía's specialty) pray here. Notice the especially nice eyes in the painted statue of Lucía.

• At the far end of the cloister, you'll find the...

❽ Altarpiece Museum (Museu Capitular)

The little museum (entry possible only during paid visiting hours) has the six-foot-tall 14th-century Great Monstrance, a ceremonial display case for the communion wafer. Made of gold and studded with jewels, it's really three separate parts: a church-like central section, topped with a crown canopy, standing on a golden chair. This huge monstrance with its wafer is paraded through the streets during the Corpus Christi festival. Nearby is a gold-plated silver statue of Santa Eulàlia, carrying the X-shaped cross she was crucified on. An 11th-century baptismal font from the Romanesque church is also on view.

The next room, the Sala Capitular, has several altarpieces, including a pietà (*Desplà,* 1490) by Bartolomé Bermejo. An anguished Mary cradles a twisted Christ against a bleak, stormy landscape. It's unique in Spanish art for its Italianesque, Renaissance 3-D. Rather than your basic gold backdrop, this has a strong foreground (the mourners), middle distance (the cross), and background (the city and distant hills). The kneeling donors who paid for the painting are photorealistic, complete with reading glasses and five o'clock shadows. These are just two of the countless Barcelona faithful who helped make their cathedral great.

• *Our tour is over. Go in peace.*

EL BORN WALK

From Via Laietana to the Waterfront

The neighborhood called El Born (a.k.a. "La Ribera") is bohemian-chic, with funky shops, upscale cafés and wine bars, a colorful market hall, unique boutiques, gritty bars and nightclubs, and one of Barcelona's top museums (exhibiting the early works of Picasso). Anchored by the Church of Santa Maria del Mar and just a short stroll from the waterfront, El Born is a rewarding quarter to explore and a welcome escape from the sightseeing grind.

Back when Barcelona was Barcino—a walled Roman town—this area was farmland. As the city sprawled beyond its walls, El Born was established.

With its proximity to the harbor, El Born became the neighborhood of sailors, shippers, and skilled craftsmen. During the medieval city's trading heyday, wealthy shipping magnates built grand mansions here and a local church, Santa Maria del Mar, that rivaled the cathedral.

But all that came crashing down in 1714, when the Spanish crown crushed Catalan resistance to Madrid's rule and, in a show of force, razed a big chunk of this district to erect an imposing citadel (now a delightful park). The focus of the city shifted west, to the Barri Gòtic, and El Born became a largely forgotten backwater.

But in recent years, as tourists have overrun the Barri Gòtic, El Born has regained attention. While it has gentrified and is now one of the city's most in-demand residential areas, El Born retains a pleasantly rough-around-the-edges appeal. Its tight lanes are still lined with innovative one-off shops that, very often, make what they sell. Although we'll cover some history, this walk includes some enticing boutique streets; think of it as a route for making your own discoveries.

Orientation

Length of This Walk: About one hour, not including shopping stops.

When to Go: Sightseers and shoppers should do this walk during the day. But to take advantage of the neighborhood's lively night scene, go in the late afternoon/early evening to visit the sights you want, then stay for dinner and nightlife. By the way, if your answer to "when to go" was "10 years ago"—you're right. El Born is no longer the city's most happening place— the "next El Born" is the Raval neighborhood (described on page 49).

Getting There: This walk begins at Plaça d'Antoni Maura, where the pedestrian area in front of the Barcelona Cathedral meets Via Laietana. The closest Metro stop is Jaume I.

Santa Caterina Market: Mon-Sat 7:30-15:30, open until 20:30 on Tue and Thu-Fri, closed Sun.

El Born Cultural Center: Center—free and open Tue-Sun 10:00-20:00, Oct-Feb until 19:00, closed Mon year-round; Barcelona 1700 exhibit—€4.40, free all day first Sun of month and other Sun from 15:00, includes audioguide, same hours; Plaça Comercial 12, www.elbornculturaimemoria.barcelona.cat.

Picasso Museum: €12, Tue-Sun 9:00-19:00, Thu until 21:30, closed Mon (advance ticketing recommended; see the Picasso Museum Tour chapter).

Church of Santa Maria del Mar: Free during worship times: Mon-Sat 9:00-13:00 & 17:00-20:30, Sun 10:00-14:00 & 17:00-20:30; otherwise, €5 to visit Mon-Sat 13:00-17:00, Sun from 14:00; Plaça Santa Maria.

The Walk Begins

• *Our walk starts in front of the Barcelona Cathedral. As you stand facing the church, head left toward the Santa Caterina Market. You'll see its colorful, undulating roof in the distance. To get there, you'll cross...*

❶ Via Laietana

This traffic-choked street slices through Barcelona's Old City. It marks the boundary between the Barri Gòtic (behind you) and El Born (in front of you). When the road was built in 1908, Barcelona was turning its back on its Gothic past and racing into its Modernista future—and hundreds of historic buildings were torn down to create this new artery. (The most treasured structures, nicknamed "traveling buildings," were saved—taken down one brick at a time and reassembled in a more workable location.) Fortunately, even as

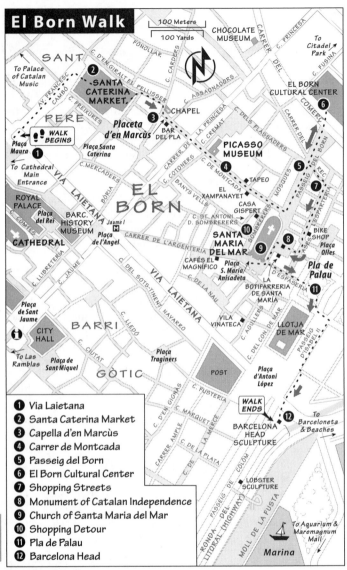

El Born Walk

① Via Laietana
② Santa Caterina Market
③ Capella d'en Marcùs
④ Carrer de Montcada
⑤ Passeig del Born
⑥ El Born Cultural Center
⑦ Shopping Streets
⑧ Monument of Catalan Independence
⑨ Church of Santa Maria del Mar
⑩ Shopping Detour
⑪ Pla de Palau
⑫ Barcelona Head

much of Barcelona modernized, El Born retained much of its medieval character and the low-key charm we're about to see.

• *Across Via Laietana, continue ahead to the crazy building that looks like it's wearing a giant, colorful sunhat.*

❷ Santa Caterina Market

While tourists swarm the more famous La Boqueria Market on the

Ramblas, Santa Caterina is a lively dose of local color, still primarily serving its neighborhood. This is the place to buy *jamón* and cheese without the crowds or tourist markup.

Check out the exterior. The market was originally built atop the ruins of an old monastery in 1845 to keep El Born's blue-collar workers well fueled with quality foods. A 2006 renovation added the swooping roof and a shell around its original arcaded white walls. The roof's bright colors evoke Gaudí and the colorful produce within.

Its Catalan architect, Enric Miralles, is best known for designing the Scottish parliament building in Edinburgh—an unlikely connection that's also oddly fitting, since both the Catalans and the Scots consider themselves "nations without states."

Enter and browse your way to the far left end. Inside are beautifully lit produce stalls with mouthwatering presentations and surprising variety (one stall displays 20 kinds of tomato). There are lots of tempting eateries—locals eat before shopping so as not to overbuy. For tips on where to eat in the market, see page 192.

As you exit at the far left end, find the archaeological area (with diagrams and English explanations) of the old monastery. (If the market is closed, you can reach this spot by looping around the left side to the back.) You're standing in what was once the sacristy, located just off the apse of the monastery's church.

• *Leaving the market, angle left and continue down narrow Carrer d'en Giralt el Pellisser, a lane of tiny boutiques and cafés. Look up and see the neighborhood. At the T-intersection, turn right, where you'll immediately find a tiny church.*

❸ Capella d'en Marcùs

This humble Romanesque chapel, from the 1100s, is supposedly the oldest church in town. Made of stone and topped with two small bells, it was a neighborhood center, where El Born's working-class medieval folk would pause to share the news. Back then, this part of El Born was where guilds—the laborers specializing in a particular trade—were located. The streets were named after the trades plied there, like beltmakers (on Carrer dels Corders, near the church entrance), or tanners (on Carrer dels Assaonadors, behind the church).

The church stands at what was once a major intersection. Across the street from its front door, above the plaque for #1, notice the sign with the horse and the word ***entrada*** (entrance). This is an old-fashioned one-way sign, marking the direction of carriage traffic in this tight tangle of lanes. Along the right side of the chapel, at the far end of the tiny square, find the sign's twin, *salida* (exit), above the street sign for Carrer dels Assaonadors. You'll spot signs like these all over El Born and the Barri Gòtic.

• *Passing between the chapel and the recommended Bar del Pla, continue straight down the lane called Carrer de Montcada. Next to Bar del Pla is the Barcelona Legalize head shop. Drop in for a lesson on pot politics in Spain (they sell seeds and "hemp" products with plenty of CBD but maximum 0.2% THC; ask about the cannabis social clubs). After one block, glance right at Carrer de la Princesa to notice its many lively bars. If you turned right here, you'd go to the Jaume I Metro stop, Barri Gòtic, and cathedral area. Instead, cross Princesa and continue straight ahead, entering the most historic stretch of...*

❹ Carrer de Montcada

This was the medieval neighborhood's main street, connecting the blue-collar tradesmen's quarter (where we were) with the wealthy merchant district near the waterfront (up ahead). El Born's rich and famous built their mansions here. The street is lined with rustic stone palazzos with elaborately carved windows and wide-arched entrances leading to interior courtyards.

Carrer de Montcada has become the most touristy street in El Born—thanks to the **Picasso Museum** (on the left), which sprawls through five mansions laced together (formerly owned by the noble Montcada family, who give the street its name). Even without a ticket, you can generally pop into the museum courtyards and make out the typical mansion layout: built around a quiet, interior open-air courtyard with servants' quarters on the ground floor and staircases up to the living rooms above.

Continuing down the street, pause at #25 (on the left, now an art gallery) to see another historic palazzo, and yet another at #20 (right) with its rainspout gargoyles. As the street widens up, you'll find palm trees, other art galleries, cafés, shops, and restaurants (mostly touristy, though I recommend El Xampanyet and Tapeo).

• *At the end of the street, you'll pop out onto a long square stretching to the left.*

❺ Passeig del Born

This long square—actually a "passeig," or boulevard—has been El Born's center for a thousand years. At one end of the square is the neighborhood church; at the other is the neighborhood market hall. Enjoy the square's cobbled pavement, tree-lined ambience, ironwork lanterns, apartments with small balconies, and a couple of fine stone medieval facades.

Passeig del Born grew as a neighborhood center because (as we'll see) it was located very close to the waterfront, where all the commercial action was. Sailors, traders, merchants, and travelers came here, all looking for a meal, a drink, a church to worship at, and a place to shop. In medieval times, Passeig del Born served as a jousting square (as its Roman circus-esque shape indicates), giving it the name "El Born," from an old Catalan word for "tournament." Eventually the square's name was given to the entire district that grew up around it.

Over the centuries, the Passeig has hosted festivals, religious processions during Holy Week, Inquisition-era heretic burnings, carnival celebrations, and other public spectacles. These days, Passeig del Born is a popular springboard for exploring inviting tapas bars, fun restaurants, and nightspots in the narrow streets all around.

• *At the far end of Passeig del Born is the former market hall, now known as the...*

❻ El Born Cultural Center

This vast, iron-and-glass construction once housed the El Born produce market, which not only served this neighborhood but was a major distribution point for the entire city. In 1971, the merchants moved their wholesale business to the suburbs, and the neighborhood went into a steep decline. Only in the last decade or so has El Born revived.

Today the market hall has reopened as the El Born Cultural Center, an exhibition and event space (free to enter). The first such iron-and-glass structure in town, the building, from 1876, was inspired by similar market halls that were then the rage in France.

Visiting the Center: When the hall was renovated in the 20th century, workers discovered remains of the Old City below. Belly up to the railing and look down at the exposed excavations and foundations. This was the neighborhood around the year 1700. In the central zone (near the cultural center's entrance) you can make out a cobbled plaza, flanked by houses and shops. In the area to the left, a canal brought in water, near where the laundry was located. A nearby street (still in the left zone) was once lined with guitar-making shops, and there's a rectangular 17th-century paddleball court. Heading over to the right zone, find the round vat of a brandy distillery and the all-important ice house, for stocking snow shipped in from nearby mountains to refrigerate food. Yes, this was clearly a vibrant neighborhood—until the tragic events of 1714.

Independence for Catalunya?

In much of Spain, you'll find four languages on ATM screens, and all are native to Spain: Spanish—spoken by most of the population; Euskara—used by the Basques in the far north; Galician—used by the Celtic people of the northwest; and Catalan—the language of the northeast Catalunya region, including Barcelona. The country is more complicated than many realize.

For decades, the ETA, a Basque group, dominated separatist news from Spain. But that group dissolved in 2018, laying down its weapons after an almost 50-year and, at times, violent struggle for independence. Today it's Catalunya that's in the news, with its own bold independence movement, and Spain, for its hard stance against Catalan separatists.

Pro-independence Catalans explain the situation to me like this: Tensions rose in 2017 when Catalunya wanted the right to put a referendum on independence before voters (like Scotland). The central government in Madrid said "no" and sent 4,000 police officers to Barcelona to enforce a ban on the vote. But in October the Catalan people held the referendum anyway: stay or leave.

Despite peaceful demonstrations (even in the face of police violence), Spain maintained the vote to leave was illegal and charged several Catalan leaders with rebellion and sedition. The Catalan president fled the country rather than go to jail.

Many Europeans were shocked by the harsh reaction from Madrid. Many Spaniards were upset that it wasn't stronger. And Catalunya itself is sadly divided. Those who oppose Catalan independence still feel loyal to the region—they're just not in favor of splitting away. And those passionate for a completely independent Catalunya consider those who oppose them to be turncoats.

Catalunya has lived as part of Spain for centuries. So why did the Catalans decide to break? They tell me it's because the central government in Madrid has become

Information plaques explain the story, which still resonates with locals. In the early 1700s, Barcelona's Catalan patriots took advantage of the chaos of the War of Spanish Succession to rise up against their Spanish overlords. But Barcelona fell in 1714, and the Spaniards suppressed the rebellion brutally. Residents were forced to destroy their homes and use those very stones to build a citadel for the Spanish just east of here (now a park). The citadel came with a one-kilometer buffer zone, so no buildings were allowed where the market stands today.

right-wing and regressive—repeatedly overriding domestic initiatives better left to the Catalan people.

Just as Vermont is more liberal than Wyoming, Catalunya is more liberal than mainstream Spain. Catalan laws that would have prohibited bullfighting, banned fracking, protected Catalunya's cultural heritage, and taxed nuclear energy, corporations, and banks in creative ways to help society (common initiatives among other European nations) were opposed and overturned by Madrid. The central government even decreed that if one child in a Catalan school asks that the Spanish language be used, the entire class must be taught in Spanish rather than Catalan. From a Barcelona perspective, national news coverage of these issues is biased in favor of Madrid. And in much of the Catalan press, it's biased in the other direction.

Catalunya has become a divided society, split by the question: Are you for independence or are you a Spanish nationalist? In Catalunya, pro-independence is politically correct, and Spanish nationalists are often insulted as "fascists." Catalans who want to stay with Spain feel that the separatists are driving a wedge between themselves and the rest of society. Many very patriotic Catalans believe they can be adequately autonomous without leaving Spain. It's an awkward discussion (much like the political dynamic in the US today).

The unfortunate thing about independence votes is that they are all or nothing. Most people would like something in the middle—which so far hasn't been an option. Madrid's aggressive response to this latest surge for Catalan independence is driving many longtime Spanish nationalists and moderates into the independence camp.

It's a bit like David and Goliath. But David is not always right. A Catalan friend who is against separating makes the case that the real victim is Catalan society, as now there is no longer a single "Catalan people." The society is losing its ability to talk together. He misses the good old days when, on the feast of St. George (Jordi, Catalunya's patron saint), the roses given in his honor were all red—not (as now) yellow, the color of protest. Only time will tell what the future holds for Catalunya.

A permanent display called *Barcelona 1700* brings that age to life with paintings, artifacts, and videos (buy tickets from the info point near the entry; includes audioguide explaining the excavations). There are usually other temporary exhibits to explore as well. Or just enjoy a drink in the modern café on-site.

• The **Chocolate Museum** *is just two blocks from here if you want to make an interesting and delicious detour (see page 48). Otherwise, from the cultural center, backtrack into Passeig del Born and turn left* *on the arcaded Carrer del Rec. This part of El Born has a high concentration of...*

❼ Shopping Streets

Fashion boutiques populate the area around **Carrer del Rec.** Take the first right turn, down **Carrer de l'Esparteria,** a great shopping street. On the side lanes, you can see local "fashions" flapping in the breeze from characteristic wrought-iron balconies. While strict building codes prohibit people from drying laundry outside in most of the city, an exception is made for El Born—since parts of this medieval quarter lacks interior courtyards.

As elsewhere in El Born, most street names are tied to a particular craft or product. An *"esparteria"* is a place where things (like baskets) made from esparto grass are woven; Carrer de la Formatgeria (third street on the right) was home to the cheesemakers.

Stick with Esparteria as it passes a recommended bike rental shop. (It's cheap and easy to rent a bike here to explore the nearby beach and harbor strip.) The lane jogs slightly left and becomes Carrer dels Ases. Pause at **Carrer del Malcuinat,** literally "the street of bad cooking." Looking left, you'll notice you're just a block off what was once the bustling old port. In the Middle Ages, unpretentious eateries here served fill-the-tank meals to undiscerning sailors who were fresh off the boat. These days, no self-respecting restaurateur has the nerve to open an eatery along here (except, strangely, an Irish pub).

• *Turn right down the short Carrer del Malcuinat, emerging at a big square with the...*

❽ Monument of Catalan Independence

The square is called Plaça del Fossar de les Moreres ("The Burial Place of the Mulberry Trees"). The lone mulberry tree and modern monument honor a 300-year-old massacre that's still fresh in the Catalan consciousness. On September 11, 1714, the Bourbon king Philip V, ruling from Madrid, completed a successful 14-month siege of Barcelona (the "Catalan Alamo"). In retaliation for the local resistance to Bourbon rule, he massacred Catalan patriots. From that day on, the king outlawed Catalan language, culture, and institutions, kicking off more than two centuries of cultural suppression. For example, no university was allowed in Barcelona from 1720 to 1850. To establish his hold, the king demolished homes in the nearby fishermen's quarter and built a gigantic citadel. The suddenly homeless seafarers were

moved to the tight, grid-planned Barceloneta area that juts into the harbor just east of here. Meanwhile, besides this depopulation of El Born, the neighborhood declined further as shipping shifted west, to the Barri Gòtic's harbor at Port Vell.

This square marks the site of a mass grave of the massacred Catalans. The **eternal flame** burns atop this monument, and 9/11 remains a sobering anniversary for the Catalans, who still harbor a grudge against the Bourbon king. They say when heading to the toilet, "I'm going to Philip's house."

Here or elsewhere in El Born, you may see displayed the *estelada* **flag,** the symbol of Catalan separatists: It features the typical red-and-gold horizontal stripes of the Catalunya flag, but with a blue triangle and white star on the hoist side. This design comes from the flag of a former Spanish colony that fought hard for its independence—Cuba. It's a provocative image to Spaniards who want to keep Catalunya in their country.

• *The hulking building dominating this square is the Church of Santa Maria del Mar. Turn left and walk to the small square in front of the church.*

❾ Church of Santa Maria del Mar

This 14th-century church, the proud centerpiece of El Born, is where shipwrights and merchants came to worship. It was dubbed

"Del Mar" (meaning "of the sea"), as it was right near the water's edge when it was built. Proud shippers built this church in less than 60 years, so it has a harmonious style that is considered pure Catalan Gothic. Located outside the city walls, this was a defiantly independent symbol of neighborhood pride; to this day, it's fully supported not by the Church or the city, but by the community.

Exterior: The church, with its twin lighthouse-like towers, has an impressively ornate facade. On the big front doors, notice the figures of workers who donated their time and sweat to build the church. The stone they used was quarried at Montjuïc and had to be carried across town on the backs of porters called *bastaixos.* Although it's always been celebrated by residents, their work is now more widely appreciated, following the release of the historical novel *Cathedral of the Sea* (2006), which tells the story of the church's construction from the perspective of an ambitious *bastaixo.*

Indulgences near the Church

The colorful neighborhood around the Church of Santa Maria del Mar offers plenty of inviting places to eat, drink, and shop (with recommended eateries nearby—see page 191). Explore!

For liquid and gourmet food souvenirs, try **Vila Vinateca,** a wine shop with (they claim) the widest selection in Barcelona (Mon-Sat 8:30-20:30, closed Sun, Carrer des Agullers 7—as you face the church it's buried about 100 yards away in the streets over your right shoulder, tel. 902-327-777). Across the lane is their gifty-edibles shop, with a wild cheese selection. To go with your wine and cheese, try the very Catalan sausage *botifarra* from **La Botifarreria de Santa Maria.** Take a number and join the locals in line; be sure to ask for *botifarra* that doesn't require cooking (Mon-Sat 8:30-14:30 & 17:00-20:30, closed Sun; Carrer Santa Maria 4; tel. 933-199-123).

A caffeine jolt awaits at **Cafés El Magnífico,** selling what's reputed to be the city's best coffee beans and takeout coffee (Mon-Sat 10:00-20:00, closed Sun, one block up Carrer de l'Argenteria at #64—immediately to the left as you face the church's front door, tel. 933-196-081). For a fragrant snack, head to **Casa Gispert,** which has been roasting nuts in the same wood-fired oven since 1851. Drop in to enjoy the aroma of fire-roasted nuts and pick up a snack (Mon-Sat 10:00-14:00 & 16:00-20:00, closed Sun; facing front door of church, circle around left side and walk almost all the way to the end—store is on the left at Carrer dels Sombrerers 23, tel. 933-197-535).

Inside the Church: Stepping inside, take in the nave. The church is stripped down—naked in all its Gothic glory. The tree-like columns with their extreme vertical thrust inspired Gaudí (the influence on the columns inside his Sagrada Família church is obvious). As within the Barcelona Cathedral, here you see the characteristic Catalan Gothic buttresses flying inward, defining the chapels that ring the nave. Brilliant stained glass—most notably the rose window over the main entry—floods the interior with soft light.

The church was once highly decorated with Baroque frills. But during the Spanish Civil War (1936-1939), when the Catholic Church sided with the conservative forces of Franco, working-class leftists took their anger out on this church. They torched the interior, and it burned for 11 days straight—destroying all of its wood furnishings and decor (carbon still blackens the ceiling). Since then, some things have been replaced; the local sculptor Frederic Marès began the restoration. At the altar, there's a statue of St. Mary of the Sea, to whom this church is dedicated. Just as 16th-century sailors left models of their ships at the altar for Mary's protection, even today, a classic old Catalan ship remains at Mary's feet.

EL BORN WALK

• *If you've seen enough, you can end your walk now and give in to El Born's many buyable and edible temptations (see sidebar for ideas). A good place to start is around the left side of the church ("left" as you face the main facade), on the street called Carrer dels Banys Vells, which makes for an excellent...*

⑩ Shopping Detour

Follow Carrer dels Banys Vells all the way up to Carrer de la Princesa; a bunch of great shops hide along the lanes branching off to the left. Many of them have workshops where the goods for sale are actually produced. You'll see small boutiques, leather stores, one-of-a-kind dress shops, and art studios. The warren of streets wedged between here and Carrer de l'Argenteria are particularly interesting and an easy place to score cool finds, including handmade clothing, accessories, and bags.

• *Backtrack to the Church of Santa Maria del Mar. Facing the main facade, turn right and head down Carrer d'Espaseria. You'll pop out at...*

⑪ Pla de Palau

Goods arriving from the harbor were received and traded on this square. The hulking building on your right (with columns and a triangular pediment) is the **Llotja de Mar,** or commercial exchange. It originated in medieval times as a place to trade fish and goods brought in on boats. Then, as Barcelona grew into a major shipping center and El Born was its ritziest neighborhood, the Llotja went from trading fish and livestock to becoming one of Europe's first stock exchanges. From the late 17th through late 20th century, the building also housed the prestigious Barcelona Arts and Crafts School, providing state-subsidized instruction to budding artists—including Pablo Picasso and Joan Miró.

• *From Llotja de Mar, cross the wide street (Passeig d'Isabel II), and turn right to walk under the shaded arches of the big arcaded building. At the busy intersection at the end of the arcade, you'll come face-to-face with the...*

⑫ *Barcelona Head*

This sculpture, created for the 1992 Summer Olympics by American Pop artist Roy Lichtenstein, instantly became an icon of the city. Depicting a woman's head in an abstract style, it brings together the colors of Miró, the tiles of Gaudí, the Cubism of Picasso, and the trademark dots of Lichtenstein. He created paintings that have the look of a comic strip, blown up to a size where you can see individual printing color dots.

The grand main post office stands across the main avenue. Also nearby is a giant, whimsical **lobster sculpture** waving hello. Designed by Javier Mariscal, this cheery crustacean is just one more piece of invigorating public art on Barcelona's fine waterfront. In fact, El Born, with its history, shops, and galleries, is itself a veritable open-air art museum.

• *Barcelona's inviting waterfront beckons. From here, you could continue into the neighborhood of Barceloneta and the beach (or consider renting a bike at the recommended Bike Tours Barcelona shop for a pedal down the beach promenade to the Fòrum—see page 21). Or walk along the delightful art-lined promenade next to the Old Port (bristling with sailboats) to the Columbus Monument at the bottom of the Ramblas.*

PICASSO MUSEUM TOUR

Museu Picasso

This museum has the best collection in Spain of the work of Pablo Picasso (1881-1973), and the best collection anywhere of his earliest works. The Spaniard Picasso spent his formative years (from age 14 to 23) in Barcelona, and a visit to this museum intimately reveals the young man finding his way as an artist. By experiencing his youthful, realistic art, you can better understand his later, more challenging art and more fully appreciate his genius.

Picasso's personal secretary, Jaume Sabartés, amassed many examples of his friend's work and bequeathed them to Barcelona. The artist, happy to have a museum showing off his work in the city of his youth, added to the collection over the years. The museum and artworks are now housed in several connected Catalan Gothic palaces in the El Born neighborhood.

Orientation

Cost and Hours: €12, more with special exhibits, book tickets in advance online; open Tue-Sun 9:00-19:00, Thu until 21:30, closed Mon.

Free Entry: The museum is free—and crowded—Thu after 18:00 and all day on the first Sun of the month (must reserve online up to four days in advance).

Information: Tel. 932-563-000, www.museupicasso.bcn.cat.

Reservations and Ticketing Tips: While technically you can buy a ticket at the door, there's nearly always a long line, and the museum often sells out entirely. Buy a **timed-entry ticket** in advance at the museum website (the site can be temperamental—keep trying). An **Articket BCN** (see page 20) allows you to enter the galleries whenever you wish (stop first at the Articket window to receive a ticket; you can also buy an Articket at the window).

Day-of tickets (when available) are also sold online (must purchase at least 2 hours before your visit). The museum's busiest times are mornings before 13:00, all day Tue, and during the free entry times.

Getting In: The galleries sit one floor above a free-to-enter courtyard with several entrances. Tickets are sold at the center ground-floor entry; those with timed tickets can enter at either side.

Getting There: It's on Carrer de Montcada; the general ticket office is in the courtyard at #19, and the Articket BCN booth is at #23. From the Jaume I Metro stop, it's a quick five-minute walk. It's a 10-minute walk from the cathedral and many parts of the Barri Gòtic.

Tours: The 1.5-hour audioguide (€5) offers descriptions for 51 paintings. Occasional English-language tours are announced on the museum website.

Length of This Tour: Allow at least an hour.

Services: The ground floor has a required bag check, a bookshop, and WC.

Cuisine Art: Along Carrer de Montcada in either direction are several recommended tapas bars: With your back to the museum, a few steps to the left are **El Xampanyet** and **Tapeo,** while to the right (across Carrer de la Princesa and up a block) is **Bar del Pla.** For details about these and other characteristic places nearby, see page 192.

The Tour Begins

The Picasso Museum's collection of nearly 300 paintings is presented more or less chronologically. With good text panels in every room providing context, it's easy to follow the evolution of Picasso's work. This tour (like the museum itself) is arranged by the stages of his life and art. Don't be surprised if a painting described here is not on view. Individual paintings are rotated in and out constantly (to keep it interesting for locals and repeat visitors). But the themes and chronology remain constant.

Boy Wonder (Room 1)

Pablo's earliest art is realistic and earnest. His work quickly advanced from childish pencil drawings (from about 1890), through a series of technically skilled **art-school works** (copies of plaster feet and arms), to oil paintings of impressive technique. Pablo was born in 1881, so you can easily calculate how amazingly young he was when he painted these works. His **portraits**—of grizzled peasants,

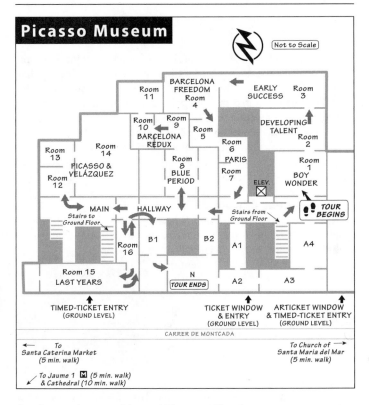

Picasso Museum

Not to Scale

BARCELONA
FREEDOM
Room 11 | Room 4 | EARLY SUCCESS | Room 3

Room 10 | Room 9 | DEVELOPING TALENT
BARCELONA REDUX | Room 5 | Room 2

Room 13 | Room 14 | Room 6 | PARIS
PICASSO & VELÁZQUEZ | Room 8 BLUE PERIOD | Room 7
Room 12 | ELEV. ☒ | Room 1 BOY WONDER

TOUR BEGINS

MAIN HALLWAY | Stairs from Ground Floor
Stairs to Ground Floor
Room 16 | B1 | B2 | A1 | A4

Room 15 LAST YEARS | N TOUR ENDS | A2 | A3

TIMED-TICKET ENTRY (GROUND LEVEL) | TICKET WINDOW & ENTRY (GROUND LEVEL) | ARTICKET WINDOW & TIMED-TICKET ENTRY (GROUND LEVEL)

CARRER DE MONTCADA

← To Santa Caterina Market (5 min. walk)
To Church of Santa Maria del Mar (5 min. walk) →
To Jaume 1 Ⓜ (5 min. walk) & Cathedral (10 min. walk)

family members, and himself (at age 15)—demonstrate surprising psychological insight. Because his dedicated father—himself a curator and artist—kept everything his son ever did, Picasso must have the best-documented youth of any great painter. Though Pablo dabbled in landscapes, still lifes, and everyday scenes, he was always, first and foremost, a painter of people.

Developing Talent (Room 2)

Pablo moved to Barcelona at age 14. During a summer trip to Málaga (his birthplace and boyhood home) in 1896, he experimented with a series of fresh, Impressionistic-style landscapes (relatively rare in Spain at the time). As a 15-year-old, Pablo dutifully entered art-school competitions. A case along the wall shows off his art-school studies, Barcelona scenes from 1896 (allowing you to see the city through Picasso's eyes), and classical studies of the human body.

His first big work, *First Communion,* tackled a prescribed religious subject, but Picasso made it an excuse to paint his family. His sister Lola was the model for the communicant, and the man beside her has the face of Picasso's father. Notice Lola's exquisitely painted

PICASSO MUSEUM

veil. This piece was heavily influenced by the academic style of local painters.

Picasso's relatives star in a number of portraits from this time. You may find a touching portrait of his mother, with a cameo-like face and fine details in her white blouse. Find the portrait of his aunt **Tía Pepa,** painted in Málaga in 1896 (this and other family portraits are frequently rotated). It's said Picasso painted this in less than a day. Notice how ably he captured the toughness of his aunt. Look at Picasso's signature on some paintings in this room. Spaniards keep both parents' surnames, with the father's first, followed by the mother's: Pablo Ruiz Picasso.

Early Success (Room 3)

In the large, classically painted *Science and Charity* (1897), Picasso used realistic means to represent subjects of social concern—a

technique typical of the social realism movement of the late 19th century. The doctor (modeled on Pablo's father) represents science. The nun represents charity and religion. From the hopeless face and lifeless hand of the sick woman, it seems that Picasso believes nothing will save her from death. Pablo painted a little perspective trick: Walk back and forth across the room to see the bed stretch and shrink. Three small studies (to the left) show the preparatory work Picasso did for this major painting.

Science and Charity won second prize at a fine-arts exhibition, earning Picasso the chance to study in Madrid. Stifled by the stuffy art school there, he hung out instead in the Prado Museum and learned by copying earlier Spanish masters, especially Diego Velázquez, with whom he developed a virtual friendship. An example of Picasso's impressive mimicry is sometimes displayed in this room—a nearly perfect copy of a **portrait of Philip IV** by Velázquez. (Near the end of this tour, we'll see a much older Picasso riffing on another Velázquez painting.)

In this room you'll also see outdoor views of Madrid (mostly in Retiro Park) and rural village scenes. In 1898 Pablo fell sick and was sent to convalesce in the mountain village of Horta de Sant Joan. Away from his father and the conservative art establishment in Madrid, his creative spirit was freed. You can sense that Picasso was finding his artistic independence as he painted these landscapes and scenes of village life. The artist later credited his time at Horta de Sant Joan as an important step in his artistic evolution.

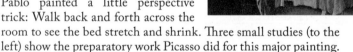

PICASSO MUSEUM

Barcelona Freedom (Room 4)

After regaining his health, Picasso returned to Barcelona in 1900. Art Nouveau was all the rage there. Upsetting his dad, he quit art school and fell in with an avant-garde crowd. These bohemians congregated daily at Els Quatre Gats ("The Four Cats," a popular restaurant to this day—see page 188). Picasso even created the **menu cover** for this favorite hangout. Further establishing his artistic freedom, he painted often dark and brooding **portraits** of his new friends (including Carlos Casagemas and Jaume Sabartés, who later became Picasso's personal assistant and donated the foundational

works of this museum). Still a teenager, Pablo exhibited his first one-man show—a series of neighborhood sketches in the style of Toulouse-Lautrec—at Els Quatre Gats in 1900.

Paris (Rooms 6-7)

In 1900 Picasso made his first trip to Paris, a city bursting with life, light, and love. Dropping the paternal surname Ruiz (which is a kind of Spanish "Smith"), Pablo established his commercial brand name: simply "Picasso." Here the explorer Picasso went bohemian and befriended poets, prostitutes, and artists. He began sampling the contemporary art styles around him: He painted **cancan dancers** like Toulouse-Lautrec, **still lifes** like Paul Cézanne, brightly colored **Fauvist** works like Henri Matisse, and Impressionist **landscapes** like Claude Monet (you may see examples on the walls of this room). In *The Waiting (Margot)*, the subject—with her bold outline and strong gaze—pops out from the vivid, mosaic-like background. Picasso was learning Cézanne's technique of "building" a figure with "cubes" of paint—a step toward Picasso's invention of Cubism.

Blue Period (Room 8)

Picasso would travel to Paris several times before settling there permanently in 1904. The suicide of his best friend Casagemas, his own poverty, and the influence of new ideas linking color and mood led Picasso to abandon jewel-bright color for his Blue Period (1901-1904). He cranked out stacks of blue art just to stay housed and fed. With blue backgrounds (the coldest color) and depressing subjects, this period was revolutionary in art history. Now the artist was painting not what he saw, but what he felt. Painting misfits and

Pablo Picasso
(1881-1973)

Pablo Picasso was the most famous and, for me, the greatest artist of the 20th century. Always exploring, he became the master of many styles (Cubism, Surrealism, Expressionism) and of many media (painting, sculpture, prints, ceramics, assemblages). Still, he could make anything he touched look unmistakably like "a Picasso."

Born in Málaga, Spain, Picasso was the son of an art teacher. At a very young age, he quickly advanced beyond his teachers. Picasso's teenage works are stunningly realistic and capture the inner complexities of the people he painted. As a youth in Barcelona, he fell in with a bohemian crowd that mixed wine, women, and art.

In 1900, at age 19, Picasso started making trips to Paris. Four years later, he moved to the City of Light and absorbed the styles of many painters (especially Henri de Toulouse-Lautrec) while searching for his own artist's voice. His paintings of beggars and other social outcasts show the empathy of a man who was himself a poor, homesick foreigner. When his best friend, Spanish artist Carlos Casagemas, committed suicide, Picasso plunged into a **Blue Period** (1901-1904)—so called because the dominant color in these paintings matches their melancholy mood and subject matter (emaciated beggars, hard-eyed pimps).

In 1904, Picasso got a steady girlfriend (Fernande Olivier) and suddenly saw the world through rose-colored glasses—the **Rose Period.** He was further jolted out of his Blue Period by the "flat" look of the Fauve paintings being made around him. Not satisfied with their take on 3-D, Picasso played with the "building blocks" of line and color to find new ways to reconstruct the real world on canvas.

At his studio in Montmartre, Picasso and his neighbor Georges Braque worked together, in poverty so dire they often didn't know where their next bottle of wine was coming from. And then, at age 25, Picasso reinvented painting. Fascinated by the primitive power of African tribal masks, he sketched human faces with simple outlines and almond eyes. Intrigued by his girlfriend's body, he sketched Fernande from every angle, then experimented with showing several different views on the same canvas. A hundred paintings and nine months later, Picasso gave birth to a monstrous canvas of five nude, fragmented prostitutes with mask-like faces—*Les Demoiselles d'Avignon* (1907).

This bold new style was called **Cubism.** With Cubism, Picasso shattered the Old World and put it back together in a new way. The subjects are somewhat recognizable (with the help of the titles), but they're built with geometric shards (let's call them "cubes")—it's like viewing the world through a kaleidoscope of brown and gray. Cubism presents several different angles of the subject at once—say, a woman seen from the front and side simultaneously, resulting in two eyes on the same side of the nose. Cubism showed the traditional three dimensions, plus Einstein's new fourth dimension—the time it takes to walk around the subject to see other angles.

In 1918, Picasso married his first wife, Olga Kokhlova. He then traveled to Rome and entered a **Classical Period** (1920s) of more realistic, full-bodied women and children, inspired by the three-dimensional sturdiness of ancient statues. While he flirted with abstraction, throughout his life Picasso always kept a grip on "reality." His favorite subject was people. The anatomy might be jumbled, but it's all there.

Though he lived in France and Italy, Picasso remained a Spaniard at heart, incorporating Spanish motifs into his work. Unrepentantly macho, he loved bullfights, seeing them as a metaphor for the timeless human interaction between the genders. The horse—clad with blinders and pummeled by the bull—is just a pawn in the battle between bull and matador. To Picasso, the horse symbolizes the feminine, and the bull, the masculine. Spanish imagery—bulls, screaming horses, a Madonna—appears in Picasso's most famous work, *Guernica* (1937). The monumental canvas of a bombed village summed up the pain of Spain's brutal civil war (1936-1939) and foreshadowed the onslaught of World War II.

At war's end, Picasso left Paris, his wife, and his emotional baggage behind, finding fun in the **south of France.** Sun! Color! Water! Freedom! Senior citizen Pablo Picasso was reborn, enjoying worldwide fame. He lived at first with the beautiful young painter Françoise Gilot, mother of two of his children, but it was another young beauty, Jacqueline Roque, who became his second wife. Dressed in rolled-up white pants and a striped sailor's shirt, bursting with pent-up creativity, Picasso often cranked out a painting a day. Picasso's Riviera works set the tone for the rest of his life. They're sunny, lighthearted, and childlike; filled with motifs of the sea, Greek mythology (fauns, centaurs), and animals; and freely experimental in their use of new media. The simple drawing of doves Picasso made at this time become emblematic of the artist and an international symbol of peace.

Picasso made collages, built "statues" out of wood, wire, ceramics, papier-mâché, or whatever, and even turned everyday household objects into statues (like his famous bull's head made of a bicycle seat with handlebar horns). **Multimedia** works like these have become so standard today that we forget how revolutionary they once were. His last works have the playfulness of someone much younger. As it is often said of Picasso, "When he was a child, he painted like a man. When he was old, he painted like a child."

PICASSO MUSEUM

street people, Picasso, like Velázquez and Toulouse-Lautrec before him, revealed the beauty in ugliness.

During a visit back to Barcelona, Picasso painted a nighttime view over the **rooftops** of the city. His palette is still blue, but here we see proto-Cubism...five years before the first real Cubist painting.

Rose Period

Picasso finally lifted out of his funk after meeting a new lady, Fernande Olivier (a bronze bust of her from 1906 may be on view). He moved out of the blue and into the happier Rose Period (1904-1907), dominated by soft pink and reddish tones. (Other than the rarely displayed *Portrait of Bernadetta Bianco*, the museum is weak on Rose Period works.)

Cubism

Pablo's role in the invention of the groundbreaking Cubist style (with his friend Georges Braque) is well known—at least I hope so, since this museum has no true Cubist paintings. What made the style revolutionary is that it's free from conventional perspective. A Cubist work gives not only the basic shape of a subject—it shows every aspect of it simultaneously. The technique of "building" a subject with "cubes" of paint simmered in Picasso's artistic stew for years. The idea was to simultaneously see several 3-D facets of the subject.

Barcelona Redux (Rooms 9-10)

Picasso spent six months back in Barcelona in 1917 (yet another girlfriend, a Russian ballet dancer, had a gig in town). The paintings in these rooms demonstrate the artist's irrepressible versatility: He had already developed Cubism, but he also continued to play with other styles. In *Woman with Mantilla*, we see a little Post-Impressionistic Pointillism in a portrait that is as elegant as a classical statue. Nearby, *Gored Horse* has all the anguish and power of his iconic *Guernica* (painted years later).

Remember that this museum has very little from the most famous and prolific "middle" part of Picasso's career—basically, from his adoption of Cubism to his sunset years on the French Riviera. (To fill in the gaps in his middle career, see the sidebar in this chapter.)

Picasso and Velázquez (Rooms 12-14)

Whoosh. We've skipped ahead a few decades in Picasso's life, and suddenly he is 40 years older. We left him at age 36 in 1917. Now it's 1957 and he's 76. As a mature artist, Picasso had few peers. He turned to the great Old Masters for inspiration.

He decided to make a series of works related to what many

PICASSO MUSEUM

Velázquez's Las Meninas *(left) inspired many versions by Picasso (right).*

consider the greatest painting by anyone, ever: Diego Velázquez's
Las Meninas. The 17th-century original (in Madrid's Prado Museum) depicted the young maids of honor (or *meninas*) of the Spanish
royal court. Heralded as the first completely realistic painting, *Las
Meninas* became, centuries later, an obsession for Picasso.

Pablo, who had great respect for Velázquez, painted more than
40 interpretations of the masterwork. He seemed to enjoy a rela-
tionship of equals with Velázquez, and like artistic soul mates, the
two geniuses sparred and teased. Picasso deconstructed Velázquez
and then injected light, color, and perspective as he improvised on
the earlier masterpiece. In Picasso's big, black and white canvas,
he more or less re-created Velázquez's painting in its entirety. But
here, the king and queen (reflected in the mirror in the back of the
room) are hardly seen, while the painter—the great Velázquez—
towers above everyone. In other paintings in the series, Picasso
focused on details—one maid of honor or a pair of them, or he
zeroed in on just their faces. Browse the various studies (in Rooms
13-14), a playground of color and perspective. See the fun Picasso
had playing paddleball with Velázquez's tour de force—filtering
Velázquez's realism through the kaleidoscope of Cubism.

Last Years (Room 15)

Picasso spent the last 36 years of his life living simply in the south
of France. He said many times that "paintings are like windows
open to the world." We see his sunny Riviera world: With simple
black outlines and Crayola colors, Picasso painted sun-splashed
nature, peaceful doves, and the joys of the beach. He's enjoyed life
with his second (and much younger) wife, Jacqueline Roque.

His last works have the playfulness of someone much younger.
As is often said of Picasso, in his youth he was taught to see the
world like an adult, and in his golden years he enjoyed seeing and
portraying the world with the freedom of a child.

Nearby (in Rooms B1, N, and B2), you'll see how in his later years
Picasso became a master of other media besides painting. With his
ceramics, he made bowls and vases in fun animal shapes, decorated

PICASSO MUSEUM

with simple motifs. You'll also find **portraits of Jaume Sabartés,** whose initial donation made this museum possible.

Picasso died with brush in hand, still growing as an artist. Picasso—who had vowed never to set foot in fascist, Franco-ruled Spain—sadly died two years before Franco, in 1973. Picasso never returned to his homeland...and never saw this museum. But to the end, Picasso continued exploring and loving life through his art.

EIXAMPLE WALK

From the Top of Passeig de Gràcia to Plaça de Catalunya

Literally "The Expansion," the Eixample is where Barcelona spread when it burst at the seams in the 19th century. Rather than allowing unchecked growth, city leaders funneled Barcelona's newfound wealth into creating a standardized yet refreshingly open grid plan—quite the opposite of the claustrophobic Gothic lanes that had contained locals for centuries.

The creation of the Eixample coincided with a burst in architectural creativity as the great Modernista builders Antoni Gaudí, Lluís Domènech i Montaner, and Josep Puig i Cadafalch adorned Barcelona's new boulevards with fanciful facades. It was a perfect storm of urban planning, unbridled architectural innovation, Industrial Age technology, ample wealth, and Catalan cultural pride.

This walk takes you gently downhill through the Eixample's "Golden Quarter" (Quadrat d'Or) to see two of the city's Modernista musts—the Block of Discord and La Pedrera (Casa Milà)—as well as several other sights. We'll wind through some pleasant, relatively untouristy residential neighborhoods that showcase modern Barcelona's unusual street plan, inviting restaurant and shopping options, and everyday life in this elegant quarter.

Orientation

Length of This Walk: Allow one hour (more if you tour the sights).

Sightseeing Tip: If you want to see the interiors, advance purchase is essential for Casa Batlló and La Pedrera.

Getting There: This walk starts at the Diagonal Metro station.

La Pedrera (Casa Milà): €22 for timed-entry ticket—buy online, daily 9:00-20:30, Nov-Feb until 18:30.

Casa Batlló: €24.50 for timed-entry ticket—buy online, daily 9:00-21:00.

Casa Museu Amatller: €24 for one-hour English tour, €19 for 40-minute videoguide group tour, daily 10:30-18:30.

La Concepció Market: Open Mon and Sat 8:00-15:00, Tue-Fri until 20:00, closed Sun, Carrer de València 317.

Church of the Holy Conception: Free, daily 8:00-13:00 & 17:00-21:00, enter at Carrer de Roger de Llúria 70, through the cloister, if entrance on Carrer d'Aragó is locked.

Tours: ∩ Download my free Eixample Walk audio tour (available in 2019).

Eateries: La Concepció Market is the handiest spot on this walk for a tasty, budget bite. Several fine tapas bars and restaurants are on or near this route (see page 193).

BACKGROUND

Barcelona boomed in the 1800s, with its population doubling (from a half-million to a million) over the course of one century. After a long period of stagnation—caused by changing sea-trading routes and political repression from Madrid—the city was finding new success. Catalunya's abundant coal deposits and many rivers were powering lucrative textile mills. The factories brought workers from all over Spain and beyond. By 1850, Barcelona was becoming an industrial powerhouse.

Unfortunately, Barcelona was all jacked up with nowhere to grow. Two hundred thousand residents were still crammed into the Barri Gòtic. It was a slum of steep and crowded tenements where disease was rampant, the air was choked with coal soot, and the quality of life was miserable. It was clear there was only one solution—expansion *(eixample)*.

Other European cities (like Paris, Vienna, and Copenhagen) were dealing with similar growing pains by tearing down antiquated defensive walls, draining moats, and converting the unused land into circular boulevards, parks, and housing.

But because the Madrid government was still wary of a Catalan uprising, Barcelona by law had to stay within its medieval walls. Finally, in 1854, Queen Isabella II allowed the city to tear down the old walls and expand northward. Because very little existed outside the Old City, urban planners had a blank slate.

Civil engineer Ildefons Cerdà (1815-1876) proposed a carefully plotted, remarkably modern plan. It would be an efficient grid of streets that would surround the convoluted tangle of Barcelona's Old City. He added a unique twist to the

Modernisme and the Renaixença

Modernisme is Barcelona's unique contribution to the Europe-wide Art Nouveau movement. Meaning "a taste for what is modern"—such as streetcars, electric lights, and big-wheeled bicycles—this free-flowing organic style lasted from 1888 to 1906.

Broadly speaking, there were two kinds of Modernisme (otherwise known as Catalan Art Nouveau). Early Modernisme has a Neo-Gothic flavor, clearly inspired by medieval castles and towers—logically, since architects wanted to recall the days when Barcelona was at its peak. From that starting point, Antoni Gaudí branched off on his own, adding the color and curves we most associate with the look of Barcelona's Modernisme.

The aim was to create buildings that were both practical and decorative. To that end, Modernista architects experi-

mented with new construction techniques. Their most important material was concrete, which they could mold to curve and ripple like a wave, and enliven with brightly colored glass and tile. Their structures were fully modern, but the decoration was a clip-art collage of natural images, exotic Moorish or Chinese themes, and fanciful Gothic crosses and knights to celebrate Catalunya's medieval glory days.

It's ironic to think that Modernisme was a response against the regimentation of the Industrial Age—and that all those organic shapes were only made possible thanks to Eiffel Tower-like iron frames. As you wander through the Eixample looking at all those fanciful facades and colorful, leafy, blooming shapes in doorways, entrances, and ceilings, remember that many of these homes were built at the same time as the first skyscrapers in Chicago and New York City.

Underpinning Modernisme was the Catalan cultural revival movement, called the Renaixença. Across Europe, it was a time of national resurgence. It was the dawn of the modern age, and downtrodden peoples—from the Basques to the Irish to the Hungarians to the Finns—were throwing off the cultural domination of other nations and celebrating what made their own culture unique. Here in Catalunya, the Renaixença encouraged everyday people to get excited about all things Catalan—from their language, patriotic dances, and inspirational art to their surprising style of architecture.

usual rectangular grid. By snipping off the corners of buildings, he created light and spacious octagonal "squares" at every intersection.

Work began in 1860 on Cerdà's progressive plan. In his vision, each block-square district of the Eixample would have all the services its residents would need: hospital, park, market, schools, and day-care centers. Restrictions on the height, width, and depth of buildings ensured that sunlight would reach every dwelling unit. The hollow space found inside each "block" of apartments would form a neighborhood park. Cerdà's vision proved to be an urban-planning success story.

The birth of the Eixample also coincided with two other important moments in the city's history: The revival of Catalan cultural pride (the Renaixença) and the emergence of Catalunya's version of Art Nouveau—Modernisme (see the sidebar). These progressive movements found expression not only in enlightened urban planning but also in the beauty built into the buildings.

Rich-and-artsy big shots bought plots along the Eixample grid and hired some of the best and brightest architects in the business, including Antoni Gaudí. It's no accident that Modernista mansions come with big bay windows and outlandish decoration: The people who paid for them wanted both to be seen and recognized for their forward-thinking embrace of the new art. They built as close to the center as possible—that's why the most distinctive buildings are near Passeig de Gràcia.

Today's Eixample remains Barcelona's upscale and genteel uptown. The heart of the Eixample is the Quadrat d'Or, or "Golden Quarter," with the richest collection of Modernista facades...and the richest local residents. As you walk through the streets, peek into the big, ornate iron and glass doorways of almost any apartment building to see the eclectic decorative entrance halls and old-fashioned elevators. This remains one of the city's most desirable neighborhoods.

The Walk Begins

• *Begin at the Diagonal Metro stop. Take the Passeig de Gràcia exit and surface at the street of the same name.*

❶ Passeig de Gràcia (Top End)

Stand at the head of this broad boulevard and gaze downhill. This is the Eixample's grand, 50-yard-wide, tree-lined "main street,"

Eixample Walk

GRÀCIA

CASA DE LES PUNXES

AVINGUDA DIAGONAL

To Sagrada Família

Verdaguer Ⓜ

CARRER DE CÒRSEGA

C. DEL ROSSELLÓ

CARRER

PROVENÇA

CARRER DE BAILEN

CARRER DE GIRONA

WALK BEGINS

PALAU BARÓ DE QUADRAS

EIXAMPLE

LA CONCEPCIÓ MARKET

CARRER D'ARAGÓ

Ⓑ #24

Ⓜ Diagonal

ℹ

LA PEDRERA (CASA MILÀ)

❶

❷

CENTRE CULTURAL LA CASA ELIZALDE

CASA JUNCOSA

CARRER MALLORCA

VALÈNCIA

CHURCH OF THE HOLY CONCEPTION

❻

❺

❼

DEL BRUC

C. DEL CONSELL DE CENT

Ⓜ Girona

MAURI PASTRIES

C. Provença

PASSEIG DE GRÀCIA

CARRER DE

J. MURRIA QUEVIURES GROCERY

PASS. MEDIZVIGO

C. DE ROGER

TOWER

C. DE DIPUTACIÓ

QUADRAT D'OR

RAMBLA

❸ FUNDACIÓ TÀPIES

CASA BATLLÓ

CASA AMATLLER

PASSEIG DE GRÀCIA TRAIN STN. Ⓜ Passeig de Gràcia

BLOCK OF DISCORD

❹

PASSATGE PERMANYER

C. DE PAU CLARIS

DE LLÚRIA

200 Meters
200 Yards

CASA LLEÓ MORERA

PASSEIG DE GRÀCIA

COMEDIA THEATER

Passeig de Gràcia

Ⓜ ❽

CATALANES

DE

CATALUNYA

GRAN VIA DE LES CORTS

GRÀCIA

EL CORTE INGLÉS DEP'T STORE

WALK ENDS

❾

RONDA DE LA UNIVERSITAT

Ⓜ Universitat

Catalunya Ⓜ

Plaça de Catalunya

ℹ

To Las Ramblas

OLD CITY

❶ Passeig de Gràcia (Top End)
❷ La Pedrera (a.k.a. Casa Milà)
❸ Rambla de Catalunya
❹ Block of Discord
❺ Carrer de València
❻ La Concepció Market
❼ Church of the Holy Conception
❽ Passeig de Gràcia (Bottom End)
❾ Plaça de Catalunya

which runs through the heart of the district. At the far end—seven blocks down—is Plaça de Catalunya, where we'll end our walk.

Passeig de Gràcia was built as a kind of Champs-Elysées of Barcelona. The richest folks built their mansions along here (as we'll see). It was a place to dress up, promenade in your carriage, linger for a drink at a café, or shop at a high-fashion boutique. Gazing around, it's clear that the street still retains that same chic character. International high-fashion stores abound, like Dolce & Gabbana, Jimmy Choo, and Montblanc.

Passeig de Gràcia actually dates back to pre-Eixample times, when it was a narrow (but aptly named) path to the town of Gràcia. That former town is now the neighborhood of **Gràcia,** just a couple of blocks uphill from here, across Avinguda Diagonal. Gràcia is known for its old-time character, narrow streets, and upper-middle-class intellectual feel, with many design schools and a youthful scene.

• *Before moving on, if you're a Modernista completist, it's just a short walk from here to three more fine buildings—"extra credit" for those fascinated by this era (see the sidebar, "A Modernista Detour," for directions).*

Otherwise, stroll gently downhill along Passeig de Gràcia for a block or two. On your left will be the unmistakable wavy stone facade of...

❷ La Pedrera (a.k.a. Casa Milà)

Of all the over-the-top mansions built in the Eixample, this one was the most daring. A wealthy developer and his wealthier wife hired the city's most famous architect, Antoni Gaudí, and gave him a free hand. Even today, this Gaudí exterior laughs down on the crowds filling Passeig de Gràcia. La Pedrera ("The Quarry") has a much-photographed roller coaster of melting-ice-cream eaves. It remains Barcelona's quintessential Modernista building and was Gaudí's last major commission (1906-1910) before he dedicated his final years to the Sagrada Família.

The building has an iron structural skeleton to support its weight (a new construction technique at the time). Gaudí's planned statues of the Virgin Mary and archangels were vetoed by the owner.

The best views of La Pedrera are from kitty-corner across the street. From there, notice the century-old elegance of this fancy neighborhood. The ornate metal street lamps (from 1906) were originally gas-lit. At the base of the lampposts, spot the two little doors curbside—these were actually equipped with wood-burning ovens to heat benches for aristocratic bums. Across the street, notice the circular stone sofa corralling a plane tree.

• *From Passeig de Gràcia, turn right on Carrer de Provença and go one block. Each block is exactly 250 meters (so walking around the block is exactly one kilometer). As you stroll, look up and appreciate the details. You'll pass tony shops and apartments with nice bay windows in this exclusive neighborhood. Notice the dedicated bike lane and the long lines of parked motor scooters. To maintain the Eixample's quality of life, car*

A Modernista Detour

Several Modernista buildings are clustered near the Diagonal Metro stop. To reach them, cross Avinguda Diagonal, and continue two long blocks on Passeig de Gràcia. Where the street curves around the tree-lined median, you'll find the **Hotel Casa Fuster,** a fine Modernista building by Lluís Domènech i Montaner. This top-of-the-top luxury hotel is a favorite of Woody Allen (who featured the city in his film *Vicky Cristina Barcelona*). Seeking a place to play jazz in town, Allen prodded the hotel to sponsor jazz concerts. The hotel's Café Vienés now hosts a weekly jazz night (for details, see the Nightlife in Barcelona chapter).

Backtrack to Diagonal to reach two works by Josep Puig i Cadafalch. Take a left (go east) down the busy Diagonal boulevard. After a block, you reach the **Palau Baró de Quadras** (Diagonal 373, on the right across the street). Puig i Cadafalch's plateresque facade (in Spain's medieval "silverwork" style of intricate decoration) celebrates a time when Catalunya was powerful, and the statues flanking the door—of St. George defeating the dragon—make the building's Catalan pride even more evident. Today the building houses the Institut Ramón Llul, a public cultural center dedicated to promoting Catalan language and culture (www.llull.cat). You can walk into the foyer and peek at some of the interior for free.

Continuing down another block and a half, Diagonal leads to the distinctively turreted Casa Terrades (at #416, on the left)—better known as **Casa de les Punxes** ("House of Spikes"). Here Puig i Cadafalch lassoed together what had been three separate buildings into one large complex, wrapping them in a fanciful Gothic castle cloak (no inside access). The turrets, spires, balconies, and ceramic tiles celebrate Catalan culture.

traffic is restricted, so locals find other ways to get around. At the first corner you'll find the Mauri pastry shop—where it's always tea time for local grandmothers. But we're turning left on...

❸ Rambla de Catalunya

First, pause to notice the cut-off corners of the intersection. Octagonal intersections like this showed off the fine building facades, allowed for freer traffic movement, and gave citizens some breathing room in the crowded city.

Now head down Rambla de Catalunya—a narrow, manageable street with a median strip lined with inviting cafés. The boutiques along here are still upscale, but generally more local and unique than those on the main drag.

The area a few blocks to the west of here (around Carrer d'Aribau) is a center of the local gay community, earning it the nickname "Gayxample."

Rambla de Catalunya has many classy buildings. After a block, on the left (at #78), you'll find the elaborately carved Casa Juncosa. It was built in 1909, around the same time as Gaudí's La Pedrera, from similar materials—stone and iron—but its curved balconies and bay windows show the touch of a more traditional architect. If open, step inside to see the atrium leading to condos, and say hi to the doorman.

Despite the great architectural variation in their facades, most Eixample homes were used identically: The entire building was owned by one family who lived on the high-ceilinged middle level and rented out the floors above and below. Shops and businesses occupied the ground floor; tenants lived on the less grand floors higher up. Throughout the Eixample, you'll see that the first floor up is usually taller and more elaborate than the rest—often with balconies or bay windows that higher floors are lacking. (Most of these houses predate the elevator; after that convenience was invented and widely installed, penthouse living became popular.) Many houses have two doors—one for the owners and another for the upstairs tenants. Most house blocks had an interior garden courtyard for ventilation and light, although over time many of these spaces have been covered over by one-story structures or parking lots.

Because the Eixample was developed during the Renaixença of local culture, you'll spot decorative Catalan themes such as St. George—the local patron saint—slaying the dragon.

Not all the architecture of this neighborhood is artful. In fact, lots of tasteless buildings, erected in the 1970s, punctuate the older elegance. Locals are fully aware that when a building hits the age of 50, it becomes protected—and many of the greatest eyesores of the Eixample are about to reach that threshold, at which time they will become a permanent part of the cityscape. Also notice how many buildings have what locals call "caps." A mayor in the 1980s allowed landowners to add extra floors to older buildings; many structures have a simple addition capping an otherwise elegant facade.

A block farther down, cross Carrer d'Aragó and turn left for a better view of the **Fundació Antoni Tàpies** (on the left). This

brick building with a crazy hairdo of fanciful iron-work (called "The Cloud and the Chair") was de-signed by one of the holy trinity of Modernista ar-chitects, Lluís Domènech i Montaner. It serves as a nice introduction to the more famous Modernista buildings we're about to see, and sums up the credo of the movement: modern brick, iron, and glass ma-terials; playful decorative motifs; and a spacious, functional, and light-filled interior.

• *Continue along on Carrer d'Aragó. For a fun little stop, pop into the hardware store* **Servei Estació** *(at #270). One floor up, they have an open terrace in the back with self-serve coffee from where you can peek at the back side of the Block of Discord. Continue down Carrer d'Aragó to Passeig de Gràcia; turn right (downhill), and take in the view from the corner. This begins the city block of Modernista facades known as the...*

❹ Block of Discord (Illa de la Discòrdia)

One block, three buildings, three creative Modernista architects, and a lot of visual commotion—that's the Block of Discord. Over a short span of time, the big names of Catalunya's bold Art Nou-veau architectural movement erected innovative facades along this one short stretch of Passeig de Gràcia. Although each architect has better works elsewhere in town, this is a convenient place to see their sharply contrasting visions side by side. In fact, the whole block is a jumble of delightful architectural whimsy. Reliefs, coats of arms, ironwork, gables, and bay windows adorn otherwise ordi-nary buildings.

• *Work your way down the block, beginning with the unmistakably Gaudí-style facade that's situated one build-ing in from the corner.*

Casa Batlló (#43)

The most famous facade on the block is Antoni Gaudí's green-blue, ceram-ic-speckled Casa Batlló (pronounced BAHT-yoh). It's thought that Gaudí based the work on the popular legend of St. George (Jordi) slaying the dragon: The humpback roofline suggests a crest-ing dragon's back, and the smallest, top balcony is shaped like a rosebud (a rose is said to have grown in the place where St.

George spilled the dragon's blood). The building's tibia-like pillars and skull-like balconies evoke the dragon's victims. Look at the first-floor bay window. If you squint (and perhaps smoke some pot, the consumption of which is legal here, by the way), you might see a bat with outstretched wings, relating to a Catalan folk legend. Notice also the random broken tiles, a Gaudí trademark that only later became appreciated. The tiled roof has a soft-ice-cream-cone turret topped with a cross. But some see instead a Mardi Gras theme, with mask-like balconies, a facade flecked with purple and gold confetti, and the ridge of a harlequin's hat up top. The inscrutable Gaudí preferred to leave his designs open to interpretation.

Before moving on, turn 180 degrees and look across the boulevard to see the linear iron-framed apartment building at #52—structurally the same as Casa Batlló. In 1904, when Gaudí was hired to renovate Casa Batlló, it looked like that.

• *Next door is…*

Casa Amatller (#41)

Josep Puig i Cadafalch completely remodeled this house for the Amatller family. The facade features a creative mix of three of Spain's historical traditions: Moorish-style pentagram and vine designs; Gothic-style tracery, gargoyles, and bay windows; and the step-gable roof from Spain's Habsburg connection to the Low Countries. Notice the many layers of the letter "A": The house itself (with its gable) forms an A, as does the decorative frieze over the bay window on the right side of the facade. Within that frieze, you'll see several more A's sprouting from branches (*amatller* means "almond tree"). The reliefs above the smaller windows show off the hobbies of the Amatller clan: Find the little animals holding the early box camera,  the open book, and the amphora jug (which the family collected). Look through the second-floor bay window to see the corkscrew column. You can step inside the interior courtyard for a sense of the livability of a residence like this, with its braided columns, marble floors, pink walls, wood-beam ceiling, and stone staircase topped with eagles. As you leave, note the servants' door on the right, ornamented with St. George and the dragon.

For another dimension of Modernisme, peek into the ground-floor windows of the Bagues Joieria jewelry shop and notice the slinky pieces by Spanish Art Nouveau jeweler Masriera.

• *Continue down the street to the end of the block. On the corner, you'll find…*

Casa Lleó Morera (#35)

This paella-like mix of styles is the work of the architect Lluís Domènech i Montaner, who also designed the Palace of Catalan Music. The lower floors have classical columns and a bay window reminiscent of a Greek temple. (Notice the real marble column—supporting nothing but some aristocrat's ego—placed for all to see behind the bay window.) Farther up are Gothic balconies of rosettes and tracery, while the upper part has faux Moorish stucco work. The whole thing is ornamented with fantastic griffins, angels, and fish. Flanking the third-story windows, four muses, representing the fine arts, hold exciting inventions of the day—the camera, lightbulb, and gramophone—demonstrating just how modern these homeowners were in this age of Modern-isme.

• *From here, cross the street and backtrack up the Block of Discord, enjoying a more distant view of the facades. Take time to notice the swirling sidewalk (by Gaudí), the nice benches slathered with broken white tile mosaics, and the arcing ironwork streetlamps (by other architects).*

Turn right on Carrer d'Aragó. Go one block and turn left on Carrer de Pau Claris, then right onto...

❺ Carrer de València

A half-block down (on the right at #302) is the **Centre Cultural La Casa Elizalde.** This city center is a hive of creative and personal growth activities. You're welcome to explore the building, which often has free temporary exhibits on art or community life. Head into the passage, noticing the community bulletin board listing classes and events. Continuing down the hall, you'll pop out into an appealing interior courtyard with benches. Look up and around the buildings for a taste of the typical inner patios that are a quiet sanctuary from the busy Eixample streets. (Upstairs there's more, including WCs: women, first floor; men, second floor.)

Continue down Carrer de València to the next intersection, with a couple of interesting facades. On the right is the classic Modernista grocery of **J. Murria Queviures.** This old-fashioned gourmet deli is stocked with pricey ingredients for a top-end picnic. Breathe deep to smell the cheese aging in the cellar. The vintage ad outside, facing the corner—dubbed *La Mona y el Mono (The Classy Lady and the Monkey)*—advertised anise liquor to Modernista-era clients.

A half-block farther down, at #293 (on the left) is a fine Modernista building with wrought-iron railings and matching bay

Modernista Masters: Gaudí and Beyond

Yes, you'll hear plenty about Gaudí, but he's merely one of many who contributed to the architectural revolution of Modernisme. Here's a rundown of the movement's talented stars.

The Stars of Modernisme

Antoni Gaudí (1852-1926), Barcelona's most famous Modernista artist, was a proud descendant of four generations of metalwork-

ers. He incorporated ironwork into his architecture and came up with novel approaches to architectural structure and space. Gaudí's work strongly influenced his younger Catalan contemporary, Salvador Dalí. Notice the similarities: While Dalí was creating unlikely and shocking juxtapositions of surrealistic images, Gaudí did the same in architecture—using the spine of a reptile for a bannister or a turtle-shell design on windows. Entire trips (and lives) are dedicated to seeing the works of Gaudí, but on a brief visit, the highlights include his great unfinished church, the Sagrada Família; the La Pedrera, Casa Batlló, and Palau Güell mansions; and Park Güell, his ambitious and never-completed housing development.

While Gaudí gets most of the attention and certainly was a remarkable innovator, these next two architects are just as important—and perhaps more purely representative of the Modernista style.

Lluís Domènech i Montaner (1850-1923), a professor and politician, was responsible for some major civic buildings, including his masterwork, the Palace of Catalan Music, and the sprawling Hospital de Sant Pau complex. Domènech i Montaner also designed Casa Lleó Morera on the Block of Discord and Casa Fuster (now a luxury hotel), along with several works in the small towns of Canet de Mar and Comillas.

windows. Unfortunately, that's followed by a modern brick monstrosity that breaks up the Eixample harmony. Across the street (#320), step into the **Navarro flower shop.** It's open daily 24 hours so there's just no excuse if a loved one is deserving flowers. Take a fragrant stroll, looping deep into the shop.

Continue a few steps more to the intersection, with the twin-turreted Municipal Conservatory of Barcelona on the corner. You'll often see students hurrying into this city-run music academy with violin cases on their backs.

Josep Puig i Cadafalch (1867-1956) was a city planner who oversaw the opening up of Via Laietana through the middle of the Old City, the redevelopment of Montjuïc for the 1929 World Expó, and a redesign of the monastery at Santa Maria de Montserrat. Later he flourished as a Modernista architect, best known for the manor houses Casa de les Punxes and Casa Amatller on the Block of Discord. He also designed the brick Casaramona factory complex (now the Caixa-Forum exhibition space) and Casa Martí—the home for the Modernista hangout bar Els Quatre Gats, which became a cradle of sorts for the whole movement.

Supporting Cast

All the architects worked with a team of people who made real contributions. For example, Gaudí's colleague **Josep Maria Jujol** (1879-1949) is primarily responsible for much of what Gaudí became known for—the broken-tile mosaic decorations (called *trencadís*) on Park Güell's benches and La Pedrera's chimneys.

Joan Martorell i Montells (1833-1906) was a professor, mentor, and employer of a young Gaudí. Although an accomplished architect, Martorell's most important role was as a facilitator for his prized student: He oversaw the committee that hired Gaudí to build Sagrada Família, and introduced Gaudí to his most important benefactor, **Eusebi Güell** (1846-1918). Güell used his nearly $90 billion fortune to bankroll Gaudí and others, much as the Medici financed Michelangelo and Leonardo da Vinci. Güell's name still adorns two of Gaudí's most important works: Palau Güell and Park Güell.

• *Continue another half-block down Carrer de València. On the right is the entrance to...*

❻ La Concepció Market

While it has many of the same features as La Boqueria (on the Ramblas) and the Santa Caterina Market (in El Born), this market (with a modern supermarket in the basement and a garage below that) has virtually zero tourists. Walk through the building, from one end to the other. It's a good place to sample local cheeses, buy olives, pick up some fruit, or sit at a counter for cheap, ultra-fresh tapas.

Ponder the fact that in just a few blocks, we've passed a municipal building, a school, and a market. This is very much in keeping with the original vision for the Eixample as a series of self-sufficient neighborhood zones with easy access to important services. Each neighborhood here is served by a market like this one.

• *Exiting the market at the far end, you'll emerge into a delightful flower market crowding the sidewalk. Turn right on Carrer d'Aragó. At the intersection with Carrer del Bruc, notice (on the right) the detailed iron gate and columns. This is the entrance to the Seu del Districte Eixample—the Eixample's own branch of city hall.*

Now, cross Carrer del Bruc and continue another half-block, to the church. Step inside. (If it's locked, enter via the cloister, just ahead and around the corner.)

❼ Church of the Holy Conception
(Basílica de la Puríssima Concepció)

This purely Gothic, 14th-century church once stood in the Old City. But when the city walls came down as part of Barcelona's expansion, a few historic churches like this one were moved, brick by brick, to new locations in the 1870s. The bell tower came from a different Gothic church. (These relocated historic structures are nicknamed "traveling buildings.")

Step inside and take a seat. Ahhhh. The interior has many classic features of Barcelona Gothic: gray stone, interior buttresses forming side chapels, statues to many local saints, intricate chandeliers, and crisscross vaults on the ceiling culminating in medallions with more local saints. A statue of Mary crowns the prickly Gothic altar.

Exit the church midway up the nave, to the left. This leads you outside into a delightful 15th- and 16th-century cloister. The slender columns and delicate arches mingle with palm, banana, magnolia, and orange trees to create a peaceful oasis.

• *From the cloister, return to Carrer d'Aragó, turn right and follow it back to the big and busy Passeig de Gràcia (and the Block of Discord). There turn left, and head straight downhill to the end of this walk. Up ahead, an angel atop a monumental building says, "Plaça de Catalunya is this way."*

❽ Passeig de Gràcia (Bottom End)

As we saw earlier, this main street of the Eixample was once prime real estate for stately residences. But times change, and this stretch of  Passeig de Gràcia shows the encroachment of the modern world.

As the city continued to grow and real estate was at a premium, it became more lucrative to tear down those mansions and replace them with multistory apartments and businesses. The domed building topped with an angel on a phoenix went up in the 1920s for an insurance company. A block down (by the fountain), one of the few surviving original mansions was converted to the **Comedia theater.**

As you walk down Passeig de Gràcia, see how the elegant 19th-century Eixample melds into the 21st-century city. Softly rounded buildings give way to stern rectangular skyscrapers. Now travel the final stretch down to the sprawling Times Square of this country, Plaça de Catalunya.

❾ Plaça de Catalunya

Dotted with fountains, statues, and pigeons, and ringed by grand buildings, this plaza is Barcelona's center. Plaça de Catalunya—where four great thoroughfares cross—is the heart of the city. Historically, Plaça de Catalunya links the modern city with its past. As you cross this square and slip back into the old town, those last 500 feet take you back 500 years. You can step back into the Barri Gòtic knowing you've seen the best of Barcelona's ambitiously modern town, the Eixample.

SAGRADA FAMÍLIA TOUR

Architect Antoni Gaudí's most famous and awe-inspiring work is this unfinished, super-sized church. With its cake-in-the-rain facade and otherworldly spires, the church is not only an icon of Barcelona and its trademark Modernisme, but also a symbol of its greatest practitioner. As an architect, Gaudí relied on the foundation of the classics, nature, and religion, and this church represents all three.

Gaudí labored on Sagrada Família for 43 years, from 1883 until his death in 1926. Nearly a century on, people continue to toil to bring Gaudí's designs to life. There's something inspirational about a community of committed people with a vision, who've worked on a church that wouldn't be finished in their lifetimes—as was standard in the Gothic age. The progress of this remarkable building is a testament to the generations of architects, sculptors, stonecutters, fundraisers, and donors who shared Gaudí's astonishing vision. After paying the admission price (becoming a partner in this building project), you will actually feel good. If there's any building on earth I'd like to see, it's the Basílica de la Sagrada Família...finished.

Orientation

Cost: Buy in advance online—basic ticket-€15 (church only), Guided Experience ticket-€24 (church and live guide), Audio Tour ticket-€22 (church and audioguide), Top Views ticket-€29 (church, audioguide, and one tower elevator). All options are 20 percent more if you buy at the church rather than online.

Hours: Mon-Sat 9:00-20:00, Sun 10:30-20:00, March and Oct until 19:00, Nov-Feb until 18:00. The church is busiest mornings, weekends, and Mondays.

Information: Tel. 932-073-031, www.sagradafamilia.org.

Advance Tickets Recommended: While you can try to buy a ticket at the church, on busy days the ticket office simply shuts down with a sign on the door saying: "Tickets for today are all sold out." The only smart way to visit is to book and pay in advance online for a timed-entry ticket.

Getting There: The Metro stop Sagrada Família puts you right on the church's doorstep. Exiting toward Plaça de Gaudí (follow silhouette logos of the church) will save a little walking.

Getting In: With ticket in hand (or on your phone), go through security and enter at the Nativity Facade side.

Church Services: Mass is held each Sunday at 9:00; those who actually want to worship here are admitted at no charge.

Tours: The 50-minute English tours run year-round; choose a tour time when you buy your ticket. Or rent the good 1.5-hour audioguide (€8 if purchased separately on-site, credit cards only, at desk to the right as you enter). There are often scalpers outside the gate selling admission with tours for those who don't have tickets.

Tower Elevators: Elevators on opposite sides of the church take you partway up the towers—one on the Passion Facade, and one on the Nativity Facade. The elevators go up only—to get down, you'll use a tightly wound, narrow staircase.

To ride an elevator, you must buy a Top Views combo-ticket. You'll choose the tower you want to visit and reserve an entry time (your entrance to the church will be assigned automatically, usually 15 minutes before your tower time). Towers can close when windy or rainy (if that happens, the tower portion of your ticket will be refunded).

The **Passion Facade elevator** takes you up a touch higher, and the stairs to come down are slightly wider than those descending from the **Nativity Facade elevator.** The facades are not joined, so it isn't possible to cross from one facade to the other, but you can cross a dizzying bridge between towers on the same facade. From either side, you'll have great views of the city and a gargoyle's-eye perspective of the loopy church.

Baggage Check: Bags are allowed in the church but are scanned. Small lockers are available at each elevator when the towers are open (bigger bags not allowed in towers). Though intended for those riding the elevators, the lockers can be used by anyone.

Length of This Tour: Allow 1.5 hours. While the actual church is the highlight, save time for the museum in the basement.

Nearby: Inviting parks flank the two completed facades.

A Dream Made Real

For over 130 years, Barcelona has labored to bring Antoni Gaudí's vision to reality. Local craftsmen often cap off their careers by spending a couple of years on this exciting construction site. The present architect has been at it since 1985. The work is funded exclusively by private donations and entry fees, which is another reason its completion has taken so long. Your admission helps pay for the ongoing construction.

Like Gothic churches of medieval times, the design has evolved over the decades. At heart, it's Gothic, a style much admired by Gaudí. He added his own Art Nouveau/Modernisme touches, guided by nature and engineering innovations. Today the site bristles with cranking cranes, rusty forests of rebar, and scaffolding. Sagrada Família offers a fun look at a living, growing, bigger-than-life building.

Sagrada Família Timeline

1882: The church is begun in Gothic-revival style by architect Francisco de Paula del Villar.

1883: Paula del Villar quits, and Antoni Gaudí is hired—and proceeds to completely re-envision the church's design.

1892: Gaudí begins the Nativity Facade.

1914: Gaudí turns his attention exclusively to the Sagrada Família.

1925: The first bell tower is completed.

1926: Gaudí dies, with the project about 20 percent complete.

1936-1939: The Spanish Civil War halts all work; the crypt is burned, along with many of Gaudí's plans.

1950s: Building resumes in earnest with the start of the Passion Facade.

1976: The four Passion spires are finished, bringing the total of completed spires to eight (out of 18 planned).

1980s: Computer technology is introduced, greatly accelerating the pace of construction.

2000: The nave roof is completed.

2005: Passion statues are completed.

2010: Crossing vaults are finished (enclosing the roof), and Pope Benedict XVI dedicates the church as a basilica.

2026? The church could be finished by the 100th anniversary of Gaudí's death. Make a date to attend the dedication with your kids...to teach them a lesson in delayed gratification.

The Tour Begins

• *Before entering the church, start on the far side of the pond in the park that faces the Nativity Facade (east side, where the entry lines for individuals are located). From there, you're back far enough to take in the entire towering facade.*

❶ View of the Exterior from Beyond the Pond

Stand and imagine how grand this church will be when completed. The eight 330-foot spires topped with crosses are just a fraction of this mega-church. When finished, it will have 18 spires. Four will stand at each of the three entrances. Rising above those will be four taller towers, dedicated to the four Evangelists. A tower dedicated to Mary (expected to be completed soon) rises still

higher—400 feet. And in the very center of the complex will stand the grand 560-foot Jesus tower, topped with a cross that will shine like a spiritual lighthouse, visible even from out at sea.

The Nativity Facade—where tourists enter today—is only a side entrance to the church. The grand main entry will be around to the left. To accommodate the church's planned entrance esplanade, a nine-story apartment building will have to be torn down. (This is an ongoing controversy as authorities negotiate with landowners.)

The three facades—Nativity, Passion, and Glory—will chronicle Christ's life from birth to death to resurrection. Inside and out, a goal of the church is to bring the lessons of the Bible to the world. Despite his boldly modern architectural vision, Gaudí was fundamentally traditional and deeply religious. He designed the Sagrada Família to be a bastion of solid Christian values in the midst of what was a humble workers' colony in a fast-changing city.

When Gaudí died, the only section that had been completed was the Nativity Facade (with its themes of birth and new life). Notice the dove-covered Tree of Life on top, with playful little creatures carved into nooks and crannies throughout, and a white pelican at the bottom. Because it was believed that this noble bird would feed its young with its own blood, the pelican was a common symbol in the Middle Ages for the self-sacrifice of Jesus.

The Nativity Facade's four spires are dedicated to apostles, and they repeatedly bear the word "sanctus," or holy. Their colorful ceramic caps symbolize the miters (formal hats) of bishops. The shorter spires (to the left) symbolize the Eucharist (communion),

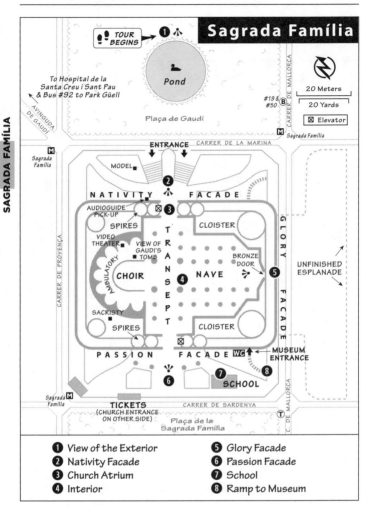

Sagrada Família

- ① View of the Exterior
- ② Nativity Facade
- ③ Church Atrium
- ④ Interior
- ⑤ Glory Facade
- ⑥ Passion Facade
- ⑦ School
- ⑧ Ramp to Museum

alternating between a chalice with grapes and a communion host with wheat.

The rest of the church, while inspired by Gaudí's long-range vision, has been designed and executed by others. This artistic freedom was amplified in 1936, when civil war shelling burned many of Gaudí's blueprints. Supporters of the ongoing work insist that Gaudí, who enjoyed saying, "My client [God] is not in a hurry," knew he wouldn't live to complete the church and recognized that later architects and artists would rely on their own muses for inspiration. Studying the various plans and models in the museum below the church, it's clear that Gaudí's plan evolved dramatically the longer he worked. And the plan continues to evolve to this day.

• *Now move up to the viewing plaza in front of the Nativity Facade. Check out the small **bronze model** of how the church might look when completed. Then stand as far back as you can to take it all in.*

❷ Nativity Facade

This is the only part of the church essentially finished in Gaudí's lifetime (although the architect had intended for this facade to be painted). The four spires decorated with his naturalistic sculpture mark this facade as unmistakably part of his original design. Mixing Gothic-era symbolism, images from nature, and Modernista asymmetry, the Nativity Facade is the best example of Gaudí's original vision, and it established the template for future architects. Cleverly, this attractive facade was built and finished first to bring in financial support for the project.

The theme of the facade, which faces the rising sun, is Christ's birth. A statue above the doorway shows Mary, Joseph, and Baby Jesus in the manger, while a curious cow and donkey peek in. It's the Holy Family—or "Sagrada Família" (literally "sacred family")—to whom this church is dedicated. Flanking the doorway are the three Magi and adoring shepherds. Other statues at this height show Jesus as a young carpenter (right), the Holy Family fleeing to Egypt (left), and angels playing musical  instruments. Much higher up, in the arched niche, Jesus crowns Mary triumphantly.

The doors in the middle of the facade were designed by head sculptor Etsuro Sotoo. Born in Japan, Sotoo visited Barcelona for the first time in 1978 and fell in love with the project. He worked hard to become a part of it and even converted to Catholicism. Go up to the bronze doors and examine the surface, covered with small colorful bugs and leaves.

• *Now join the line and enter the ❸ **church atrium** (within your allotted window of time). If you purchased a tower ticket, a guard will direct you to your elevator. If you purchased an audioguide (or would like to rent one now), go to that desk (on the right). Continue to the center of the church, near the altar, to survey the magnificent…*

❹ Interior

Typical of even the most traditional Catalan and Spanish churches, the floor plan is in the shape of a Latin cross, 300 feet long and 200 feet wide. Ultimately, the church will accommodate 8,000 worshippers. The crisscross arches of the ceiling (the vaults) show off Gaudí's distinctive engineering. The church's roof and flooring were only completed in 2010—just in time for Pope Benedict XVI to arrive and consecrate the church.

Part of Gaudí's religious vision was a love for nature. He said, "Nothing is invented; it's written in nature." Like the trunks of trees, these **columns** (56 in all) blossom with life, complete with branches, leaves, and knot-like capitals. The columns vary in color and material—brown clay, gray granite, dark gray basalt.

Partway up, the columns angle off to form many **arches.** Gaudí's starting point was the medieval Gothic pointed arch, which he tweaked to achieve maximum weight-bearing effect.

Light filtering through the stained-glass windows has the dappled effect of a rainforest canopy. Notice how splashes of color breathe even more life into this amazing space. The morning light shines in through blues, greens, and other cool colors, whereas the evening light glows through reds, oranges, and warm tones. Gaudí envisioned an awe-inspiring symphony of colored light to encourage a contemplative mood.

At the center of the church stand four main columns, each marked with an Evangelist's symbol and name in Catalan: angel (Mateu), lion (Marc), bull (Luc), and eagle (Joan). These columns support a ceiling vault that's 200 feet high—and eventually will also support the central steeple (the Jesus tower with the shining cross). It will be the tallest church steeple in the world, though still a few feet shorter than the city's highest point at the summit of Montjuïc hill, as Gaudí believed that a creation of man should not attempt to eclipse the creation of God.

The Holy Family is looking down from on high: Jesus is above the altar, Mary is in the left transept, and Joseph in the right transept.

Behind the high altar, peer down to see a surprisingly traditional space—the 19th-century Neo-Gothic building that Gaudí was originally hired to finish (talk about mission creep!). Today this is a **crypt** holding the tomb of Gaudí himself. A few steps away are two small theaters in adjacent side chapels. One shows a short **video** about the architect and his work. Immediately behind the altar (possibly accessed on the other side) is a small chapel set aside for prayer and meditation.

• *Walk through the forest of massive columns to the opposite end of the church. The view from here is best for appreciating the majesty of the* *building's interior. (A big mirror is placed here to make admiring the ceiling easier.) Suspended high above the nave, the U-shaped **choir** can seat a thousand singers, who will eventually be backed by four organs.*

Doors here will one day open to the...

❺ Glory Facade

While you can't go out what will one day be the main entrance, you can study a life-size image of the **bronze door** intended for

this spot, emblazoned with the Lord's Prayer in Catalan and surrounded by "Give us this day our daily bread" in 50 languages. If you were able to exit through the actual door, you'd be face-to-face with drab, doomed apartment blocks. In the 1950s, the mayor of Barcelona, figuring this day would never really come, sold the land destined for the church project. Now the city must buy back these buildings in order to complete Gaudí's vision of a grand esplanade leading to this main entry. Four towers will rise. The facade's sculpture will represent how the soul passes through death, faces the Last Judgment, avoids the pitfalls of hell, and finds its way to eternal glory with God. Gaudí purposely left the facade's design open for later architects—stay tuned.

• *Head back up the nave, and exit through the left transept. To the left, notice the second **elevator** up to the towers. Before exiting, look down at the fine porphyry floor with scenes of Jesus' entry into Jerusalem. To the right, stroll through the **sacristy**, where you will find benches, candelabras, and sacristy furniture designed by Gaudí. Now head outside and down the ramp. Step away to take in the...*

❻ Passion Facade

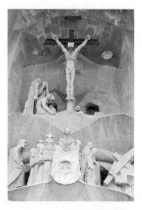

Judge for yourself how well Gaudí's original vision has been carried out by later artists. The Passion Facade's four spires were designed by Gaudí and completed (quite faithfully) in 1976. But the lower part was only inspired by Gaudí's designs. The sculptures intended for this facade were interpreted freely and sternly (also controversially) by Josep Maria Subirachs (1927-2014), who completed the work in 2005.

Subirachs tells the story of Christ's

torture and execution. The various scenes—Last Supper, betrayal, whipping, and so on—zigzag up from bottom to top, culminating in Christ's crucifixion over the doorway. The style is severe and un-adorned, quite different from Gaudí's signature naturalism. Large letters spell out "Iesus Nazarenus Rex Iudæorum" (Jesus the Naza-rene, King of the Jews). The bone-like archways are closely based on Gaudí's original designs. And Gaudí had made it clear that this facade should be grim and terrifying.

The facade is full of symbolism. A stylized Alpha and Omega is over the door (which faces the setting sun). Jesus, hanging on the cross, has hair made of an open book, symbolizing the word of God. To the left of the door is a grid of numbers, always adding up to 33—Jesus' age at the time of his death. The distinct face of the man below and to the left of Christ (in profile, next to what looks like two stormtroopers) is a memorial to Gaudí.

• *Now, for a fun little break from all this church architecture, head into the small building outside the Passion Facade. This is the...*

❼ School

Gaudí erected this school for the children of the workers building the church. Today, it displays a replica classroom and old photos of school activities during Gaudí's time.

• *Back outside, head down the ramp, where you'll find WCs and the entrance to the...*

❽ Museum

Housed in what will someday function as the church crypt, the museum takes you through the past, present, and future of Sagrada Família's development.

It starts with a photo of the master himself and a timeline il-lustrating how construction has progressed from Gaudí's day until now. Walking the hall, you'll pass pieces of Gaudí's original plaster model of the church (damaged dur-ing Spain's civil war, on the left) and his reconstructed studio (left). Com-pare Gaudí's old-fashioned space with a nearby photo of the current team, working with the latest technology.

In a room at the end of the hall, four plaster models show the evolution of Gaudí's thinking (clockwise from left): 1) the Neo-Gothic design by the church's first architect, Francisco de Paula del Villar; 2) Gaudí's re-en-visioned plan, with a nave formed of narrow parabolic arches; 3) a plan with the middle story opened up; and 4) finally, an even more open plan with tree-like columns fanning out at the top.

Exploring further, you'll find exhibits dedicated to the sculptor Subirachs and the stained-glass artist Joan Vila-Grau; an exhibit about nature as the father of architecture; and a small theater showing a worthwhile 11-minute movie. Sit down and enjoy this fine review of all you've seen.

Gaudí lived on the site for more than a decade and is buried here in the Neo-Gothic 19th-century crypt. You can look (steeply) down at his tomb. There's a move afoot to beatify Gaudí and make him a saint. Gaudí prayer cards provide words of devotion. Perhaps someday his tomb will be a place of pilgrimage.

Back in the main hall, peer into the actual workshop where artists employ the latest technology (such as 3-D printing) to test ideas and create models. An intriguing "Hanging Model" for Gaudí's unfinished Church of Colònia Güell (in a suburb of Barcelona) can be found here as well. Featuring a design similar to Sagrada Família, the model illustrates how the architect used gravity to calculate the arches that support the church. Wires dangle like suspended chains, forming perfect hyperbolic arches. Attached to these are bags, representing the weight the arches must support. Flip these arches over, and they can bear the heavy weight of the roof. The mirror above the model shows how the right-side-up church is derived from this.

The final part of the museum has photos of Pope Benedict XVI's 2010 visit and consecration of the church, as well as dedications to the architects and sculptors who have worked on this project.

From here, step outside. You can either exit the complex through a gift shop (on the right), or circle left and uphill to return to the church, exiting through the Passion Facade.

Once outside, look back and pause for a moment to pay homage to the man who made all this possible. Gaudí—a faithful Catholic whose medieval-style mysticism belied his career as a Modernista architect—was certainly driven to greatness by his passion for God.

• *Our tour is over. From here, you have several options.*

Return to Central Barcelona: *It's simple to hop on the Metro back to the* **center.** *Bus #50 goes to the heart of the* **Eixample** *(corner of Gran Via de les Corts Catalanes and Passeig de Gràcia), then continues on to Plaça Espanya where you can hop off for the* **Montjuïc** *sights.*

Visit Park Güell: *The park sits nearly two (uphill) miles to the northwest. By far the easiest way to get there is by taxi (around €12).*

But if you prefer public transportation and don't mind a little walking, here's a scenic way to get there that also takes you past another, often overlooked Modernista masterpiece: the striking **Hospital de la Santa Creu i Sant Pau** *(see page 55). With the Nativity Facade at your back, walk to the near-left corner of the park across the street. Then walk about 10 minutes along Avinguda de Gaudí, a pleasantly shaded, café-lined pedestrian street, to reach the hospital.*

After your visit, facing the main entrance, go right to catch bus #92 on Carrer de Sant Antoni Maria Claret, which will take you to the side entrance of Park Güell.

PARK GÜELL TOUR

Tucked in the foothills at the edge of Barcelona, this fanciful park—designed by Antoni Gaudí—combines playful architecture, inviting spaces, and a one-of-a-kind terrace offering sweeping views over the rooftops of the city.

In recent years, this unique park became so popular that it was nearly trampled by tourists. To control crowds, the iconic areas with Gaudí features were declared a Monumental Zone, requiring an admission fee and a timed entry to visit. Even so, big crowds swarm this fairly compact zone containing a pair of gingerbread-style houses, a grand staircase monitored by a colorful dragon, a forest of columns supporting a spectacular view terrace, and an undulating balcony slathered in tile shards.

Outside the zone, the rest of the park contains the Gaudí House Museum, the Calvary viewpoint, a picnic area, and a pleasant network of nature trails—all of which (except the museum) are free.

No matter where you visit—inside the zone or out—you'll see Barcelonans and tourists alike enjoying a day at the park.

Orientation

Cost: €7.50 for timed-entry Monumental Zone ticket (buy online); the rest of the park is free. The only smart way to visit is with a prepaid entry purchased online. While you can buy a ticket at the park (€8.50), you'll likely have to wait hours for an open entry time.

Hours: Daily 8:00-20:30 (May-Aug until 21:30), Nov-March 8:30-18:15.

Information: Tel. 934-091-831, www.parkguell.cat.

Getting There: Park Güell is about 2.5 miles from Plaça de Cata-

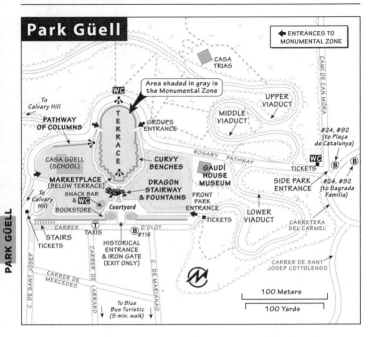

Park Güell

← ENTRANCES TO
MONUMENTAL ZONE

CAMÍ DE CAN MORA

CASA
TRIAS

Area shaded in gray is
the Monumental Zone

WC

To
Calvary Hill

PATHWAY
OF COLUMNS

T
E
R
R
A
C
E

GROUPS
ENTRANCE

UPPER
VIADUCT

MIDDLE
VIADUCT

#24, #92
(to Plaça
de Catalunya)

CASA GÜELL
(SCHOOL)

ROSARY PATHWAY

CURVY
BENCHES

GAUDÍ
HOUSE
MUSEUM

TICKETS

B

B

MARKETPLACE
(BELOW TERRACE)

DRAGON
STAIRWAY
& FOUNTAINS

SIDE PARK
ENTRANCE

#24, #92
(to Sagrada
Família)

To
Calvary
Hill

SNACK BAR
& WC

FRONT
PARK
ENTRANCE

WC

BOOKSTORE

Courtyard

LOWER
VIADUCT

CARRETERA
DEL CARMEL

TICKETS

CARRER

STAIRS
TICKETS

T

TAXIS

B

D'OLOT
#116

HISTORICAL
ENTRANCE
& IRON GATE
(EXIT ONLY)

CARRER DE SANT
JOSEP COTTOLENGO

C. DE SANT JOSEP

CARRER DE LARRARD

C. DE MARIANAO

CARRER DE
MERCEDES

100 Meters

100 Yards

To Blue
Bus Turístic
(5 min. walk)

lunya, beyond the Gràcia neighborhood in Barcelona's foot-hills. If asking for directions, ask for "Park Gway" (sounds like "parkway").

A **taxi** from downtown will take you to the front entrance for about €15. Otherwise, from Plaça de Catalunya, hop on either the blue **Bus Turístic** (stops about four blocks down-hill from front entrance, on Travessera de Dalt) or **public bus** #24, which drops you at a side entrance (described below). Or do a **Metro-plus-bus combination** to the front entrance (ride Metro to Joanic stop, look for Carrer de l'Escorial exit, walk up Carrer de l'Escorial to bus stop in front of #20, and hop on bus #116 to the park). If coming from Sagrada Família, take a taxi or public bus #92 (for directions on connecting these two sights, see page 164).

Getting In: The Monumental Zone has several entrances; the most practical way in for tourists is on Carrer d'Olot (front entrance) or on Carretera del Carmel (side entrance). At either, you'll find a ticket office, WCs, and plenty of park staff to help orient you. Hang on to your ticket; you'll need to show it when you exit.

Length of this Tour: An hour is plenty to take this tour, but the park is a pleasant place to linger longer.

Gaudí House Museum: €5.50, daily 9:00-20:00, Oct-March until

18:00, located outside the Monumental Zone, tickets easily available at the door, www.casamuseugaudi.org.

Eating: Options are limited. The park has a simple **snack bar** with tables by the historical entrance. There are a few basic cafés on the streets leading to the historical entrance. If you've packed a **picnic** (a good idea), head anywhere outside the Monumental Zone—eating is not allowed inside the ticketed area.

OVERVIEW

Gaudí intended this 30-acre garden to be a high-end community, with 60 upscale residences. Funded by his frequent benefactor Eusebi Güell, he began work on the project in 1900; however, the project stalled in 1914, with the outbreak of World War I, and it never resumed. Only two houses were built, neither designed by Gaudí (one is now the Gaudí House Museum). Be thankful that the housing development faltered—as a park, this place is a delight. It offers a novel peek into Gaudí's eccentric genius in a setting that's wonderfully in keeping with the naturalism that pervades his work.

Many sculptures and surfaces in the park are decorated with colorful *trencadís* mosaics—broken ceramic bits rearranged into new patterns. This Modernista invention, made of discarded tile, dishes, and even china dolls from local factories, was an easy, cheap, and aesthetically pleasing way to cover curvy surfaces like benches and columns. Most of the mosaics you see in the park are by Gaudí's collaborator, Josep Maria Jujol.

The Tour Begins

• *This tour assumes you're arriving at the front entrance on Carrer d'Olot, near the historical entryway to the park. Before entering the park, notice the* **mosaic medallions** *along the outside wall that say "park" in English—a reminder that Park Güell was modeled on the British "garden city" concept of integrating housing with green space.*

If you arrive at the side entrance, walk past the ticket office there and along the path (to the left of the building) to the view terrace. Enter the Monumental Zone there and walk down to the stairway, picking up this tour inside the historical entrance.

Historical Entrance

Enjoy Gaudí's historical front entrance (now exit only) with its palm-frond **gate** and gas lamps on either side, made of wrought iron. Gaudí's dad was a blacksmith, and he always enjoyed this medium.

Two Hansel-and-Gretel gingerbread lodges flank this former entrance, signaling to visitors that the park is a magical space. One building houses a bookshop; the other is home to the skippable **La Casa del Guarda,** a branch of the Barcelona History Museum. The sparse exhibit inside has no real artifacts—just video slideshows about Gaudí's building methods and old movies of the age. But true Gaudí fans should take a close look at the structure, as it's one of the few built examples of his ideas for simple housing.

• *Now face the grand...*

Dragon Stairway

Twin staircases curve upward, separated by three **fountains** stacked between them. The first, at the base of the steps, is rocky and leafy,

typical of Gaudí's naturalism. Next is a red and gold Catalan shield, with the head of a serpent poking out. The third fountain is an icon of the park—and of Barcelona: a smiling dragon, slathered in colorful tile. As for the ornamental brown tripod at the top of the stairs: Is it the Oracle of Delphi? The tail of the serpent? Or something else entirely?

The **two grottos** flanking the stairs were functional: One was a garage for Eusebi Güell's newfangled automobiles; the other was a cart shelter.

• *At the top of the dragon stairs, enter the...*

Marketplace (Hypostyle Room)

This space was designed to house a **produce market** for the neighborhood's inhabitants. Eighty-six Doric columns—each lined at the base with white ceramic shards—populate the marketplace and add to its vitality. (Their main job, though, is to hold up the view terrace above.) Shards of white ceramic also cover the multiple domes of the ceiling. The four giant mosaic decorations overhead repre-

sent the four seasons. Notice the hook in the middle of each one, where a lantern could be hung.

• *Continue up the left-hand staircase, looking left, down the playful...*

Pathway of Columns

Gaudí drew his inspiration from nature, and this arcade is like a surfer's perfect tube. Both structural and aesthetic, it is one of

many clever double-decker **viaducts** that Gaudí designed for the grounds: vehicles up top, pedestrians in the portico down below. Gaudí intended these walkways to remind visitors of the pilgrim routes that crisscross Spain (such as the famous Camino de Santiago).

The big pink house flanking the stairs is where Eusebi Güell lived. Now a school, this house predates the park project and was not designed by Gaudí.

• *At the top of the stairway, you pop out on the...*

View Terrace (Nature Square)

Sit on a colorful bench and enjoy one of Barcelona's best views. (Find the Sagrada Família in the distance.) Functioning as both a

seat and a balustrade, the 360-foot-long bench is designed to fit your body just so. Supposedly, Gaudí enlisted a construction worker as his guinea pig to figure out exactly where to place the lumbar support. To Gaudí, this terrace evoked ancient Greek the-

aters that burrowed scenically into the sides of hills—but it is more like an ancient Greek agora, a wide-open meeting place, jammed with people feasting on the view.

Gaudí engineered a catchment system to collect rainwater hitting this plaza and funnel it through the columns of the market below to an underground cistern. The collected water was used to irrigate the surrounding gardens and power the park's fountains. Notice the lion's-head gargoyles and the big stone droplets that cling to the outside edge of the terrace, which hint at this hidden function.

• *From here, with the city at your back, the **Gaudí House Museum** is to your right, and the **Calvary Hill** is high up on your left, hidden behind* *trees. These sights are outside the Monumental Zone; once you leave the zone, you can't return.*

Gaudí House Museum

This pink house with a steeple was Gaudí's home for 20 years. Designed by a fellow architect (not Gaudí), it was originally built as a model home to attract prospective residents. Gaudí himself lived here from 1906 until 1925. His belongings are mostly gone, but the house is now a museum with some quirky Gaudí furniture, and it offers an idea of what the envisioned housing development might have been (but it's not worth the entry fee for most travelers).

The lane connecting this house to the view terrace, called the **Rosary Pathway,** is lined with giant stone balls that represent the beads of a rosary. During the years he lived here, the reverent Gaudí would pray the rosary while walking this path.

Calvary Hill

High on a wooded hill beyond the pink school building is a stubby stone tower topped with three crosses, meant to evoke where Jesus was crucified. Gaudí envisioned Park Güell as a metaphor for the soul's progress: starting low, but toiling upward toward spiritual enlightenment. And indeed, the park's higher paths seem to converge to lead pilgrims to this summit. The tower rewards those who huff up with grand views over Barcelona and its bay.

Rest of the Park

Like any park, this one is made for aimless rambling, whether in or out of the Monumental Zone. As you wander, consider that, as a high-end housing development, Gaudí's project flopped (back then, high-society ladies didn't want to live so far from the cultural action). But a century later, as a park, it's a magnificent success.

• *To return to the city center, take a taxi (you'll find some waiting outside the historical entrance), catch bus #24 at the side entrance back to Plaça de Catalunya, or reverse the Metro-plus-bus combination outlined at the top of the chapter.*

SLEEPING IN BARCELONA

Choosing the right neighborhood in Barcelona is as important as choosing the right hotel. All of my recommended accommodations are in safe areas convenient to sightseeing. The area around Plaça de Catalunya, Barcelona's central square, is filled with business-class hotels. Near the Ramblas—the city's pedestrian boulevard—you'll find cheaper, less-refined places with more character. For Old World charm, stay in Barcelona's Old City. For an uptown feel, sleep in the Eixample.

Despite being Spain's most expensive city, Barcelona has reasonably priced rooms. Cheap places are more crowded in summer; fancier business-class hotels fill up in winter and may offer discounts on weekends and in summer. When considering relative hotel values, in summer and on weekends you can often get modern comfort in centrally located business-class hotels for about the same price (€130) as you'll pay for ramshackle charm. For some travelers, short-term, Airbnb-type rentals can be a good alternative to hotels; search for places in my recommended hotel neighborhoods.

I rank accommodations from $ budget to $$$$ splurge. Any special prices, discounts, and offers of breakfast included are valid only when you book directly with the hotel. Book your accommodations well in advance if you'll be traveling during peak season or if your trip coincides with a major holiday or festival (see the appendix). Note, though, that Barcelona can be busy any time of year.

For more information on rates and deals, making reservations, finding a short-term rental, and more, see the "Sleeping" section in the Practicalities chapter.

NEAR PLAÇA DE CATALUNYA

These hotels have sliding-glass doors leading to shiny reception areas, air-conditioning, and modern bedrooms. Most are on big streets within two blocks of Barcelona's exuberant central square, where the Old City meets the Eixample. As business-class hotels, they have hard-to-pin-down prices that fluctuate with demand. In summer and on weekends, supply often far exceeds the demand, and many of these places cut prices. Most of these are located between two Metro stops: Catalunya and Universitat; if arriving by Aerobus, note that the bus also stops at both places. Some of my recommended hotels are on Carrer Pelai, a busy street; for these, request a quieter room in back, although double-paned windows limit much of the noise.

$$$$ Hotel Catalonia Plaça Catalunya has four stars, an elegant old entryway with a modern reception area, splashy public spaces, slick marble and hardwood floors, 150 comfortable rooms, and a garden courtyard with a pool a world away from the big-city noise. It's a bit pricey for the quality of the rooms—you're paying for the posh lobby (air-con, elevator, a half-block off Plaça de Catalunya at Carrer de Bergara 11, Metro: Catalunya, tel. 933-015-151, www.hoteles-catalonia.com, catalunya@hoteles-catalonia.es).

$$$$ Hotel Midmost (owned by the same people as Hotel Denit, listed later) is an oasis a little west of Plaça de Catalunya. It has 56 rooms with luxurious, four-star style; a seaside-lounge-inspired rooftop terrace; and a mini pool to relax (family rooms, air-con, elevator, Carrer de Pelai 14, Metro: Universitat, tel. 935-051-100, www.hotelmidmost.com, info@hotelmidmost.com).

$$$ Hotel Ginebra is a modern version of the old-school *pension,* with 18 rooms in a classic, well-located building at the corner of Plaça de Catalunya (RS%—use code "HGinebra-RickSteves" and print voucher, family rooms, breakfast extra, laundry, air-con, elevator, Rambla de Catalunya 1, Metro: Catalunya, tel. 932-502-017, www.hotelginebra.com.es, info@barcelonahotelginebra.com, Brits Alfred and Ivon).

$$$ Hotel Reding Croma, on a quiet street a 10-minute walk west of the Ramblas and the Plaça de Catalunya action, is a slick and sleek place renting 44 basic but mod rooms on color-themed floors at a reasonable price (RS%, air-con, elevator, Carrer de Gravina 5, Metro: Universitat, tel. 934-121-097, www.hotelreding.com, recepcion@hotelreding.com).

$$$ Hotel Lleó (YAH-oh) is well-run, with 92 big, bright, and comfortable rooms; a great breakfast room; and a generous lounge (air-con, elevator, small rooftop pool, Carrer de Pelai 22, midway between Metros: Universitat and Catalunya, tel. 933-181-312, www.hotel-lleo.com, info@hotel-lleo.com).

$$ Hotel Atlantis is solid, with 50 big, nondescript, slightly dated rooms and fair prices for the location (includes breakfast, air-con, elevator, Carrer de Pelai 20, midway between Metros: Universitat and Catalunya, tel. 933-189-012, http://hotelatlantis-atbcn. com, inf@hotelatlantis-bcn.com).

$$ Hotel Denit is a small, stylish, 36-room hotel on a pedestrian street two blocks off Plaça de Catalunya. It's chic, minimalist, and fun: Guidebook tips decorate the halls, and the rooms are sized like T-shirts, from small to extra-large (includes breakfast, air-con, elevator, Carrer d'Estruc 24, Metro: Catalunya, tel. 935-454-000, www.denit.com, info@denit.com).

ON OR NEAR THE RAMBLAS

These places are generally family-run, with ad-lib furnishings, more character, and lower prices.

$$$ Hotel Continental Barcelona, in a building overlooking the top of the Ramblas, offers classic, tiny view-balcony opportunities if you don't mind the noise. Its 40 rooms are quite comfortable and the staff is friendly. Choose between your own little Ramblas-view balcony (where you can eat your breakfast) or a quieter back room. J. M.'s (José María's) free breakfast and all-day snack-and-drink bar are a plus (RS%, air-con, elevator, quiet terrace, Ramblas 138, Metro: Catalunya, tel. 933-012-570, www.hotelcontinental. com, barcelona@hotelcontinental.com).

$$ Hostal Grau is a homey, family-run, and extremely eco-conscious hotel with custom recycled furniture and organic bedding. It has 25 crisp, impeccable, and cheery rooms a few blocks off the Ramblas in the colorful university district. Double-glazed windows keep it quiet (some rooms with balconies, family rooms, strict cancellation policy, air-con, elevator, 200 yards up Carrer dels Tallers from the Ramblas at Ramelleres 27, Metro: Catalunya, tel. 933-018-135, www.hostalgrau.com, bookgreen@hostalgrau.com, Monica).

$$ Hostal Operaramblas, with 68 simple rooms 20 yards off the Ramblas, is clean, modern, and a great value. The street can feel a bit seedy at night, but it's safe, and the hotel is very secure (RS%—use code "operaramblas," air-con in summer, elevator, Carrer de Sant Pau 20, Metro: Liceu, tel. 933-188-201, www. operaramblas.com, info@operaramblas.com).

OLD CITY

These accommodations are buried in Barcelona's Old City, mostly in the Barri Gòtic. The Catalunya, Liceu, and Jaume I Metro stops

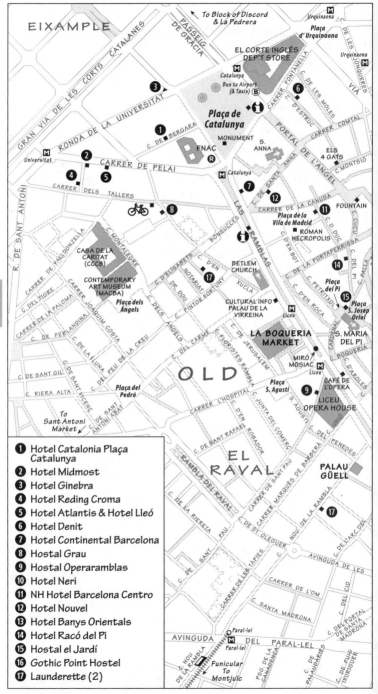

EIXAMPLE

To Block of Discord & La Pedrera

EL CORTE INGLÉS DEP'T STORE

Plaça d'Urquinaona

Catalunya Bus to Airport (& Taxis)

Plaça de Catalunya

MONUMENT

FNAC

S. ANNA

ELS 4 GATS

ROMAN NECROPOLIS

Plaça de la Vila de Madrid

FOUNTAIN

BETLEM CHURCH

CULTURAL INFO PALAU DE LA VIRREINA

CASA DE LA CARITAT (CCCB)

CONTEMPORARY ART MUSEUM (MACBA)

Plaça dels Àngels

LA BOQUERIA MARKET

MIRÓ MOSIAC

Plaça del Pi

Plaça S. Josep Oriol

S. MARIA DEL PI

Plaça del Pedró

CAFÉ DE L'OPERA

LICEU OPERA HOUSE

Plaça S. Agustí

To Sant Antoni Market

O L D

EL RAVAL

PALAU GÜELL

Paral·lel

Funicular To Montjuic

SLEEPING

1 Hotel Catalonia Plaça Catalunya
2 Hotel Midmost
3 Hotel Ginebra
4 Hotel Reding Croma
5 Hotel Atlantis & Hotel Lleó
6 Hotel Denit
7 Hotel Continental Barcelona
8 Hostal Grau
9 Hostal Operaramblas
10 Hotel Neri
11 NH Hotel Barcelona Centro
12 Hotel Nouvel
13 Hotel Banys Orientals
14 Hotel Racó del Pi
15 Hostal el Jardí
16 Gothic Point Hostel
17 Launderette (2)

Barcelona's Old City Hotels

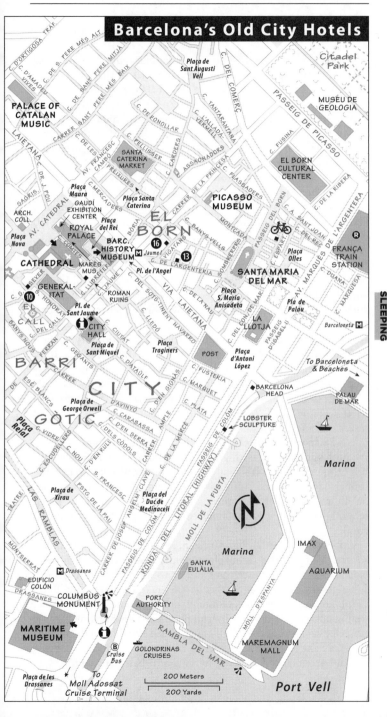

flank this tight tangle of lanes; I've noted which stop(s) are best for each.

$$$$ Hotel Neri is posh, pretentious, and sophisticated, with 22 rooms spliced into the ancient stones of the Barri Gòtic, overlooking an overlooked square (Plaça Sant Felip Neri) a block from the cathedral. It has pricey modern art on the bedroom walls, dressed-up people in its gourmet restaurant, and high-class service (air-con, elevator, rooftop tanning deck, Carrer de Sant Sever 5, Metro: Liceu or Jaume I, tel. 933-040-655, www.hotelneri.com, info@hotelneri.com).

$$$ NH Hotel Barcelona Centro, with 156 rooms and tasteful chain-hotel predictability, is professional yet friendly, buried in the Barri Gòtic just three blocks off the Ramblas (air-con, elevator, Carrer del Duc 15, Metro: Catalunya or Liceu, tel. 932-703-410, www.nh-hotels.com, nhbarcelonacentro@nh-hotels.com).

$$$ Hotel Nouvel, in an elegant, Victorian-style building on a handy pedestrian street, is less business oriented and offers more character than the others listed here. It boasts royal lounges and 78 comfy rooms (air-con, elevator, Carrer de Santa Anna 20, Metro: Catalunya, tel. 933-018-274, www.hotelnouvel.com, info@hotelnouvel.com).

$$$ Hotel Banys Orientals, a modern, boutique-type place, has a people-to-people ethic and refreshingly straight prices. Its 43 restful rooms are located in the El Born district on a pedestrianized street between the cathedral and Church of Santa Maria del Mar (air-con, elevator, Carrer de l'Argenteria 37, 50 yards from Metro: Jaume I, tel. 932-688-460, www.hotelbanysorientals.com, reservas@hotelbanysorientals.com).

$$$ Hotel Racó del Pi, part of the H10 hotel chain, is a quality, professional place with generous public spaces and 37 modern, bright, quiet rooms. It's located on a wonderful pedestrian street immersed in the Barri Gòtic (air-con, around the corner from Plaça del Pi at Carrer del Pi 7, three-minute walk from Metro: Liceu, tel. 933-426-190, www.h10hotels.com, h10.raco.delpi@h10hotels.com).

$ Hostal el Jardí offers 40 clean, remodeled rooms on a breezy square. Many of the tight, plain, comfy rooms come with petite balconies (for an extra charge) and enjoy an almost Parisian feel. It's a good deal only if you value the quaint-square-with-Barri-Gòtic ambience—you're definitely paying for the location. Book well in advance, as this family-run place has an avid following (air-con, elevator, some stairs, halfway between Ramblas and cathedral at Plaça Sant Josep Oriol 1, Metro: Liceu, tel. 933-015-900, www.eljardi-barcelona.com, reservations@eljardi-barcelona.com).

EIXAMPLE

For an uptown, boulevard-like neighborhood, sleep in the Eixample, a 10-minute walk from the Ramblas action. Most of these places use the Passeig de Gràcia or Catalunya Metro stops. Because these stations are so huge—especially Passeig de Gràcia, which sprawls underground for a few blocks—study the maps posted in the station to establish which exit you want before surfacing.

$$$$ Hotel Granvía, filling a palatial, brightly renovated 1870s mansion, offers a large, peaceful sun patio, several comfortable common areas, and 58 spacious, modern, business-style rooms (free breakfast for Rick Steves readers, family rooms, air-con, elevator, Gran Via de les Corts Catalanes 642, Metro: Passeig de Gràcia, tel. 933-181-900, www.hotelgranvia.com, hgranvia@nnhotels.com).

$$$$ Hotel Yurbban Trafalgar is a small, classy boutique hotel with 56 rooms and a masculine-minimalist decor. Their rooftop bar, tiny pool, and views alone are worth the price of your stay (air-con, free self-service laundry, gym, near the Palace of Catalan Music at Carrer de Trafalgar 30, a long block from Metro: Urquinaona, tel. 932-680-727, www.yurbban.com, trafalgar@yurbban.com).

$$$ Hotel Continental Palacete, with 22 small rooms, fills a 100-year-old chandeliered mansion. With flowery wallpaper and ornately gilded stucco, it's gaudy in the city of Gaudí, but it's also friendly, quiet, and well located. Guests have unlimited access to the outdoor terrace and the "cruise-inspired" fruit, veggie, and drink buffet (RS%, includes breakfast, air-con, two blocks northwest of Plaça de Catalunya at corner of Rambla de Catalunya and Carrer de la Diputació, Rambla de Catalunya 30, Metro: Passeig de Gràcia, tel. 934-457-657, www.hotelcontinental.com, palacete@hotelcontinental.com).

$$ BacHome B&B has two bright and comfortable locations in traditional Eixample buildings on Carrer Bruc. BacHome Terrace (at #14) has 10 rooms and a pleasant outdoor terrace. BacHome Gallery (#96) has seven rooms and common areas with big windows looking out onto the city (includes breakfast, air-con, elevator, Metro: Urquinaona, tel. 620-657-810, www.bachomebarcelona.com, reservations@bachomebarcelona.com).

$$ Hostal Oliva, family-run with care, is a spartan, old-school place with 15 basic, bright, high-ceilinged rooms. It's on the fourth floor of a classic old Eixample building—with a beautiful mahogany elevator—in a perfect location, just a couple of blocks above Plaça de Catalunya (corner of Passeig de Gràcia and Carrer de la Diputació, Passeig de Gràcia 32, Metro: Passeig de Gràcia, tel. 934-880-162, www.hostaloliva.com, info@hostaloliva.com).

SLEEPING

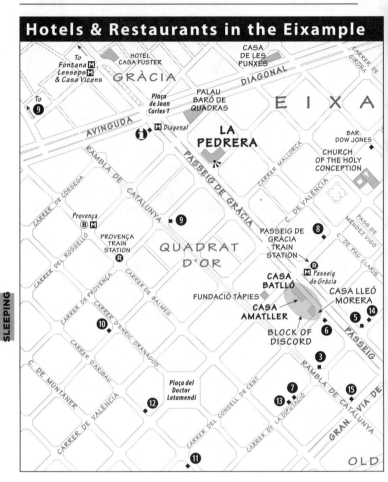

Hotels & Restaurants in the Eixample

OTHER ACCOMMODATIONS

Hostels

¢ **Equity Point Hostels:** Barcelona has a terrific chain of well-run and centrally located hostels, offering plenty of opportunities to meet other backpackers (tel. 932-312-045, www.equity-point. com). All three locations—in the Eixample, in the Barri Gòtic, and near the beach—enforce quiet hours after 23:00. **Centric Point Hostel** is a huge place renting 400 beds in the heart of the Eixample (bar, kitchen, Passeig de Gràcia 33, Metro: Passeig de Gràcia, tel. 932-151-796). **Gothic Point Hostel** rents 130 beds a block from the Picasso Museum (roof terrace, Carrer Vigatans 5, Metro: Jaume I, reception tel. 932-687-808). **Sea Point Hostel** has 70 beds

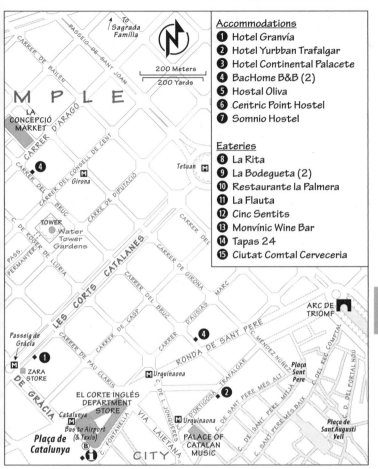

Accommodations
1. Hotel Granvía
2. Hotel Yurbban Trafalgar
3. Hotel Continental Palacete
4. BacHome B&B (2)
5. Hostal Oliva
6. Centric Point Hostel
7. Somnio Hostel

Eateries
8. La Rita
9. La Bodegueta (2)
10. Restaurante la Palmera
11. La Flauta
12. Cinc Sentits
13. Monvínic Wine Bar
14. Tapas 24
15. Ciutat Comtal Cerveceria

by the beach (closed roughly Nov-Feb, Plaça del Mar 4—see the map on page 74, Metro: Barceloneta, reception tel. 932-247-075).

¢ **Somnio Hostel,** a smaller place, has nine simple rooms (RS%, cheaper rooms with shared bath, private rooms available, air-con, Carrer de la Diputació 251, second floor, Metro: Passeig de Gràcia, tel. 932-725-308, www.somniohostels.com, info@ somniohostels.com). They have a second location that's five blocks farther out.

Apartments

Consider this option if you're traveling as a family, in a group, or staying several days. Websites such as Airbnb and VRBO let you correspond directly with property owners or managers. Or consider one of the sites listed below. Some specialize in Barcelona, while others also cover other European cities. For more information on renting apartments, see page 284 in the Practicalities chapter.

Friendly Rentals (www.friendlyrentals.com) has a number of listings in Barcelona (and other European cities), or you can try a local agency, such as **Top Barcelona Apartments** (http://top-barcelona-apartments.com) or MH Apartments (www.mhapartments.com). I've had good luck with **Cross-Pollinate,** a reputable booking agency representing B&Bs and apartments in a handful of European cities, including Barcelona (US tel. 800-270-1190, www.cross-pollinate.com, info@cross-pollinate.com).

Many Barcelona residents see turn-key vacation rentals as damaging to the fabric of traditionally residential neighborhoods, especially when they're rented to rowdy bachelor/bachelorette parties. I like to counterbalance this trend by treating my temporary Barcelona home—and neighbors—with a little extra courtesy.

SLEEPING

EATING IN BARCELONA

Barcelona, the capital of Catalan cuisine, offers a tremendous variety of colorful places to eat, ranging from workaday eateries to homey Catalan bistros *(cans)*, crowded tapas bars, and avant-garde restaurants. In general, restaurants in Barcelona rise to a higher level than elsewhere in Spain, propelled by talented chefs who aren't afraid to experiment, the relative affluence of the region, and the availability of good, fresh ingredients—especially fish and seafood.

I rank eateries from **$** budget to **$$$$** splurge. In my recommendations, I've distinguished tapas places (which serve small plates throughout the afternoon and evening) from more formal restaurants (with generous portions, no tapas, and service that starts much later than the American norm). Most of my recommended eateries—grouped by neighborhood and handy to the sights—are practical, characteristic, affordable, and lively, with a busy tapas scene at the bar, along with restaurant tables where larger plates can be enjoyed family-style. To avoid bad, touristy restaurants, a good rule of thumb is not to eat (or drink) on the Ramblas or Passeig de Gràcia.

Catalan tapas menus most often include seafood (cod, hake, tuna, squid, and anchovies), delicious local olives, and a traditional sausage called *butifarra*. In restaurants, you'll see Catalan favorites such as *fideuà*, a thin, flavor-infused noodle served with seafood—a kind of Catalan paella—and *arròs negre,* black rice cooked in squid ink. *Pa amb tomàquet* is the classic Catalan way to eat bread—toasted white bread with olive oil, tomato, and a pinch of salt. It's often served free with your plate and used to make sandwiches. While the famous cured *jamón* (ham) is more Spanish than it is Catalan, you'll still find lots of it in Catalunya (see the "Sampling *Jamón*" sidebar on page 291). All this food is accompanied by local beers, wines, and, of course, the beloved sweet vermouth.

EATING TIPS

For general advice on eating in Barcelona, including details on ordering, dining (at restaurants and in tapas bars), and tipping, along with information on typical cuisine and beverages, see page 287. For help deciphering menus, see the "Tapas Menu Decoder" on page 294. I've tried to make this information on eating in Barcelona appropriately Catalan—as opposed to just Spanish with a Barcelona accent.

Hours: As in the rest of Spain, the people of Catalunya eat late—lunch around 14:00 (and as late as 16:00), and dinner after 21:00. The earliest you can go to a restaurant for dinner is about 20:30, when the place is empty or filled with tourists. Going after 21:00 is better, but if you wait until 22:00, it can be hard to get into popular restaurants. Note that many restaurants close in August (or July), when the owners take a vacation.

Although tapas are served throughout the day, the real action begins late—21:00 or after. For less competition at the bar, go early or on Monday and Tuesday (but check to see if the place is open, as many close on Sunday or Monday).

For advice on adapting to the Spanish eating schedule, see page 287.

Bread and Water: Most places don't automatically give you bread with your meal. If you ask for it, you'll usually receive *pa amb tomàquet* (bread with tomato spread), and you will be charged. Barcelona's tap water is safe to drink and free, but some bar owners are rather insistent on not serving it to their clientele, as it doesn't taste particularly good. For details on how to ask for water, see page 297.

Local-Style Tapas: Catalans have an affinity for Basque culture, so you'll find a lot of Basque-style tapas places here, where they lay out bite-size tapas (called *pintxos,* or *pinchos*) on the countertop. These places are user-friendly, as you are free to take what you want, and you don't have to look at a menu or wait to be served; just grab what looks good, order a drink, and save your toothpicks (they'll count them up at the end to tally your bill). I've listed several of these bars (including Taverna Basca Irati and Sagardi Euskal Taberna), but there are many others. Look for signs reading *basca* or *euskal taberna* (*euskal* means "Basque")—or just keep an eye out for places with lots of toothpicks. You'll also find traditional Catalan tapas bars and *bodegas* (originally a name denoting wine cellars but preserved as many *bodegas* evolved into restaurants).

Market Halls: Try eating at one of Barcelona's covered market halls at least once—either at La Boqueria (on the Ramblas) or Santa Caterina (in El Born; both described later). I far prefer Santa Caterina, as La Boqueria is so touristy now. It's hard to walk through any market and not pick up something—either traditional or fun and touristy.

Catalan in Restaurants: Catalan and Spanish (in that order) are the official languages of Barcelona. While menus are usually in both languages, and many times English as well, these days—with the feisty spirit of independence stoked—you may find some menus in just Catalan, or Catalan and English without Spanish. Throughout this book, I've given most food terms in Spanish and added Catalan where helpful. For terms in Spanish and Catalan, consult the "Tapas Menu Decoder" on page 294 and the list of drink terms on page 296.

In any Catalan bar or restaurant, an occasional *"si us plau"* (please) or *"moltes gràcies"* (thank you very much) will go a long way with the locals. An *"adéu"* (good-bye), *"que vagi bé"* (have a good one!), or, in the evening, *"bona nit"* (good evening/night) on your way out the door will certainly earn you a smile. And, as they say in Catalan, *"Bon profit!"* (Bon appétit!)

NEAR THE RAMBLAS

The entire length of the Ramblas itself is a tourist trap. Simply put: Do not eat or drink on the Ramblas (to make the rip-off prices even worse, when it comes time to pay, you may find that your bag has been stolen). But within a few steps of the Ramblas, you'll find handy lunch places, an inviting market hall, and some good vegetarian options.

Lunching Simply yet Memorably near the Ramblas

Although these places are enjoyable for a lunch break from sightseeing, many are also open for dinner.

$$ Taverna Basca Irati serves 40 kinds of hot and cold Basque *pintxos* for €2 each. These are small open-faced sandwiches—a baguette slice topped with something tasty. Muscle in through the hungry crowd, get an empty plate from the waiter, and then help yourself. Every few minutes, waiters circulate with platters of new,

EATING

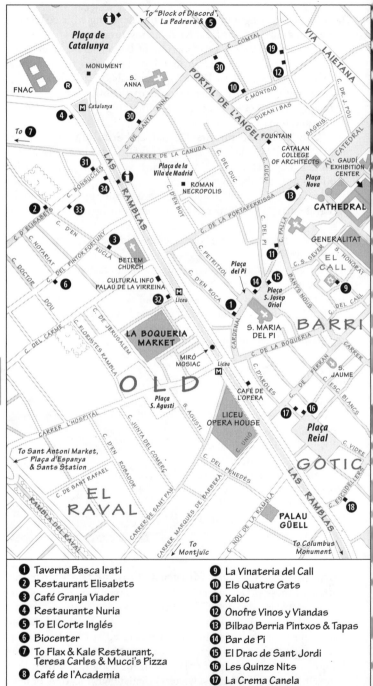

1 Taverna Basca Irati
2 Restaurant Elisabets
3 Café Granja Viader
4 Restaurante Nuria
5 To El Corte Inglés
6 Biocenter
7 To Flax & Kale Restaurant, Teresa Carles & Mucci's Pizza
8 Café de l'Academia
9 La Vinateria del Call
10 Els Quatre Gats
11 Xaloc
12 Onofre Vinos y Viandas
13 Bilbao Berria Pintxos & Tapas
14 Bar de Pi
15 El Drac de Sant Jordi
16 Les Quinze Nits
17 La Crema Canela

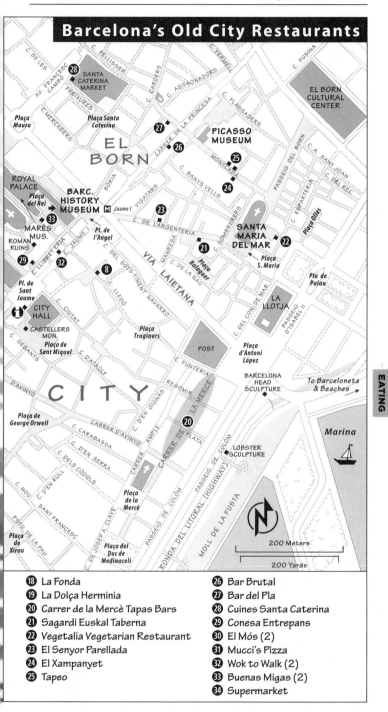

Barcelona's Old City Restaurants

EATING

18 La Fonda
19 La Dolça Herminia
20 Carrer de la Mercè Tapas Bars
21 Sagardi Euskal Taberna
22 Vegetalia Vegetarian Restaurant
23 El Senyor Parellada
24 El Xampanyet
25 Tapeo

26 Bar Brutal
27 Bar del Pla
28 Cuines Santa Caterina
29 Conesa Entrepans
30 El Mós (2)
31 Mucci's Pizza
32 Wok to Walk (2)
33 Buenas Migas (2)
34 Supermarket

Budget Meals Around Town

Bright, clean, and inexpensive **sandwich shops** proudly hold the cultural line against the fast-food invasion that has hamburgerized the rest of Europe. You'll see two big Catalan chains (Bocatta and Pans & Company) everywhere, but these serve mass-produced McBaguettes ordered from a multilingual menu. I've had better luck with hole-in-the-wall sandwich shops—virtually as numerous as the chains—where you can see exactly what you're getting.  Other good alternatives include Conesa Entrepans (on Plaça de Sant Jaume) and the good local chain **El Mós,** with speedy service, fresh ingredients, and long hours daily (two locations near Plaça de Catalunya, at Carrer Comtal 12 and Carrer Santa Anna 9).

Kebab places are also a good, super-cheap standby; you'll see them all over town. Another popular budget option is the **empanada**—a pastry turnover filled with seasoned meat and vegetables. In basic restaurants and bars, you'll often find daily lunch specials *(menú del día)* for about €12. And you can always graze cheaply in bars offering an array of affordable **tapas** and individual bites called *pintxos* (or *pinchos*).

For other options, try **Mucci's Pizza,** with good, fresh pizza slices and empanadas (two locations just off the Ramblas, at Bonsuccés 10 and Tallers 75). **Wok to Walk** makes tasty food on the run, serving up noodles and rice in takeaway containers with your choice of meat and/or veggies and finished with a savory sauce (convenient branches near Plaça de Sant Jaume and Liceu Metro station). **Buenas Migas** is another Barcelona chain serving focaccia, quiche, salads, and pastas (locations include behind the cathedral at Baixada de Santa Clara 2, at Plaça de la Sagrada Família 17, and off the Ramblas at Plaça del Bonsuccés 6).

still-warm munchies. Grab one as they pass by...it's addictive (you'll be charged by the number of toothpicks left on your plate when you're done). For drink options, look for the printed menu on the wall in the back. Wash down your food with Rioja (full-bodied red wine), Txakolí (sprightly Basque white wine), or *sidra* (apple wine). Open daily (11:00-24:00, a block off the Ramblas, behind arcade at Carrer del Cardenal Casanyes 17, Metro: Liceu, tel. 933-023-084).

$$ Restaurant Elisabets is a rough little neighborhood eatery packed with antique radios. It's popular with young locals and tourists alike for its €12 "home-cooked" three-course lunch special; even cheaper *menú rapid* options are available (13:00-16:00 only). Stop by for lunch, survey what those around you are enjoying, and order what looks best. Apparently, locals put up with the service for the tasty food (cash only, Mon-Sat 7:30-23:00, closed Sun and Aug, 2 blocks west of Ramblas on far corner of Plaça del Bonsuccés at Carrer d'Elisabets 2, Metro: Catalunya, tel. 933-175-826).

$$ Café Granja Viader is a quaint time capsule, family-run since 1870. They boast about being the first dairy business to bottle and distribute milk in Spain. This feminine-feeling place—specializing in baked and dairy treats, toasted sandwiches, and light meals—is ideal for a traditional breakfast. Or indulge your sweet tooth: Try a glass of *orxata* (or *horchata*—*chufa*-nut milk, summer only), *llet mallorquina* (Majorca-style milk with cinnamon, lemon, and sugar), *crema catalana* (crème brûlée, their specialty), or *suis* ("Swiss"—hot chocolate with a snowcap of whipped cream). *Mel i mató* is fresh cheese with honey...very Catalan (Mon-Sat 9:00-13:00 & 17:00-21:00, closed Sun, a block off the Ramblas behind Betlem Church at Xuclà 4, Metro: Liceu, tel. 933-183-486).

$$ Restaurante Nuria is a big, venerable standby that's been overlooking all the Ramblas action since 1926. It's a low-stress, hardworking place with a menu designed to please tourists: pizza, burgers, paellas, and salads (daily 24/7, Rambla de Canaletes 133, tel. 933-023-847). They have a fancier place upstairs.

Cafeteria on Plaça de Catalunya: For a quick, affordable lunch with an almost 360-degree view, the ninth-floor cafeteria at **$$ El Corte Inglés** can't be beat. Grab a tray and browse; there's always fresh paella, and the food is often cooked to order (Mon-Sat 9:30-21:00, until 22:00 in summer, closed Sun, Metro: Catalunya, tel. 933-063-800).

Picnics: Shoestring tourists buy groceries at **El Corte Inglés** (supermarket in basement) and **Carrefour Market** (Mon-Sat 10:00-22:00, closed Sun, Ramblas 113, Metro: Liceu).

La Boqueria Market: If you're in La Boqueria and ready for lunch, a snack, or a drink, there are several high-energy bars that would love to take your money. The Pinotxo Bar (just to the right as you enter) has a waiter beloved for his smile and his double thumbs up. If you see fun-loving Juan, give him a wink and a double thumbs up yourself. For more on La Boqueria, see the Ramblas Ramble chapter. For a market hall that's far less touristy, try Santa Caterina in El Born (described later).

Vegetarian Eateries near the Ramblas

$$ Biocenter, a Catalan soup-and-salad restaurant busy with local vegetarians, takes its cooking very seriously and feels a bit more like a real restaurant than most (weekday lunch specials include soup or salad and plate of the day, Mon-Sat 13:00-23:00, Sun until 16:00, two blocks off the Ramblas at Carrer del Pintor Fortuny 25, Metro: Liceu, tel. 933-014-583).

$$ Flax & Kale is a top-end vegetarian place, and the nearby campus gives it a university vibe. As its name suggests, this place serves seriously healthy dishes and juices in a delightful, spacious indoor setting (daily 9:30-23:30, five-minute walk from the top of the Ramblas at Carrer Tallers 74, tel. 933-175-664). Its sister location, named for the founder, **Teresa Carles,** is also good but has a standard and more forgettable setting (same hours, closer to the Ramblas, just off Carrer Tallers at Carrer Jovellanos 2, Metro: Universitat or Catalunya, tel. 933-171-829).

BARRI GÒTIC

These eateries populate Barcelona's atmospheric Gothic Quarter, near the cathedral. Choose between a sit-down meal at a restaurant or a string of tapas bars.

Restaurants

$$$ Café de l'Academia is a delightful place on a pretty square tucked away in the heart of the Barri Gòtic—but patronized mainly by the neighbors. They serve refined cuisine with Catalan roots, using what's fresh from the market. The candlelit, air-conditioned interior is rustic yet elegant, with soft jazz, flowers, and modern art. And if you want to eat outdoors on a convivial, mellow square... this is the place. Reservations are a must, though if you show up without one, try asking to sit at the bar (lunch specials, open Mon-Fri 13:00-15:30 & 20:00-23:00, closed Sat-Sun, near the City Hall square, off Carrer de Jaume I up Carrer de la Dagueria at Carrer dels Lledó 1, Metro: Jaume I, tel. 933-198-253).

$$$ La Vinateria del Call, buried deep in the Jewish Quarter, is one of the oldest wine bars in town. It offers a romantic restaurant-style meal of tapas with fine local wines. Eating at the small bar by the entrance is discouraged, so I'd settle in at a candlelit table. They have more than 100 well-priced wines, including a decent selection of Catalan wines at €2.50 a glass. Three or four plates of their classic tapas will fill two people (daily 19:30-24:00; with back to church, leave Plaça de Sant Felip Neri and walk two short blocks to Sant Domènec del Call 9; Metro: Jaume I, tel. 933-026-092).

$$$ Els Quatre Gats ("The Four Cats") was once the haunt of the Modernista greats—including a teenaged Picasso, who first publicly displayed his art here, and architect Josep Puig i Cada-falch, who designed the building. Inspired by Paris' famous Le Chat Noir café/cabaret, Els Quatre Gats celebrated all that was modern at the turn of the 20th century (for more on the illustrious history of the place, see page 97 in the Barri Gòtic Walk). You can snack or drink at the bar, or go into the back for a sit-down meal after 19:00. While touristy (less so later), the food and service are good, and the prices aren't as high as you might guess (weekday lunch specials, daily 9:00-24:00, just steps off Avinguda del Portal de l'Angel at Carrer de Montsió 3, Metro: Catalunya, tel. 933-024-140).

$$$ Xaloc is a good place in the old center for nicely presented gourmet tapas. It has a woody, modern, relaxed, and spacious dining room with a fun energy, attentive service, and reasonable prices. The walls are covered with *ibérico* hamhocks and wine bottles. They focus on home-style Catalan classics—and though the food here doesn't impress locals, tourists find the place comfortable. A bowl of gazpacho, plate of ham, *pa amb tomàquet* (comes free), and nice glass of wine make a fine light meal (daily, 13:00-17:00 & 19:00-23:00, a block toward the cathedral from Plaça de Sant Josep Oriol at Carrer de la Palla 13, Metro: Catalunya, tel. 933-011-990).

$$$ Onofre Vinos y Viandas, owned and run by Marisol and Ángel, is a tiny wine bar (20 wines by the glass) with a few simple tables behind walls of wine bottles. Foodie but without pretense, it has few tourists and a fun, creative, accessible menu—be adventurous and try the brandy foie shavings. For a gastronomic treat highlighting house favorites and seasonal specials, you can trust your hosts and order the €40-per-person "Marisol Extravaganza" (daily 10:00-16:30 & 19:30-24:00, near the Palace of Catalan Music, Carrer de les Magdalenes 19, tel. 933-176-937).

$$ Bilbao Berria Pintxos and Tapas is a hardworking tapas bar, like its Basque sisters around town. It faces the cathedral, with tables outside on the square (15 percent surcharge to sit there), and sells little open-faced sandwiches and fun bites for €2 per toothpick. Grab a plate and pick what you want, buffet-style (Plaça Nova 3, tel. 933-170-124).

On Plaça de Sant Josep Oriol: For me, this is the most inviting square in the Gothic Quarter. To enjoy the ambience with a meal, there are two very simple eateries to consider, both with a few tables on the square: **$$ Bar del Pi** is a hardworking bar serving salads, sandwiches, and tapas (daily 9:00-23:00). **$ El Drac de Sant Jordi** has a fun budget formula—€10 for any four tapas, a drink, and a tiny dessert (daily 12:00-22:00).

The Andilana Chain for a Little Dining Sanity

This group of **$$** restaurants offers the impression of fine dining at a budget price. While many tapas bars can be intense and sloppy, these restaurants offer a calm sit-down meal featuring good, solid, local dishes. They are popular for their artfully presented Spanish and Mediterranean cuisine; crisp, modern ambience; and unbeatable prices (three-course lunches for about €11 and €16-21 dinners—both with wine; open daily generally 13:00-15:45 & 20:00-23:00). These places are a hit with tourists—be warned that they are notoriously busy.

Three branches are on or near atmospheric Plaça Reial: **Les Quinze Nits** has great seating right on the square (line for dinner starts forming around 20:30, at #6, tel. 933-173-075, takes reservations). **La Crema Canela,** a few steps above Plaça Reial, feels cozier than the others (Passatge de Madoz 6, tel. 933-182-744, takes reservations). **La Fonda** is a block below Plaça Reial (Carrer dels Escudellers 10, tel. 933-017-515).

Near the Palace of Catalan Music is a branch called **La Dolça Herminia** (Carrer de les Magdalenes 27, Metro: Jaume I, tel. 933-170-676).

The Eixample hosts another restaurant in the chain, **La Rita** (described later).

Tapas on Carrer de la Mercè in the Barri Gòtic

This area lets you experience a rare, unvarnished bit of old Barcelona with great *tascas*—colorful local tapas bars. Get small plates (for maximum sampling) by asking for "tapas," not the bigger "*raciones.*" Glasses of *vino tinto* go for about €1. And though trendy uptown restaurants are safer, better-lit, and come with English menus and less grease, these places will stain your journal. The neighborhood's dark, the regulars are rough-edged, and you'll get a glimpse of a crusty Barcelona from before the affluence hit.

Of the many bars on Carrer de la Mercè, I'd visit these three: **$ Bar Celta** (marked *la pulpería,* at #9) eases you into the scene with fried fish, octopus, and *patatas bravas,* all with Galician Ribeiro wine. Farther down at the corner, **$ La Plata** (#28) keeps things wonderfully simple, serving extremely cheap plates of sardines, little salads, and small glasses of keg wine. **$ Cerveceria Vendimia,** at the north end of Carrer de la Mercè (#46), is a dive that slings tasty clams and mussels. You can sit at the bar and point to what looks good. Their *pulpo* (octopus) is more expensive than other choices but is the house specialty.

EL BORN

El Born sparkles with eclectic and trendy as well as subdued and classy little restaurants hidden in the small lanes surrounding the Church of Santa Maria del Mar. While I've listed a few well-established tapas bars that are great for light meals, to really dine, simply wander around for 15 minutes and pick the place that tickles your gastronomic fancy. Consider starting off your evening with a glass of fine wine at one of the *enotecas* on the square facing the Church of Santa Maria del Mar (such as La Vinya del Senyor). Sit back and admire the pure Catalan Gothic architecture. Most of my listings are nearby. Many restaurants and shops in this area are, like the Picasso Museum, closed on Mondays. For all of these eateries, use Metro: Jaume I.

(If El Born feels too touristy, I feel your pain. The "next El Born" is El Raval. For a quick review of places you might eat there, see the brief overview description on page 49.)

Near the Church of Santa Maria del Mar

$$ Sagardi Euskal Taberna offers an array of Basque goodies—tempting *pintxos* and *montaditos* (small open-faced sandwiches) at €2 each—along its huge bar. Ask for a plate and graze (just take whatever looks good). You can sit on the square with your plunder for about 20 percent extra. Wash it down with Txakolí, a Basque white wine poured from the spout of a huge wooden barrel into a glass as you

watch. When you're done, they'll count your toothpicks to tally your bill. Study the two price lists—bar and terrace—posted at the bar (daily 12:00-24:00, Carrer de l'Argenteria 62, tel. 933-199-993). Note that Sagardi serves the same *pintxos* as Taverna Basca Irati, described earlier.

$$ Vegetalia Vegetarian Restaurant, facing the Monument of Catalan Independence and the Church of Santa Maria del Mar, is a basic vegetarian diner with a cheery, healthy-feeling interior (good three-course lunch special, daily from 11:00, tel. 930-177-256).

$$$ El Senyor Parellada, filling a former cloister, is an elegant restaurant with a smart, tourist-friendly waitstaff. It serves a fun menu of Mediterranean and Catalan cuisine with a modern twist, all in a classy chandeliers-and-white-tablecloths setting (daily 13:00-15:45 & 20:30-23:30, Carrer de l'Argenteria 37, 100 yards from the Jaume I Metro stop, tel. 933-105-094).

Near the Picasso Museum

$$ El Xampanyet ("The Little Champagne Bar"), a colorful family-run bar with a fun-loving staff (Juan Carlos, his mom, and the man who may be his father). It specializes in tapas and anchovies—and their cheap homemade *cava* (Spanish champagne) goes straight to your head. Don't be put off by the seafood from a tin: Catalans like it this way. A *sortido de fumats* (assorted plate of small fish) with *pa amb tomàquet* makes for a fun meal. This place is filled with tourists during the sightseeing day, but it's jam-packed with locals after dark. The scene is great, but—especially during busy times—it's tough without Spanish skills. When I asked about the price, Juan Carlos said, "Who cares? The ATM is just across the street" (same price at bar or table, Tue-Sun 12:00-15:30 & 19:00-23:00, closed Sun evening and Mon, a half-block beyond the Picasso Museum at Carrer de Montcada 22, tel. 933-197-003).

$$ Tapeo is a mod, classy alternative to the funky Xampanyet across the street. It serves high-end tapas at a long, sit-down bar and tiny tables with stools. This small space fills quickly so go early to get a seat (Tue-Sun 12:00-16:00 & 19:00-24:00, closed Mon, Carrer de Montcada 29, tel. 933-101-607).

$$$ Bar Brutal is a creative and edgy bohemian-chic place with a young, local following. It serves a mix of Spanish and Italian dishes with an emphasis on wines—especially natural wines, with plenty available by the glass (Mon-Sat 13:00-24:00, closed Sun, Carrer de Princesa 14, tel. 932-954-797).

$$$ Bar del Pla is a favorite near the Picasso Museum. This classic diner/bar—overlooking a tiny crossroads next to Barcelona's oldest church—serves traditional Catalan dishes, *raciones,* and tapas. Their *croquetas,* mushrooms with wasabi, and crispy oxtail with foie gras are highlights. They also have a local IPA on tap. Prices are the same at the bar or at a table; eating at the bar puts you in the middle of a great scene (Mon-Sat 12:00-23:00, closed Sun, reservations smart; leaving the Picasso Museum, head right two blocks past Carrer de la Princesa to Carrer de Montcada 2; tel. 932-683-003, www.bardelpla.cat).

At Santa Caterina Market

$$ Cuines Santa Caterina, bright and modern, has shared tables under the open rafters of a modern market hall. There's also a handy tapas bar and fine self-service outdoor seating on the square. Their menu—with vegetarian, international, and Mediterranean dishes, all made from market-fresh and seasonal ingredients—cross-references everything on an innovative grid (outside tables OK for both restaurant and tapas bar, daily 12:30-16:00 & 19:30-23:00, Avinguda de Francesc Cambó 16, tel. 932-689-918, no reservations).

$ Tapas Bars: Several lively tapas bars are great for a quick and characteristic bite. Sitting here at one of these bars, immersed in the local scene, nets you a cheap and wonderful meal along with great market memories.

EIXAMPLE

The people-packed boulevards of the Eixample are lined with appetizing eateries featuring breezy outdoor seating. Choose between a real restaurant or an upscale tapas bar (for the best variety, I prefer Rambla de Catalunya). For locations, see the map on page 178.

Restaurants

$$ La Rita is a fresh and dressy little restaurant serving Catalan and Mediterranean cuisine near the Block of Discord. Their €11 lunch and €16 dinner *menú* specials are a great value. Like at most of its sister Andilana restaurants—described earlier—its prices attract a loyal following, so arrive early...or wait (daily 13:00-15:45 & 20:00-23:00, near corner of Carrer de Pau Claris and Carrer d'Aragó at d'Aragó 279, a block from Metro: Passeig de Gràcia, tel. 934-872-376).

$$ La Bodegueta is an atmospheric below-street-level bodega serving hearty wines, homemade vermouth, *anchoas* (anchovies), tapas, and *flautas*—sandwiches made with flute-thin baguettes. On a nice day, it's great to eat outside, sitting in the median of the boulevard under shady trees. Its three-course lunch special with wine is a deal (Mon-Fri only, 13:00-16:00). A long block from Gaudí's La Pedrera, this makes a fine sightseeing break (Mon-Sat 7:00-24:00, Sun from 18:00, at intersection with Carrer de Provença, Rambla de Catalunya 100, Metro: Provença, tel. 932-154-894). La Bodegueta has another location nearby—similar style and format but more comfortable and spacious (Carrer de Balmes 213).

$$$ Restaurante la Palmera serves a mix of Catalan, Mediterranean, and French cuisine in an elegant room with bottle-lined walls. This untouristy place offers great food, service, and value—for me, a very special meal in Barcelona. They have three zones: the classic main room, a more forgettable adjacent room, and a few outdoor tables. I like the classic room. Reservations are smart (creative €24 six-plate *degustation* lunch—also available at dinner Sun and Tue-Thu, open Mon-Sat 13:00-15:45 & 19:45-23:30, closed Sun, Carrer d'Enric Granados 57, at the corner with Carrer Mallorca, Metro: Provença, tel. 934-532-338, www.lapalmera.cat).

$$ La Flauta fills two floors with enthusiastic eaters (I prefer the ground floor). It's fresh and modern, with a fun, no-stress menu featuring small plates, creative *flauta* sandwiches, and a three-course lunch deal. Consider the list of *tapas del día*. Good wines by the glass are listed on the blackboard, and solo diners get great service at the bar (Mon-Sat 7:00-24:00, closed Sun, upbeat and helpful staff, no reservations, just off Carrer de la Diputació at Carrer d'Aribau 23, Metro: Universitat, tel. 933-237-038).

$$$$ Cinc Sentits ("Five Senses"), with only about 30 seats, is my gourmet recommendation for those who want to dress up and spend more money. At this chic, minimalist, slightly snooty place, all the attention goes to the fine service and beautifully presented dishes. The €55 *formula* lunch *menú* and the *quatre plats* (€90) and *sis plats* (€120) dinner *menús* are unforgettable extravaganzas. Each comes with a wine-pairing option (€65-70). Expect *menús* only—no à la carte. It's run by Catalans who lived in Canada (so there's no language barrier) and serve avant-garde cuisine inspired by Catalan traditions and ingredients. Reservations are essential (Tue-Sat 13:30-15:00 & 20:30-22:00, closed Sun-Mon, near Carrer d'Aragó at Carrer d'Aribau 58, between Metros: Universitat and Provença, tel. 933-239-490, www.cincsentits.com, maître d' Eric).

$$$$ Monvínic ("World of Wine")—a sleek, trendy wine bar that's evangelical about local wine culture—has an open kitchen, a passion for fine food, and little pretense. Considered one of the top wine bar/restaurants in town, their renowned chef creates Catalan and Mediterranean dishes for enjoying with the wine. Diners can use an iPad to read descriptions of the 50 or so open bottles, virtually "visit" each winery, and "meet" the vintner. The faces of farmers—the unsung heroes of the food industry—are projected on the wall. Staff don't turn the tables and hope you'll spend the evening, so reserve in advance. For a more casual visit, they have a tapas bar (no reservations) in front where you'll also be empowered by an iPad and wine (Tue-Fri 13:00-23:00, Mon and Sat from 19:00, closed Sun, starters designed to share, creative tapas, lunch specials, Diputació 249, Metro: Passeig de Gràcia, tel. 932-726-187, www.monvinic.com).

Tapas Bars

Many trendy and touristic tapas bars in the Eixample offer a cheery welcome and slam out the appetizers. These two are particularly handy to Plaça de Catalunya and the Passeig de Gràcia artery (closest Metro stops: Catalunya and Passeig de Gràcia).

$$$ Tapas 24 makes eating fun. This local favorite, with a few street tables, fills a spot a few steps below street level with happy energy, funky decor, and good yet pricey tapas. Along with daily specials and fine breakfasts, the menu has all the typical standbys and quirky inventions. The *tapas del día* list is particularly good. The owner, Carles Abellan, is one of Barcelona's hot chefs; although his famous fare is pricey, you can enjoy it without going broke. Prices are the same whether you dine at the bar, a table, or outside. Come early or wait; no reservations are taken (daily 9:00-24:00, just off Passeig de Gràcia at Carrer de la Diputació 269, tel. 934-880-977).

$$ Ciutat Comtal Cerveceria is an Eixample favorite, full of tourists, with an elegant bar and tables plus good seating out on the Rambla de Catalunya for all that people-watching action. It's packed after 21:00, when you'll likely need to put your name on a list and wait. While it has no restaurant-type menu, the varied list of tapas and *montaditos* is easy, fun, high-quality, and includes daily specials (daily 8:00-24:00, facing the intersection of Gran Via de les Corts Catalanes and Rambla de Catalunya at Rambla de Catalunya 18, tel. 933-181-997).

BARCELONETA AND THE BEACH

The nearest Metro stop to this former sailors' quarter is Barceloneta; the bus will get you closer—the best ones are #V15 (catch it at Plaça de Catalunya or along Via Laietana), #59 (from the top of the Ramblas), or #D20 (from the Columbus Monument). For the locations of these eateries, see the map on page 74.

At the Center of Barceloneta

The main square of Barceloneta (Plaça del Poeta Boscà) is homey, with a 19th-century iron-and-glass market, families at play in the park, and lots of hole-in-the-wall eateries and bars. The main drag—Passeig de Joan de Borbó—faces the city and is lined with many interchangeable seafood restaurants and cafés.

$$$$ La Mar Salada is a traditional seafood restaurant with a slightly modern twist and both indoor and outdoor seating (weekday lunch *menú*, open Wed-Mon 13:00-16:00 & 20:00-23:00, closed Tue, Passeig de Joan de Borbó 59, tel. 932-212-127).

$$$$ Restaurante Can Solé, serving seafood since 1903, hides on a nondescript lane between the square and the marina one block off the harborfront promenade, this venerable yet homey restaurant draws a celebrity crowd, judging by the autographed pictures of the famous and not-so-famous that line the walls (Tue-Sat 13:30-16:00 & 20:30-23:00, closed Sun-Mon, Carrer de Sant Carles 4, tel. 932-215-012, www.restaurantcansole.com).

$$ El Guindilla Taverna del Mercat, in the market and spilling onto the main square, is a good value for a basic local meal in a neighborhood family setting (great outdoor tables, daily, Plaça del Poeta Boscà 2, tel. 932-215-458).

$ Baluard, one of Barcelona's most highly regarded artisan bakeries, faces one side of the big market hall. Line up with the locals to get a loaf of heavenly bread, a pastry, or a slice of pizza

(Mon-Sat 8:00-21:00, closed Sun, Carrer del Baluard 38, tel. 932-211-208).

On the Beach

The *chiringuito* tradition of funky eateries lining Barcelona's beach now has serious competition from trendy bars and restaurants. A piece of modern art in the sand—a bunch of cubical shacks piled high—stands like a memorial to these beloved-but-seasonal beach joints. Now the spendy places have moved in, and all along the beach you have restaurants offering both indoor and terrace tables with a sea view. My favorites are at the far south end near the towering Hotel W.

$$$$ Pez Vela is the top-end option with a fashionable local crowd and its own DJ (daily 13:00-23:30, Passeig del Mare Nostrum 19, tel. 932-216-317).

$$$ Mamarosa Beach, just next door, is a family-friendly place with Italian classics and local favorites (daily 13:00-24:00, Passeig del Mare Nostrum 21, tel. 933-123-586).

BARCELONA WITH CHILDREN

Barcelona is a great place to travel with kids; it's bubbling with inexpensive, quirky sights and an infectious human spirit. Sure, there's an amusement park, a zoo, and a science museum, but your kids will have an adventure simply wandering down the city's tangled streets. And when it's time for a break, Barcelona has one of Europe's best urban beach scenes.

Trip Tips

PLAN AHEAD

Involve your kids in trip planning. Have them read about the places that you may include in your itinerary (even the hotels you're considering), and let them help with your decisions.

Where to Stay

- Choose hotels in an area with wide, strollable streets, small parks, and a family-friendly feel—try Eixample or Barceloneta.
- If you're staying a week or more, or if your kids love playing in the sand, consider renting an apartment near one of Barcelona's many beaches.
- Aim for hotels with restaurants, so older kids can go back to the room while you finish a pleasant dinner.
- Barcelona's hotels often give price breaks for kids. Most have some sort of crib you can use.
- Your kids will thank you for avoiding the few remaining hotels without air-conditioning.

What to Bring

- If traveling with infants, plan on bringing or buying a light stroller for neighborhood walks, and a child backpack for riding the Metro.
- Bring your own drawing supplies and English-language picture books, as these supplies can be pricier in Europe.

EATING

Your kids may be surprised to find out that Catalan food is nothing like Mexican food back home. Picky eaters may have a hard time with *jamón*, deep-fried dishes, and strange seafood. Try these tips to keep your kids content throughout the day.

What to Eat (and Drink)

- Seek out commonly available, kid-friendly food choices such as a *tortilla de patatas* (potato-egg omelette), *bikinis* or *sandwich mixto* (grilled ham-and-cheese sandwich), *empanada de atún, pollo, carne picada,* or *jamón y queso* (savory pastry filled with tuna, chicken, ground beef, or ham and cheese), or *bocadillo* (French-bread sandwich usually filled with meat, cheese, or egg). For breakfast, try *una tostada con mantequilla y mermelada* (toast with butter and jam) or a croissant, along with *zumo natural* (fresh-squeezed orange juice). Fruit, cereal, and yogurt are available at the supermarket.
- Sweet treats popular with little travelers include *churros con chocolate* (fried dough strips with a dense chocolate drink for dipping), *ensaimada* (a Mallorca-style croissant with powdered sugar), *crema catalane* (like a crème brûlée), and *torró/turrón* (a nougat confection).

Where to Eat

- Picnic lunches or dinners work well. Try large grocery stores such as Carrefour Market or El Corte Inglés. Or drop by a *panadería* (bakery), which will likely have baguette sandwiches, pizza by the slice, and empanadas. There are also plenty of tiny, convenient shops with long hours throughout the old town. Near the beach? Head to the market—El Mercat de la Barceloneta—near the Barceloneta Metro stop (closed Sun; Plaça Poeta Bosca 1, tel. 932-216-471). Having snacks on hand can avoid meltdowns (and can help your kids avoid them, too).
- Choose easy eateries. A good, safe (though not exotic) bet is the cafeteria/restaurant at the **$ El Corte Inglés** department store on Plaça de Catalunya (service all day, kids menu). Quick chain restaurants such as Bocatta or Pans & Company serve reasonably priced *bocadillos* (sandwiches) and fries—and grownups can order a beer. For a sweet break for both you and

---

Barcelona Books for Kids

Get your kids into the spirit of Barcelona with these books about the city and some of its most influential former residents. (Also see my recommended books and films list in the appendix, which includes some good choices for teenagers.)

A Stroll with Mr. Gaudí (Pau Estrada, 2013). In this fun introduction to Barcelona's architecture, Antoni Gaudí takes a walk through the city, visiting famous landmarks.

Building with Nature: The Life of Antoni Gaudí (Rachel Rodriguez and Julie Paschkis, 2009). Beautiful, folksy illustrations enliven the biography of Barcelona's most famous architect.

Let's Visit Barcelona!: Adventures of Bella & Harry (Lisa Manzione and Kristine Lucco, 2012). Two Chihuahuas visit Barcelona with their family, learning basic Spanish phrases and visiting famous landmarks.

Mission Barcelona: A Scavenger Hunt Adventure (Catherine Aragon, 2014). This interactive scavenger hunt will keep your youngsters engaged throughout your trip.

Molly and the Magic Suitcase: Molly Goes to Barcelona (Chris Oler and Amy Houston Oler, 2013). With the help of a magic suitcase, Molly and her brother trek to Barcelona in search of adventure.

Pablo Picasso: Meet the Artist (Patricia Geis, 2014). Young readers will enjoy this look at Picasso's art, and may just be inspired to create some of their own.

Picasso and Minou (P.I. Maltbie and Pau Estrada, 2005). This beautifully illustrated book tells the story of Picasso and his work through the eyes of his cat, Minou.

---

the kids, try the **$ Pudding** café. You can snack or have a light meal sitting next to a giant mushroom or in the kids' play area (books and board games). It's near the Plaça de Catalunya; look for it around the corner from the Gran Vía about two blocks from the Passeig de Gràcia (cakes, sandwiches/quiche, daily 11:00-21:00, Carrer de Pau Claris 90, tel. 936-678-748).

When to Eat

- Catalans eat late—usually about 21:00 or 22:00—and dinner can take two hours. If you're eating late with your kids at a restaurant, bring something to occupy them and seek out places on squares where kids can run free while you dine. Catalan children go out and stay out late, so don't worry about your kids disturbing others as they gambol around the plaza.

CHILDREN

SIGHTSEEING

The key to a successful Barcelona family vacation is to slow down. Tackle one or two key sights each day, mix in a healthy dose of pure fun at a park or beach, and take extended breaks when needed.

Planning Your Time

- Let your kids make some decisions, such as choosing lunch spots or deciding which stores or museums to visit. Deputize your child to lead you on my self-guided walks and museum tours.
- Older children and teens can help plan sightseeing details, such as what to see, how to get there, and ticketing details.
- Take advantage of Time Out Barcelona's website, which includes kids' activities, shows, and family restaurants (www.timeout.com/barcelona/barcelona-for-kids).
- Don't overdo it. Tackle only one or two key sights a day. Encourage your kids to endure an hour to see a sight, then relent if they've had enough.
- Balance your museum-going with fun and energetic activities, like boating in Citadel Park or biking along the beach.
- Barcelona's sights generally offer free admission to children and reduced admission for students—always ask before buying tickets for your kids.
- Follow this book's crowd-beating tips to the letter. Kids despise long lines even more than you do.
- Public WCs are hard to find: Try museums, ice cream shops, and fast-food restaurants.

Successful Sightseeing

- Get kids engaged in age-appropriate museum fun. Younger kids might enjoy a scavenger hunt approach: Buy postcards of sights in the museum gift shop (or give them this book with its photos) and let them find the art. Museum audioguides are great for older children.
- Bring a sketchbook to a museum and encourage kids to select a painting or statue to draw. It's a great way for them to slow down and observe.
- Seek out kid-friendly museums, such as CosmoCaixa or the Maritime Museum.

Making or Finding Quality Souvenirs

- Buy your child a trip journal, and encourage him or her to write down observations, thoughts, and favorite sights and memories. This journal could end up being your child's favorite souvenir.

- For a group project, keep a family journal. Pack a small diary and a glue stick. While relaxing over ice cream, take turns writing or drawing about the day's events and include mementos such as ticket stubs from museums and postcards.
- Teens might love shopping (or even window-shopping). See the Shopping in Barcelona chapter for fun areas.

MONEY, SAFETY, AND STAYING CONNECTED

Before setting them loose, talk to your kids about safety and money.

- Give your child a money belt and an expanded allowance; you are on vacation, after all. Let your kids budget their funds by comparing and contrasting the dollar and euro.
- If you allow older kids to explore a museum or neighborhood on their own, be sure to establish a clear meeting time and place.
- For kids of all ages, have a "what if" procedure in place in case something goes wrong. Give your kids your hotel's business card, your phone number (if you brought a mobile phone), and emergency taxi fare. Let them know to ask to use the phone at a hotel if they are lost. And if they have mobile phones, show them how to make calls in Barcelona.
- Teens traveling with a mobile device can keep in touch with friends at home—and Europeans they meet—via apps such as WhatsApp (common in Europe), Snapchat, Google Talk, FaceTime, or Skype. Readily available Wi-Fi helps keep online time affordable, or consider buying an international data plan (see the "Staying Connected" section of the Practicalities chapter).

Top Kids' Sights and Activities

ATTRACTIONS

Tibidabo

This 100-year-old amusement park (the city's oldest) sits atop the Tibidabo foothills above town; visiting it could easily fill an entire day.

At the top are Disneyland-like rides and some vintage attractions appealing to younger children, teens, and adults alike. Many enjoy the maze of mirrors—you have to wear gloves so the mirrors stay fingerprint-free. Older kids might like modern attractions such as a 4-D cinema show and the Tibidabo Express rollercoaster. Those on a budget can enjoy the entrance labeled *Panoramic views,* which allows access to an old-fashioned carousel, a Ferris wheel with breathtaking views of Barcelona, and a handful of other old-fashioned rides (see page 56).

CosmoCaixa

One of Europe's most advanced science museums, CosmoCaixa features hands-on exhibits, many of which are specifically geared toward small children. Youngsters will love *¡Toca toca!* (Touch touch!), an exhibit exploring the natural world, while the 3-D planetarium (€4 extra) may entice older kids and teens. Other kid-focused highlights include a jungle greenhouse and a treasure hunt.

Cost and Hours: €4, free for kids 15 and under and on first Sun of the month; Tue-Sun 10:00-20:00, closed Mon; Metro: Tibidabo, then hop on bus #196 for one stop or walk about 15 minutes to the museum, Carrer d'Isaac Newton 26; tel. 932-126-050, www.cosmocaixa.com.

Barcelona Zoo (Zoo de Barcelona)

This enormous zoo, which gained fame in the 1960s as the home of the only known albino gorilla in the world, Copito de Nieve (Snowflake), is inside Citadel Park. The zoo features tigers, hippos, zebras, Komodo dragons, and more. Daily shows with the dolphins and sea lions in "Aquamara," the small SeaWorld-like marina arena, may impress the young and old.

Cost and Hours: €13 for kids 3-12, free for kids 2 and under, €22 for teens and adults, cheaper online; hours vary by season, summer hours daily 10:00-20:00, last entrance one hour before closing; Metro: Barceloneta, Ciutadella-Vila Olímpica, Marina, or Arc de Triomf; tel. 902-457-545, www.zoobarcelona.cat.

Barcelona Aquarium at Port Vell (L'Aquàrium de Barcelona Port Vell)

Located on the waterfront not far from the Columbus Monument, the aquarium is home to more than 11,000 animals. Its star attraction is the "Oceanarium," a 262-foot underwater glass tunnel that lets you walk beneath schools of deep-sea creatures such as sharks and stingrays. The IMAX Theater next door shows movies in Spanish or Catalan, sometimes with English subtitles. The Port Vell area is an inviting mix of towering sailboats and a steady flow of people on the boardwalk in the midst of daily life; the green space offers room for a picnic or quick rest from sightseeing.

Cost and Hours: €15 for kids 5-10, €7 for kids 3-4, free for kids 2 and under, €20 for visitors 11 and over, cheaper online; daily 10:00-20:00, July-Aug until 21:30; Metro: Drassanes or Barceloneta, Moll d'Espanya del Port Vell, tel. 932-217-474, www.aquariumbcn.com.

Magic Fountains (Font Màgica)

This popular, free spectacle uses classic and modern tunes—including film scores—as the soundtrack for a fanciful water show. Built for the 1929 World's Fair and renovated before the 1992 Olympics, it's part of a web of ponds and waterfalls on Avinguda Maria Cristina in Montjuïc (see page 70).

MUSEUMS AND EXHIBITS

Art Museums

A short visit to some of Barcelona's modern and contemporary art museums could dazzle your kids. All of the following offer educational programs aimed at children and their families.

Museu d'Art Contemporani (MACBA) houses a vast collection of artwork from the past 50 years and offers lectures, video screenings, and special exhibits covering contemporary culture and art. The museum's square is also a roller-skaters' hangout; it's fun to watch the tricks before going inside (€10, free for kids 13 and under; Mon and Wed-Fri 11:00-19:30, Sat 10:00-21:00, Sun 10:00-15:00, closed Tue, Metro: Universitat or Catalunya, Plaça dels Àngels 1, tel. 934-120-810, www.macba.cat).

The Picasso Museum gives kids a chance to marvel at the artist's early works (see page 45).

If you feel like venturing outside of the city for a surreal experience, a two-hour drive or train ride will take you to the **Dalí Theater-Museum** in the town of Figueres (see page 242).

Chocolate Museum (Museu de la Xocolata)

Satisfy everyone's sweet tooth while learning the history of traditional Catalan confectionery through a range of kid-friendly exhibits. You'll see chocolate statues of just about anything and everything—including FC Barcelona soccer players. Family activities may even include painting with chocolate (see page 48).

Maritime Museum (Museu Marítim de Barcelona)

This museum illuminates the history of Catalunya's rich maritime past from the 13th to the 20th century (though part of the permanent collection is not on display while the museum completes a major renovation project). Boat aficionados and sailors-to-be enjoy the collection of model boats and seafaring gadgets, as well as the sprawling marina. Museum admission includes the **Santa Eulàlia** (docked on the Moll de la Fusta quay), a historic three-masted schooner from 1918 that was meticulously restored to its original state. It's especially fun to visit on Saturday mornings, when the schooner sails around the harbor—reserve well in advance (see page 37).

Natural Science Blue Museum
(Museu Blau de Ciencies Naturals)

A good choice for any kid interested in nature, this natural history museum—home to more than three million specimens—celebrates the diversity in flora, fauna, and geology in Catalunya and beyond. Its main exhibit, Planet Earth, follows the birth of our planet and the evolution of life. A special space, the "Science Nest," has activities designed for preschoolers, but you'll need to reserve your visit in advance (closed Aug, though museum is open).

Cost and Hours: €6, free for kids 15 and under, free on Sun after 15:00, €7 combo ticket with Botanical Gardens; Tue-Sat 10:00-19:00, Sun until 20:00, shorter hours Oct-Feb, closed Mon year-round; Metro: El Maresme-Fòrum, Plaza Leonardo da Vinci 4, tel. 932-566-002, www.museuciencies.cat.

Botanical Gardens

Montjuïc is the home of the natural history museum's Botanical Gardens and its Botanical Institute, as well as the recently reopened Historical Botanical Garden. A network of paths follows the natural terrain, taking visitors past 87 outdoor exhibits known as "phytoepisodes."

Cost and Hours: €3.50, free for kids 15 and under, €7 combo-ticket with Natural Science Blue Museum; daily June-Aug 10:00-20:00, closes earlier off-season; take bus #193 from Plaça d'Espanya or the Montjuïc funicular from Paral-lel, main entrance between Olympic Stadium and castle—see map on page 58, Carrer Dr. Font i Quer 2; tel. 932-564-160, www.museuciencies.cat.

Olympic and Sports Museum
(Museu Olímpic i de l'Esport)

Barcelona hosted the Olympics in 1992 and has never been the same since. Sports-crazed kids might enjoy this museum, as well as exploring what is left of the adjacent, anticlimactic 1992 Olympic Stadium. The mod-yet-tacky museum offers up several kid-friendly multimedia installations, such as a virtual race

against an Olympic athlete, but it ultimately appeals only to Olympics fanatics (see page 65).

Camp Nou Soccer Stadium

"Barça" is to Barcelona what the Cowboys are to Dallas; the city lives and breathes for this top-ranked soccer team, as evidenced by their motto, "More Than a Club." The team's pricey visitors center has an interactive museum, features memorabilia from past seasons of glory, and includes a behind-the-scenes visit onto the soccer field. An English audioguide helps explain the exhibits—and the city's soccer obsession. The crowded, energetic FC Barcelona superstore *(La FC Botiga)* is a cool spot for kids and teens as well. Pick up a scarlet-and-blue jersey or scarf as a souvenir (see page 57).

PARKS AND BEACHES
Citadel Park (Parc de la Ciutadella)

Barcelona's most central park sprawls its grassy fields and large avenues across the grounds of an old fortress, and offers plenty for curious kids to discover. Attractions include a giant mammoth statue, a small lake with rental rowboats and duck feeding, a large Baroque fountain (La Cascada), and several outdoor events held throughout the year. The Barcelona Zoo is also accessible from the park. Bikes can be rented from the bike-rental shop opposite the entrance to the park on Passeig de Picasso and Avinguda del Marquès de l'Argentera (see page 75).

Horta Labyrinth Park (Parc del Laberint d'Horta)

Away from the city center in an unassuming location lies the most tranquil green space in town. With barely a tourist in sight, the park holds a handful of Neoclassical and Romantic gardens, highlighted by a small central maze that was used in the filming of Guillermo del Toro's hit, *Pan's Labyrinth* (2006) and Tom Tykwer's *Perfume* (2006). There are more than 20 water features—pools, fountains, reservoirs, canals, and an artificial waterfall—and the tricky labyrinth should provide ample entertainment for kids.

Cost and Hours: €1.50 for kids 5-14, free for kids 4 and under, €2.25 for adults, free on Wed and Sun; daily 10:00-21:00, closes earlier off-season, last entry one hour before closing; Metro: Mundet, then a 15-minute walk, the park is behind a velodrome.

Sant Sebastià, Barceloneta, and Nova Icària Beaches

These are the closest, longest, and busiest beaches (with Sant Sebastià preferred by locals). Both are near the city center, making them a good stop before or after sightseeing. A long boardwalk with food, drink, and ice-cream options lines Sant Sebastià and Barceloneta; on the sand, you'll come upon children's play areas (including one with a cool climbing frame). Expect beach sports

CHILDREN

such as Ping Pong, beach volleyball, and the Basque hand-
ball game, *pelota*. Look out on
the waves, and you'll also spot a
surfer or two.

If you don't care for crowds,
head instead for the nearby Nova
Icària beach; this more tranquil
beach is frequented by families.
Nova Icària is within walking distance of the 1992 Olympic Marina, a popular place for sailing and boating. All of these beaches
are accessible from the Old City area by bus or Metro; see page 73
for directions.

OTHER EXPERIENCES

Sardana Dance

The easy-to-do *sardana* is a beloved traditional symbol of Catalan
unity and pride. Kids might enjoy this spectacle of local culture
(see page 42).

Cable Car (El Transbordador Aeri del Port)

This is a fun and scenic ride between the Barcelona waterfront and
Montjuïc, providing spectacular views of the city. Note that the car
is often crowded and very slow-moving; if there's a long line, it may
not be worth the wait (see page 60).

CHILDREN

SHOPPING IN BARCELONA

Barcelona is a fantastic shopping destination, whatever your taste or budget. The streets of the Barri Gòtic and El Born are bursting with characteristic hole-in-the-wall shops and delightful neighborhood boutiques, while the Eixample is the upscale "uptown" shopping district. The area around Avinguda del Portal de l'Angel (at the northern edge of the Barri Gòtic) has a number of department and chain stores.

Most shops are open Monday through Friday from about 9:00 or 10:00 until lunchtime (13:00 or 14:00). After the siesta, they reopen in the evening (16:30 or 17:00) and stay open until 20:00 or 21:00. Large stores and some smaller shops in touristy zones may remain open through the afternoon—but don't count on it. On Saturdays, many shops are open in the morning only. On Sundays, most shops are closed (though the Maremagnum complex on the harborfront is open).

For information on VAT refunds and customs regulations, see the "Money" section of the Practicalities chapter. For clothing size comparisons between the US and Europe, see the appendix.

What to Buy

Home and Design Goods

Consider picking up prints, books, posters, decorative items, or other keepsakes featuring works by your favorite artist (Picasso, Dalí, Miró, Gaudí, etc.). Gift shops at major museums are open to the public (such as the Picasso Museum and Gaudí's La Pedrera) and are a bonanza for art and design lovers. Model-ship builders will be fascinated by the offerings at the Maritime Museum shop.

In this design-oriented city, home decor shops are abundant and fun to browse, offering a variety of Euro-housewares unavailable back home. For something more classic, look for glassware or other items with a dash of Modernista style.

Decorative tile and pottery can be a good keepsake. Eixample sidewalks are paved with distinctively patterned tiles, which are sold in local shops.

Foodie Items

Home cooks might enjoy shopping for olive oil, wine, spices (such as saffron or sea salts), high-quality canned foods and preserves, dried beans, and other Spanish food items. Remember, these must be sealed to make it back through US customs. But keep in mind that cured meat can never get past US customs, even if it is vacuum-packed and sealed. Cooks can look for European-style gadgets at kitchen-supply stores.

Torró (or *turrón* in Spanish) is the beloved nougat treat that's traditionally eaten around Christmastime, but has become popular anytime.

Market halls are great places to shop for Catalan edibles. The best are La Boqueria (described in the Ramblas Ramble chapter) and Santa Caterina (described in the El Born Walk chapter).

Clothing, Jewelry, and Accessories

Department and chain stores can be fun places to browse for clothing—including styles you won't find back home.

An *espardenya* (or *alpargata* in Spanish) is a soft-canvas, rope-soled shoe (known in the US as an espadrille). It originated as humble peasant footwear in the 14th century in the Pyrenean region (including Catalunya, Occitania, and the Basque Country), but has become popular in modern times for its lightweight comfort in hot weather. A few shops in Barcelona (including La Manual Alpargatera, described later) still make these the traditional way.

Jewelry shops are popular here. While the city doesn't have a strictly local style, finding a piece with a Modernista flourish gives it a Barcelona vibe.

Accessories crafted from discarded materials into stylish, useful products (such as handbags) sell well in "green" Barcelona.

Catalan Pride

If you're drawn to Catalunya's culture, consider a Catalan flag (gold and red stripes). And if you're a fan of Catalunyan independence, pick up one with the blue triangle and star.

Sports fans love jerseys, scarves, and other gear associated with the wildly popular Barça soccer team. As you wander, you'll likely see official football team shops. Knockoffs can be found at any tourist gift shop for less.

Shopping Spots

THE OLD CITY

The Barri Gòtic bursts with shops, from international chain stores to creative artisan boutiques. Neighboring El Born is another good area for boutique-hopping (see my El Born Walk chapter, which takes you through the heart of this district and points you to some appealing shopping streets). Keep in mind that many shops are closed during the midafternoon siesta and have shorter hours or are closed altogether on Sundays.

Barri Gòtic Shopping Walk
(From the Cathedral to the Ramblas)

Most visitors going between the cathedral and the Ramblas follow the straight shot along the wide Carrer de la Portaferrissa. This drag

is lined with mostly international clothing stores catering to teens and young adults (H&M, Mango, etc.). For a more characteristic route—leading you through far more interesting streets lined with little local shops—plunge into some lanes just to the south. This brief, U-shaped walk is designed to lead you through some of the Barri Gòtic's most enjoyable shopping streets. For shop locations, see the "Barri Gòtic Walk" map on page 94.

• Begin on **Plaça Nova**, *the long square in front of the cathedral. At the west end of that square, stand facing the old Roman towers and the big BARCINO letters. Turn 90 degrees to the right, and just to the left of the restaurant (Bilbao Berria "BB"—good for a quick tapas bite with fine seating facing the cathedral), head up the tight lane called...*

Carrer de la Palla: This is ideal for antiques, with a half-dozen ancient-feeling shops crammed with mothballed treasures. (You'll also find, on the left, a fenced-in area with fragments of the old Roman walls, which functions today as a schoolyard soccer field at recess time.) Mixed in are a few contemporary art galleries, offbeat shops (such as **Librería Angel Batlle** at #23, selling books and vintage posters), and a motorcycle museum. Stay on this street until you reach the fork, marked by the building with **Caelum**—a casual but classy-feeling café that sells a wide range of nun-made pastries from convents around Spain. Peruse the boxes of sisterly goodies, and consider sticking around for a coffee—either on the charming main floor or down in the cellar (Carrer de la Palla 8).

The big news in this area is the recent lifting of rent controls. This change has brought a sudden, massive increase in rents, driving many venerable shops out of business and threatening the character of this delightful neighborhood.

From here, detour left and head down **Carrer dels Banys Nous,** which curves gracefully south as it follows the route of the original Roman wall; while you'll have to backtrack a bit, it's another great shopping street with antiques, locally made colorful dresses (at #17), and a bridal shop. About 100 yards down this street, on the left at #10, the sprawling **Oliver** shop (selling home decor, women's clothing, and accessories) has the remains of an old Arabic bath in the back. Directly across the lane, **Artesania Catalunya** (at #11) is a large market-space run by the city, featuring handmade items from Catalan artisans. You can typically find ceramics, jewelry, leather goods, and accessories, but the artisans and merchandise change every few months.

Backtrack to Caelum, and take a hard left down Carrer de la Palla to another fine shop, **Oro Líquido** ("Liquid Gold," at #8), which sells a wide range of high-quality olive oils from around Spain.

• *After another block, you'll pop out on the charming, café-lined Plaça de Sant Josep Oriol, facing the Church of Santa Maria del Pi (a popular venue for guitar concerts). Skirt around the right side of the church to find...*

Plaça del Pi: While small, this square—named for its *pi* (or pine) tree—has some worthwhile shops. Enjoy checking out the genteel **Josep Roca,** a *ganiveteria* (cutlery shop) selling knives, shaving gear, and other manly items (at #3). Nearby is a small outlet branch of the colorful Barcelona clothing designer, **Custo** (at #2; for the full Custo experience, visit their shop on the Ramblas, at #120). On many days, local food and crafts markets set up on this square.

• *Head up the street immediately left of Josep Roca...*

Carrer de Petritxol: This fun, narrow, characteristic lane (pronounced peht-ree-CHUHL) is decorated with historic tiles. It's a fun combination of art galleries (such as **Sala Parés,** at #5, where Picasso had his first professional exhibition in town—step in and enjoy the latest in 150 years of art exhibits), fancy jewelry shops, and simple local places for hot chocolate and churros or other treats.

For a great *churros con chocolate* break, stop into **Granja La Pallaresa,** near the end of the street on the left (at #11). Elegant, older ladies gather here for the Spanish equivalent of teatime. For a more local treat, try an *ensaimada* (Mallorca-style croissant with powdered sugar) or the *crema catalane* (like a crème brûlée). Three doors further down (at #15) is **Vicens,** a fancy sweets shop specializing in *torró.* They offer generous plates of samples, lots of varieties on sale in small quantities, and a warm welcome.

And if you're looking for handmade-in-Barcelona ballet flats, you'll find them in a rainbow of colors at the family-run **Kokua** (at #18); they also sell bags, with a bigger selection of colors and sizes at their nearby shop at Carrer de la Boquería 30.

• *You'll dead-end onto touristy Carrer de la Portaferrissa. Head one block left to get to the Ramblas, or five blocks right to return to the cathedral. Or retrace your steps, this time poking into side streets to discover more shops.*

More Shops in the Barri Gòtic

The streets described in the above walk are just the beginning. While exploring the many other characteristic lanes of the Barri Gòtic, keep an eye out for these shops (for most of these shop locations, see the "Barri Gòtic Walk" map on page 96).

Sabater Hermanos (abbreviated "Hnos." on the sign) continues a family tradition of making and selling handmade, natural, colorful soaps. The simple but fragrant shop feels like an artisanal Lush. To buy soap and call it a culturally redeemable souvenir, look for the bars shaped like characteristic Barcelona sidewalk tiles (Plaça Sant Felip Neri 1).

Papirum is an inviting, classic, artisan shop selling craft paper, stationery, and hand-bound blank books (Baixada de la Llibreteria 2, run by Dolores Crespo and family).

Som Naturals sells earthy baby and toddler clothing, designed and handmade by locals Dora Garriga and Jordi Cugat. They use 100-percent natural burlap and cotton. Their wares also regularly appear in artisan markets around town (Carrer Santa Anna 37).

La Manual Alpargatera, dating from the 1940s, is an *espardenya* store famous for making and selling these affordable, comfy shoes (7 Carrer d'Avinyó, just off Carrer de Ferran between the Ramblas and Plaça Sant Jaume).

Herbolari Ferran, on Plaça Reial (to the right as you enter the square from the Ramblas), is a fine and aromatic shop of herbs, with fun souvenirs such as top-quality saffron, or *safra*, and a pleasant little café (closed Sat-Sun, downstairs at Plaça Reial 18).

Carrer Ample, the street one block up from the tapas-loaded Carrer de la Mercè (in the lower part of Barri Gòtic—just above the waterfront), feels local but with little bursts of trendy energy. For example, **Papabubble** is a candy shop where you can watch treats being made the old-fashioned way (Carrer Ample 28).

On the other side of the Ramblas (two blocks below Plaça de Catalunya), stroll down skinny **Carrer de Bonsuccés** (it turns into **Carrer d'Elisabets**) and poke into the boutiques along the way (such as the tiny, fashionable clothing store, **Passé Composé,** at #12).

THE EIXAMPLE

This ritzy "uptown" district is home to some of the city's top-end shops. In general, you'll find a lot of big international names along **Passeig de Gràcia,** the main boulevard that runs from Plaça de Catalunya to the Gaudí sights—an area fittingly called the "Golden Quarter" (Quadrat d'Or). Appropriately enough, the "upper end" of Passeig de Gràcia has the fancier shops—Gucci, Luis Vuitton, Escada, Chanel, and so on—while the southern part of the street is relatively "low-end" (Zara, Mango, H&M). One block to the west, **Rambla de Catalunya** holds more local (but still expensive) options: fashion, home decor, jewelry, perfume, and so on. The streets that connect Rambla de Catalunya to Passeig da Gràcia are also home to some fine shops.

Cubiñá, three blocks east and a block south, is a furniture and home-decor shop—worth a peek for its upscale-mod collection, as well as for the Domènech i Montaner building that houses it (Carrer Mallorca 291).

Farther south, the street called **Consell de Cent** has a variety of art galleries (close to Plaça de Catalunya, roughly between Passeig de Gràcia and Carrer d'Enric Granados). And much farther to the west, the broad main boulevard **Diagonal** is another popular shopping zone—especially the stretch between Plaça de Francesc Macià and where it crosses Gran Via de Carles III (at the Maria Cristina Metro stop).

This neighborhood is also home to some fun kitchen stores: Try **Gadgets & Cuina** (Carrer d'Aragó 249) or **The Kitchen Company** (Carrer de Provença 246).

AVINGUDA DEL PORTAL DE L'ANGEL

Barcelona natives do most of their shopping at big department stores. You'll find these and a high concentration of chain stores on one convenient street: Avinguda del Portal de l'Angel, which connects Plaça de Catalunya with the cathedral.

Chain Stores: Chains along this street include Zara, Massimo Dutti (upscale business attire, like Banana Republic), Bershka (teens), Pull and Bear (young adults—sort of the Spanish Gap), Barcelona-based Mango (clothing), Desigual (bold and colorful clothing), Camper shoes (which started in Mallorca), and Yamamay and Women's Secret (the Spanish answer to Victoria's Secret). Most of these chains have several locations scattered around the city, and some even have different offerings based on their location (for instance, the Zara in the Barri Gòtic has more casual clothes, while the one along the ritzy Diagonal street emphasizes business attire).

Department Stores: At the top of Avinguda del Portal de l'Angel, Plaça de Catalunya has a gigantic **El Corte Inglés,** with

everything you can imagine—clothes, housewares, furniture, electronics, bonsai trees, a travel agency, haircuts, and cheap souvenirs (get the complete list by picking up an English directory at their info desk). It also has a supermarket in the basement and a ninth-floor view cafeteria (Mon-Sat 9:30-21:00, until 22:00 in summer, closed Sun). Across the square is **FNAC**—a French department store that sells electronics, music, books, and tickets for major concerts and events (Mon-Sat 10:00-22:00, closed Sun).

LAS ARENAS MALL

While the shops inside it are nothing special, the Las Arenas shopping mall itself is—since it fills Barcelona's repurposed bullring. After Catalunya outlawed bullfighting in 2010, the former *plaça de toros* was converted into a modern mall with chain stores, a food court, a view terrace on top, and an escalator that trundles all the way up through its wide-open atrium (daily 10:00-22:00, don't pay the small fee to take the exterior elevator—the escalators are free, Gran Via de les Corts Catalanes 373-385). Located on Plaça d'Espanya, it's convenient to combine with a visit to the Montjuïc sights (described in the Sights in Barcelona chapter).

NIGHTLIFE IN BARCELONA

Like all of Spain, Barcelona is extremely lively after hours. People head out for dinner at 22:00, then bar-hop or simply wander the streets until well after midnight. Some days it seems that more people are out and about at 2:00 in the morning (party time) than at 2:00 in the afternoon (lunch time). The most "local" thing you can do here after sunset is to explore neighborhood watering holes and find your favorite place to enjoy a glass of wine. I've described several parts of town ideally suited to doing just that. For a musical event, consider taking in a serious performance at a fancy venue (such as the Palace of Catalan Music or the Liceu Opera House), or opt for a jazz, flamenco, or classical guitar show.

Information: The TI hands out the free, monthly, user-friendly *Time Out BCN Guide* and *Visit Barcelona* (both in English, with descriptions of each day's main events and ticket information). The TI's culture website is also helpful: http://lameva.barcelona.cat/barcelonacultura/en. The weekly *Guía del Ocio,* sold at newsstands (or free in some hotel lobbies), is a Spanish-language entertainment listing (with guidelines for English speakers inside the back cover; also available at www.guiadelocio.com). Other resources are the monthly *Barcelona Planning.com* (www.barcelonaplanning.com), quarterly *See Barcelona* (www.seebarcelona.com), and monthly *Barcelona Metropolitan* (www.barcelona-metropolitan.com); all are available for free from the TI.

Palau de la Virreina, an arts-and-culture information office, provides details on Barcelona cultural events—music, opera, and theater (daily 10:00-20:30, Ramblas 99—see the map on page 79, tel. 933-161-000, www.lavirreina.bcn.cat). A ticket desk is next door.

Getting Tickets: Most venues sell tickets through their websites, or you can book through TicketMaster or TelenTrada for most events. You can also get tickets through the box offices in the main El Corte Inglés department store or the giant FNAC electronics store (both on Plaça de Catalunya, extra booking fee), or at the ticket desk in Palau de la Virreina (see previous page).

MUSIC AND DANCE
Concerts
Several classy venues host high-end performances.

The **Palace of Catalan Music** (Palau de la Música Catalana), with one of the finest Modernista interiors in town (see the listing on page 45), offers a full slate of performances, ranging from symphonic to Catalan folk songs to chamber music to flamenco (€20-150 tickets, purchase online or in person, box office open Mon-Sat 9:30-21:00, Sun 10:00-15:00, Carrer Palau de la Música 4, Metro: Urquinaona, box office tel. 902-442-882).

The **Liceu Opera House** (Gran Teatre del Liceu), right in the heart of the Ramblas, is a pre-Modernista, sumptuous venue for opera, dance, children's theater, and concerts (tickets from €10, buy tickets online up to 1.5 hours before show or in person, Ramblas 51, box office just around the corner at Carrer Sant Pau 1, Metro: Liceu, box office tel. 934-859-913, www.liceubarcelona.cat).

Another, much less architecturally interesting venue for classical music is **L'Auditori,** the home of the city's orchestra (boxy modern building northeast of Old City at Lepant 150; Metro: Glòries, Marina, or Monumental; tel. 932-479-300, www.auditori.cat).

Some of Barcelona's top sights host good-quality concerts. Try **La Pedrera** (described later under "Jazz"), **Fundació Joan Miró** (www.fundaciomiro-bcn.org), and **CaixaForum** (https://caixaforum.es/barcelona, choose *"actividades"*).

Touristy Performances of Spanish Clichés
Two famously Spanish types of music—flamenco and Spanish guitar—have little to do with Barcelona or Catalunya, but are performed to keep visitors happy. If you're headed for other parts of Spain where these musical forms are more typical (such as Andalucía for flamenco), you might as well wait until you can experience the real deal. But if this is your only stop in Spain, here are some options.

Flamenco: While flamenco is foreign to Catalunya (locals say that it's like going to see country music in Boston), there are some good places to view this unique Spanish artform. Head to **Palau Dalmases,** in an atmospheric old palace courtyard in the heart of El Born, for the highest-quality performances I've found (€25 includes a drink, daily at 19:30, additional shows Fri-Sun at 21:30, also hosts opera and jazz, Carrer de Montcada 20, tel. 933-100-673, www.palaudalmases.com).

Sights Open Late

Many of Barcelona's major sights are open well into the evening (and the hop-on, hop-off **Tourist Bus** runs until 20:00 daily in summer). If you'd like to extend your sightseeing day, here's where to do it:

Near the Ramblas

Maritime Museum: Daily until 20:00 (*Santa Eulàlia* schooner: April-Oct Tue-Sun until 20:30)

Palau Güell: April-Oct Tue-Sun until 20:00

La Boqueria Market: Mon-Sat until 20:00

Barri Gòtic and El Born

Barcelona Cathedral: Mon-Fri until 19:30, Sat-Sun until 20:00

Gaudí Exhibition Center: March-Oct daily until 20:00

Frederic Marès Museum: Sun until 20:00

Barcelona History Museum: Sun until 20:00

Picasso Museum: Thu until 21:30

Santa Caterina Market: Tue and Thu-Fri until 20:30

Church of Santa Maria del Mar: Daily until 20:30

Eixample and Beyond

Sagrada Família: April-Sept daily until 20:00

La Pedrera (Casa Milà): March-Oct daily until 20:00; also hosts nighttime visits

Casa Batlló: Daily until 21:00

Park Güell: Daily until 20:30 in peak season (May-Aug until 21:30)

Montjuïc and Vicinity

Fundació Joan Miró: Thu until 21:00 year-round, also April-Oct Tue-Wed and Fri-Sat until 20:00

Catalan Art Museum: May-Sept Tue-Sat until 20:00

Magic Fountains: June-Sept Wed-Sun 21:30-22:30, April-May and Oct Thu-Sat 21:00-22:00, winter Thu-Sat 20:00-21:00 (no shows Jan-Feb)

CaixaForum: Daily until 20:00

Las Arenas (Bullring Mall): Shops daily until 22:00, terrace restaurants until 24:00

NIGHTLIFE

Tarantos, on Plaça Reial in the heart of the Barri Gòtic, puts on brief (30 minutes), riveting flamenco performances several times nightly—an easy and inexpensive way to see it. Performances are in a touristy little bar/theater with about 50 seats (€15; nightly at 19:30, 20:30, 21:30, and 22:30; Plaça Reial 17, tel. 933-191-789, go to www.masimas.com and click on "Tarantos").

Another option is the pricey (and relatively high-quality) **Tablao Cordobés** on the Ramblas (€45 includes a drink, €80 includes mediocre buffet dinner and better seats, 3 performances/day, Ramblas 35, tel. 933-175-711, www.tablaocordobes.com).

For flamenco in a concert-hall setting, try one of the Palace of Catalan Music's regular performances (see listing earlier, under "Concerts").

Spanish Guitar: "Masters of Guitar" concerts are offered nearly nightly at 21:00 in the Barri Gòtic's Church of Santa Maria del Pi (€23 at the door, €4 less if you buy at least 3 hours ahead or online—look for ticket sellers in front of church and scattered around town, Plaça del Pi 7; at Carrer de Ferran 28; tel. 647-514-513, www.maestrosdelaguitarra.com). The same company also does occasional concerts in the Palace of Catalan Music (€39-45). Similar guitar concerts are performed at the Church of Santa Anna featuring different artists (tel. 662-698-547, www.spanishguitarbarcelona.es, see page 96).

Jazz

On summer weekends, a classy option is the **"Summer Nights at La Pedrera"** concerts at Gaudí's Modernista masterpiece in the Eixample. This evening rooftop concert series generally features live jazz and also gives you the chance to see the La Pedrera (Casa Milà) rooftop illuminated (€27, late June-early Sept Thu-Sat at 22:30, book advance tickets online or by phone, tel. 902-101-212, www.lapedrera.com).

Hotel Casa Fuster, a Modernista landmark designed by Lluís Domènech i Montaner, is a luxury hotel that hosts a weekly Woody Allen-inspired jazz night (€19, Thu 21:00-23:00, in the basement of Café Vienés, reservations recommended, across Avinguda Diagonal from the Eixample at Passeig de Gràcia 132, tel. 932-553-006, www.hotelcasafuster.com).

Jamboree jazz and dance club, right on Plaça Reial, features two jazz sets nightly, at 20:00 and 22:00, in a cellar under brick vaults (€12-25 in advance, a euro or two more at the door, check schedule online or stop by to pick one up, Plaça Reial 17, Metro: Liceu, tel. 933-191-789, go to www.masimas.com and click on "Jamboree").

Also consider the divey **Harlem Jazz Club** (€6-10, a couple of blocks off Plaça Reial at Comtessa de Sobradiel 8, tel. 933-100-755, www.harlemjazzclub.es).

AFTER-HOURS HANGOUT NEIGHBORHOODS

Most Barcelonans' idea of "nightlife" is hopping from bar to bar with a circle of friends, while nibbling tapas and enjoying drinks. The streets are jammed with people. In general, the weekend pro-

NIGHTLIFE

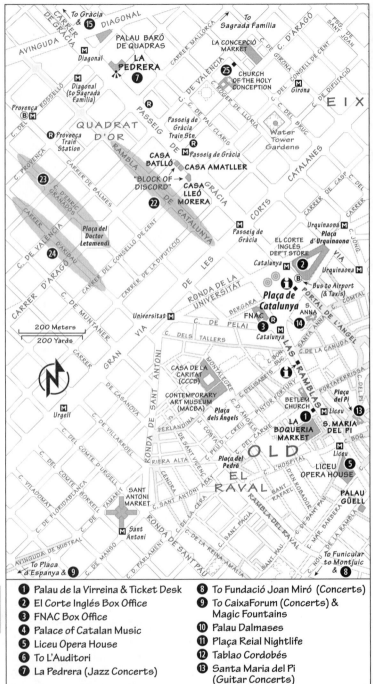

1 Palau de la Virreina & Ticket Desk

2 El Corte Inglés Box Office

3 FNAC Box Office

4 Palace of Catalan Music

5 Liceu Opera House

6 To L'Auditori

7 La Pedrera (Jazz Concerts)

8 To Fundació Joan Miró (Concerts)

9 To CaixaForum (Concerts) & Magic Fountains

10 Palau Dalmases

11 Plaça Reial Nightlife

12 Tablao Cordobés

13 Santa Maria del Pi (Guitar Concerts)

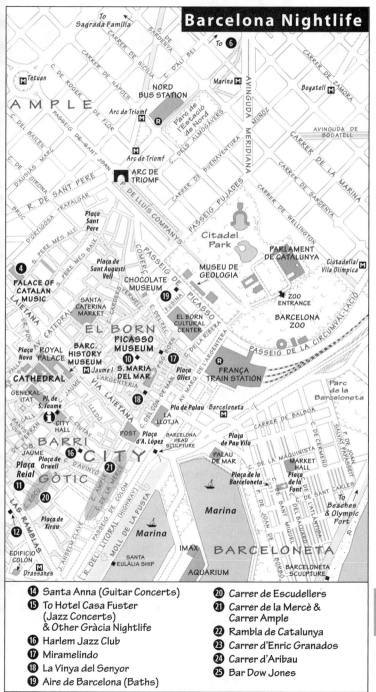

Barcelona Nightlife

To Sagrada Família

To 6

Tetuan

NORD BUS STATION

Marina

Bogatell

AVINGUDA MERIDIANA

MUÑOZ

AVINGUDA DE BOGATELL

Arc de Triomf

Parc de l'Estació de Nord

Arc de Triomf

ARC DE TRIOMF

Plaça Sant Pere

Citadel Park

PARLAMENT DE CATALUNYA

Ciutadella/ Vila Olímpica

Plaça de Sant Augustí Vell

MUSEU DE GEOLOGIA

ZOO ENTRANCE

4
PALACE OF CATALAN MUSIC

CHOCOLATE MUSEUM 19

BARCELONA ZOO

SANTA CATERINA MARKET

EL BORN CULTURAL CENTER

EL BORN

Plaça Nova

ROYAL PALACE

BARC. HISTORY MUSEUM

PICASSO MUSEUM 10

S. MARIA DEL MAR

17 Plaça Olies

FRANÇA TRAIN STATION

Parc de la Barceloneta

CATHEDRAL

Jaume I

18

Pla de Palau

Barceloneta

GENERAL- ITAT

Pl. de S. Jaume

LA LLOTJA

CITY HALL

POST

Plaça d'A. López

BARCELONA HEAD SCULPTURE

Plaça de Pau Vila

BARRI

16

Plaça de Orwell

21

PALAU DE MAR

Plaça de la Barceloneta

MARKET HALL

Plaça de la Font

CITY GÒTIC

Plaça Reial

11

20

Plaça de Xirau

Marina

To Beaches & Olympic Port

12

EDIFICIO COLÓN

Drassanes

Marina

SANTA EULÀLIA SHIP

IMAX

BARCELONETA

AQUARIUM

BARCELONETA SCULPTURE

14 Santa Anna (Guitar Concerts)

15 To Hotel Casa Fuster (Jazz Concerts) & Other Gràcia Nightlife

16 Harlem Jazz Club

17 Miramelindo

18 La Vinya del Senyor

19 Aire de Barcelona (Baths)

20 Carrer de Escudellers

21 Carrer de la Mercè & Carrer Ample

22 Rambla de Catalunya

23 Carrer d'Enric Granados

24 Carrer d'Aribau

25 Bar Dow Jones

gression (Thu-Sat) goes like this: dinner at around 22:00; a music club for cocktails and DJ music from midnight; then, at about 2:00 or 3:00 in the morning, hit the discos until dawn. The following neighborhoods let you join in this social ritual.

El Born

Passeig del Born, a broad park-like strip stretching from the Church of Santa Maria del Mar up to the old market hall, is lined with inviting bars and nightspots. The side streets also teem with options. Wander to find a place that appeals to you.

Right on Passeig del Born is **Miramelindo,** a local favorite—mellow yet convivial, with two floors of woody ambience and a minty aura from all those mojitos the bartenders are mashing up (Passeig del Born 15). **Palau Dalmases,** in the atmospheric court-yard of an old palace, slings cocktails when it's not hosting flamenco shows (described earlier). **La Vinya del Senyor** is a fine place for a glass of high-quality wine out on the square in front of the Church of Santa Maria del Mar.

The **Aire de Barcelona** Arab-style thermal baths, across from Citadel Park, are open late and have great style. They are ideal for recovering from a busy day of sightseeing (€38-45/person for 1.5 hours, massage also possible; reserve ahead—a week ahead for weeknights, a month ahead for weekends; Passeig Picasso 22, tel. 902-555-789, www.airedebarcelona.com).

Plaça Reial and Nearby

This elegant-feeling square, just off the Ramblas in the Barri Gòtic, has a trendy charm. It bustles with popular bars and restaurants offering inflated prices at pleasant outdoor tables. While not a great place to eat (the only one worth seriously considering for a meal is the recommended **Les Quinze Nits**), this is a great place to sip a before- or after-dinner drink. **Bar Club Ocaña,** at #13, has a dilapi-dated-mod interior, a see-through industrial kitchen that serves up

tapas, rickety-chic secondhand tables out on the square, and an-other cocktail bar downstairs (open nightly, can reserve a table on-line at www.ocana.cat). Or there's always the student option: Buy a cheap €1 beer from a convenience store (you'll find several just off the square, including a few along Carrer dels Escudellers, just south of Plaça Reial), then grab a free spot on the square, either sitting on one of the few fixed chairs, perched along the rim of the fountain, or simply leaning up against a palm tree.

Plaça Reial is also home to the **Tarantos** flamenco bar and **Jamboree** jazz club (both described earlier). You'll find a variety of nightclubs here, including the hip **Sidecar Factory Club** (at #7, often live music, www.sidecarfactoryclub.com) and the hidden, mellow, pipe-happy **Barcelona Pipa Club** (at #3—find and ring the doorbell to get inside, this member's club opens to the public around 22:00, www.bpipaclub.com).

Wandering the streets near the square leads to other nightlife options. **Carrer de Escudellers** is a significantly rougher scene—a few trendy options are mixed in with several sketchy dives. Much closer to the harbor, **Carrer de la Mercè** (described in the Eating in Barcelona chapter) has its share of salty sailors' pubs and more youthful bars. The next street up, **Carrer Ample,** has a similar scene.

Barceloneta

A broad beach stretches for miles from the former fishermen's quarter at Barceloneta to the Fòrum. Every 100 yards or so is a *chiringuito*—a shack selling drinks and light snacks. Originally these sold seafood, but now they keep locals and tourists well-lubricated. It's a very fun, lively scene on a balmy summer evening and a nice way to escape the claustrophobic confines of the Old City to enjoy some sea air and the day's final sun rays.

Barceloneta itself has a broad promenade facing the harbor, lined with interchangeable seafood restaurants. But the best beach experience is beyond the tip of Barceloneta. From here, a double-decker boardwalk runs the length of the beach, with a cool walkway up above and a series of fine seafood restaurants with romantic candlelit beachfront seating tucked down below. Pricey but well-regarded places featuring high-quality Catalan cuisine are **Agua, Ca la Nuri,** and **Arenal.** Farther along, **Carpe Diem Lounge Club** (a.k.a. CDLC) is a fun Turkish-themed bar with cozy lounging sofas—ideal for a post-dinner drink; later, it becomes an edgier disco.

Around Frank Gehry's glittering fish sculpture (at the former Olympic village) are several popular discos, crowded with twentysomethings (including the famous—and exclusive—**Opium Mar,** a haunt of Barça footballers and other celebrities). Beyond the beach, at the Olympic port, you'll find more bars with chill-out music (which later turn into livelier discos).

Montjuïc

With a little hustle, in summer it's possible to string together a fun evening of memorable views from the Montjuïc hilltop. Start with sweeping city vistas as you ride the Aeri del Port cable car (catch it at the tip of the Barceloneta peninsula; see page 60) up to the park's Miramar viewpoint. From there, head up to Montjuïc Castle on foot for more breathtaking views. Finally, wind your way around the hilltop to the Catalan Art Museum and reward yourself with a drink at its terrace café—a prime spot for taking in the Magic Fountains show (for details, see the listing on page 70; café open Tue-Sun 10:00-19:30 but closing time varies with fountain schedule, can close as late as 23:00 in summer). For a splurge, consider dinner at the museum's **Òleum Restaurant** (open until 23:30), which also overlooks the fountains and the entire 1929 Expo site.

The Eixample

Barcelona's upscale uptown isn't quite as lively or funky as some other neighborhoods, but a few streets have some fine watering holes. Walk along the inviting, park-like **Rambla de Catalunya,** or a couple of blocks over, along **Carrer d'Enric Granados** and **Carrer d'Aribau** (near the epicenter of the Eixample's gay community); all of these streets are speckled with cocktail bars offering breezy outdoor seating. In the opposite direction (east of Passeig de Gràcia), **Bar Dow Jones**—popular with the American expat student crowd—has a clever gimmick: Drink prices rise and fall like the stock market (Carrer del Bruc 97).

Gràcia

A bit farther flung, and more local-feeling because of it, the Gràcia neighborhood sits between the Eixample and Park Güell. Known for its design schools and its international art-house cinema (the Cines Verdi, www.cines-verdi.com/barcelona), it's the unpretentious but intellectual corner of town. Though it lacks the twisty-Gothic-lanes ambience of the Old City, Gràcia feels more like a small town (which it was, before it was swallowed up by an expanding Barcelona). It's popular with students—both local and international—and can be a bit rowdy. The district is even more vibrant in August, when it hosts the Festa Major de Gràcia, with street music everywhere (see page 26).

The most interesting stretch of Gràcia is squeezed between two Metro stops: Fontana, on the L3 (green) line; and Joanic, on the L4 (yellow) line. Here's a handy bar-crawl route: From the Fontana stop, exit and turn left, heading down the shop-lined Carrer d'Astúries. After crossing the busy Carrer del Torrent de l'Olla, keep going straight two short blocks to **Carrer de Verdi.** You'll find several nightspots up and down this street, and a block over, at **Plaça de la Virreina** (where several places fill the square in front of the church with outdoor tables). From there you can head down Carrer de Torrijos, with more options—including **Café Salambo,** with an Art Deco vibe (at #51). A right turn at Carrer de Ramón y Cajal leads you (in three blocks) to your grand finale, **Plaça del Sol,** the epicenter of Gràcia nightlife.

Tibidabo

Many people enjoy heading up to Tibidabo for drinks with a great view—ideal for watching the sunset. At the top of the Tramvía Blau (blue trolley)—which is also the bottom of the Tibidabo funicular—you'll find two places: **Mirabé** (nightly from 19:00, Manuel Arnús 2) and **Mirablau** (Plaça Dr. Andreu). While this probably isn't worth the long trip from downtown (unless you're a panorama seeker), it's handy to combine with a visit to Tibidabo or Park Güell.

Come here for a pricey drink with a view—not for dinner. And remember that the bus back downtown (bus #196) stops running at 22:00; after that, take a taxi.

BARCELONA CONNECTIONS

This chapter covers Barcelona's airports, main train station, cruise port, and main bus station.

I don't advise driving in Barcelona—thanks to its excellent public transportation and taxis, you won't need a car here, and the parking fees are outrageously expensive (for example, the lot behind La Boqueria Market charges upwards of €25/day).

By Plane

Most flights use Barcelona's **El Prat de Llobregat Airport;** a few budget flights use a smaller airstrip 60 miles away, called **Girona–Costa Brava Airport.** Information on both airports can be found on the official Spanish airport website, www.aena-aeropuertos.es.

EL PRAT DE LLOBREGAT AIRPORT
Barcelona's primary airport is eight miles southwest of town (airport code: BCN, info tel. 913-211-000). It has two large terminals, linked by shuttle buses. Terminal 1 serves Air France, Air Europa, American, British Airways, Delta, Iberia, Lufthansa, United, Vueling, and others. EasyJet, Ryanair, and minor airlines use the older Terminal 2, which is divided into sections A, B, and C.

Terminal 1 and the bigger sections of Terminal 2 (A and B) each have a post office, a pharmacy, a left-luggage office, plenty of good cafeterias in the gate areas, and ATMs.

Getting Between the Airport and Downtown
To get downtown cheaply and quickly, take the bus or train (about 30 minutes on either).

By Bus: The Aerobus (#A1 and #A2, corresponding with Terminals 1 and 2) picks up immediately outside the arrivals lobby of both terminals and makes several stops downtown, including at Plaça de Catalunya, near many of my recommended hotels (returning from downtown, buses leave from in front of El Corte Inglés). Either way it's very easy: Buses depart about every five minutes (30-40 minutes, runs from 5:30 to 24:00, buy €6 ticket from driver, tel. 902-100-104, www.aerobusbcn.com).

By Train: The Renfe train (on the "R2 Nord" Rodalies line) leaves from Terminal 2 and involves more walking. Head up the escalators and down the long orange-roofed skybridge to reach the station (2/hour at about :08 and :38 past the hour, 20 minutes to Sants station, 25 minutes to Passeig de Gràcia station—near Plaça de Catalunya; €4.10 or covered by T10 Card—described on page 22—which you can purchase from machines at the airport train station). If you are arriving or departing from Terminal 1, you will have to use the airport shuttle bus to connect with the train station, so leave extra time (10 buses/hour, 7-minute ride between terminals).

Long-term plans call for the Renfe train and eventually the AVE to be extended to Terminal 1. Stay tuned.

By Metro: Take Metro's L9 Sud (orange) line from either Terminal 1 or 2, to Zona Universitária, then transfer to the L3 (green) line and ride to a downtown stop (Passeig de Gràcia, Plaça de Catalunya, or Liceu). To reach the airport from downtown via Metro, take line L3 to Zona Universitária, and transfer to line L9 in the direction of Aeroport T1 (runs about every 10 minutes 5:00 until late; 20-30 minute ride; use €4.60 *Billet Aeroport* or any "Hola BCN!" travel card—the T10 and single-ride Metro tickets do not work for this ride).

By Taxi: A taxi between the airport and downtown costs about €32 (including €3 airport supplement). For good service, you can round up to the next euro on the fare—but keep in mind that the Spanish don't tip cabbies. To get to the cruise port, ask for *"tarifa cuatro"*—a €39 flat rate between the airport and the cruise port, all fees included.

GIRONA-COSTA BRAVA AIRPORT
Some budget airlines use this airport, located 60 miles north of Barcelona near Girona (airport code: GRO, tel. 972-186-600, www.aena-aeropuertos.es). If you're arriving on a Ryanair flight, you can take a **bus** (#604), run by Ryanair and operated by Sagalés, to the Barcelona Nord bus station (departs airport about 20-25 minutes after each arriving flight, 1.25 hours, €16, tel. 902-361-550, www.sagales.com). You can also take a Sagalés bus (#602, about every 10 minutes, 1.5 hours, €2.75) or a taxi (€25) to the town of Girona, then catch a train to Barcelona (at least hourly, 1.5

hours, €15-20). A taxi between the Girona airport and Barcelona costs at least €130.

CHEAP FLIGHTS

Check the reasonable flights from Barcelona to Sevilla or Madrid. **Vueling** is Iberia's most popular discount airline (tel. 902-333-933, www.vueling.com). Other airlines that fly to Madrid include **Iberia** (tel. 902-400-500, www.iberia.com) and **Air Europa** (tel. 902-401-501 or 932-983-907, www.aireuropa.com). For more information on flights within Europe, see the Practicalities chapter.

By Train

Virtually all trains end up at Barcelona's **Sants train station,** west of the Old City. AVE trains from Madrid go only to Sants sta-

tion. But many other trains also pass through other stations en route, such as **França station** (between the El Born and Barceloneta neighborhoods), or the downtown **Passeig de Gràcia** or **Plaça de Catalunya** stations (which are also Metro stops— and very close to most of my recommended hotels). Figure out which stations your train stops at (ask the conductor), and get off at the one most convenient to your hotel.

SANTS TRAIN STATION

Barcelona's big white main train station offers many services. In the large lobby area, you'll find a TI, ATMs, a world of handy shops and eateries, pay WCs, car-rental kiosks, and, in the side concourse, a classy, quiet Sala Club lounge for travelers with first-class reservations. Sants is the only Barcelona station with luggage storage (€6/up to 2 hours, €10/day, daily 5:30-23:00, follow signs to *consigna*; go toward track 14, then exit the main building toward parking lot and go down to level -1).

In the vast main hall is a very long wall of ticket windows. Figure out which one you need before you wait in line (all are labeled in English). Generally, windows 1-7 (on the left) are for local commuter and *media distancia* trains, such as to Sitges; windows 8-21 handle advance tickets for long-distance *(larga distancia)* trains beyond Catalunya; windows 22-26 give information—go here first if you're not sure which window you want; and windows 27-31 sell tickets for long-distance trains leaving today. These window assignments can shift in the off-season. The information booths by windows 1 and 21 can help you find the right line and can provide some train schedules.

Scattered nearby are train-ticket vending machines. The red-and-gray machines sell tickets for local and *media distancia* trains within Catalunya. The purple machines are for national Renfe trains; these machines can also print out prereserved tickets if you have a confirmation code. And the orange machines sell local *Rodalies* train tickets. There are usually attendants around the machines to help you.

An easier option for English-speaking travelers is to buy your tickets at the travel agencies inside El Corte Inglés department stores. See page 308 for more info.

Getting Downtown: To reach the center of Barcelona, take a train or the Metro. To ride the subway, follow signs for the Metro (red *M*), and hop on the L3 (green) or L5 (blue) line, both of which link to useful points in town. Purchase tickets for the Metro at touch-screen machines near the tracks (where you can also buy the cost-saving T10 Card, explained on page 22).

To zip downtown even faster (just five minutes), you can take any Rodalies de Catalunya suburban train from track 8 (R1, R3, or R4) to Plaça de Catalunya (departs at least every 10 minutes). Your long-distance Renfe train ticket comes with a complimentary ride on Rodalies, as long as you use it within three hours before or after your travels. Look for a code on your ticket labeled *Combinat Rodalies* or *Combinado Cercanías*. Go to the orange commuter ticket machines, touch *Combinat Rodalies,* type in your code, and the machine will print your ticket. There is usually an attendant around to help you.

TRAIN CONNECTIONS

Unless otherwise noted, all of the trains listed below depart from Sants station; however, remember that some trains also stop at other stations more convenient to the downtown tourist zone: França station, Passeig de Gràcia, or Plaça de Catalunya. Figure out if your train stops at these stations (and board there) to save yourself the trip to Sants.

If departing from the downtown Passeig de Gràcia station, where three Metro lines converge with the rail line, you might find the underground tunnels confusing. You can't access the Renfe station directly from some of the entrances. Use the northern entrances to this station (rather than the southern "Consell de Cent" entrance, which is closest to Plaça de Catalunya).

Train info: Tel. 912-320-320, www.renfe.com.

From Barcelona by Train to Madrid: The AVE train to Madrid is faster than flying (when you consider that you're zipping from downtown to downtown). The train departs at least hourly. The nonstop train is a little more expensive but faster (€130, 2.5 hours) than the train that makes a few stops (€110, 3 hours). Regular reserved AVE tickets can be prepurchased (often with a discount) at the Renfe website and printed from an email or at the station. You can also download a ticket QR code on a smartphone. If you have a rail pass, most trains require paid reservations; see the "Transportation" section of the Practicalities chapter.

From Barcelona by Train to: Sitges (departs from both Passeig de Gràcia and Sants, 4/hour, 40 minutes), **Montserrat** (departs from Plaça d'Espanya—*not* from Sants, 1-2/hour, 1 hour, €22 round-trip, includes cable car or rack train to monastery—see details on page 232), **Figueres** (hourly, 1 hour via AVE or Alvia to Figueres-Vilafant; hourly, 2 hours via local trains to Figueres station), **Sevilla** (2/day direct, more with transfer in Madrid, 5.5 hours), **Granada** (2/day, 8 hours via AVE and connecting bus, transfer in Antequera), **Córdoba** (4/day direct, 5 hours, many more with transfer in Madrid), **Salamanca** (6/day, 7 hours, change in Madrid from Atocha station to Chamartín station via Metro or *cercanías* train; also 1/day with a change in Valladolid, 8.5 hours), **San Sebastián** (2/day direct, 6 hours), **Málaga** (8/day via AVE, 6.5 hours; some with transfer), **Lisbon** (no direct trains, head to Madrid and then catch night train to Lisbon, 17 hours—or fly).

From Barcelona by Train to France: Direct high-speed trains run to **Paris** (2-4/day, 6.5 hours), **Lyon** (1/day, 5 hours), and **Toulouse** (1/day, 3 hours), and there are more connections with transfers.

By Bus

Most buses depart from the Nord bus station at Metro: Arc de Triomf, but confirm when researching schedules (www.barcelonanord. com). Destinations served by Alsa buses (www.alsa.es) include **Madrid** and **Madrid's Barajas Airport** (nearly hourly, 8 hours), and **Salamanca** (2/day, 12 hours). Sarfa buses (www.sarfa.com) serve many **coastal resorts,** including **Cadaqués** (1-2/day, 3 hours). Reservations are smart for long-distance destinations, especially during the busy summer season.

The Mon-Bus leaves from the university and Plaça d'Espanya in downtown Barcelona to **Sitges** (2/hour, 1 hour, www.monbus. cat). One bus departs daily for the **Montserrat** monastery, leaving from Carrer de Viriat near Sants station (1.5 hours, see page 234).

By Cruise Ship

Cruise ships arrive in Barcelona at one of three ports, all just southwest of the Old City, beneath Montjuïc. If your trip includes cruising beyond Barcelona, consider my guidebook, *Rick Steves Mediterranean Cruise Ports.*

Most cruise ships arrive in Barcelona at the **Moll Adossat/ Muelle Adosado** port, about two miles from the bottom of the Ramblas. This port has four modern, airport-like terminals (lettered A through D); most have a café, shops, and TI kiosk; some have Wi-Fi and other services. Two other terminals are far less commonly used: the **World Trade Center,** just  off the southern end of the Ramblas (a 10-minute walk from the Columbus Monument), and **Moll de la Costa,** tucked just beneath Montjuïc (ride the free, private shuttle bus to World Trade Center; from there, it's a short walk or taxi ride to the Columbus Monument).

Getting Downtown: From any of the cruise terminals, it's easy to reach the Ramblas. **Taxis** meet arriving ships outside terminal building exits (about €15-20 to downtown, as much as €10 more in heavy traffic; €3.10 cruise-port surcharge). To get to the airport, ask for *"tarifa cuatro"*—a €39 flat rate between the airport and the cruise port, all fees included. Taxis on this rate must use the most direct route or face fines.

You can also take a **shuttle bus** from Moll Adossat/Muelle Adosado to the bottom of the Ramblas, then walk or hop on public transportation to various sights. The blue *Cruise Bus* departs from the parking lot in front of each of the port's four terminals and drops you right on the waterfront near the Columbus Monument (€4 round-trip, €3 one-way, 2-3/hour, timed to cruise ship arrival, 5-15 minutes, tel. 932-986-000). The return bus to the port leaves from where you were dropped off (look for a covered bus stop bench and blue-and-white sign reading *Cruise Bus*).

DAY TRIPS FROM BARCELONA

Montserrat • Figueres • Cadaqués • Sitges

Four fine sights are day-trip temptations from Barcelona. Pilgrims with hiking boots head 1.5 hours into the mountains for the most sacred spot in Catalunya: Montserrat. Fans of Surrealism can enjoy a fantasy in Dalí-land by combining a stop at the Dalí Theater-Museum in Figueres (one to two hours from Barcelona) with a day or two in the classy, often sleepy port-town getaway of Cadaqués (pictured above, an hour from Figueres). Or for a quick escape from the city, head 40 minutes south to the charming and free-spirited beach town of Sitges.

Montserrat

Montserrat—the "serrated mountain"—rocks dramatically up from the valley floor northwest of Barcelona. With its unique rock formations, a mountaintop monastery (also called Montserrat), and spiritual connection with the Catalan people, it's a popular day trip. This has been Catalunya's  most important pilgrimage site for a thousand years. Hymns explain how the mountain was carved by little angels with golden saws. Geologists blame nature at work.

Once upon a time, there was no mountain. A river flowed here, laying down silt that solidified into sedimentary layers of hard rock. Ten million years ago, the continents shifted, and the land around the rock massif sank, exposing this series of peaks that

reach upward to 4,000 feet. Over time, erosion pocked the face with caves and cut vertical grooves near the top, creating the famous serrated look.

The monastery is nestled in the jagged peaks at 2,400 feet, but it seems higher because of the way the rocky massif rises out of nowhere. The air is certainly fresher than in Barcelona. In a quick day trip, you can view the mountain from its base, ride a funicular up to the top of the world, tour the basilica and museum, touch a Black Virgin's orb, hike down to a sacred cave, and listen to Gregorian chants by the world's oldest boys' choir.

Montserrat's monastery is Benedictine, and its 30 monks carry on its spiritual tradition. Since 1025, the slogan *"ora et labora"* ("prayer and work") has pretty much summed up life for a monk here.

The Benedictines welcome visitors—both pilgrims and tourists—and offer this travel tip: Please remember that the most important part of your Montserrat visit is not enjoying the architecture, but rather discovering the religious, cultural, historical, social, and environmental values that together symbolically express the life of the Catalan people.

GETTING TO MONTSERRAT

Barcelona is connected to the valley below Montserrat by a convenient train; from there, a cable car or rack railway (your choice) takes you up to the mountaintop. You have to decide whether to take the cable car or the rack railway when you buy your ticket in Barcelona—see the "Tickets to Montserrat" sidebar. Both options are similar in cost and take about the same amount of time. (It's about 1.5 hours each way from downtown Barcelona to the monastery.)

Driving or taking the bus round out your options.

By Train Plus Cable Car or Rack Railway

Trains leave from Barcelona's Plaça d'Espanya to Montserrat. Take the Metro to Espanya, then follow signs for Montserrat (showing a graphic of a train and the *FGC* symbol—for Ferrocarrils de la Generalitat de Catalunya) through the tunnels to the FGC station. Once there, check the overhead screens or ask for help (staff are usually at the ticket machines) to find the track for train line R5 (direction: Manresa, 1-2/hour—usually at :36 and/or :56).

Hang onto your train ticket; you'll need it to exit the FGC station when you return to Plaça d'Espanya. You'll ride about an hour on the train. As you reach the base of the mountain, get out at the Montserrat-Aeri station for the cable car, or continue another few minutes to the next station—Monistrol de Montserrat (or simply "Monistrol de M.")—for the rack railway.

Cable Car or Rack Train? For the sake of scenery and fun, I enjoy the little German-built cable car more than the rack railway. Departures are more frequent (4/hour rather than hourly on the railway), but because the cable car is small, you may wait a while to get on (up to an hour when crowded). If you're afraid of heights, take the rack train. Paying extra (about €5) to ride both isn't worthwhile.

Cable Car, from Montserrat-Aeri Station: Departing the train, follow signs to the cable-car station (covered by your train or combo-ticket; 4/hour, 5-minute trip, daily 10:00-19:00, www.aeridemontserrat.com). Don't linger on the platform: Make your way to the cable car quickly, or you may have to wait to go up.

On the way back down, cable cars depart from the monastery

Tickets to Montserrat

Various combo-tickets cover your journey to Montserrat, as well as some sights there. All begin with the train from Barcelona's Plaça d'Espanya and include either the cable car or rack railway—you'll have to specify one or the other when you buy the ticket (same price for either option). You can't go one way and come back the other unless you pay extra (about €5) for the leg that's not included in your ticket.

The basic option is to buy a **train ticket** to Montserrat (€22 round-trip, includes cable car or rack railway to monastery, Eurail pass not valid, tel. 932-051-515, www.fgc.es). Note that if you buy this ticket in Barcelona, then decide at Montserrat that you want to use the funiculars to go higher up the mountain or to the Sacred Cave, you can buy a €16.50 ticket covering both funiculars at the TI or at either funicular.

If you plan to do some sightseeing once at Montserrat, it makes sense to spend a little more on one of two combo-tickets offered by the train company: The €35 **Trans Montserrat** ticket includes your round-trip Metro ride in Barcelona to and from the train station, the train trip, the cable car or rack railway, unlimited trips on the two funiculars at Montserrat, and entry to the disappointing audiovisual presentation. The €54 **Tot Montserrat** ticket includes all of this, plus the good Museum of Montserrat and a self-service lunch (served daily 12:00-16:00). If you expect to do it all, you'll save at least €5 with either of these combo-tickets. But during the off-season, ask the TI whether one of the funiculars or the cable car is closed for maintenance; if so, the combo-ticket may not be worth it (or available).

You can get advice about your ticket choice and return schedules at the Montserrat Cremallera (rack railway) or cable-car information booths at Plaça d'Espanya station (daily 8:00-14:00). Then purchase any of these options from the ticket machines—if you need help, ask one of the TI officials standing by in the morning. To use your included round-trip Metro ride to get *to* the station, buy the ticket in advance at the Plaça de Catalunya TI. If you buy your ticket online (www.montserratvisita.com), you must take your purchase voucher to the Cremallera rack-railway information booth during open hours (daily 8:00-14:00) to receive an actual ticket. Combo-tickets may be available at the Barcelona TI's online shop (http://bcnshop.barcelonaturisme.com).

every 15 minutes; make sure to give yourself enough time to catch a Barcelona-bound train (these leave at :05 and :45 past the hour Mon-Fri, only at :45 Sat-Sun).

Rack Railway (Cremallera), from Monistrol de Montserrat Station: From this station you can catch the Cremallera rack railway up to the monastery (covered by your train or com-

bo-ticket; cheaper off-season, hourly, 20-minute trip, www.
cremallerademontserrat.com). On the return trip, this train departs the monastery at :15 past the hour, allowing you to catch the
Barcelona-bound train leaving Monistrol de Montserrat at :45 past
the hour. The last convenient connection leaves the monastery at
19:15 (Sat-Sun at 20:15). Confirm the schedule when you arrive,
as specific times can change year to year. Note that there is one
intermediate stop on this line (Monistrol-Vila, at a large parking
garage), but—either coming or going—you want to stay on until
the end of the line.

By Car

Once drivers get out of Barcelona (Road A-2, then C-55), it's a
short 30-minute drive to the base of the mountain, then a 10-min-
ute series of switchbacks to the actual site (where you can find parking for €5/day). It may be easier to park your car down below and
ride the cable car or rack railway up; there is plenty of free parking
at the Monistrol-Vila rack-railway station (cable car—€7 one-way,
€11 round-trip; rack railway—€6.90 one-way, €11.50 round-trip,
€16 version also includes Museum of Montserrat).

By Bus

One bus per day connects downtown Barcelona directly to the
monastery at Montserrat (departs from Carrer de Viriat near Barcelona's Sants station daily at 9:15, returns from the monastery to
Barcelona at 18:00 June-Sept, at 17:00 Oct-May, €5 each way, 1.5
hours, operated by Autocares Julià, www.autocaresjulia.es). You
can also take a four-hour **bus tour** offered by the Barcelona Guide
Bureau (€52, leaves Mon-Sat at 15:00 from Plaça de Catalunya;
see page 28). However, since the other options are scenic, fun, and
relatively easy, the only reason to take a bus is to avoid transfers.

Orientation to Montserrat

When you arrive at the base of the mountain, look up the rock face
to find the cable-car line, the monastery near the top, and the tiny
building midway up (marking the Sacred Cave).

However you make your way up to the Montserrat monastery,
it's easy to get oriented once you arrive at the top. Everything is
within a few minutes' walk of your entry point. All of the transit
options—including the rack railway and cable car—converge at the
big train station. Above those are both funicular stations: one up
to the ridge top, the other down to the Sacred Cave trail. Across
the street is the TI, and above that (either straight up the stairs or
up the ramp around the left side) is the main square. To the right
of the station, a long road leads along the cliff to the parking lot; a

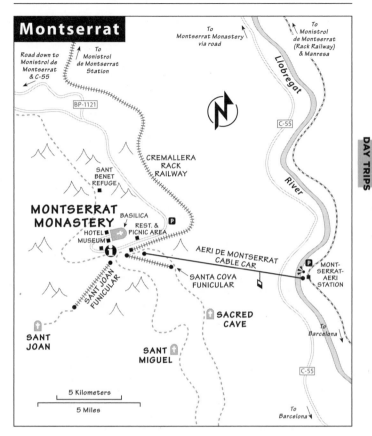

humble farmers market along here sells *mel y mató,* a characteristic Catalan cheese with honey.

Crowd-Beating Tips: Arrive early or late, as tour groups mob the place midday. Crowds are less likely on weekdays and worst on Sundays.

TOURIST INFORMATION

The square below the basilica houses a helpful TI, right across from the rack-railway station (daily from 9:00, closes just after last train heads down—roughly 18:45, Sat-Sun until 20:00; tel. 938-777-701, www.montserratvisita.com). A good audioguide, available only at the TI, describes the general site and basilica (€7 includes book; €16 includes entrance to museum, bland audiovisual presentation, and book). If you're a hiker, ask for the handout outlining hiking options here. Trails offer spectacular views (on clear days) to the Mediterranean and even (on clearer days) to the Pyrenees.

The audiovisual center (upstairs from the TI) provides some

The History of Montserrat

The first hermit monks built huts at Montserrat around AD 900. By 1025, a monastery was founded. The Montserrat Escolania, or Choir School, soon followed, and is considered to be the oldest music school in Europe (they still perform—see "Choir Concert" at the end of "Sights in Montserrat").

Legend has it that in medieval times, some shepherd children saw lights and heard songs coming from the mountain. They traced the sounds to a cave (now called the Sacred Cave, or Santa Cova), where they found the Black Virgin statue (La Moreneta), making the monastery a pilgrim magnet.

In 1811 Napoleon's invading French troops destroyed Montserrat's buildings, though the Black Virgin, hidden away by monks, survived. Then, in the 1830s, the Spanish royalty—tired of dealing with pesky religious orders—dissolved the monasteries and convents.

But in the 1850s, the monks returned as part of Catalunya's (and Europe's) renewed Romantic appreciation for all things medieval and nationalistic. (Montserrat's revival coincided with other traditions born out of rejuvenated Catalan pride: the much-loved FC Barcelona soccer team; Barcelona's Palace of Catalan Music; and even the birth of local sparkling wine, *cava*.) Montserrat's basilica and monastery were reconstructed and became, once more, the strongly beating spiritual and cultural heart of the Catalan people.

Then came Francisco Franco, the dictatorial leader who wanted a monolithic Spain. To him Montserrat represented Catalan rebelliousness. During Franco's long rule, from 1939 to 1975, the *sardana* dance was still illegally performed here (but with a different name), and literature was published in the outlawed Catalan language. In 1970, 300 intellectuals demonstrating for more respect for human rights in Spain were locked up in the monastery for several days by Franco's police.

But now Franco is history. The 1990s brought another phase of rebuilding (after a forest fire and rain damage), and the Montserrat community is thriving once again, unafraid to display its pride for the Catalan people, culture, and faith.

cultural and historical perspective—and an entrance to their big gift shop. The lame interactive exhibit—nowhere near as exciting as the mountains and basilica outside—includes touch screens and a seven-minute video (available in English when there is enough demand). Learn about the mountain's history, and get a glimpse into the daily lives of the monastery's resident monks (€5, covered by Trans Montserrat and Tot Montserrat combo-tickets, same hours as TI).

Sights in Montserrat

Montserrat Spin Tour

From the main square in front of the basilica complex, face the main facade and take this spin tour. Like a good pilgrim, face Mary, the high-up centerpiece of the facade. Below her to the left is St. Benedict, the sixth-century monk who established the rules that came to govern Montserrat's monastery. St. George, the symbol of Catalunya, is on the right (amid victims of Spain's Civil War).

Five arches line the base of the facade. The one on the far right leads pilgrims to the high point of any visit, the Black Virgin (a.k.a. La Moreneta). The center arch leads into the basilica's courtyard, and the arch second from left directs you to a small votive chapel filled with articles representing prayer requests or thanks.

Now look left of the basilica, where delicate arches mark the 15th-century monks' cloister. The monks have planted four trees here, hoping to harvest only their symbolism (palm = martyrdom, cypress = eternal life, olive = peace, and laurel = victory). Next to the trees are a public library and a peaceful reading room. The big archway is the private entrance to the monastery. Still turning to your left, then comes the modern hotel and, below that, the glass-fronted museum. Other buildings provide cells for pilgrims. The Sant Joan funicular lifts hikers up to the trailhead (you can see the tiny building at the top). From there you can take a number of fine hikes (described later). Another funicular station descends to the Sacred Cave. And, finally, five arches separate statues of founders of the great religious orders. Step over to the arches for a commanding view (on a clear day) of the Llobregat River, meandering all the way to the Mediterranean.

▲▲Basilica

Although there's been a church here since the 11th century, the present structure was built in the 1850s, and the facade only dates from 1968. The decor is Neo-Romanesque, so popular with the Romantic artists of the late 19th century. The basilica itself is ringed with interesting chapels, but the focus is on the Black Virgin (La Moreneta) sitting high above the main altar.

Cost and Hours: Free; La Moreneta viewable Mon-Sat 8:00-10:30 & 12:00-18:30, Sun 19:30-20:15; church itself has longer hours and daily services (Mass at 11:00 at the main altar, at 12:00 or 13:00 and 19:30 in side chapels, vespers at 18:45); www.abadiamontserrat.net.

Visiting the Basilica: Montserrat's top attraction is **La Moreneta,** the small wood statue of the Black Virgin, discovered in the Sacred Cave in the 12th century. Legend says she was carved by St. Luke (the gospel writer and supposed artist), brought to Spain by St. Peter, hidden away in the cave during the Moorish invasions, and miraculously discovered by shepherd children. (Carbon dating says she's 800 years old.) While George is the patron saint of Catalunya, La Moreneta is its patroness, having been crowned as such by the pope in 1881. "Moreneta" is usually translated as "black" in English, but the Spanish name actually means "tanned." The statue was originally lighter, but it darkened over the centuries from candle smoke, humidity, and the natural aging of its original varnish. Pilgrims shuffle down a long, ornate passage leading alongside the church for their few moments alone with the Virgin (keep an eye on the time if you want to see the statue; there are no visits Mon-Sat 10:30-12:00, Sun viewing is only 19:30-20:15—a short window if you want to catch the last train).

Join the line of pilgrims (along the right side of the church). Though Mary is behind a protective glass case, the royal orb she cradles in her hands is exposed. Pilgrims touch Mary's orb with one hand and hold their other hand up to show that they accept Jesus. Newlyweds in particular seek Mary's blessing.

Immediately after La Moreneta, to the right, is the delightful Neo-Romanesque prayer **chapel,** where worshippers can sit behind the Virgin and pray. The ceiling, painted in the Modernista style in 1898 by Joan Llimona, shows Jesus and Mary high in heaven. The trail connecting Catalunya with heaven seems to lead through these serrated mountains. The lower figures symbolize Catalan history and culture.

You'll leave by walking along the **Ave Maria Path** (along the outside of the church), which thoughtfully integrates nature and the basilica. Thousands of colorful votive candles are all busy helping the devout with their prayers. Before you leave the inner courtyard and head out into the main square, pop in to the humble little room with the many votive offerings. This is where people leave personal belongings (wedding dresses, baby's baptism outfits, wax replicas of body parts in need of healing, and so on) as part of a prayer request or as thanks for divine intercession.

Museum of Montserrat

This bright, shiny, and cool collection of paintings and artifacts was mostly donated by devout Catalan Catholics. While it's nothing really earth-shaking, you'll enjoy an air-conditioned wander past lots of antiquities and fine artwork. Head upstairs first to see some lesser-known works by the likes of Picasso, Caravaggio, Monet, Renoir, Pissarro, Degas, and local Modernista artists (Ramón Casas, Santiago Rusiñol, Isidro Nonell, and Joaquim Mir). One gallery shows how artists have depicted the Black Virgin of Montserrat over the centuries in many different styles. Down on the main floor, you'll see ecclesiastical gear, a good icon collection, and more paintings, including—at the very end—works by Dalí and a few Picasso sketches and prints.

Cost and Hours: €7, covered by Tot Montserrat combo-ticket, daily 10:00-17:45, Sat-Sun until 18:45, tel. 938-777-745.

▲Sant Joan Funicular and Hikes

This funicular climbs 820 feet above the monastery in five minutes. At the top of the funicular, you are at the starting point of a 20-minute walk that takes you to the Sant Joan Chapel (follow sign for *Ermita de St. Joan*). Other hikes also begin at the trailhead by the funicular (get details from TI before you ascend; basic map with suggested hikes posted by upper funicular station).  For a quick and easy chance to get out into nature and away from the crowds, simply ride up and follow the most popular hike—a 45-minute, mostly downhill loop through mountain scenery back to the monastery. To take this route, go left from the funicular station; the trail—marked *Monestir de Montserrat*—will first go up to a rocky crest before heading downhill.

Cost and Hours: Funicular—€8.45 one-way, €13 round-trip, €16.50 combo round-trip for both Sant Joan and Santa Cova, covered by Trans Montserrat and Tot Montserrat combo-tickets, goes every 20 minutes, more often with demand.

Sacred Cave (Santa Cova)

The Moreneta was originally discovered in the Sacred Cave (or Sacred Grotto), a 40-minute hike down from the monastery (then another 50 minutes back up). The path (c. 1900) was designed by devoted and patriotic Modernista architects, including Gaudí and Josep Puig i Cadafalch. It's lined with Modernista statues depicting scenes corresponding to the Mysteries of the Rosary. While the original Black Virgin statue is now in the basilica, a replica sits in the cave. A three-minute funicular ride cuts 20 minutes off the hike. (The funicular may be closed for repairs—check locally.) If you're here late in the afternoon, check the schedule before you head into the Sacred Cave to make sure you don't miss the final ride back down the mountain. Missing the last funicular could mean catching a train back to Barcelona later than you had planned.

Cost and Hours: Funicular—€3.40 one-way, €5.20 round-trip, €16.50 combo round-trip for both Sant Joan and Santa Cova, covered by Trans Montserrat and Tot Montserrat combo-tickets, goes every 20 minutes, more often with demand.

Choir Concert

Montserrat's Escolania, or Choir School, has been training voices for centuries. Fifty young boys, who live and study in the monastery itself, make up the choir, which performs daily except Saturday. The boys sing for only 10 minutes, the basilica is jam-packed, and it's likely you'll see almost nothing. Also note that if you attend the evening performance, you'll miss the last train or cable-car ride down the mountain.

Cost and Hours: Free, generally Mon-Fri at 13:00, Sun at 12:00, and Sun-Thu at 18:45, choir on vacation late June-late Aug, check schedule at www.montserratvisita.com.

Sleeping and Eating in Montserrat

An overnight here gets you monastic peace and a total break from the modern crowds. There are ample rustic cells for pilgrim visitors, but tourists might prefer **$$ Hotel Abat Cisneros.** A three-star hotel with 82 rooms and all the comforts is low-key and appropriate for a sanctuary (half- and full-board available, elevator, tel. 938-777-701, www.montserratvisita.com, reserves@larsa-montserrat.com).

Montserrat is designed to feed hordes of pilgrims and tourists. You'll find a cafeteria along the main street (across from the train station) and a grocery store and bar with simple sandwiches where the road curves on its way up to the hotel. In the other direction, follow the covered walkway below the basilica to reach the Mirador dels Apòstols, with a bar, cafeteria, restaurant, and picnic area. The Hotel Abat Cisneros also has a restaurant, and the Montserrat-Aeri train station has a ramshackle but charming family-run bar with outdoor tables, simple food, and views of the mountain and the cable cars. The best option is to pack a picnic from Barcelona, especially if you plan to hike.

Figueres

The town of Figueres (feeg-YEHR-ehs)—conveniently connected by train to Barcelona—is of sightseeing interest mainly for its Dalí Theater-Museum. In fact, the entire town seems Dalí-dominated. But don't be surprised if you also see French shoppers bargain-hunting. Some of the cheapest shops in Spain—called *ventas*—are here to lure French visitors.

GETTING TO FIGUERES

Figueres is an easy day trip from Barcelona, or a handy stopover en route to France. It has two train stations on opposite sides of town: **Figueres-Vilafant** (served by the high-speed train from Barcelona's Sants station, about hourly, 1 hour) and **Figueres** (served by the less expensive but slower regional train; departs from Barcelona's Sants station or from the Renfe station at Metro: Passeig de Gràcia; hourly, 2 hours; slightly more expensive *media distancia* trains are 20 minutes faster). If you're on your way to Paris, it's possible to take the high-speed train from Barcelona in the morning, visit the Dalí Theater-Museum, and catch the late afternoon TGV train (also called "InOui") to Paris. Neither train station has baggage storage, but the bus station (across from Figueres station) and the Dalí Theater-Museum do. For bus connections to Cadaqués, see "Getting to Cadaqués," later.

Orientation to Figueres

You'll find the town's museums and sights clustered within a couple of blocks of one other—the Rambla shopping street, church, city hall, toy museum (Museu del Joguet), and Catalan art museum (Museu Empordà)—as well as the only sight that matters for most visitors: the Dalí Theater-Museum.

Arrival in Figueres: The most important sights are all clearly marked with red directional signs.

To reach the Dalí museum from Figueres-Vilafant station, take the **bus** marked *Estació AVE-Figueres* (€1.70, departs only with the arrival of each train, buy ticket from driver), and get off at the Rambla stop—ask the driver for the museum. From there, it's a five-minute walk uphill to the museum. **Taxis** charge €10 to and from the station.

To get to the museum from Figueres station, simply follow *Museu Dalí* signs (and the crowds) for the 15-minute walk to the museum.

Sights in Figueres

DALÍ THEATER-MUSEUM

This ▲▲▲ museum is *the* essential Dalí sight—and, if you like his work, one of Europe's most enjoyable museums, period. Inaugurated in 1974, the Dalí Theater-Museum (Teatre-Musei Dalí) is a work of art in itself. Ever the entertainer and promoter, Dalí personally conceptualized, designed, decorated, and painted it to showcase his life's work. The museum fills a former theater and contains the artist's mausoleum (his tomb is in the crypt below center stage). It's also a kind of mausoleum to Dalí's creative spirit.

Dalí had his first public art showing at age 14 here in this building when it was a theater, and he was baptized in the church just across the street. He felt sentimental about the place. After the theater was destroyed in the Spanish Civil War (along with most of Figueres—the town was the last Republican stronghold before France), Dalí struck a deal with the mayor: Dalí would rebuild the theater as a museum to his works, Figueres would be put on the sightseeing map...and the money's been flowing in ever since.

Dalí worked here over many years and personally designed the core of the museum (Rooms 1 through 18). Even the building's exterior—painted pink, studded with golden loaves of bread, and topped with monumental eggs and a geodesic dome—exudes the artist's outrageous public persona. The Dalí Theater-Museum is called the largest Surrealist object in the world.

Cost: €14; purchase a timed-entry ticket online in advance. Your ticket includes the nearby Museu Empordà (two floors of Catalan paintings).

Hours: July-Sept daily 9:00-20:00; April-June same hours but closed Mon, Oct-March Tue-Sun 9:30-18:00—except from 10:30 Nov-Feb, closed Mon; last entry 45 minutes before closing, tel. 972-677-500, www.salvador-dali.org.

Advance Tickets Recommended: It's important to reserve

ahead online for this museum, which can be a mob scene, especially when bad weather drives beach crowds here (they let in no more than 250 people each half-hour). You can make a reservation as little as two hours in advance.

Bag Check: The free and required bag check will have your belongings waiting for you at the exit. (It's OK to leave checked backpacks/small suitcases here while you browse the town.)

Sightseeing Tip: Much of Dalí's art is movable and coin-operated—bring a few €0.20 and €1 coins, and keep an eye out for the machines where you insert them. It's fun to gather other museumgoers in a group to experience these animated works together.

DAY TRIPS

Background

Dalí's art can be playful, but also disturbing. He was passionate about the dark side of things, but with his wife, Gala, for balance, he managed never to go off the deep end. Unlike Pablo Casals (the Catalan cellist) and Pablo Picasso (another local artist), Dalí didn't go into exile under Franco's dictatorship. Pragmatically, he accepted both Franco and the Church, and was supported by the dictator. Apart from the occasional *sardana* dance, you won't find a hint of politics in Dalí's art.

You could spend hours here, wandering around and wondering: Is it real or not real? Am I crazy, or is it you? Beethoven is painted with squid ink applied by a shoe on a stormy night. Jesus is made with candle smoke and an eraser. It's fun to see the Dalí-ization of art classics. Dalí, like so many modern artists, was inspired by the masters—especially Velázquez.

❍ Self-Guided Tour

The museum has two parts—the theater-mausoleum and the "Dalí's Jewels" exhibit in an adjacent building. There's no logical order for a visit (that would be un-Surrealistic). Naturally, there's no audioguide (but there is a good museum book for sale). Dalí said there are two kinds of visitors: those who don't need a description, and those who aren't worth a description. At the risk of offending Dalí, I've written this loose commentary to attach some meaning to your visit.

Courtyard (Ground Floor): Step into the courtyard (with its audience of golden statues) and face the stage (visible through the window wall). You know how you can never get a cab when it's raining? Pop a coin

Salvador Dalí (1904-1989)

When Salvador Dalí was asked, "Are you on drugs?" he replied, "I am the drug...take me."

Labeled by various critics as sick, greedy, paranoid, arrogant, and a clown, Dalí produced some of the most thought-provoking and trailblazing art of the 20th century. His erotic, violent, disjointed imagery continues to disturb and intrigue to this day.

Born in Figueres to a well-off family, Dalí showed talent early. He was expelled from Madrid's prestigious art school—twice—but formed longtime friendships with playwright and poet Federico García Lorca and filmmaker Luis Buñuel.

After a breakthrough art exhibit in Barcelona in 1925, Dalí moved to Paris. He hobnobbed  with fellow Spaniards Pablo Picasso and Joan Miró, along with a group of artists exploring Sigmund Freud's theory that we all have a hidden part of our mind, the unconscious "id," which surfaces when we dream. Dalí became the best-known spokesman for this group of Surrealists, channeling his id to create photorealistic dream images (melting watches, burning giraffes) set in bizarre dreamscapes.

His life changed forever in 1929, when he met an older, married Russian woman named Gala who would become his wife, muse, model, manager, and emotional compass. Dalí's popularity

into Dalí's personal 1941 Cadillac and it rains inside the car. Look above, atop the tire tower: That's the boat Dalí enjoyed with his soul mate, Gala—his emotional life preserver, who kept him from going overboard. When she died, so did he (for his last seven years). Blue tears made of condoms drip below the boat.

Stage/Cupola (Ground Floor): Now cross through the courtyard and go up to the stage. On the left, squint at the big digital Abraham Lincoln, and president #16 comes into focus. Approach the painting to find that Abe's facial cheeks are Gala's butt cheeks—or use the coin-operated telescope (at the far end) or your phone's camera to focus on his face.

Treasures Room (Ground Floor): Under Lincoln, a door leads to the **Treasures Room** (Room 4), with the best collection of original Dalí oil paintings in the museum. (Many of the artworks displayed elsewhere in the building are prints.) You'll see Cubist visions of Cadaqués and dreamy portraits of Gala. One portrays her half nude, as if her arms are a woven basket supporting her spread to the US, where he (and Gala) weathered the WWII years.

In the prime of his career, Dalí's work became less Surrealist and more classical, influenced by past masters of painted realism (Velázquez, Raphael, Ingres, Vermeer) and by his own study of history, science, and religion. He produced large-scale paintings of historical events (e.g., Columbus discovering America, the Last Supper) that were collages of realistic scenes floating in a surrealistic landscape, peppered with thought-provoking symbols.

Dalí—an extremely capable technician—mastered many media, including film. *An Andalusian Dog* (*Un Chien Andalou*, 1929, with Luis Buñuel) was a cutting-edge montage of disturbing, eyeball-slicing images. He designed Alfred Hitchcock's big-eye backdrop for the dream sequence of *Spellbound* (1945). He made jewels for the rich and clothes for Coco Chanel, wrote a novel and an autobiography, and pioneered what would come to be called "installations." He also helped develop "performance art" by showing up at an opening in a diver's suit or by playing the role he projected to the media—a super-confident, waxed-mustached artistic genius.

In later years, Dalí's over-the-top public image contrasted with his ever-growing illness, depression, and isolation. He endured the scandal of a dealer overselling "limited editions" of his work. When Gala died in 1982, Dalí retreated to his hometown, living his last days in the Torre Galatea of the Theater-Museum complex, where he died of heart failure.

Dalí's legacy as an artist includes his self-marketing persona, his exceptional ability to draw, his provocative pairing of symbols, and his sheer creative drive.

exposed breast like a crust of bread. Dalí said, "She has become my basket of bread." In the tiny-but-powerful *Specter of Sex Appeal,* crutches—a recurring Dalí theme—also represent Gala, who kept him supported whenever a meltdown threatened.

Downstairs Crypt (Lower Level): Make your way downstairs, below the stage, and pay respect at the artist's crypt, within dimly lit rooms filled with golden sculptures. True to the irreverent spirit of Dalí, the public toilets are right next to his tomb.

Mae West Room (First Floor): Back upstairs and to the right (as you face the stage), head into the famous Mae West Room (Room 11), a tribute to the sultry seductress. Dalí loved her atti-

tude. Saying things like, "Why marry and make one man unhappy, when you can stay single and make so many so happy?" Mae West was to conventional morality what Dalí was to conventional art. Climb to the vantage point where the sofa lips, fireplace nostrils, painting eyes, and drapery hair come together to make the face of Mae West.

If you side-trip up to the second and third floors from here, you can visit Rooms 12-14, where you'll find numbered prints from various book illustrations Dalí did and his private collection of works by other artists who inspired him.

Smoking Lounge (First Floor): Circle around to the Room 15, with purple walls, labeled "Palace of the Wind" (just above the entrance). Formerly the theater's smoking lounge, it displays por-traits of Gala and Dalí (with a big eye, big ear, and a dark side) bookending a Roman candle of creativity. The fascinating ceil-ing painting shows the feet of Gala and Dalí as they bridge the earth and the heavens. Dalí's drawers are wide open and  empty, indicating that he gave everything to his art. It was in this hall that the young Dalí first exhibited his art to the public.

Final Section (First Floor): Circle clockwise around the the-ater and pass above the stage once more, then go through the Bra-mante's Temple Room, followed by several more exhibits in Rooms 19 to 22. You'll be routed back downstairs and through the gift shop.

Nearby: As you leave the theater through the turnstile gate, hook right around the corner to pop into the adjacent, not-to-be-missed Dalí's Jewels exhibit (*Dalí-Joies,* covered by your theater ticket). It shows sketches and paintings of jewelry Dalí designed, and the actual pieces jewelers made from those surreal visions: a mouth full of pearly whites, a golden finger corset, a fountain of diamonds, and the breathing heart. Explore the ambiguous per-ception worked into the big painting titled *Apotheosis of the Dollar.* The upstairs section includes the exquisite, jeweled creation titled *Chalice of Life.*

OTHER SIGHTS IN TOWN

While everything else in Figueres pales compared to the Dalí Theater-Museum, you're right in the heart of town, near a few en-joyable sights and countless eateries. (Remember, you can check your bag in the Dalí museum and pick it up later.)

A few blocks downhill from the museum, you'll hit the **Rambla,** Figueres' grand boulevard, with the **Museu Empordà**

(19th- and 20th-century Catalan paintings, free with Dalí ticket, Tue-Sun 11:00-20:00, closed Mon, at Rambla 2). The nearby Museu del Joguet de Catalunya—a **toy museum**—offers a delightful trip back to grandpa's Catalan childhood with three floors of old playthings (€7 includes audioguide, daily 10:00-19:00, Oct-May until 18:00 and closed Mon, Carrer Sant Pere 1).

Cadaqués

Since the late 1800s, Cadaqués (kah-dah-KEHS) has served as a haven for intellectuals and artists alike. The fishing village's craggy coastline, sun-drenched colors, and laid-back lifestyle inspired Fauvists such as Henri Matisse and Surrealists such as René Magritte, Marcel Duchamp, and Federico García Lorca. Even Picasso, drawn to this enchanting coastal haunt, painted some of his Cubist works here.

Salvador Dalí, raised in nearby Figueres, brought international fame to this sleepy Catalan port in the 1920s. As a kid Dalí spent summers here in the family cabin, where he was inspired by the rocky landscape that would later be the backdrop for many Surrealist canvases. In 1929, he met his future wife, Gala, in Cadaqués. Together they converted a fisherman's home in nearby Port Lligat into their semipermanent residence, dividing their time between New York, Paris, and Cadaqués. It was here that Dalí did his best work.

In spite of its fame, Cadaqués is mellow and feels off the beaten path. At the easternmost tip of Spain, it's remote, with no train service and only a tiny access road that dead-ends, making it less developed than it might otherwise be. If you want a peaceful beach-town escape near Barcelona, this is it. From the moment you descend into the town, taking in whitewashed buildings and deep blue waters, you'll be struck by the port's tranquility and beauty. Join the locals playing chess or cards at the cavernous harborfront Casino Coffee House. Have a glass of *vino tinto* or *cremat* (a traditional rum-and-coffee drink served flambé-style) at one of the seaside cafés. Savor the lapping waves, brilliant sun, and gentle breeze.

The Salvador Dalí House at Port Lligat, a 20-minute walk

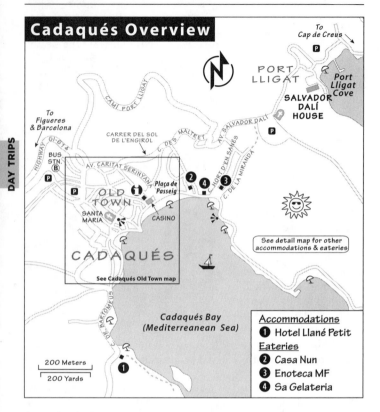

Cadaqués Overview

To Cap de Creus

PORT LLIGAT

Port Lligat Cove

SALVADOR DALÍ HOUSE

To Figueres & Barcelona

HIGHWAY GI-614

CARRER DEL SOL DE L'ENGIROL

BUS STN. B

AV. CARITAT SERINYAN

OLD TOWN

SANTA MARIA

Plaça de Passeig

CASINO

CADAQUÉS

See Cadaqués Old Town map

Cadaqués Bay (Mediterreanean Sea)

See detail map for other accommodations & eateries

CAMI PORT LLIGAT

C. DES MALTRET

AV. SALVADOR DALÍ

C. HORT D'EN SANÉS

C. DE LA MIRANDA

C. DE BARTOMEU

200 Meters
200 Yards

Accommodations
1 Hotel Llané Petit

Eateries
2 Casa Nun
3 Enoteca MF
4 Sa Gelateria

from the Cadaqués town center, is the main sightseeing attraction (reservations required). And at the gateway to Cadaqués, you'll see a Statue of Liberty with both arms raised, based on a Dalí drawing inspired by his visit to New York City. He thought, "Why not two?"

GETTING TO CADAQUÉS

Reaching Cadaqués is very tough without a car. There are no trains and only a few buses a day. A taxi from Figueres is another option.

By Car: Cadaqués is about an hour's drive from Figueres. The road is flat at first, then twists dramatically over a desolate mountain range (with sweeping views over town). As only one small road goes in and out of Cadaqués, you may run into traffic during the summer months.

To visit the town center, park in the big lot just above the city—don't try to park near the harborfront. The handiest free parking is on Riera de Sant Vicenç, the long, generally dry riverbed that flows through the center of town (but steer clear on Monday when the town market happens here).

To drive to the Salvador Dalí House, carefully track *Port Lligat* signs at the big, elongated roundabout as you enter Cadaqués (as you approach from Figueres, you'll loop all the way around the roundabout and exit at its top corner—near where you entered). A big parking lot is just past the Salvador Dalí House, an easy five-minute walk along a gravel beach.

By Bus: Sarfa buses serve Cadaqués from **Figueres** (3/day, 1 hour) and from **Barcelona** (1-2/day, 3 hours). You can buy bus tickets to Cadaqués at Barcelona TIs on Plaça de Catalunya, Plaça Sant Jaume, and at the Columbus Monument. Bus info: Cadaqués tel. 972-258-713, Figueres tel. 972-674-298, www.sarfa.com. On busy summer days, it's wise to book your ride in advance.

By Taxi: A taxi from Figueres costs about €60. It's just a little more for a round-trip—including the drive to Port Lligat and a couple of hours' wait—as it is to be dropped off. You can arrange a ride over the phone in advance (tel. 972-505-043; good Spanish skills help—or ask your hotelier), or in person at the taxi stand on the Rambla in Figueres (from the Dalí Theater-Museum, walk down Carrer Sant Pere to the Rambla). Driver Josep María has an official taxi-and-van service and offers the same rates (mobile 696-906-476).

Orientation to Cadaqués

TOURIST INFORMATION

The TI is near the waterfront at Carrer Cotxe 2 (July-Sept Mon-Sat 9:00-21:00, shorter hours Sun and off-season plus closed for lunch, tel. 972-258-315, www.visitcadaques.org).

HELPFUL HINTS

Golf Carts: The only "taxi" service in town, EcoCar has a handful of electric golf carts that can take you around, including to Port Lligat, the bus station, and out to Cap de Creus—with spectacular clifftop views (short rides-€4/person, Cap de Creus-€8/person, cash only, tel. 618-883-656, www.ecocarcadaques. com, Diego speaks English).

Local Guide: Simply a delight to be with, **Merce Donat** (pronounced "mercy doughnut") organizes tours in and around Cadaqués. Merce knows everyone and loves to show off her town. For €60, she's all yours for a two-hour town walk. She also does tours with her car (up to 4 people, €120/half-day, €180/day) and can tailor a "Discover Dalí" day. Other options are on her website (mobile 686-492-369, www.rutescadaques. com, rutescadaques@gmail.com).

Tourist Train: The **Es Trenet de Cadaqués** tourist train goes around town and to Port Lligat and back, with a recorded nar-

DAY TRIPS

DAY TRIPS

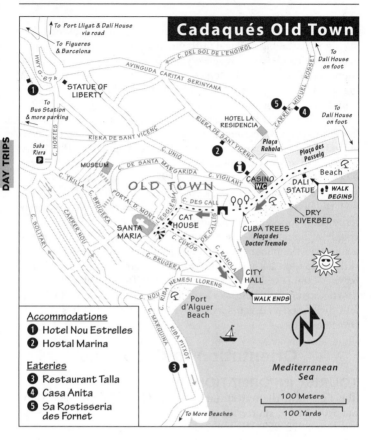

Cadaqués Old Town

Accommodations
1 Hotel Nou Estrelles
2 Hostal Marina

Eateries
3 Restaurant Talla
4 Casa Anita
5 Sa Rostisseria des Fornet

ration and a few photo stops—but it doesn't stop at the Dalí House (€10, departs at 11:00 and on the hour 15:00-18:00, 1 hour). It also does a loop to the lighthouse at Cap de Creus, where you can enjoy the views for about 20 minutes before returning to Cadaqués (€16, departs at 12:00, 2 hours; for either tour, purchase tickets at the booth in the square just below the casino, tel. 653-829-442, www.estrenetdecadaques.cat).

Market Day: If you're here on a Monday, be sure to stroll through the sprawling market that fills the paved riverbed through the center of town (Riera de Sant Vicenç).

Cadaqués Walk

Cadaqués has no really important "sights" other than the Dalí House. But the old town is remarkably interesting and easy to miss. Here's a quick eight-point walk. Having strolled this, you can better relax along the harbor knowing you've "done" Cadaqués.

Dalí Statue on Beach: Start near the statue of Salvador Dalí. The artist called Cadaqués home (he lived a 20-minute walk away in the 1920s and 1930s). He did his best work here and put this small town on the map. From the Dalí statue, walk down to the water's edge and survey the harbor. Looking inland, you can see the Hotel La Residencia. This was the only hotel in town when Dalí arrived, and it remains a kind of time warp.

• *Notice the street that runs below grade, beneath a short bridge that's nearly at the water's edge.*

Riverbed Street: This street, just in front of the casino building, is actually a paved and usually dry riverbed. A couple of times each year, after big rains, this big drain becomes a raging river, saving the city from flash floods—which washed out several earlier bridges. Old-timers remember previous bridges on this spot, which separates the old town from the new. Traditionally, the bridge was where people hung out on benches, but the new bridge is too narrow to host loungers. Now, people make do with the wide windowsills of the casino.

• *Walk over to the casino entrance.*

Casino: This place feels like the timeless clubhouse of the town, where the old boys gather to play cards and pool. Wander inside. There's a public WC next to the pool table. Enjoy the old photos on the walls.

• *Just past the casino is a small park with three...*

Cuba Trees: These stubby "elephant trees" were imported by locals who left Cuba when it won its independence from Spain in 1897. These trees are a reminder that lots of Catalans moved to Cuba in the 19th century and came back home when Spanish rule ended. Just uphill from the top tree are bits of the beloved (and well-used) old bridge benches. From here, try to imagine when Cadaqués was a small walled town filling the bluff above you.

• *Climb uphill to the right, through the old gate, into the...*

Old Town and Jewish Quarter: Stepping through the main gate, you enter a different world. Climb up Carrer des Call, the old Jewish street. There was a strong Jewish community in Spain from the first century until 1492. That's when Christian fanaticism (gone wild with the final Reconquista victory) led to the expulsion of Jews and Muslims from Catholic Spain. Notice the characteristic slate pavers underfoot.

• *Keep climbing until the T-intersection. There, at the top, turn left to the church.*

Church of Santa Maria: Enjoy the commanding view from in front of the church. This spot marks the high point of the old town. If open, step inside to enjoy its amazing Baroque altar from the 1700s (generally 10:00-13:00 & 16:00-20:00). Pop a euro into the light box to appreciate this treasure (and support the church).

Carved from pine wood with 365 figures, it's covered with gold from the Americas. Peter (with the keys) and Paul (with his trusty sword) are actually part of the doors that lead into the sacristy. Fishermen paid for this altar—as you're reminded by the two guys in red and green, dressed as fishermen would have been in the mid-1700s. Treasures like this throughout Spain survived until the rampant destruction of churches during the civil war in the 1930s. This altar exists today because industrious locals built a protective wall in front of it all the way to the ceiling.

• *From the church, walk steeply down Carrer Curós. But first, on the left, notice the Cat House, a one-woman mission to care for the town's homeless cats. (She lives here with 20 cats and one dog.)*

Carrer Curós or Gallery Street: This characteristic lane is lined with art galleries. Near the lower end, local painters show off by painting the covers on electrical panels.

• *The street bottoms out at city hall (on the left) and a small terrace overlooking the harbor.*

City Hall: You're at the Casa de la Vila, or city hall. The top of the old city wall here now serves as a balustrade for a view terrace, and it's a delightful spot to look out for pirates. The last Barbary pirate raid (from North Africa) was in 1828. You should be safe. Hey...it's cerveza-o'clock!

Sights near Cadaqués

SALVADOR DALÍ HOUSE AND GARDEN

Once Dalí's home and worth ▲▲▲, this house (Casa Salvador Dalí) in Port Lligat gives fans a chance to explore a labyrinthine compound. This is the best artist's house I've toured in Europe. It shows how a home can really reflect the creative spirit of an artistic genius and his muse. The ambience, both inside and out, is perfect for a Surrealist hanging out with his creative playmate. The bay is ringed by sleepy islands. Fish-

ing boats are jumbled on the beach. After the fishermen painted their boats, Dalí asked them to clean their brushes on his door—creating an abstract work of art he adored (which you'll see as you line up to get your ticket).

Cost and Hours: House—€11, garden only—€5; mid-June-mid-Sept daily 9:30-21:00; rest of year Tue-Sun 10:30-18:00, closed many Mondays—see website; closed early Jan-mid-Feb. Last tour departs 50 minutes before closing. No bags are allowed in the house; the baggage check is free.

Reservations Required: You must reserve in advance to visit the house (tel. 972-251-015, www.salvador-dali.org). In summer, book at least a week in advance. You must arrive 30 minutes early to pick up your ticket, or they'll sell it. Really! For a full visit, see the home (with a timed entry and escorted tour) followed by the garden.

No Reservation?: Those without a ticket to the home can easily get a garden ticket and see all the exteriors (including the pool).

Getting There: Parking is free nearby. There is no public bus service to the house, but from Cadaqués you can arrange a ride to and from in an **EcoCar** (see "Helpful Hints," earlier). On foot, the house is a 20-minute, one-mile walk over the hill from Cadaqués to Port Lligat. (The path, which cuts across the isthmus, is simple: straight up and over. It's much shorter than the road.) Follow signs to *Casa S. Dalí.*

Visiting the House

Across from the entry is a wooden boat with a tree growing through it, symbolically connecting earth and sky with the fishermen's culture. A few small-time fishermen still work out of this bay and sell their catch at the pier each morning. (The bag check desk is near the boat).

Only eight people are allowed inside the house every 10 minutes. There are five sections, each with a guard who gives you a brief explanation and then turns you loose for a few minutes. (As the content shared is light, talk with your guide for more info.) The entire visit takes 50 minutes. Before (or after) your tour, enjoy the 15-minute video (alternates in four languages) that plays in the waiting lounge (with walls covered in Dalí media coverage) just across the lane from the house.

The **house's interior** is left almost precisely as it was in 1982, when Gala died and Dalí moved out—never to return. (He died in 1989.) You'll see Dalí's studio (the clever easel cranks up and down to allow the artist to paint while seated, as he did eight hours a day); the bohemian-yet-divine living room (complete with a mirror to reflect the sunrise onto their bed each morning); and the painter's study (with his favorite mustaches all lined up). Like Dalí's art, his home is offbeat, provocative, and fun.

Visiting the Garden

While you'll get a guided tour of Dalí's home, you're on your own in his playful garden—which is where your house tour ends. It's a one-way circle (following numbered signs, 14-20). Here's what to look for:

Dalí's **patio** is where you can enjoy a little playful Dalí hide-and-seek, with crickets in cages, a horseshoe-shaped, slate dining table, and cool corridors leading to the olive garden out back (#14-16). From a platform, you'll view *Christ of the Rubbish*, a huge **statue** (#17) that sprawls on the ground, created from collected junk.

In the **olive grove** (#18), relax on Dalí's six-legged chairs ("they never fall"). And then enjoy a commanding view of the bay, including an island where hippies slept back in the 1960s. At the top of the garden is a theater with video documentaries (rarely with English subtitles).

Descend through Dalí's "historic garden," noting that he preserved this oasis to honor the hard labor and time it took to create. At a little patio you reach a broken eggshell sculpture (symbolizing how Dalí and Gala were "hatched")—climb in for some photo fun.

Next you enter the **"egg terrace"** (#19, the egg symbolizes fertility), protected from the steady wind. Above, in a niche is a sink—a reminder of Dalí's belief (or joke) that to gain salvation you must be clean. He was ambiguous about his religion.

Now it's party time, and you're poolside. Dalí's penis-shaped **pool** (#20) is surrounded by stylish kitsch (Mae West lips sofa, fountain with cheap Spanish sherry bottles)—decor as eclectic as his circle of friends. Imagine the parties. Dalí hosted lots of hedonism but would himself only observe. That's why Gala had many lovers, and he accepted it. Just beyond the head of the "penis" is the old pre-electric lamp from the lighthouse at Cap de Creus.

Your exit was Dalí's entry. Dalí had a national phone booth placed here for the convenience (and expense) of friends who needed to make a call. Notice the white sculpture of a warrior with a small child (see the two little feet) emerging from it. The message: Leave your warrior outside and let your inner child enter.

NEAR CADAQUÉS
Cap de Creus
The top excursion for nature lovers is the easternmost point of mainland Spain—Cap de Creus. The cape, marked by a lighthouse, is a popular nine-mile round-trip hike (get details at the Cadaqués TI). There are swimming coves along the way and a restaurant at the lighthouse. The easy way to get there is on the tourist train (see "Helpful Hints," earlier).

Drive to France
Just over the Spanish border is the charming French town of Collioure (which seems like Cadaqués' sister city). It's a scenic 90-minute drive; you'll pass an evocative abandoned border post along the way—where the Pyrenees mountains hit the Mediterranean.

Sleeping in Cadaqués

$$ Hotel Llané Petit, with 32 spacious rooms (half with view balconies), is a small resort-like hotel with its own little beach, a 10-minute walk south of the town center (RS%, some view rooms, air-con, elevator, pay parking, Carrer del Doctor Bartomeus 37, tel. 972-251-020, www.llanepetit.com, info@llanepetit.com).

$ Hotel Nou Estrelles is a big, concrete exercise in efficient, economic comfort. Facing the bus stop a few blocks in from the waterfront, this family-run hotel offers 15 rooms at a great value (air-con, elevator, Carrer Sa Tarongeta 3, tel. 972-259-100, www.hotelnouestrelles.com, reservas@hotelnouestrelles.com, Emma).

$ Hostal Marina is run by a local family with care and enthusiasm and has 30 fresh rooms at a great location a block from the harborfront main square (RS%—use code "Rick Steves" when reserving, some rooms with balcony, family rooms, no elevator, Riera de Sant Vicenç 3, tel. 972-159-091, www.hostalmarinacadaques.com, info@hostalmarinacadaques.com, Pau and Isabel).

Eating in Cadaqués

$$$$ Restaurant Talla, grandly situated across from the old town with a harbor view, serves modern Mediterranean top-end cuisine. It has a rustic-yet-elegant interior and some fine harborside tables outside. There are two seatings (20:00 and 22:00) for this popular place, and you must reserve (open 12:30-15:30 & 20:00-23:00, closed Tue-Wed April-June, Riba Pitxot 18, tel. 972-258-739, tallacadaques@gmail.com).

$$$ Casa Nun, serving wonderful traditional Catalan dishes and the freshest seafood, has been run by Paco since 1979 (fun photos in the back). Its cozy interior is whitewashed and tiled, and the little front porch gives a few tables great harbor views. Portions are big—don't hesitate to split first courses family-style (daily, Plaça Portixó 6, tel. 972-258-856).

$$ Casa Anita is good for an entertaining meal. You'll sit with others around a big table and enjoy fresh local fish and homemade *helado* (ice cream). There's no menu—you'll just eat what they serve you. Finish your meal with a glass of sweet Muscatel (closed Mon, Carrer Miquel Rosset 16, tel. 972-258-471, Joan and family).

$$$ Enoteca MF is popular for their creative tapas and *raciones,* prepared with local ingredients that they mostly produce or catch themselves (Riba des Poal, mobile 682-107-142).

$ Sa Rostisseria des Fornet is a very simple deli designed mostly for takeout but with a couple of humble tables. There's no atmosphere, but it's cheap (you pay by weight), fast, and tasty (Carrer Miquel Rosset 3, tel. 972-258-501).

DAY TRIPS

For Dessert: The venerable ice-cream shop **Sa Gelateria** faces the harbor (east of the center). Along with gelato, they serve home-made popsicles. Speaking of popsicles, pop in for the interesting historic photos of Cadaqués and its people.

Sitges

Sitges (SEE-juhz) is one of Catalunya's most popular resort towns. Because the town beautifully mingles sea and light, it's long been an artists' colony. Here you can still feel the soul of the Modernis-tas...in the architecture, the museums, the salty sea breeze, and the relaxed rhythm of life. Today's Sitges is a world-renowned vaca-tion destination among the gay community. Despite its jet-set sta-tus, the Old Town has managed to retain its charm. With a much slower pulse than Barcelona, Sitges is an enjoyable break from the big city.

If you visit during one of Sitges' two big **festivals** (St. Bar-tholomew on Aug 24 and St. Tecla on Sept 23), you may see teams of *castellers* competing to build human pyramids.

To reach Sitges, you can take the train or bus. Southbound **trains** depart Barcelona from the Sants and Passeig de Gràcia sta-tions (take frequent Rodalies train on the dark-green line R2sud toward Sant Vicenç de Calders, 40 minutes). The **TI** is to the left after you exit the train station. They can provide information about beaches and the town in general (Plaça Eduard Maristany 2, tel. 938-944-251, www.sitgestur.cat). The Mon-Bus Company runs an easy and frequent **bus** from downtown Barcelona (with stops near the university and Plaça d'Espanya) that stops at Barcelona's air-port en route to Sitges (1 hour, www.monbus.cat).

Visiting Sitges: Sitges basically has two attractions—its tight-and-tiny Old Town (with a couple of good museums) and its long, luxurious beaches. To head into the heart of town, exit the train sta-tion straight ahead and walk down Carrer Francesc Gumà. When it dead-ends, continue right onto Carrer de Jesús, which takes you to the town's tiny main square, Plaça del Cap de la Villa. Cross the square and turn left down Carrer Major ("Main Street"), which after several blocks leads you past the old market hall (now Casa Bacardí, a museum and lounge bar telling the history of Sitges na-tive Facundo Bacardí Masso, founder of Bacardí rum in Cuba) and the town hall to a beautiful terrace next to the main church.

Take time to explore the **Old Town**'s narrow streets. They're crammed with cafés, boutiques, and all the resort staples. The focal point, on the waterfront, is the 17th-century Baroque-style **Sant**

Bartomeu i Santa Tecla Church. The terrace in front of the church will help you get the lay of the land. Poke into the Old Town or take the grand staircase down to the beach promenade.

As an art town, Sitges has seen its share of creative people—look for the sculptures by local artists scattered all over town, then head to the two appealing museums that share one entrance and fee, located along the water behind the church (tel. 938-940-364, www.museusdesitges. com). The **Museu Maricel** displays the eclectic artwork of a local collector, including some Modernista works, pieces by Sitges artists, and a collection of maritime-themed works. The **Museu Cau Ferrat** bills itself as a "temple of art," as collected by local intellectual Santiago Rusiñol. In addition to paintings and drawings, it has ironwork, glass, and ceramics. Also on  this square, you'll see **Palau Maricel**—a sumptuous old mansion that's sometimes open to the public for concerts in the summer (ask at TI).

Nine **beaches,** separated by breakwaters, extend about a mile southward from town. Stroll down the seaside promenade, which stretches from the town to the end of the beaches. Anyone can enjoy the sun, sea, and sand, or you can rent a beach chair to relax like a pro. The crowds thin out about halfway down, and the last three beaches are more intimate and cove-like. Along the way, restaurants and *chiringuitos* (beach bars) serve tapas, paella,  and drinks. If you walk all the way to the end, you can continue inland to enjoy the nicely landscaped **Terramar Gardens** (Jardins de Terramar).

Sleeping in Sitges: Hotel values are not much better in this swanky beach resort than in Barcelona. As this is a party town, expect some noise after hours (request a quiet room). Consider **$$ Hotel Celimar** (small but modern rooms in a classic Modernista building facing the beach, Paseo de la Ribera 20, tel. 938-110-170, www.hotelcelimar.com) or the larger, family-run **$$ Hotel Romàntic** (an old-fashioned-elegant, quirky place in a villa a few blocks from the beach, Sant Isidre 33, tel. 938-948-375, www.hotelromantic.com).

BARCELONA: PAST & PRESENT

Barcelona has thrived for 2,500 years. Its location is ideal: on a gently sloping plain facing the Mediterranean, where east-west sea trade meets the natural north-south highway to northern Europe. In its day, Barcelona has been a Roman retirement colony, a maritime power, a dynamo of the Industrial Age, and a cradle for all things modern. Today it cobbles together all these elements into a one-of-a-kind culture.

Keep in mind that Catalunya's history is quite distinct from that of the rest of Spain. Catalans pride themselves on their different language and independent traditions. When the rest of Spain was riding high, Catalunya was often in the doldrums, and vice versa.

The painter Joan Miró said, "We Catalans believe that you must plant your feet firmly on the ground in order to jump high in the air." This optimistic Catalan spirit—earthy but creative—has blossomed again and again through their history. Free spirits like Dalí, Miró, Gaudí—and even Wilfred the Hairy—have all come from this small corner of Europe.

PREHISTORY AND ROMAN ORIGINS (c. 500 BC-AD 500)

The original Iberian inhabitants settled atop Barcelona's hills overlooking the harbor, creating settlements on Montjuïc and around today's Plaça de Sant Jaume. They called their town "Barkeno." The name may (or may not) derive from the famous family of Hannibal Barca—the

Carthaginian general who passed through the area with his war elephants en route to attacking Rome, in 218 BC.

In 19 BC, the (future) Roman Emperor Augustus conquered Iberia. The Romans made "Hispania" their agricultural breadbasket to feed the vast Empire. In Catalunya, they planted grapes on large farming estates and shipped the wine abroad from Barcelona's busy port. Roman "Barcino"—a pleasant, sunbathed valley with Mediterranean breezes—became a retirement colony for soldiers.

Like most Roman cities, Barcino had a forum in the center of town (today's Plaça de Sant Jaume) and a grid pattern of streets. It was a tight, 30-acre town of some 4,000 inhabitants contained within a wall (the area around today's cathedral). More broadly, the Romans brought Barcelona the Latin language (which became modern Catalan) and a connection to the wider world.

Sights

- Barcelona History Museum (with Roman ruins in basement)
- Temple of Augustus
- Big, sculpted BARCINO letters on Plaça Nova
- Remnants of the Roman wall (especially the towers on Plaça Nova, near the cathedral)
- Roman necropolis near the Ramblas

MEDIEVAL (500-1000)

As the Roman Empire crumbled, Barcelona made a peaceful transition, coming under the protection of Christian Visigoths from Germany who had strong Roman ties. Christianity had entered Barcelona during Rome's last years (when martyrs such as Santa Eulàlia were persecuted). The feisty Christians built their cathedral—the core of today's cathedral—atop the Roman Temple of Jupiter.

In 711, the Moors (Muslim invaders from North Africa) swept through Spain, and Barcelona surrendered without a fight. While Moorish culture went on to dominate much of Spain for the next 700 years, its impact on Catalunya was minimal. In 801, Barcelona was liberated by Charlemagne's son, who made it part of the Frankish empire under the rule of Frankish "Counts." When Count Wilfred the Hairy (so called because he was; ruled 878-898) declared himself independent of the Franks, he launched a Golden Age in Barcelona.

Sights
- Cathedral (with its original fourth-century font)
- Santa Eulàlia's tomb and silver statue in the cathedral

KINGDOM OF ARAGON (1000-1500)

Wilfred the Hairy's heirs sprouted and grew into powerful sea trad-ers who connected Catalunya to the world. When Count Ramon of Barcelona married Petronila of Aragon in 1137, it united their two realms, creating the powerful king-dom of Aragon.

King Jaume I the Conqueror (1208-1276) led Aragon's powerful army and navy in acquiring rich trading ports in the Mediterranean. He also estab-lished the Catalan Generalitat, one of Europe's first parliaments, which still governs the region today. By 1450, the Crown of Aragon ruled a mercantile em-pire that stretched across the Mediterranean, from eastern Spain to southern Italy to Greece. Barcelona flourished.

In 1469 came another powerful marriage: King Ferdinand II of Aragon married Isabel of Castile. This power couple—the so-called Catholic Monarchs—united the peninsula's two largest kingdoms. They drove the last Moors out of Granada, expelled the Jews, and created a unified nation-state. They sent Christopher Columbus to explore new lands under the Spanish flag. And where did Columbus come first to debrief the Catholic Monarchs upon his return? To Barcelona.

Sights
- The medieval legacy lives on in lots of Neo-Gothic and medi-eval motifs in Modernisme (especially the city symbol of St. George slaying the dragon)
- The El Born neighborhood, which flourished during this time
- Catalan Art Museum (excellent Romanesque collection)
- Columbus Monument
- Plaça del Rei and the Royal Palace, where Columbus met Fer-dinand and Isabel
- The coffin of Count Ramon in the cathedral
- Generalitat building and statue of Jaume I on Plaça de Sant Jaume
- The churches of Santa Maria del Mar, Santa Maria del Pi, and the Chapel of St. Agatha (at the Royal Palace), plus the *extra muro* ("outside the walls") Church of Santa Anna
- Montserrat monastery, dating from medieval times

Church Architecture

History comes to life when you visit a centuries-old church. Even if you don't know your apse from a hole in the ground, learning a few simple terms will enrich your experience. Note that not every church will have every feature, and a "cathedral" isn't a type of architecture, but rather a designation for a church that's a governing center for a local bishop.

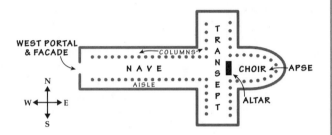

Aisles: The long, generally low-ceilinged arcades that flank the nave.

Altar: The raised area with a ceremonial table (often adorned with candles or a crucifix), where the priest prepares and serves the bread and wine for Communion.

Apse: The space beyond the altar, generally bordered with small chapels.

Barrel Vault: A continuous round-arched ceiling that resembles an extended upside-down U.

Choir: A cozy area, often screened off, located within the church nave and near the high altar, where services are sung in a more intimate setting, often blocking the common people from viewing the altar.

Cloister: Covered hallways bordering a square or rectangular open-air courtyard, traditionally where monks and nuns got fresh air.

Facade: The exterior surface of the church's main (west) entrance, generally highly decorated.

Groin Vault: An arched ceiling formed where two equal barrel vaults meet at right angles. Less common usage: term for a medieval jock strap.

Narthex: The area (portico or foyer) between the main entry and the nave.

Nave: The long, central section of the church (running west to east, from the entrance to the altar) where the congregation sits or stands during the service.

Transept: In a traditional cross-shaped floor plan, the transept is one of the two parts forming the "arms" of the cross. The transepts run north-south, perpendicularly crossing the east-west nave.

West Portal: The main entry to the church (on the west end, opposite the main altar).

DECLINE (1500-1800)

Ironically, the glorious age of Ferdinand and Isabel also sowed the seeds of Barcelona's decline. Columbus' discoveries opened new Atlantic trade routes that made Barcelona's Mediterranean trade routes obsolete. Meanwhile, the center of royal power slowly shifted from Barcelona to the region midway between Aragon and Castile—the growing city of Madrid. While the rest of Spain enjoyed an unprecedented Golden Age of fabulous New World wealth and influence (producing artists such as El Greco, Velázquez, Goya, and Murillo), Barcelona became a poor and forgotten backwater.

On September 11, 1714—a date that is still marked by Catalunya's most sobering holiday—Catalan independence ended. Barcelona found itself on the losing end in the War of Spanish Succession (1701-1714), having sided against the eventual winner, the French-backed King Philip V. On September 11, Philip's forces overran the city walls and massacred those who had stood against him.

For more than a century, the Spanish crown centered in Madrid would punish the rebellious Catalans. They suppressed the Catalan language, culture, and institutions. The Generalitat was disbanded. Trade with the Americas was forbidden. For surveillance and control, the Castilians built an imposing citadel on one side of town and a fortress atop Montjuïc on the other, and ordered that nothing could be built beyond the reach of the fort's cannons. Barcelona spiraled down into a dirty, cramped city contained within its medieval wall.

Sights
- Monument to Catalan Independence in El Born (honoring the victims of September 11, 1714)
- El Born Cultural Center (archaeological site with 18th-century artifacts, plus exhibits on the 1714 siege)
- Castle of Montjuïc
- Citadel Park (previously the site of the citadel)
- Barceloneta fishermen's quarter (built to house those displaced by Citadel construction)
- Betlem Church on the Ramblas (rare example of Baroque)

INDUSTRIAL REVIVAL AND CULTURAL RENAISSANCE (1800-1900)

In the 1800s, another revolution was brewing—the Industrial Revolution. Blessed with soft coal and rushing rivers from the Pyrenees, Barcelona harnessed the power to stoke textile mills. Having finally been given permission to trade with the Americas (1788), they imported cotton and shipped the finished cloth abroad from their busy harbor. Workers flocked in from the countryside, drawn by good-paying jobs. Barcelona's population doubled, reaching a million, and it created a thriving middle class.

By 1850—while the rest of Spain stagnated as a fading colonial power—Catalunya was humming. In 1854, Queen Isabella II finally loosened Madrid's death-grip, allowing the growing city to tear down the medieval wall and expand northward, creating the Eixample neighborhood of modern boulevards. They used new technology to make life better for everyday citizens, bringing in modern plumbing, streetlights, and the first rail line in Spain. The city hosted a World's Fair in 1888 that renovated the city (and gave us the Columbus Monument and other urban improvements).

There was a cultural renaissance of the Catalan language and the arts. Historians divide the movement (somewhat arbitrarily) into two parts. The Renaixença (roughly 1840-1880) was a rediscovery of Catalunya's historic roots and national identity, similar to the Romantic movements sweeping all of Europe. Suddenly, people were embracing the language and traditions of their forebears. Writers wrote in Catalan, and artists revived the medieval motifs of Barcelona's 14th-century glory days. This energy flowed naturally into Modernisme (roughly 1890-1910), which continued the love affair with Catalunya's traditions while championing all things modern—things like streetcars and electric lights. The new technology was also meant to be beautiful, and Modernisme is Barcelona's version of the curvy, wistful Art Nouveau style found elsewhere in Europe. As the old city walls came down, Modernista architects like Antoni Gaudí remade the city with fanciful buildings—made of a modern concrete-and-iron substructure but decorated with colorful, playful, medieval motifs.

Sights
- Eixample neighborhood, with the Block of Discord, La Pedrera, and other buildings
- Sagrada Família
- Other Gaudí and Modernista sights

TURBULENT 20TH CENTURY

By the turn of the 20th century, Barcelona was seething with change. Industrialization had made factory owners rich, but the working class was still poor, living in dirty slums and working in unsafe factories. Barcelona's Socialists fought for the right to bathroom breaks, while anarchists bombed the Liceu Opera House. The unrest culminated in the bloody riots of "Tragic Week" (1909), during which dozens of churches were vandalized and demonstrators were shot in the streets.

Barcelona developed a reputation across Spain as a breeding ground for liberals, troublemakers, and nonconformists. In the art world, young Pablo Picasso captured the plight of society's disenfranchised (in his Blue Period), then moved to Paris and—with fellow artist Georges Braque—broke all the rules of art by pioneering Cubism. Joan Miró perplexed the masses with his childlike doodles, and Salvador Dalí shocked and astonished with his Surrealistic dreamscapes.

When Spain splintered into its bitter civil war (1936-1939)—pitting democratic Republicans against fascist Nationalists—left-

leaning Barcelona became the natural capital of the Republican side. The fascists, under General Francisco Franco (1892-1975), invited Mussolini's Italian air force to bomb Barcelona, killing a thousand citizens. When Barcelona finally fell in 1939, the war was effectively over. For the next four decades, Franco would rule Spain with an iron fist.

Catalunya was punished. The Generalitat was abolished after having been restored just a few years earlier, and the Catalan president was executed by firing squad. Franco began a program of Castilianization to assimilate the region into greater Spain. The Catalan language and traditions were suppressed. You couldn't buy a newspaper in Catalan or hear the people's language spoken on TV. You couldn't dance the *sardana*. Simultaneously, the region was flooded with poor, Castilian-speaking farmers from the rest of Spain, looking for work. The city expanded way too fast, throwing up dusty gray concrete buildings amid suburban sprawl.

But Catalunya kept the flame alive with underground newspapers and a president-in-exile living in France. Finally, Franco died in 1975, and—on September 11, 1977—millions of Catalan patriots flooded the streets to demand their culture back.

It ushered in a third Golden Age for Catalunya. The Generalitat and Catalan president returned. Catalan became the sole

Catalans You May Know

Catalans invented the submarine, assassinated Leon Trotsky, and founded San Diego. Here are a few names you may be familiar with.

Pablo Picasso (1881-1973): Though he was born in Andalucía (to Spanish, not Catalan, parents) and spent his adult life in France, Picasso's formative teenage years were spent in Barcelona's Barri Gòtic.

Salvador Dalí (1904-1989): The master Surrealist was born in Figueres, spent holidays in Cadaqués, and passed his formative years in Barcelona, where he exhibited his early works and soaked up Gaudí's dreamlike architecture.

Joan Miró (1893-1983): Raised in the Barri Gòtic, he divided his adulthood living between Barcelona and Paris. His whimsical sculptures and ceramics adorn Barcelona.

Antoni Gaudí (1852-1926): Resident of the Barri Gòtic (in his youth), the Eixample (in young adulthood), and Park Güell (in his twilight years). Gaudí designed many of Barcelona's iconic Modernista buildings.

Pau (Pablo) Casals (1876-1973): A world-class cellist who's often described as one of the best musicians ever to pick up the instrument, Casals retired to French Catalunya in protest against Franco.

Bacardi Rum Family: The world-famous rum company was founded in Cuba in 1814 by a man from Sitges; it's now run by his great-great-grandson.

Juan Antonio Samaranch (1920-2010): The longtime president of the International Olympic Committee (r. 1980-2001) was born and raised in Barcelona.

Ferran Adrià (b. 1962): This celebrity chef revolutionized cuisine with his innovations in molecular gastronomy at the (now-closed) Costa Brava restaurant El Bulli.

Antoni Tàpies (1923-2012): Spain's best-known postwar artist is most famous for his distinctive mud-caked canvases.

Pau Gasol (b. 1980) and **Marc Gasol** (b. 1985): These basketball-playing brothers grew up in Barcelona.

Rafael Nadal (b. 1986): From the Catalan-speaking island of Mallorca, this multiple Grand Slam-winning tennis star is known as the "King of Clay" for his dominance on that surface.

official language in schools. Barcelona reinvented itself, spiffing up old quarters with new buildings and expanding the Metro system. The Sagrada Família, after nearly a century of false starts, made dramatic progress. In 1992, a revived Barcelona hosted the Summer Olympic Games—for which they rebuilt Montjuïc and the waterfront—and put on a modern face for the world.

Sights

- Picasso Museum
- Fundació Joan Miró, plus Liceu mosaic in the Ramblas, *Woman and Bird* sculpture, and other public works by Miró
- Figueres, hometown of Salvador Dalí
- Cadaqués, a mecca for modern artists
- 1929 World Expo Fairgrounds, including Magic Fountains (at the base of Montjuïc, near Plaça d'Espanya)
- Fresh-looking Montjuïc (with Olympic Stadium) and the rejuvenated waterfront
- *Barcelona Head* sculpture by Roy Lichtenstein, on the waterfront

CATALUNYA TODAY: FEISTY AND PROUD

Today Catalunya navigates a path that may diverge from the rest of Spain. With each visit, I seem to hear more Catalan and less Spanish spoken in the streets. With a population of over 1.6 million, Barcelona is Spain's second city, and the focal point of a polarizing drive for self-rule. (For more on this topic, see the "Independence for Catalunya?" sidebar in the El Born Walk chapter.)

Along with the rest of Spain, Catalunya has suffered from the global economic downturn that began in 2008. Spain's real-estate bubble burst, banks stopped lending, and unemployment soared. So many young Spaniards were out of work that a new name was coined to describe them: *"generación ni-ni"* (the neithernor generation). Under pressure from the European Union, Spain is working to dig itself out of debt.

Regular, massive demonstrations fill Plaça de Catalunya, as the people fight to retain their cultural heritage. As if to underscore their cultural distance from greater Spain, in 2010 Barcelona outlawed the popular Spanish pastime of bullfighting. The Las Arenas bullring is now a shopping mall.

In 2014—300 years after the massacre that ended its autonomy—Catalunya held a referendum on leaving Spain. Eighty percent of those who voted backed independence (though polls indicate that residents are fairly evenly split on the matter). The national government called the vote illegal under the Spanish constitution.

But the secessionist movement was only warming up; upon winning a majority in 2015 regional elections, Catalan nationalist parties passed a motion to begin the secession process. Their 18-month "roadmap" to statehood included plans for a Catalan constitution, army, central bank, and judicial system. The Spanish government, unsurprisingly, proclaimed the plans unconstitutional.

In January 2016, the Catalan parliament elected separatist Charles Puigdemont as president of the regional government. His determination to "chase the invaders out" enlivened the secessionist movement after months of political deadlock.

In October 2017, the Catalan people scheduled another independence referendum, which once again was declared illegal by the central government. National police were sent to Catalunya to suppress voting, and peaceful protests were met with police violence. The Catalans persisted, many voted, and the results favored independence. Puigdemont declared Catalunya a sovereign nation.

In response, Spain's prime minister at the time, Mariano Rajoy, enacted a never-before-used article of Spain's constitution to dissolve the Catalan parliament. Several Catalan politicians were arrested, and Puigdemont fled to Belgium to avoid imprisonment. The whole affair has left the Catalan people deeply divided.

No matter how this political uncertainty is ultimately resolved, it's clear Catalunya will continue to chart its own course.

Sights

- Plaça de Catalunya
- *Sardana* dances in front of the cathedral
- The red-and-gold flag of Catalunya flapping in the breeze

For more on history, consider Europe 101: History and Art for the Traveler, *by Rick Steves and Gene Openshaw (available at www. ricksteves.com).*

PRACTICALITIES

This chapter covers the practical skills of European travel: how to get tourist information, pay for things, sightsee efficiently, find good-value accommodations, eat affordably but well, use technology wisely, and get between destinations smoothly. For more information on these topics, see www.ricksteves.com/travel-tips.

Tourist Information

Spain's national tourist office **in the US** will fill brochure requests and answer your general travel questions by email (newyork. information@tourspain.es). Scan their website (www.spain.info) for practical information and sightseeing ideas; you can download many brochures free of charge. Also see www.barcelonaturisme. cat.

In Barcelona, a good first stop is generally at any of its tourist information offices (abbreviated TI in this book; see page 16 for locations). TIs are in business to help you enjoy spending money in their town, but even so, I still make a point to swing by to confirm sightseeing plans, pick up a city map, and get information on public transit, walking tours, special events, and nightlife. Anticipating a harried front-line staffer, prepare a list of questions and a proposed plan to double-check.

Websites for Barcelona: In addition to the TI websites listed earlier, try www.barcelonaplanning.com and www.guiadelocio. com/barcelona (for events).

Travel Tips

Emergency and Medical Help: For any emergency service—ambulance, police, or fire—call **112** from a mobile phone or landline. If you get sick, do as the locals do and go to a pharmacist for advice. Or ask at your hotel for help—they'll know the nearest medical and emergency services. Operators, who in most countries speak English, will deal with your request or route you to the right emergency service.

Theft or Loss: To replace a passport, you'll need to go in person to an embassy or consulate (see next). If your credit and debit cards disappear, cancel and replace them (see "Damage Control for Lost Cards" later). File a police report, either on the spot or within a day or two; you'll need it to submit an insurance claim for lost or stolen rail passes or travel gear, and it can help with replacing your passport or credit and debit cards. For more information, see www. ricksteves.com/help.

US Consulate: Tel. 932-802-227, after-hours emergency tel. 915-872-200 (Passeig de la Reina Elisenda de Montcada 23, https://es.usembassy.gov).

Canadian Consulate: Tel. 932-703-614, after-hours emergency tel. in Ottawa—call collect 613-996-8885 (Plaça de Catalunya 9, www.spain.gc.ca, click on "Contact Us," then "Consulate of Canada in Barcelona").

Avoiding Theft and Scams: Like anywhere in Europe, thieves target tourists, especially in Barcelona. They break into cars, snatch purses, and pick pockets. Thieves have been known to zip by on motorbikes to grab handbags from pedestrians or even from cars in traffic. A fight or commotion is often created to enable pickpockets to work unnoticed. Someone in a small group pushing you as you enter or exit a crowded subway car may have one hand in your pocket.

Be on guard, use a money belt, and treat any disturbance around you as a smoke screen for theft. Don't believe any "police officers" looking for counterfeit bills. When traveling by train, keep your luggage in sight. Drivers should read the tips on page 313.

Time Zones: Spain, like most of continental Europe, is generally six/nine hours ahead of the East/West coasts of the US. The exceptions are the beginning and end of Daylight Saving Time:

Europe "springs forward" the last Sunday in March (two weeks after most of North America), and "falls back" the last Sunday in October (one week before North America). For a handy time converter, use the world clock app on your mobile phone or download one (see www.timeanddate.com).

Business Hours: For visitors, Spain is a land of strange and frustrating schedules. Many businesses respect the afternoon siesta. When it's 100 degrees in the shade, you'll understand why. The biggest museums stay open all day. Smaller ones often close for a siesta. Shops are generally open from about 9:30 to 14:00 and from 17:00 to 21:00, longer for big chain shops or touristy places. Small shops are often open on Saturday only in the morning, and closed all day Sunday. Banking hours are generally Monday through Friday from 9:00 to 14:00.

Watt's Up? Europe's electrical system is 220 volts, instead of North America's 110 volts. Most newer electronics (such as laptops, battery chargers, and hair dryers) convert automatically, so you won't need a converter plug, but you will need an adapter plug with two round prongs, sold inexpensively at travel stores in the US. Avoid bringing older appliances that don't automatically convert voltage; instead, buy a cheap replacement in Europe.

Discounts: Discounts for sights are generally not listed in this book. However, seniors (age 60 and over), youths under 18, and students and teachers with proper identification cards (www.isic.org) can get discounts at many sights—always ask. Some discounts are available only to European citizens.

Online Translation Tips: Google's Chrome browser instantly translates websites; Translate.google.com is also handy. The Google Translate app converts spoken English into most European languages (and vice versa) and can also translate text it "reads" with your phone's camera.

Money

Here's my basic strategy for using money in Europe:
- Upon arrival, head for a cash machine (ATM) at the airport and withdraw some local currency, using a debit card with low international transaction fees.
- Pay for most purchases with your choice of cash or a credit card. You'll save money by minimizing your credit and debit card exchange fees. The trend is for bigger expenses to be made by credit card, but cash is still the standby for small purchases and tips.
- Keep your cards and cash safe in a money belt.

Exchange Rate

1 euro (€) = about $1.20

To convert prices in euros to dollars, add about 20 percent: €20 = about $24, €50 = about $60. (Check www.oanda.com for the latest exchange rates.) Just like the dollar, one euro (€) is broken down into 100 cents. Coins range from €0.01 to €2, and bills from €5 to €200 (bills over €50 are rarely used; €500 bills are being phased out).

PLASTIC VERSUS CASH

Although credit cards are widely accepted in Europe, cash is sometimes the only way to pay for cheap food, taxis, tips, and local guides. Some businesses (especially smaller ones, such as B&Bs and mom-and-pop cafés and shops) may charge you extra for using a credit card—or might not accept credit cards at all. Having cash on hand helps you out of a jam if your card randomly doesn't work.

I use my credit card to book hotel reservations, to buy advance tickets for events or sights, and to cover most other expenses. It can also be smart to use plastic near the end of your trip, to avoid another visit to the ATM.

WHAT TO BRING

I pack the following and keep it all safe in my money belt.

Debit Card: Use this at ATMs to withdraw local cash.

Credit Card: Handy for bigger purchases (at hotels, shops, restaurants, travel agencies, car-rental agencies, and so on), payment machines, and ordering online.

Backup Card: Some travelers carry a third card (debit or credit; ideally from a different bank), in case one gets lost, demagnetized, eaten by a temperamental machine, or simply doesn't work.

A Stash of Cash: I always carry $100-200 as a cash backup. A stash of cash comes in handy for emergencies, such as if your ATM card stops working.

What NOT to Bring: Resist the urge to buy **euros** before your trip or you'll pay the price in bad stateside exchange rates. Wait until you arrive to withdraw money. I've yet to see a European airport that didn't have plenty of ATMs.

BEFORE YOU GO

Use this pre-trip checklist.

Know your cards. Debit cards from any major US bank will work in any standard European bank's ATM (ideally, use a debit card with a Visa or MasterCard logo). As for credit cards, Visa and

PRACTICALITIES

MasterCard are universal, American Express is less common, and Discover is unknown in Europe.

Know your PIN. Make sure you know the numeric, four-digit PIN for all of your cards, both debit and credit. Request it if you don't have one and allow time to receive the information by mail.

All credit and debit cards now have chips that authenticate and secure transactions. Europeans insert their chip cards into the payment machine slot, then enter a PIN. American cards should work in most transactions without a PIN—but may not work at self-service machines at train stations, toll booths, gas pumps, or parking lots. I've been inconvenienced a few times by self-service payment machines in Europe that wouldn't accept my card, but it's never caused me serious trouble.

If you're concerned, a few banks offer a chip-and-PIN card that works in almost all payment machines, including those from Andrews Federal Credit Union (www.andrewsfcu.org) and State Department Federal Credit Union (www.sdfcu.org).

Report your travel dates. Let your bank know that you'll be using your debit and credit cards in Europe, and when and where you're headed.

Adjust your ATM withdrawal limit. Find out how much you can take out daily and ask for a higher daily withdrawal limit if you want to get more cash at once. Note that European ATMs will withdraw funds only from checking accounts; you're unlikely to have access to your savings account.

Ask about fees. For any purchase or withdrawal made with a card, you may be charged a currency conversion fee (1-3 percent) and/or a Visa or MasterCard international transaction fee (1 percent). If you're getting a bad deal, consider getting a new debit or credit card. Reputable no-fee cards include those from Capital One, as well as Charles Schwab debit cards. Most credit unions and some airline loyalty cards have low-to-no international transaction fees.

IN EUROPE
Using Cash Machines

European cash machines have English-language instructions and work just like they do at home—except they spit out local currency instead of dollars, calculated at the day's standard bank-to-bank rate.

In most places, ATMs are easy to locate—in Spain ask for a *cajero automático*. When possible, withdraw cash from a bank-run ATM located just outside that bank. Ideally use it during the bank's opening hours so if your card is munched by the machine, you can go inside for help. Bank ATMs usually don't charge usage fees—except for Caixabank—and are generally more secure.

If your debit card doesn't work, try a lower amount—your request may have exceeded your withdrawal limit or the ATM's limit. If you still have a problem, try a different ATM or come back later—your bank's network may be temporarily down.

Avoid "independent" ATMs, such as Travelex, Euronet, Moneybox, Cardpoint, and Cashzone. These have high fees, can be less secure, and may try to trick users with "dynamic currency conversion" (see below).

Exchanging Cash

Avoid exchanging money in Europe; it's a big rip-off. In a pinch you can always find exchange desks at major train stations or airports—convenient but with crummy rates. Anything over 5 percent for a transaction is piracy. Banks generally do not exchange money unless you have an account with them.

Using Credit Cards

US cards no longer require a signature for verification, but don't be surprised if a European card reader generates a receipt for you to sign. Some card readers will accept your card as is; others may prompt you to enter your PIN (so it's important to know the code for each of your cards). If a cashier is present, you should have no problems.

At self-service payment machines (transit-ticket kiosks, parking, etc.), results are mixed, as US cards may not work in unattended transactions. If your card won't work, look for a cashier who can process your card manually—or pay in cash.

Drivers Beware: Be aware of potential problems using a US credit card to fill up at an unattended gas station, enter a parking garage, or exit a toll road. Carry cash and be prepared to move on to the next gas station if necessary. When approaching a toll plaza, use the "cash" lane.

Dynamic Currency Conversion

If merchants offer to convert your purchase price into dollars (called dynamic currency conversion, or DCC), refuse this "service." You'll pay extra for the expensive convenience of seeing your charge in dollars. If an ATM offers to "lock in" or "guarantee" your conversion rate, choose "proceed without conversion." Other prompts might state, "You can be charged in dollars: Press YES for dollars, NO for euros." Always choose the local currency.

Security Tips

Pickpockets target tourists. Keep your cash, credit cards, and passport secure in your money belt, and carry only a day's spending money in your front pocket or wallet.

Before inserting your card into an ATM, inspect the front. If anything looks crooked, loose, or damaged, it could be a sign of a card-skimming device. When entering your PIN, carefully block other people's view of the keypad.

Don't use a debit card for purchases. Because a debit card pulls funds directly from your bank account, potential charges incurred by a thief will stay on your account while the fraudulent use is investigated by your bank.

To access your accounts online while traveling, be sure to use a secure connection (see the "Tips on Internet Security" sidebar, later).

Damage Control for Lost Cards

If you lose your credit or debit card, report the loss immediately to the respective global customer-assistance centers. Call these 24-hour US numbers collect: Visa (tel. 303/967-1096), MasterCard (tel. 636/722-7111), and American Express (tel. 336/393-1111). In Spain, to make a collect call to the US, dial 900-990-011. European toll-free numbers can be found at the websites for Visa and MasterCard.

You'll need to provide the primary cardholder's identification-verification details (such as birth date, mother's maiden name, or Social Security number). You can generally receive a temporary card within two or three business days in Europe (see www.ricksteves.com/help for more).

If you report your loss within two days, you typically won't be responsible for unauthorized transactions on your account, although many banks charge a liability fee of $50.

TIPPING

Tipping in Spain isn't as automatic and generous as in the US. For special service, tips are appreciated, but not expected. As in the US, the proper amount depends on your resources, tipping philosophy, and the circumstances, but some general guidelines apply.

Restaurants: If eating at the counter of a tapas bar, there's no need to tip, though it's fine to round up the bill with a few small coins. At restaurants with table service, if a service charge is included in the bill, add about 5 percent; if it's not, leave 10 percent. For more details on tipping in restaurants and tapas bars, see pages 290 and 293.

Taxis: For a typical ride, just round up your fare a bit (for instance, if the fare is €4.85, pay €5). If the cabbie hauls your bags

PRACTICALITIES

and zips you to the airport to help you catch your flight, you might want to toss in a little more. But if you feel like you're being driven in circles or otherwise ripped off, skip the tip.

Services: In general, if someone in the tourism or service industry does a super job for you, a small tip of a euro or two is appropriate...but not required. If you're not sure whether (or how much) to tip, ask a local for advice.

GETTING A VAT REFUND

Wrapped into the purchase price of your Spanish souvenirs is a Value-Added Tax (VAT) of 21 percent (in Spain, it's called IVA—*Impuesto sobre el Valor Añadido*). You're entitled to get most of that tax back if you purchase more than €90 (about $110) worth of goods at a store that participates in the VAT-refund scheme. Typically, you must ring up the minimum at a single retailer—you can't add up your purchases from various shops to reach the required amount. (If the store ships the goods to your US home, VAT is not assessed on your purchase.)

Getting your refund is straightforward...and worthwhile if you spend a significant amount on souvenirs.

Get the paperwork. Have the merchant completely fill out the necessary refund document. You'll have to present your passport. Get the paperwork done before you leave the store to ensure you'll have everything you need (including your original sales receipt).

Get your stamp at the border or airport. Process your VAT document at your last stop in the European Union (such as at the airport) with the customs agent who deals with VAT refunds. Arrive an additional hour early before you need to check in to allow time to find the customs office—and wait. Some customs desks are positioned before airport security; confirm the location before going through security.

It's best to keep your purchases in your carry-on. If they're not allowed as carry-on (such as knives), pack them in your checked bags and alert the check-in agent. You'll be sent (with your tagged bag) to a customs desk outside security; someone will examine your bag, stamp your paperwork, and put your bag on the belt. You're not supposed to use your purchased goods before you leave. If you show up at customs wearing your new soccer jersey, officials might look the other way—or deny you a refund.

Collect your refund. You can claim your VAT refund from refund companies, such as Global Blue or Premier Tax Free, with offices at major airports, ports, or border crossings (either before or after security, probably strategically located near a duty-free shop). These services (which extract a 4 percent fee) can refund your money in cash immediately or credit your card (within two billing cycles). Otherwise, you'll need to mail the stamped refund documents to the address given by the shop where you made your purchase.

CUSTOMS FOR AMERICAN SHOPPERS

You can take home $800 worth of items per person duty-free, once every 31 days. Many processed and packaged foods are allowed, including vacuum-packed cheeses, dried herbs, jams, baked goods, candy, chocolate, oil, vinegar, mustard, and honey. Fresh fruits and vegetables and most meats are not allowed, with exceptions for some canned items. As for alcohol, you can bring in one liter duty-free (it can be packed securely in your checked luggage, along with any other liquid-containing items).

To bring alcohol (or liquid-packed foods) in your carry-on bag on your flight home, buy it at a duty-free shop at the airport. You'll increase your odds of getting it onto a connecting flight if it's packaged in a "STEB"—a secure, tamper-evident bag. But stay away from liquids in opaque, ceramic, or metallic containers, which usually cannot be successfully screened (STEB or no STEB).

For details on allowable goods, customs rules, and duty rates, visit http://help.cbp.gov.

Sightseeing

Sightseeing can be hard work. Use these tips to make your visits to sights meaningful, fun, efficient, and painless.

MAPS AND NAVIGATION TOOLS

A good map is essential for efficient navigation while sightseeing. The maps in this book are concise and simple, designed to help you locate recommended destinations, sights, and local TIs, where you can pick up more in-depth maps. More detailed maps are sold at newsstands and bookstores.

You can also use a mapping app on your mobile device. Be aware that pulling up maps or looking up turn-by-turn walking directions on the fly requires an internet connection: To use this feature, it's smart to get an international data plan. With Google Maps or CityMaps2Go, it's possible to download a map while online, then go offline and navigate without incurring data-roaming charges, though you can't search for an address or get real-time walking directions. A handful of other apps—including Apple Maps, OffMaps, and Navfree—also allow you to use maps offline.

PLAN AHEAD

Set up an itinerary that allows you to fit in all your must-see sights. For a one-stop look at opening hours, see "Barcelona at a Glance" (page 34; also see the "Daily Reminder" on page 17). Most sights keep stable hours, but you can easily confirm the latest by checking with the TI or visiting museum websites.

Don't put off visiting a must-see sight—you never know when a place will close unexpectedly for a holiday, strike, or restoration. Given how precious your vacation time is, I recommend getting reservations for any must-see sight that offers them. Many museums are closed or have reduced hours at least a few days a year, especially on holidays such as Christmas, New Year's, and Labor Day (May 1). A list of holidays is in the appendix; check online for possible museum closures during your trip. In summer, some sights may stay open late; in the off-season, hours may be shorter.

Going at the right time helps avoid crowds. This book offers tips on the best times to see specific sights. Try visiting popular sights very early or very late. Evening visits (when possible) are usually peaceful, with fewer crowds. For Barcelona, see the "Sights Open Late" sidebar on page 216.

If you plan to hire a local guide, reserve ahead by email. Popular guides can get booked up.

Study up. To get the most out of the sight descriptions in this book, read them before you visit. Gaudí seems less gaudy if you understand his artistic vision.

AT SIGHTS

Here's what you can typically expect:

Entering: Be warned that you may not be allowed to enter if you arrive less than 30 to 60 minutes before closing time. And guards start ushering people out well before the actual closing time, so don't save the best for last.

Many sights have a security check. Allow extra time for these lines. Some sights require you to check daypacks and coats. (If you'd rather not check your daypack, try carrying it tucked under your arm like a purse as you enter.)

At churches—which often offer interesting art (usually free) and a cool, welcome seat—a modest dress code (no bare shoulders or shorts) is encouraged though rarely enforced.

Photography: If the museum's photo policy isn't clearly posted, ask a guard. Generally, taking photos without a flash or tripod is allowed. Some sights ban selfie sticks; others ban photos altogether.

Temporary Exhibits: Museums may show special exhibits in addition to their permanent collection. Some exhibits are included in the entry price, while others come at an extra cost (which you may have to pay even if you don't want to see the exhibit).

Expect Changes: Artwork can be on tour, on loan, out sick, or shifted at the whim of the curator. Pick up a floor plan as you enter, and ask the museum staff if you can't find a particular item.

PRACTICALITIES

Say the title or artist's name, or point to the photograph in this book, and ask, *"¿Dónde está?"* (DOHN-day eh-STAH; meaning, "Where is?").

Audioguides and Apps: Many sights rent audioguides, which generally offer dry-but-useful recorded descriptions in English (about €3-5). Many audioguides have a standard output jack, so if you bring your own headphones, you can often enjoy better sound. To save money, bring a Y-jack and share one audioguide with your travel partner. Increasingly, museums and sights offer apps—often free—that you can download to your mobile device (check their websites). And, I've produced free, downloadable audio tours, including my Barcelona City Walk and an Eixample Walk (coming in 2019); look for the ∩ in this book. For more on my audio tours, see page 6.

Services: Important sights usually have an on-site café or cafeteria (usually a handy place to rejuvenate during a long visit). The WCs at sights are free and generally clean.

Before Leaving: At the gift shop, scan the postcard rack or thumb through a guidebook to be sure that you haven't overlooked something that you'd like to see.

Every sight or museum offers more than what is covered in this book. Use the information in this book as an introduction—not the final word.

Sleeping

Extensive and opinionated listings of good-value rooms are a major feature of this book's Sleeping sections. Rather than list accommodations scattered throughout a town, I choose hotels in my favorite neighborhoods that are convenient to your sightseeing. My recommendations run the gamut, from dorm beds to fancy rooms with all the comforts. I like places that are clean, central, relatively quiet at night, reasonably priced, friendly, small enough to have a hands-on owner, and run with a respect for Spanish traditions. I'm more impressed by a handy location and fun-loving philosophy than flat-screen TVs and a fancy gym. Most of my recommendations fall short of perfection. But if I can find a place with most of these features, it's a keeper.

In Spain, peak season runs from Easter through October, while low season is typically November until around Easter. But Barcelona can be busy any time of year. Book your accommodations well in advance, especially if you want to stay at one of my top listings or if you'll be traveling during peak times or during any holidays or festivals. See the appendix for a list of major holidays and festivals. In Barcelona, trade fairs crop up throughout the

Sleep Code

Hotels in this book are categorized according to the average price of a standard double room without breakfast in high season.

$$$$	**Splurge:** Most rooms over €170
$$$	**Pricier:** €130-170
$$	**Moderate:** €90-130
$	**Budget:** €50-90
¢	**Backpacker:** Under €50
RS%	**Rick Steves discount**

Unless otherwise noted, credit cards are accepted, hotel staff speak basic English, and free Wi-Fi is available. Comparison-shop by checking prices at several hotels (on each hotel's own website, on a booking site, or by email). For the best deal, *book directly with the hotel.* Ask for a discount if paying in cash; if the listing includes **RS%**, request a Rick Steves discount.

year and can send rates soaring (search for trade fair dates at www. firabarcelona.com/en/home).

RATES AND DEALS

I've categorized my recommended accommodations based on price, indicated with a dollar-sign rating (see sidebar). The price ranges suggest an estimated cost for a one-night stay in a standard double room with a private toilet and shower in high season, don't include breakfast, and assume you're booking directly with the hotel (not through a booking site, which extracts a commission). Room prices can fluctuate significantly with demand and amenities (size, views, room class, and so on), but relative price categories remain constant. Hoteliers are encouraged to quote prices with the IVA tax included—but it's smart to ask when you book your room. Additionally, the city of Barcelona levies a tourist tax up to a couple of euros per person per night.

Room rates are especially volatile at larger hotels that use "dynamic pricing" to set rates. Prices can skyrocket during festivals and conventions, while business hotels can have deep discounts on weekends when demand plummets. Of the many hotels I recommend, it's difficult to say which will be the best value on a given day—until you do your homework.

Booking Direct: Once your dates are set, compare prices at several hotels. You can do this by checking Hotels.com, Booking. com, and hotel websites. To get the best deal, contact family-run hotels directly by phone or email. When you go direct, the owner avoids the commission paid to booking sites, thereby leaving enough wiggle room to offer you a discount, a nicer room, or a free

PRACTICALITIES

breakfast (if it's not already included). If you prefer to book online or are considering a hotel chain, it's to your advantage to use the hotel's website.

Getting a Discount: Some hotels extend a discount to those who pay cash or stay longer than three nights. And some accommodations offer a special discount for Rick Steves readers, indicated in this guidebook by the abbreviation "**RS%.**" Discounts vary: Ask for details when you reserve. Generally, to qualify for this discount, you must book direct (not through a booking site), mention this book when you reserve, show this book upon arrival, and sometimes pay cash or stay a certain number of nights. In some cases, you may need to enter a discount code (which I've provided in the listing) in the booking form on the hotel's website. Rick Steves discounts apply to readers with either print or digital books. Understandably, discounts do not apply to promotional rates.

TYPES OF ACCOMMODATIONS
Hotels

In this book, the price for a double room ranges from about $60 (very simple, toilet and shower down the hall) to $400 (maximum plumbing and more), with most clustering at about $150.

Some hotels can add an extra bed (for a small charge) to turn a double into a triple; some offer larger rooms for four or more people (I call these "family rooms" in the listings). If there's space for an extra cot, they'll cram it in for you. In general, a triple room is cheaper than the cost of a double and a single. Three or four people can economize by requesting one big room.

Spain has stringent restrictions on smoking in public places. Smoking is not permitted in common areas, but hotels can designate 10 percent of their rooms for smokers.

Arrival and Check-In: Hotels and B&Bs are sometimes located on the higher floors of a multipurpose building with a secured door. In that case, look for your hotel's name on the buttons by the main entrance. When you ring the bell, you'll be buzzed in.

Hotel elevators are becoming more common, though some older buildings still lack them. You may have to climb a flight of stairs to reach the elevator (if so, you can ask the front desk for help carrying your bags up). Elevators are typically very small—pack light, or you may need to send your bags up without you.

The EU requires that hotels collect your name, nationality, and ID number. When you check in, the receptionist will normally ask for your passport and may keep it for anywhere from a couple of minutes to a couple of hours. (If not comfortable leaving your passport at the desk for a long time, ask when you can pick it up.) They may also ask you to sign a registration for police records.

Keep Cool

If you're visiting Spain in the summer, you'll want an air-conditioned room. Most hotel air-conditioners come with a control stick (like a TV remote; sometimes the hotel requires a deposit) that generally has similar symbols and features: fan icon (click to toggle through wind power, from light to gale); louver icon (choose steady airflow or waves); snowflake and sunshine icons (cold air or heat, depending on season); clock ("O" setting: run X hours before turning off; "I" setting: wait X hours to start); and the temperature control (21 or 22 degrees Celsius is comfortable). When you leave your room for the day, turning off the air-conditioning is good form.

If you're arriving in the morning, your room probably won't be ready. Check your bag safely at the hotel and dive right into sightseeing.

In Your Room: Most hotel rooms have a TV, telephone, and free Wi-Fi (although in old buildings with thick walls, the Wi-Fi signal might be available only in the lobby). Simpler places rarely have a room phone.

More pillows and blankets are usually in the closet or available on request. Towels and linens aren't always replaced every day, so hang your towel up to dry.

Some hotels don't use central heat before November 1 and after April 1 (unless it's unusually cold); prepare for cool evenings if you travel in spring and fall. Summer can be extremely hot. Consider air-conditioning, fans, and noise (since you'll want your window open). Many rooms come with mini-refrigerators.

Checking Out: While it's customary to pay for your room upon departure, it can be a good idea to settle your bill the day before, when you're not in a hurry and while the manager's in. That way you'll have time to discuss and address any points of contention.

Hotelier Help: Hoteliers can be a good source of advice. Most know their city well, and can assist you with everything from public transit and airport connections to finding a good restaurant, the nearest launderette, or a late-night pharmacy.

Hotel Hassles: Even at the best places, mechanical breakdowns occur: Sinks leak, hot water turns cold, toilets may gurgle or smell, the Wi-Fi goes out, or the air-conditioning dies when you need it most. Report your concerns clearly and calmly at the front desk.

Street noise in Spain is high (Spaniards are notorious night owls), and walls and doors tend to be very thin—earplugs are a necessity. Always ask to see your room first. If you suspect night noise

PRACTICALITIES

Using Online Services to Your Advantage

From booking services to user reviews, online businesses are playing a greater role in travelers' planning than ever before. Take advantage of their pluses—and be wise to their downsides.

Booking Sites

Hotel booking websites, including Priceline's Booking.com and Expedia's Hotels.com, offer one-stop shopping for hotels. While convenient for travelers, they present a real problem for small, independent, family-run hotels. Without a presence on these sites, these hotels become almost invisible. But to be listed, a hotel must pay a sizeable commission...and promise that its own website won't undercut the price on the booking-service site.

Here's the work-around: Use the big sites to research what's out there, then book direct with the hotel by email or phone, in which case hotel owners are free to give you whatever price they like. Ask for a room without the commission mark-up (or ask for a free breakfast if not included, or a free upgrade). If you do book online, be sure to use the hotel's website. The price will likely be the same as via a booking site, but your money goes to the hotel, not agency commissions.

As a savvy consumer, remember: When you book with an online booking service, you're adding a middleman who takes roughly 20 percent. To support small, family-run hotels whose world is more difficult than ever, book direct.

Short-Term Rental Sites

Rental juggernaut Airbnb (along with other short-term rental sites) allows travelers to rent rooms and apartments directly from locals, often providing more value than a cookie-cutter hotel. Airbnb fans appreciate feeling part of a real neighborhood and getting into a daily routine as "temporary Europeans." Depending on the host, Airbnb can provide an opportunity to get

will be a problem, request a quiet *(tranquilo)* room in the back or on an upper floor *(planta alta)*. In most cases, view rooms *(con vista)* come with street noise. You'll often sleep better and for less money in a room without a view.

To guard against theft in your room, keep valuables out of sight. Some rooms come with a safe, and other hotels have safes at the front desk. I've never bothered using one and in a lifetime of travel, I've never had anything stolen from my room.

For more complicated problems, don't expect instant results. Any legitimate place is legally required to have a complaint book *(libro de reclamaciones)*. A request for this book will generally prompt the hotelier to solve your problem to keep you from writing to know a local person, while keeping the money spent on your accommodations in the community.

Critics view Airbnb as a threat to "traditional Europe," saying it creates unfair, unqualified competition for established guesthouse owners. In some places, the lucrative Airbnb market has forced traditional guesthouses out of business and is driving property values out of range for locals. Some cities have cracked down, requiring owners to occupy rental properties part of the year (and staging disruptive "inspections" that inconvenience guests).

As a lover of Europe, I share the worry of those who see residents nudged aside by tourists. But as an advocate for travelers, I appreciate the value and cultural intimacy Airbnb provides.

User Reviews

User-generated review sites and apps such as Yelp and TripAdvisor can give you a consensus of opinions about everything from hotels and restaurants to sights and nightlife. If you scan reviews of a restaurant or hotel and see several complaints about noise or a rotten location, you've gained insight that can help in your decision-making.

But as a guidebook writer, my sense is that there is a big difference between the uncurated information on a review site and the vetted listings in a guidebook. A user-generated review is based on the limited experience of one person, who stayed at just one hotel in a given city and ate at a few restaurants there. A guidebook is the work of a trained researcher who forms a well-developed basis for comparison by visiting many restaurants and hotels year after year.

Both types of information have their place, and in many ways, they're complementary. If something is well reviewed in a guidebook and it also gets good online reviews, it's likely a winner.

a complaint. Above all, keep a positive attitude. If your hotel is a disappointment, spend more time out enjoying the place you came to see.

Hostales and Pensiones

Budget hotels—called *hostales* and *pensiones*—are easy to find, inexpensive, and, when chosen properly, a fun part of the Spanish cultural experience. These places are often family-owned, and may or may not have amenities such as private bathrooms and air-conditioning. Don't confuse a *hostal* with a hostel—a Spanish *hostal* is an inexpensive hotel, not a hostel with bunks in dorms.

Making Hotel Reservations

Reserve your rooms as soon as you've pinned down your travel dates. For busy national holidays (and, in Barcelona, trade fairs), it's wise to reserve far in advance (see the appendix).

Requesting a Reservation: For family-run hotels, it's generally cheaper to book your room directly via email or a phone call. For business-class hotels, or if you'd rather book online, reserve directly through the hotel's official website (not a booking website). For complicated requests, send an email. Almost all of my recommended hotels take reservations in English.

Here's what the hotelier wants to know:

- Type(s) of rooms you want and size of your party
- Number of nights you'll stay
- Your arrival and departure dates, written European-style as day/month/year (18/06/20 or 18 June 2020)
- Special requests (en suite bathroom, cheapest room, twin beds vs. double bed, quiet room)
- Applicable discounts (such as a Rick Steves reader discount, cash discount, or promotional rate)

Confirming a Reservation: Most places will request a credit-card number to hold your room. If you're using an online reservation form, look for the *https* or a lock icon at the top of your browser. If you book direct, you can email, call, or fax this information.

Canceling a Reservation: If you must cancel, it's courteous—and smart—to do so with as much notice as possible, especially for smaller family-run places. Cancellation policies can be strict; read

Short-Term Rentals

A short-term rental—whether an apartment, house, or room in a local's home—is an increasingly popular alternative, especially if you plan to settle in one location for several nights. For stays longer than a few days, you can usually find a rental that's comparable to—and cheaper than—a hotel room with similar amenities. Plus, you'll get a behind-the-scenes peek into how locals live.

Many places require a minimum stay. And you're generally on your own: There's no hotel reception desk, breakfast, or daily cleaning service.

Finding Accommodations: Aggregator websites such as Airbnb, FlipKey, Booking.com, and the HomeAway family of sites (HomeAway, VRBO, and VacationRentals) let you browse properties and correspond directly with European property owners or managers. If you prefer to work from a curated list of accommodations, consider using a rental agency such as InterhomeUSA.com or RentaVilla.com. Agency-represented apartments typically cost more, but this method often offers more help and safeguards

From:	rick@ricksteves.com
Sent:	Today
To:	info@hotelcentral.com
Subject:	Reservation request for 19-22 July

Dear Hotel Central,

I would like to stay at your hotel. Please let me know if you have a room available and the price for:
• 2 people
• Double bed and en suite bathroom in a quiet room
• Arriving 19 July, departing 22 July (3 nights)

Thank you!
Rick Steves

the fine print before you book. Many discount deals require pre-payment, with cancellation refunds.

Reconfirming a Reservation: Always call or email to reconfirm your room reservation a few days in advance. For B&Bs or very small hotels, I call again on my day of arrival to tell my host what time to expect me (especially important if arriving late—after 17:00).

Phoning: For tips on how to call hotels overseas, see page 300.

than booking direct. For a list of agencies specializing in Barcelona apartment rentals, see page 179.

Before you commit, be clear on the location. I like to virtually "explore" the neighborhood using the Street View feature on Google Maps. Also consider the proximity to public transportation and how well-connected the property is with the rest of the city. Ask about amenities (elevator, laundry, Wi-Fi, parking, etc.). Reviews from previous guests can help identify trouble spots.

Think about the kind of experience you want: Just a key and an affordable bed...or a chance to get to know a local? There are typically two kinds of hosts: those who want minimal interaction with their guests, and hosts who are friendly and may want to interact with you. Read the promotional text and online reviews to help shape your decision.

Confirming and Paying: Many places require you to pay the entire balance before your trip. It's easiest and safest to pay through the site where you found the listing. Be wary of owners who want to take your transaction offline; this gives you no recourse if things go awry. Never agree to wire money (a key indicator of a fraudulent transaction).

Apartments or Houses: If you're staying somewhere for four or more nights, it's worth considering an apartment or rental house (shorter stays aren't worth the hassle of arranging key pickup, buying groceries, etc.). Apartment and house rentals can be especially cost-effective for groups and families. European apartments, like hotel rooms, tend to be small by US standards. But they often come with laundry machines and small, equipped kitchens, making it easier and cheaper to dine in.

Rooms in Private Homes: Renting a room in someone's home is a good option for those traveling alone, as you're more likely to find true single rooms—with just one single bed, and a price to match. These can range from air-mattress-in-living-room basic to plush-B&B-suite posh. Some places allow you to book for a single night; if staying for several nights, you can buy groceries just as you would in a rental house. While you can't expect your host to also be your tour guide—or even to provide you with much info— some may be interested in getting to know the travelers who come through their home.

Other Options: Swapping homes with a local works for people with an appealing place to offer (don't assume where you live is not interesting to Europeans). A good place to start is HomeExchange. To sleep for free, Couchsurfing.com is a vagabond's alternative to Airbnb. It lists millions of outgoing members, who host fellow "surfers" in their homes.

Hostels

A hostel *(albergue juvenil)* provides cheap beds in dorms where you sleep alongside strangers for about €20-30 per night. Travelers of any age are welcome if they don't mind dorm-style accommodations and meeting other travelers. Most hostels offer kitchen facilities, guest computers, Wi-Fi, and a self-service laundry. Hostels almost always provide bedding, but the towel's up to you (though you can usually rent one for a small fee). Family and private rooms are often available.

Independent hostels tend to be easygoing, colorful, and informal (no membership required; www.hostelworld.com). You may pay slightly less by booking directly with the hostel. **Official hostels** are part of Hostelling International (HI) and share an online booking site (www.hihostels.com). HI hostels typically require that you be a member or pay a bit more per night.

Eating

Spanish cuisine is hearty, and meals are served in big, inexpensive portions. You can eat well in restaurants for about €15-20—or even

more cheaply and more varied if you graze on appetizer-sized tapas in bars.

In this guidebook, I list restaurants that are convenient to my hotel listings and sight-seeing. When restaurant-hunting, choose a spot filled with locals, not the place with the big neon signs boasting, "We Speak English and Accept Credit Cards." And avoid any restaurant that posts big photographs of its food. Venturing even a block or two off the main drag leads to higher-quality food for a better price.

The Spanish eating schedule—lunch from 13:00 to 16:00, dinner after 21:00—frustrates many visitors. Most Spaniards eat one major meal of the day—lunch *(comida)*—around 14:00, when stores close, schools let out, and people gather with their friends and family for the siesta. Because most Spaniards work until 19:30, supper *(cena)* is usually served at about 21:00 or 22:00. And, since few people want a heavy meal that late, many Spaniards eat a light tapas dinner.

Generally, no self-respecting *casa de comidas* ("house of eating"—when you see this label, you can bet it's a good, traditional eatery) serves meals at American hours. If you're looking for the "nontouristy restaurant," remember that a popular spot is often filled with tourists at 20:00; then at 22:00 the scene is entirely different—and more authentic.

Survival Tips for Spanish Eating Schedules: To bridge the gap between their coffee-and-roll breakfast and late lunch, many Spaniards eat a light meal at about 11:00 *(merienda)*. This can be a light lunch at a bar or a *bocadillo* (baguette sandwich)—hence the popularity of fast-food *bocadillo* chains such as Pans & Company. Besides *bocadillos*, bars often have slices of *tortilla española* (potato omelet) and fresh-squeezed orange juice. For your main meal of the day, you can either eat a late lunch at a restaurant at around 15:00, then have a light tapas snack for dinner; or reverse it, having a tapas meal in the afternoon, followed by a late restaurant dinner. Either way, tapas bars are the key.

RESTAURANT PRICING

I've categorized my recommended eateries based on the average price of a typical main course, indicated with a dollar-sign rating

PRACTICALITIES

Restaurant Code

Eateries in this book are categorized according to the average cost of a typical main course. Drinks, desserts, and splurge items can raise the price considerably.

$$$$	**Splurge:** Most main courses over €25
$$$	**Pricier:** €18-25
$$	**Moderate:** €12-18
$	**Budget:** Under €12

In Spain, takeout food is **$;** a basic tapas bar or no-frills sit-down eatery is **$$;** a casual but more upscale tapas bar or restaurant is **$$$;** and a swanky splurge is **$$$$.**

(see sidebar). Obviously, expensive specialties, fine wine, appetizers, and dessert can significantly increase your final bill.

The categories also indicate the personality of a place: **Budget** eateries include street food, takeaway, order-at-the-counter shops, basic cafeterias, and bakeries selling sandwiches. **Moderate** eateries are nice (but not fancy) sit-down restaurants, ideal for a straightforward, fill-the-tank meal. Most of my listings fall in this category—great for a good taste of local cuisine.

Pricier eateries are a notch up, with more attention paid to the setting, presentation, and (often inventive) cuisine. **Splurge** eateries are dress-up-for-a-special-occasion swanky—typically with an elegant setting, polished service, intricate cuisine, and an expansive (and expensive) wine list.

BREAKFAST

Hotel breakfasts are generally handy, optional, and pricey (about €6 and up). Start your day instead at a corner bar or at a colorful café near a market hall (and pay just €2-3). Ask for the *desayunos* (breakfast special, usually only available until noon), which can include coffee, a roll (or sandwich), and juice—much cheaper than ordering them separately. Sandwiches can either be on white bread (called "sandwich") or on a baguette *(bocadillo).*

A basic and standard savory breakfast item is the *tostada (torrada* in Catalan)—toasted white bread with olive oil and cured ham, *fuet* (a typical Catalan cured sausage), or cheese. Other options include the *bikini* (grilled ham-and-cheese sandwich) or a slice of *tortilla española* (potato omelet), which is often accompanied by *pa amb tomàquet* (toasted white bread with olive oil, tomato, and salt).

Those with a sweet tooth will find various sweet rolls *(bollos* or *bollería).* If you like a doughnut and coffee in American greasy-spoon joints, try the Spanish equivalent: *churros* (or the thicker *porras*) that you dip in warm chocolate pudding or your *café con leche.*

I've listed some key words for breakfast (in some cases, I've also provided the Catalan translation). For coffee and other beverages, see the section on Spanish drinks, later.

Bamba de nata: Cream puff

Bikini: Grilled ham-and-cheese sandwich, named after a Barcelona concert hall called Bikini

Bocadillo (bocata) con jamón/queso/mixto: Baguette sandwich with ham/cheese/both

Bocadillo (bocata) mixto con huevo: Baguette sandwich with ham and cheese and an over-easy egg on top

Bollos/bollería (pastisseria): Sweet pastry

Caracola: "Snail"-shaped pastry, similar to a cinnamon roll

Churros (xurros): Fried dough pastry that you dip in warm chocolate pudding or *café con leche* (*porras* is the thicker version)

Croissant a la plancha: Croissant grilled and slathered with butter

Napolitana: Rolled pastry, filled with chocolate (similar to French *pain au chocolat*) or *crema* (cream)

Palmera: Palm-shaped pastry, like a French *palmier* or "elephant ear"

Pan (pa) de molde/de barra: Bread (sandwich bread/baguette)

Rosquilla: Hard doughnut

Sandwich, tostado: White bread sandwich, toasted

Tortilla española (truita de patata): Potato omelet

Tostada (torrada) con aceite y tomate: Toasted bread with olive oil and tomato

SPANISH RESTAURANTS

While Spain's tapas bars offer small plates throughout the afternoon and evening, formal restaurants have a standard à la carte menu, serve generous portions (no tapas), and start their service much later than the American norm. But many eateries blur the distinction between a bar and a restaurant, boasting both a bar and some sit-down tables in the back or outside on the *terraza*. These more-casual places are likely to serve *raciones* (described later) rather than bite-size tapas or restaurant entrées.

Don't expect "My name is Carlos and I'll be your waiter to-night" cheery service. Service is often *serio*—it's not friendly or unfriendly...just white-shirt-and-bow-tie proficient.

At both restaurants and bars, smoking is banned in enclosed public spaces.

Ordering: While menus at formal restaurants are generally broken down by courses or categories, more casual eateries (and tapas bars) may feature dishes served in portions called *raciones* (*racions* in Catalan), or the smaller half-servings, *media-raciones* (*mitja racions* in Catalan). Smaller tapas plates are more commonly served at bars than at sit-down restaurants.

Typically, couples or small groups can share a few *raciones*, making this an economical way to eat and a great way to explore the regional cuisine. Ordering *media-raciones* may cost a bit more per ounce, but you'll broaden your tasting experience. Two people can fill up on four *media-raciones*.

For a budget meal in a restaurant, try a *plato combinado* (combination plate), which usually includes portions of one or two main dishes, a vegetable, and bread for a reasonable price; or the *menú del día* (menu of the day), a substantial three- to four-course meal that comes with a drink.

Menus in Barcelona feature lots of seafood, along with local favorites such as *fideuà* (a kind of Catalan paella made with seafood and a thin, flavor-infused noodle), and *arròs negre*—black rice cooked in squid ink. Spanish chefs love garlic and olive oil—many dishes are soaked in both. You'll see plenty of *jamón* (ham) on menus, though it is more typically Spanish than Catalan (for more on *jamón*, see the next page). The cheapest meal is a simple *bocadillo de jamón* (ham sandwich on a baguette), sold virtually everywhere.

Spanish cuisine can be a bit heavy for Americans more accustomed to salads, fruits, and grains. Good vegetarian and lighter options exist, but you'll have to seek them out. The secret to getting your veggies at restaurants is to order two courses. For your first course, resist the cheese-and-ham appetizers and instead choose the creamed vegetable soup, *parrillada de verduras* (sautéed vegetables), *ensalada mixta*, or other green option. (Spaniards rarely eat only a salad, so salads tend to be small and simple—just lettuce, tomatoes, and maybe olives and tuna.) Main courses such as meats or fish are usually served with only a garnish, not a side of vegetables.

Tipping: At restaurants with table service, a service charge is generally included in the bill (*servicio incluido; servei inclós* in Catalan). Most Spaniards tip nothing or next to nothing on top of that, but if you like to tip for good service, give up to 5 percent extra. If service is not included (*servicio no incluido; servei no inclós* in Catalan), you could tip up to 10 percent. At most places, you can leave the tip on the table. But if you're eating at an outdoor café, hand the tip to your server to avoid having it swiped by a passerby. It's best to tip in cash even if you pay with credit card. Otherwise the tip may never reach your server.

Sampling *Jamón*

The staple of Spanish cuisine, *jamón* (hah-MOHN) is prosciutto-like ham that's dry-cured and aged. It's generally sliced thin (right off the hock) and served at room temperature.

Jamón can be eaten straight, served in a *bocadillo* sandwich, or mixed into a wide variety of dishes. Bars proudly hang ham hocks from the rafters as part of the decor. *Jamón* is more than a food—it's a way of life. Spaniards treasure memories of Grandpa at Christmas, thinly carving a *jamón* supported in a special ham-hock holder, just as Americans savor the turkey carving at Thanksgiving.

Like connoisseurs of fine wine, Spaniards debate the merits of different breeds of pigs, the pig's diet, and the quality of the curing. The two major types of ham are *jamón serrano,* from white pigs whose meat is cured in the mountains of Spain, and the higher-quality *jamón ibérico,* made with the back legs of black-hooved pigs. These Iberian *pata negra* ("black foot") pigs are said to be fatter and happier (slaughtered much later than other pigs), thereby producing particularly fine ham. Another indication of quality is *de bellota,* which means the pig was raised on acorns. *Jamón ibérico de bellota* is, to Spanish eaters, as good as it gets: free-range, black-footed pigs who ate only acorns. (Ham labeled *Jamón ibérico de recebeo* or *de cebo* is still good, but comes from pigs that are grain-fed.)

To sample this delicacy without the high price tag you'll find in bars and restaurants, go to the local market. Ask for 100 grams of top-quality ham (*cien gramos de jamón ibérico;* a *ración* will run about €8), and enjoy it as a picnic with red wine and a baguette. To round out the picnic, also pick up 100 grams each of *salchichón* (salami), *chorizo* (spicy sausage), and *manchego* or *cabrales* cheese, along with some olives and pickles.

TAPAS BARS

Tapas are small portions of seafood, salads, meat-filled pastries, deep-fried tasties, and other delicious bites, typically costing €5-10 a plate. You can eat well any time of day in tapas bars. Some are sit-down, while others are more stand-up.

Chasing down a particular bar for tapas nearly defeats the purpose and spirit of tapas—they are impromptu. Just drop in at any lively place. There is nothing wrong with ordering a tapa or two to

start before deciding whether to
stay at the same bar or move on.
Part of the joy of eating at tapas
bars is turning it into a mobile
feast, visiting two or three bars
during a single meal.

I'll be blunt: The authentic tapas experience can be in-
timidating. It generally involves
elbowing up to a bar crowded
with pushy locals, squinting at
a hand-scrawled monolingual

chalkboard menu, and trying to order from a brusque bartender.

Basque-style bars, which have an array of tapas platters already laid out, are popular in Barcelona and can be less daunting,
as you simply point to or grab what you want (see page 182). These
tapas are called *pintxos* (or *pinchos*). Note that Barcelona's tapas bars
generally don't provide a free, small tapa with the purchase of a
drink as may be found elsewhere in Spain.

Where to Sit: Locate the price list (often posted in fine type
on a wall somewhere) to see the menu options and price tiers. Eating and drinking at a bar is usually cheapest if you sit or stand at
the counter *(barra)*. You may pay a little more to sit at a table *(mesa*
or *salón)* and still more for an outdoor table *(terraza)*. Traditionally,
tapas are served at the bar, and *raciones* (and *media-raciones*) are
served at tables, where food can be shared "family style." You may
be obligated to order *raciones* if sitting at a table.

It's bad form to order food at the bar, then take it to a table. If
you're standing and a table opens up, it's OK to move as long as you
signal to the waiter; anything else you order will be charged at the
higher *mesa/salón* price. In the right place, a quiet snack and drink
on a terrace on a town square is well worth the extra charge. But
the cheapest seats sometimes get the best show. Sit at the bar and
study your bartender—he's an artist.

Bars can be extremely crowded with locals, and nonnative
speakers can find it hard to get in an order—or even find a place
to sit. You'll have more room, and get better service, by showing up before the local crowd. Try to be there by 13:30 for lunch,
and 20:00-20:30 for dinner. For less competition at the bar, go on
Monday and Tuesday (but check first to make sure they're open).

Ordering: To figure out what you want, read the posted
or printed menu. Use the "Tapas Menu Decoder," later, to sort
through your options. You can also look around to see what appeals on other patrons' plates. Sometimes a few selections are displayed under glass at the counter. Handwritten signs that start out

"Hay" mean "Today we have," as in *"Hay caracoles"* ("Today we have snails").

When you're ready to order, be assertive or you'll never be served. Your bartender isn't a "waiter," in any sense. He's not there to patiently help you sort through your options—he wants to take your order, period. Hang back and observe before order-

ing. To grab his attention, say *"por favor"* (please; *"si us plau"* in Catalan); you can also say *"per-dona"* (excuse me; *"perdó"* in Catalan). Then quickly rattle off what you'd like (pointing to other people's food if necessary). To ask for the price of a dish, say *"¿Cuánto cuesta una tapa?"* (*"Quant costa una tapa?"* in Catalan).

Some bars push *raciones* (dinner plate-sized) portions rather than smaller tapas (saucer-sized). Ask for the smaller tapas portions or a *media-ración* (listed as ½ *ración* on a menu), though some bars simply don't serve anything smaller than a *ración*.

If you're undecided about what to order, it's fun to try an in-expensive sampler plate. Ask for *una tabla de canapés variados* to get a plate of various little open-faced sandwiches. Or ask for a *surtido de* (an assortment of) *charcutería* (a mixed plate of meat) or *queso* (cheese). *Un surtido de jamón y queso* means a plate of different hams and cheeses. Order bread and two glasses of red wine on the right square, and you've got a romantic (and €10) dinner for two.

Paying and Tipping: Don't worry about paying until you're ready to leave (they're keeping track of your tab). To get the bill, ask: *"¿La cuenta?"* (*"El compte?"* in Catalan). If you order a meal at a counter—as you often will when sampling tapas at a bar—there's no need to tip (though if you buy a few tapas, you can round up the bill a few small coins).

TYPICAL DESSERTS

In Spain, desserts are often an afterthought. Fruit is considered a dessert (and generally not served for breakfast or as a snack—except to kids). Dessert menus usually have a fruit option. Here are a few items you may see on Spanish menus:

Arroz con leche: Rice pudding

Brazo de gitano: Sponge cake filled with butter cream; literally "Gypsy's arm"

Crema catalana: Catalan take on crème brûlée (Barcelona)

Flan de huevo: Flan (crème caramel)

Tapas Menu Decoder

You can often just point to what you want on the menu or in the display case, say *por favor* (Spanish) or *si us plau* (Catalan), and get your food, but these words will help. I've given both Spanish and Catalan (in parentheses), when applicable.

a la parrilla (a la graella)	barbecued
a la plancha (a la planxa)	grilled (on a flat-top griddle)
aceitunas	olives
al ajillo	with garlic
albóndigas (mandonguilles)	spiced meatballs with sauce
almejas (cloïsses), a la marinera	clams, in paprika sauce
almendras (ametlles)	almonds (usually fried)
anchoas (anxoves)	cured anchovies (salted or in oil)
atún (tonyina)	tuna
bacalao (bacallà)	cod
bocadillo (entrepà/bocata)	basic baguette sandwich
bombas (bombes)	fried meat-and-potato ball
boquerones (seitons), en vinagre	fresh anchovies, marinated in olive oil, vinegar, and garlic
brocheta (broqueta)	shish kebab (on a stick)
calamares fritos (calamars fregits)	fried squid rings
canapé	tiny open-faced sandwich
caracoles (cargols)	small tree snails (May-Sept)
champiñones (xampinyons)	mushrooms
charcutería (xarcuteria)	cured meats
chorizo (xoriço)	spicy sausage
croquetas (croquetes)	croquettes—breaded, fried béchamel with fillings like ham
empanadillas (crestes)	meat or seafood hand pies
ensaladilla rusa (ensalada russa)	potato salad with lots of mayo, peas, and carrots
espinacas, con garbanzos (espinacs, amb cigrons)	spinach, with garbanzo beans
flauta	sandwich on flute-thin baguette
frito (fregit)	fried
fuet	Catalan salami-like sausage
gambas, con cáscara (gambes, amb closca)	shrimp, with shell
gazpacho	cold tomato soup
guiso (estofat)	stew
jamón (pernil)	cured ham (like prosciutto)
judías verdes (mongetes tendres)	green beans

lomo (llom)	pork tenderloin
mejillones (musclos)	mussels
merluza (lluç)	hake (whitefish)
montadito	tapa on bread, mini sandwich in Sevilla
morcilla (botifarró)	blood sausage
morro	pig snout
paella	saffron rice dish with seafood and meat
pan (pa)	bread
patatas bravas (patates braves)	fried potatoes with spicy tomato sauce
pescaditos fritos (peixet fregit)	assortment of fried little fish
pimiento, relleno (pebrot, farcit)	pepper, stuffed
pimientos de Padrón (pebrots de Padró)	fried small green peppers, a few of which are jalapeño-hot
pinchos morunos (pintxos morunos)	skewer of spicy lamb or pork
pisto (samfaina)	mixed sautéed vegetables
pollo, alioli (pollastre, all i oli)	chicken, with garlic olive-oil sauce
pulga, pulguita, or pepito (entrepà petit)	a small baguette sandwich
pulpo (pop)	octopus
queso (formatge)	cheese
queso manchego (formatge manxec)	classic Spanish sheep-milk cheese
rabas (rabes)	squid rings
rabo de toro (cua de bou)	bull's-tail stew (fatty and tender)
revuelto, de setas (remenat, de bolets)	scrambled eggs, with wild mushrooms
salchichón (llonganissa)	salami-like sausage
sandwich (sandvitx)	American-style sandwich on soft bread
sardinas (sardines)	sardines
surtido de (assortit)	assortment of
tabla serrana (assortit d'embotits i formatges)	hearty plate of meat and cheese
tortilla española (truita de patata)	potato omelet
tortilla de jamón/queso (truita de pernil/formatge)	potato omelet with ham/cheese
variado de fritos (peixet fregits)	mix of various fried fish

Fruta de la estación/fruta de temporada: Fruit in season
Helados, variados: Ice cream, various flavors
Queso: Cheese
Mel i mató: Light Catalan cheese with honey (Barcelona)
Músic de fruits secs: Selection of nuts and dried fruits (Barcelona)
Torrijas: Sweet fritters, like French toast, available during Lent and Easter

SPANISH DRINKS
Alcoholic Beverages

I encourage visiting several different tapas bars in a night, but ordering a drink at each can add up (both for your head and your wallet). To avoid getting drunk too quickly, consider ordering a *caña* (small beer), a shandy-type drink called a *clara* (beer mixed with lemon soda, or with a Sprite-style soda), or a *tinto de verano* (red wine with lemon soda), which Spaniards generally prefer to sangria (a punch of red wine with fruit pieces). For more phrases, see the lists, below.

Wine and Spirits: Spain is one of the world's leading producers of grapes, and that means lots of excellent wine: both red *(tinto)* and white *(blanco).* Major wine regions include Valdepeñas (both red and white wines made in Don Quixote country south of Toledo); Penedès (cabernet-style wines from near Barcelona); Rioja (spicy, lighter reds from the tempranillo grape, from the high plains of northern Spain); and Ribera del Duero (reds from northwest of Madrid).

For a basic glass of red wine, you can order *un tinto.* But for quality wine, ask for *un crianza* (old), *un reserva* (older), or *un gran reserva* (oldest). For good, economical wine, I always ask for *un crianza*—for little or no extra money than a basic *tinto,* you'll get a quality, aged wine. *Cava* is Spain's answer to Champagne. For nondrinkers, *mosto* is excellent Spanish grape juice that hasn't been fermented into its alcoholic cousin.

Here are some common terms (the phrases in parentheses are Catalan):

Afrutado (afruitat): Fruity
Amontillado, fino, manzanilla: Rich, dry sherries
Cava: Sparkling wine (Spanish champagne)
Chato (gotet): Small glass of house wine
Dulce (dolç): Sweet
Jerez (Xerès): Sherry (fortified wine from Jerez)
Mosto (most): Nonalcoholic grape juice—red or white

Mucho cuerpo (molt cos): Full-bodied

¡Salud! (Salut!): Cheers!

Seco (sec): Dry

Tinto de verano: Red wine, usually with lemon soda and often a slice of lemon (similar to sangria)

Un blanco (un vi blanc): Small glass of house white wine

Un crianza (un criança): Glass of nicely aged, quality wine

Un tinto (un vi negre): Small glass of house red wine

Un reserva/gran reserva: Much higher-quality (and more expensive) wine

Vermut (vermú): Vermouth (sweet, generally)

Vino blanco (vi blanc): White wine

Vino rojo (vi negre): Red wine

Beer: Spaniards rarely ask for a "cerveza." Instead, they usually specify a size or type when ordering, such as a *caña* (small beer; see the list of words below for other sizes).

Most places just have the standard local beer—a light lager—on tap. In Barcelona, local options include Estrella Damm, the trendier Moritz, and various craft beers. One of the most-appreciated Spanish lagers is Estrella Galicia (no relation to Estrella Damm; comes from Galicia region).

Caña (canya): Small glass of draft beer (a little less than a half pint)

Cerveza (cervesa): Beer

Clara con limón/casera: Shandy—small beer with lemonade/soda

Doble: Typically double a *caña*, but size can vary

Mediana: Bottle of beer (nearly three-quarters of a pint)

Quinto: Small bottle of beer (same amount as a *caña*—a little less than half a pint)

Sidra: Dry cider that's a bit more alcoholic than beer

Tubo: Tall, thin glass of beer (just over half a pint)

Una cerveza sin (una cervesa sense): Nonalcoholic beer

Water, Coffee, and Other Nonalcoholic Drinks

If ordering mineral water in a restaurant, request a *botella de agua grande* (big bottle), as they like to push the more profitable small bottles. For a glass of tap water, specify *un vaso de agua del grifo.* If you insist on *del grifo,* not *embotellada* (bottled), you'll usually get it. Note that tap water in Barcelona does not taste particularly good, and some places would rather not serve it to their customers (though it is safe to drink).

Spain's bars often serve fresh-squeezed orange juice. For something completely different, try the sweet and milky *horchata,* traditionally made from *chufa* (a.k.a. tigernuts or earth almonds).

Here are some common beverage phrases (where applicable, I've provided the Catalan translation in parentheses):

Agua con/sin gas (aigua amb/sin gas): Water with/without bubbles

Botella de agua grande: Big bottle of water
Café con leche (café amb llet): Espresso with hot milk
Café solo: Shot of espresso, sometimes with hot water added
Cortado (tallat): Espresso with a little milk
Horchata (orxata): Cold, sweet, creamy drink, similar to rice or
    almond milk
Leche: Milk
Jarra de agua: Pitcher of tap water
Refresco (Refresc): Soft drink (common brands are Coca-Cola,
    Fanta—*limón* or *naranja,* and Schweppes—*limón* or *tónica*)
Té/infusion: Tea
Vaso de agua del grifo (got d'aigua de l'aixeta): Glass of tap water
Zumo: Juice
Zumo de naranja, natural: Orange juice, freshly squeezed

Staying Connected

One of the most common questions I hear from travelers is, "How can I stay connected in Europe?" The short answer is: more easily and cheaply than you might think.

The simplest solution is to bring your own device—mobile phone, smartphone, tablet, or laptop—and use it just as you would at home (following the tips described below, such as getting an international plan or connecting to free Wi-Fi whenever possible). Another option is to buy a European SIM card for your US mobile phone. Or you can use European landlines and computers to connect. Each of these options is described below, and more details are at www.ricksteves.com/phoning. For a very practical one-hour talk covering tech issues for travelers, see www.ricksteves.com/mobile-travel-skills.

USING A MOBILE PHONE IN EUROPE

Here are some budget tips and options.

Sign up for an international plan. To stay connected at a lower cost, sign up for an international service plan through your carrier. Most providers offer a simple bundle that includes calling, messaging, and data. Your normal plan may already include international coverage (T-Mobile's does).

Before your trip, call your provider or check online to confirm that your phone will work in Europe, and research your provider's international rates. Activate the plan a day or two before you leave, then remember to cancel it when your trip's over.

Use free Wi-Fi whenever possible. Unless you have an unlimited-data plan, save most of your online tasks for Wi-Fi (pronounced *wee-fee* in Spanish). You can access the internet, send texts, and even make voice calls over Wi-Fi.

Hurdling the Language Barrier

Imported from the Old World throughout the New, Spanish is the most widely spoken Romance language in the world. With its straightforward pronunciation, Spanish is also one of the simplest languages to learn. However, Barcelona adds its own twist: About 75 percent of Barcelonans speak Catalan, the language unique to the Catalunya region. Though all Barcelonans speak Spanish, many locals insist on speaking Catalan first.

Many Barcelonans—especially those in the tourist trade—speak English. Still, many people don't. Locals visibly brighten when you know and use some key Catalan or Spanish words (see "Catalan Survival Phrases" and "Spanish Survival Phrases" in the appendix). Learn the key phrases. Travel with a phrase book, particularly if you want to interact with the Spanish people. You'll find that doors open more quickly and with more smiles when you can speak a few words of the language.

Most accommodations in Europe offer free Wi-Fi, but some—especially expensive hotels—charge a fee. Many cafés (including Starbucks and McDonald's) have free hotspots for customers; look for signs offering it and ask for the Wi-Fi password when you buy something. You'll also often find Wi-Fi at TIs, city squares, major museums, public-transit hubs, airports, and aboard trains and buses.

Minimize the use of your cellular network. Even with an international data plan, wait until you're on Wi-Fi to Skype, download apps, stream videos, or do other megabyte-greedy tasks. Using a navigation app such as Google Maps over a cellular network can take lots of data, so do this sparingly or use the app in offline mode.

Limit automatic updates. By default, your device constantly checks for a data connection and updates apps. It's smart to disable these features so your apps will only update when you're on Wi-Fi. Also change your device's email settings from "auto-retrieve" to "manual" (or from "push" to "fetch").

When you need to get online but can't find Wi-Fi, simply turn on your cellular network just long enough for the task at hand. When you're done, avoid further charges by manually turning off data roaming or cellular data (either works) in your device's Settings menu. Another way to make sure you're not accidentally using data roaming is to put your device in "airplane" mode (which also disables phone calls and texts).

Use Wi-Fi calling and messaging apps. Skype, WhatsApp, FaceTime, and Google+ Hangouts are great for making free or low-cost calls or sending texts over Wi-Fi. With an app installed on your phone, tablet, or laptop, you can log on to a Wi-Fi network and contact friends or family who use the same service. If you buy

PRACTICALITIES

How to Dial

International Calls

Whether phoning from a US landline or mobile phone, or from a number in another European country, here's how to make an international call. I've used one of my recommended Barcelona hotels as an example (tel. 933-181-312).

Initial Zero: Drop the initial zero from international phone numbers—except when calling Italy.

Mobile Tip: If using a mobile phone, the "+" sign can replace the international access code (for a "+" sign, press and hold "0").

US/Canada to Europe

Dial 011 (US/Canada international access code), country code (34 for Spain), and phone number.

▶ To call the Barcelona hotel from home, dial 011-34-933-181-312.

Country to Country Within Europe

Dial 00 (Europe international access code), country code, and phone number.

▶ To call the Barcelona hotel from Germany, dial 00-34-933-181-312.

Europe to the US/Canada

Dial 00, country code (1 for US/Canada), and phone number.

▶ To call from Europe to my office in Edmonds, Washington, dial 00-1-425-771-8303.

Domestic Calls

To call within Spain (from one Spanish landline or mobile phone to another), simply dial the phone number.

▶ To call the Barcelona hotel from Madrid, dial 933-181-312.

credit in advance, with some of these services you can call or send a text anywhere for just pennies per minute.

Some apps, such as Apple's iMessage, will use the cellular network if Wi-Fi isn't available: To avoid this possibility, turn off the "Send as SMS" feature.

USING A EUROPEAN SIM CARD

With a European SIM card, you get a European mobile number and access to cheaper rates than you'll get through your US carrier. This option works best for those who want to make a lot of local calls, need a local phone number, or want faster connection speeds than their US carrier provides. It's simple: You buy a SIM card in Europe to replace the SIM card in your "unlocked" US phone or

Toll and Toll-Free Calls: Numbers starting with 900 are toll-free, but those beginning with 901 or 902 have per-minute charges. International rates apply to US toll-free numbers dialed from Spain—they're not free.

More Phoning Help: See www.howtocallabroad.com.

European Country Codes		Ireland & N. Ireland	353 / 44
Austria	43	Italy	39
Belgium	32	Latvia	371
Bosnia-Herzegovina	387	Montenegro	382
Croatia	385	Morocco	212
Czech Republic	420	Netherlands	31
Denmark	45	Norway	47
Estonia	372	Poland	48
Finland	358	Portugal	351
France	33	Russia	7
Germany	49	Slovakia	421
Gibraltar	350	Slovenia	386
Great Britain	44	Spain	34
Greece	30	Sweden	46
Hungary	36	Switzerland	41
Iceland	354	Turkey	90

PRACTICALITIES

tablet (check with your carrier about unlocking it) or buy a basic cell phone in Europe.

SIM cards are sold at department-store electronics counters, some newsstands, and vending machines. If you need help setting it up, buy one at a mobile-phone shop (you may need to show your passport). Costing about $10, SIM cards usually include prepaid calling credit, with no contract and no commitment. Expect to pay $20-40 more for a SIM card with a gigabyte of data.

There are no roaming charges for EU citizens using a domestic SIM card in other EU countries. Theoretically, providers don't have to offer Americans this "roam-like-at-home" pricing, but most do. To be sure, buy your SIM card at a mobile-phone shop and ask if non-EU citizens also have roam-like-at-home pricing.

When you run out of credit, you can top up your SIM card

Tips on Internet Security

Make sure that your device is running the latest versions of its operating system, security software, and apps. Next, ensure that your device and key programs (like email) are password- or passcode-protected. On the road, use only secure, password-protected Wi-Fi hotspots. Ask the hotel or café staff for the specific name of their Wi-Fi network, and make sure you log on to that exact one.

If you must access your financial info online, use a banking app rather than accessing your account via a browser. A cellular connection is more secure than Wi-Fi. Avoid logging onto personal finance sites on a public computer.

Never share your credit-card number (or any other sensitive information) online unless you know that the site is secure. A secure site displays a little padlock icon, and the URL begins with *https* (instead of the usual *http*).

at newsstands, tobacco shops, mobile-phone stores, or many other businesses (look for your SIM card's logo in the window), or possibly online.

WITHOUT A MOBILE PHONE

It's possible to travel in Europe without a mobile device. You can make calls from your hotel, and check email or browse websites using public computers.

Most **hotels** charge a fee for placing calls—ask for rates before you dial. You can use a prepaid international phone card (*tarjeta telefónica con código,* usually available at newsstands, tobacco shops, and train stations) to call out from your hotel. Dial the toll-free access number, enter the card's PIN code, then dial the number.

You'll only see **public pay phones** in a few post offices and train stations. Most don't take coins but instead require insertable phone cards, which you can buy at a newsstand, convenience store, or post office. Except for emergencies, they're not worth the hassle.

Most hotels have **public computers** in their lobbies for guests to use; otherwise you can find them at public libraries (ask your hotelier or the TI for the nearest location). On a European keyboard, use the "Alt Gr" key to the right of the space bar to insert the extra symbol that appears on some keys. If you can't locate a special character (such as @), simply copy and paste it from a web page.

MAIL

You can mail one package per day to yourself worth up to $200 duty-free from Europe to the US (mark it "personal purchases"). If you're sending a gift to someone, mark it "unsolicited gift." For details, visit www.cbp.gov, select "Travel," and search for "Know Before You Go." The Spanish postal service works fine, but for quick transatlantic delivery (in either direction), consider services such as DHL (www.dhl.com).

Transportation

If your trip will cover more of Spain than just Barcelona, you may need to take a long-distance train or bus, rent a car, or fly. I give some specifics on trains, buses, car rentals, and flights here. For more detailed information on transportation throughout Europe, see www.ricksteves.com/transportation.

TRAINS
Renfe (the acronym for the Spanish national train system) used to mean "Really Exasperating, and Not For Everyone," but it has moved into the 21st century. For information and reservations, visit Renfe.com or dial Renfe's national number (tel. 912-320-320) from anywhere in Spain. You'll find tips on buying tickets later in this section.

Types of Trains
Spain categorizes trains this way:

The high-speed train called the **AVE** (AH-vay, stands for *Alta Velocidad Española*) whisks travelers between Madrid and Barce-

lona in less than three hours, and Barcelona and Sevilla in six hours. AVE trains are priced according to their time of departure. Peak hours *(punta)* are most expensive, followed by *llano* and *valle* (quietest and cheapest times). Tickets for these trains typically go on sale two months in advance. AVE trains are almost entirely covered by the Eurail pass (but book ahead). Tickets generally go on sale 60-62 days in advance.

A related high-speed train, the **Alvia,** runs on AVE lines but can switch to Iberian tracks without stopping.

Avant trains are also high-speed—typically about as fast as AVE—but designed for shorter distances. They also tend to be cheaper than AVE, even on the same route. If you're on a tight budget, compare your options before buying.

The **Talgo** is fast, air-conditioned, and expensive, and runs on AVE rails. **Intercity** and **Media Distancia** trains fall just behind

Public Transportation Routes in Iberia

Talgo in speed, comfort, and expense. **Cercanías** and **Rodalies** are commuter trains for big-city workers and small-town tourists. Trains get more expensive as they pick up speed, but all are cheaper per mile than their northern European counterparts. Spain loves to name trains, so you may encounter types of trains not listed here. The names Euromed and Altaria also indicate faster trains that require reservations. These can cost significantly less than AVE on

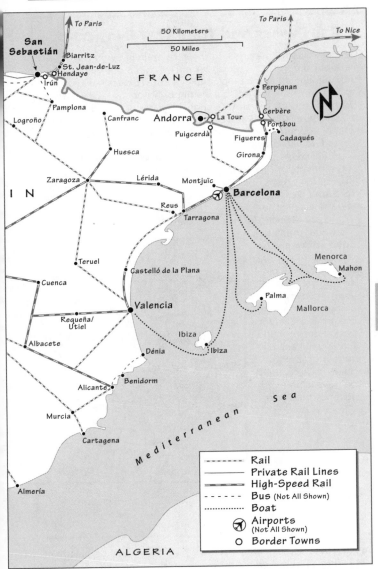

some routes. Ask about the travel time for each option when buying your tickets.

Salidas means "departures," and *llegadas* is "arrivals." On train schedules, "LMXJVSD" stands for the days of the week in Spanish, starting with Monday. A train that runs "LMXJV-D" doesn't run on Saturdays. *Laborables* can mean Monday through Friday or Monday through Saturday.

Overnight Trains: The main overnight train routes remain-

Rail Passes and Train Travel in Spain

A Eurail Spain Pass lets you travel by train in Spain for three to eight days (consecutively or not) within a one-month period. Spain can also be included in a Eurail Select Pass, which allows travel in two to four neighboring countries over two months, and it's covered (along with most of Europe) by the classic Eurail Global Pass. Discounted rates are offered for two or more people traveling together and for youths (ages 12-27). Up to two kids (ages 4-11) can travel free with each adult.

Rail passes are best purchased outside Europe (through travel agents or Rick Steves' Europe). For more on the ins and outs of rail passes, including prices, download my **free guide to Eurail Passes** (www.ricksteves.com/rail-guide) or go to www.ricksteves.com/rail.

If you're taking just a couple of train rides, look into buying individual **point-to-point tickets**. Use this map to add up approximate pay-as-you-go fares for your itinerary, and compare that to the price of a rail pass. Keep in mind that significant discounts on point-to-point tickets may be available with advance purchase.

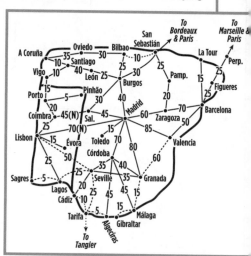

Map shows approximate costs, in US$, for one-way, second-class tickets on faster trains

ing in Spain are between Madrid, San Sebastián, or Salamanca and Lisbon (and the *only* train service on these international routes) and between Madrid or Barcelona and Galicia (A Coruña, Ferrol, or Vigo).

Overnight trains (and buses) are usually less expensive and slower than the daytime rides, not counting any sleeper fees. Most overnight trains have berths and beds that you can rent (not included in the cost of your train ticket or rail pass). A sleeping berth *(litera)* costs extra, with the price depending on the route and type of compartment. To get the space you want, it's smart to reserve in advance, even from home. Travelers with first-class reservations are entitled to use comfortable "Intercity" lounges in train stations in Spain's major cities.

Rail Passes

The single-country Eurail Spain Pass can be a reasonable value if you'll be taking three or more long train rides in Spain. But otherwise, it's unlikely to save you money. A rail pass doesn't provide much hop-on convenience in Spain, since most trains require paid seat reservations. (Passholders can't reserve online through Renfe but can reserve at www.raileurope.com before leaving the US.) Buying individual train tickets in advance or as you go in Spain can be less expensive, and gives you better access to seat reservations (which are limited for rail-pass holders). For most trains, point-to-point ticket prices already include seat reservations when required (for instance, for fast trains and longer distances).

Renfe also offers its own "Renfe Spain Pass," which works entirely differently. It counts trips instead of calendar days, requires reservations to be made in chronological order, and is sold only on their website.

If your trip extends beyond Spain, consider the Eurail Select Pass for two to four neighboring countries. Two-country options are France-Spain, Portugal-Spain, or Italy-Spain. Even if you have a rail pass, use buses when they're more convenient and direct than the trains. Remember to reserve ahead for the fast AVE trains and overnight journeys.

For more detailed advice on figuring out the smartest rail-pass options for your train trip, visit www.ricksteves.com/rail.

Buying Train Tickets

Trains can sell out, so it's smart to buy your tickets at least a day in advance, even for short rides. You have several options for buying train tickets: at the station or a Renfe office, at a travel agency, online, or by phone. Since station ticket offices can get very crowded, most travelers will find it easiest to go to a travel agency, most of which charge a nominal service fee.

At the Station: You will likely have to wait in a line to buy your ticket (and pay a five percent service fee). First find the correct line—at bigger stations, there might be separate windows for short-distance, long-distance, advance, and "today" *(para hoy)* tickets. You might have to take a number—watch others and follow their lead. While clerks accept regular US credit cards, Renfe ticket machines only take chip-and-PIN credit cards.

You can also buy tickets or reservations at the Renfe offices located in more than 100 city centers. These are more central and multilingual—and also less crowded and confusing—than most train stations.

Travel Agency: The easiest choice for most travelers is to buy tickets at an English-speaking travel agency (look for a train sticker in agency windows). El Corte Inglés department stores (with locations in most Spanish cities) often have handy travel agencies inside.

Online: Although the Renfe website is useful for confirming schedules and prices, you cannot dependably buy tickets online unless you use PayPal or have a European credit card. (The website often rejects attempts to use a US card.) But with patience and enough Spanish language skill, you may nab an online discount of up to 60 percent (limited seats at these prices, available two weeks to two months ahead of travel). Online vendors based in the US include Raileurope.com and Petrabax.com (expect a small fee from either).

By Phone: You can purchase your ticket by phone (tel. 912-240-202), then pick it up at the station by punching your confirmation code *(localizador)* into one of the machines. Discounts up to 40 percent off are offered a week or more ahead by phone (and at stations).

You can also reserve tickets by phone, then buy them at the station, which you must do a few days before departure (at a ticket window, usually signed *"venta anticipada"*). You can't pay for reserved tickets at the station on your day of travel.

BUSES

Spain's bus system is confusing (www.movelia.es is a good place to begin researching schedules and carriers). There are a number of different bus companies (though usually clustered within one building), sometimes running buses to the same destinations and using the same transfer points. If you have to transfer, make sure to look for a bus with the same name/logo as the company you bought the ticket from. Larger stations have a consolidated information desk with all schedules. In smaller stations, check the destinations and schedules posted on each office window. (If your connection requires a transfer to another company's bus in a different city, don't count on getting help from the originating clerk to figure out the onward connection.) Bus service on holidays, Saturdays, and especially Sundays can be less frequent.

If you arrive in a city by bus and plan to leave by bus, spend some time at the station upon arrival to check your departure options and buy a ticket in advance if necessary (and possible). If you're downtown, need a ticket, and the bus station isn't central, save time by asking at the TI about travel agencies that sell bus tickets.

You can (and most likely will be required to) stow your luggage under the bus. Your ticket comes with an assigned seat; if the bus is full, you should take that seat, but if it's uncrowded, most people just sit where they like. Buses are nonsmoking.

Drivers and station personnel may not speak English. Buses generally lack WCs, but they stop every two hours or so for a break (usually 15 minutes, but can be up to 30). Drivers announce how long the stop will be, but if in doubt, ask the driver, "How many minutes here?" *("¿Cuántos minutos aquí?")*. Listen for the bus horn as a final call before departure.

TAXIS AND RIDE-BOOKING SERVICES

Most European taxis are reliable and cheap. In many cities, two people can travel short distances by cab for little more than the cost of bus or subway tickets.  If you like ride-booking services such as Uber, their apps usually work in Europe just like they do in the US: Request a car on your mobile phone (connected to Wi-Fi or data), and the fare is automatically charged to your credit card. However, as of this writing, Uber is available only in Madrid and Barcelona.

RENTING A CAR

It's cheaper to arrange most car rentals from the US, so research and compare rates before you go. Most of the major US rental agencies (including Avis, Budget, Enterprise, Hertz, and Thrifty) have offices throughout Europe. Also consider the two major Europe-based agencies, Europcar and Sixt. Consolidators such as Auto Europe/Kemwel (AutoEurope.com—or the sometimes cheaper AutoEurope.eu) compare rates at several companies to get you the best deal.

Wherever you book, always read the fine print. Ask about add-on charges—such as one-way drop-off fees, airport surcharges, or mandatory insurance policies—that aren't included in the "total price."

Rental Costs and Considerations

Figure on paying roughly $250 for a one-week rental for a basic compact car. Allow extra for supplemental insurance, fuel, tolls, and parking. To save money on fuel, request a diesel car. Be warned that international trips—say, picking up in Madrid and dropping

PRACTICALITIES

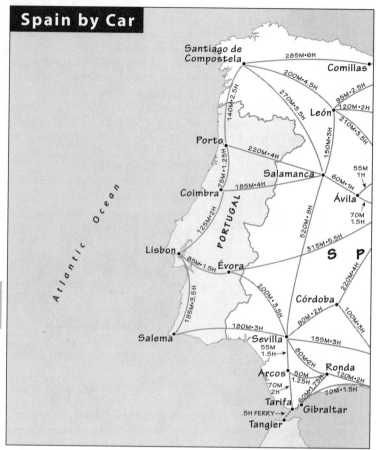

Spain by Car

Santiago de Compostela
Comillas
285M·6H
200M·4.5H
95M·2.5H
270M·5.5H
León
120M·2H
140M·2.5H
210M·3.5H
150M·3H
Porto
220M·4H
Salamanca
55M 1H
75M·1.25H
185M·4H
60M·1H
Coimbra
Ávila
PORTUGAL
70M 1.5H
125M·2H
520M·9H
Atlantic Ocean
Lisbon
315M·5.5H   S   P
85M·1.5H   Évora
220M·4H
200M·3.5H
Córdoba
195M·3.5H
90M·2H
100M·3H
Salema
180M·3H
Sevilla
155M·3H
55M 1.5H
60M·2H
Arcos
50M
Ronda
70M 2H
1.25H·1.5H
120M·2H
60M·1.75H
70M·1.5H
Tarifa
Gibraltar
.5H FERRY→
Tangier

off in Lisbon—can be expensive if the rental company assesses a drop-off fee for crossing a border.

Manual vs. Automatic: Almost all rental cars in Europe are manual by default—and cars with stick shift are generally cheaper. If you need an automatic, request one in advance. When selecting a car, don't be tempted by a larger model, as it won't be as maneuverable on narrow, winding roads or when squeezing into tight parking lots.

Age Restrictions: Some rental companies impose minimum and maximum age limits. Young drivers (25 and under) and seniors (69 and up) should check the rental policies and rules section of car rental websites. If you're considered too young or too old, look into leasing (covered later), which has less stringent age restrictions.

Choosing Pick-up/Drop-off Locations: Always check the hours of the location you choose: Many rental offices close from

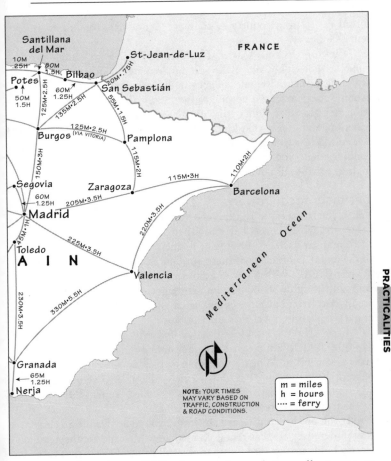

Santillana del Mar
10M·.25H
80M·1.5H
Potes
50M·1.5H
Bilbao
St-Jean-de-Luz
5H
San Sebastián
60M·1.25H
20M·.75H
55M·1.5H
FRANCE
125M·2.5H
135M·2.5H
Burgos (VIA VITORIA)
125M·2.5H
Pamplona
150M·3H
115M·2H
Segovia
60M·1.25H
Zaragoza
115M·3H
205M·3.5H
1.10M·2H
Barcelona
Madrid
220M·3.5H
Toledo
225M·3.5H
A   I   N
Valencia
230M·3.5H
330M·5.5H
Mediterranean Ocean
Granada
65M·1.25H
Nerja

NOTE: YOUR TIMES MAY VARY BASED ON TRAFFIC, CONSTRUCTION & ROAD CONDITIONS.

m = miles
h = hours
.... = ferry

PRACTICALITIES

midday Saturday until Monday morning and, in smaller towns, at lunchtime.

When selecting an office, plug the address into a mapping website to confirm the location. A downtown site is generally cheaper—and might seem more convenient than the airport. But pedestrianized and one-way streets can make navigation tricky when returning a car at a big-city office or urban train station. Wherever you select, get precise details on the location and allow ample time to find it.

Have the Right License: If you're renting a car in Spain, bring your driver's license. You're also technically required to have an International Driving Permit—an official translation of your license (sold at AAA offices for about $20 plus the cost of two passport-type photos; see www.aaa.com). While that's the letter of the law, I generally rent cars without having this permit. How this is enforced varies from country to country: Get advice from your car rental company.

Picking Up Your Car: Before driving off in your rental car, check it thoroughly and make sure any damage is noted on your rental agreement. Rental agencies in Europe tend to charge for even minor damage, so be sure to mark everything. Find out how your car's gearshift, lights, turn signals, wipers, radio, and fuel cap function, and know what kind of fuel the car takes (diesel vs. unleaded). When you return the car, make sure the agent verifies its condition with you. Some drivers take pictures of the returned vehicle as proof of its condition.

Car Insurance Options

When you rent a car in Europe, the price typically includes liability insurance, which covers harm to other cars or motorists—but not the rental car itself. To limit your financial risk in case of damage to the rental, choose one of these options: Buy a Collision Damage Waiver (CDW) with a low or zero deductible from the car-rental company (roughly 30-40 percent extra), get coverage through your credit card (free, but more complicated), or get collision insurance as part of a larger travel-insurance policy.

Basic **CDW** costs $15–30 a day and typically comes with a $1,000-2,000 deductible, reducing but not eliminating your financial responsibility. When you reserve or pick up the car, you'll be offered the chance to "buy down" the deductible to zero (for an additional $10–30/day; this is sometimes called "super CDW" or "zero-deductible coverage").

If you opt for **credit-card coverage,** you must decline all coverage offered by the car-rental company—which means they can place a hold on your card for up to the full value of the car. In case of damage, it can be time-consuming to resolve the charges. Before relying on this option, quiz your card company about how it works.

If you're already purchasing a **travel-insurance policy** for your trip, adding collision coverage can be an economical option. For example, Travel Guard (www.travelguard.com) sells affordable renter's collision insurance as an add-on to its other policies; it's valid everywhere in Europe except the Republic of Ireland, and some Italian car-rental companies refuse to honor it, as it doesn't cover you in case of theft.

For more on car-rental insurance, see www.ricksteves.com/cdw.

Leasing

For trips of three weeks or more, consider leasing (which automatically includes zero-deductible collision and theft insurance). By technically buying and then selling back the car, you save money on taxes and insurance. Leasing provides you a brand-new car with unlimited mileage and a 24-hour emergency assistance program. You can lease for as few as 21 days to as long as five and a half months. Car leases must be arranged from the US. One of several companies offering affordable lease packages is Auto Europe.

Navigation Options

If you'll be navigating using your phone or a GPS unit from home, remember to bring a car charger and device mount.

Your Mobile Phone: The mapping app on your phone works fine for navigation in Europe, but for real-time turn-by-turn directions and traffic updates, you'll need mobile data access. And driving all day can burn through a lot of very expensive data. The economical workaround is to use map apps that work offline. By downloading in advance from Google Maps, Apple Maps, Here WeGo, or Navmii, you can still have turn-by-turn voice directions and maps that recalibrate even though they're offline.

You must download your maps before you go offline—and it's smart to select large regions. Then turn off your data connection so you're not charged for roaming. Call up the map, enter your destination, and you're on your way. Even if you don't have to pay extra for data roaming, this option is great for navigating in areas with poor connectivity.

GPS Devices: If you want the convenience of a dedicated GPS unit, consider renting one with your car ($10-30/day). These units offer real-time turn-by-turn directions and traffic without the data requirements of an app. The unit may come loaded only with maps for its home country; if you need additional maps, ask. Also make sure your device's language is set to English before you drive off.

A less expensive option is to bring a GPS device from home. Be sure to buy and install the European maps you'll need before your trip.

Maps and Atlases: Even when navigating primarily with a mobile app or GPS, I always make it a point to have a paper map. It's invaluable for getting the big picture, understanding alternate routes, and filling in when my phone runs out of juice. The free maps you get from your car-rental company usually don't have enough detail. It's smart to buy a better map before you go, or pick one up at European gas stations, bookshops, newsstands, and tourist shops.

Driving

Driving in rural Spain is great—traffic is sparse and roads are generally good. But a car is a pain in big cities. Drive defensively. If you're involved in an accident, you will be in for a monumental

headache. Spaniards love to tailgate. Don't take it personally; let impatient drivers pass you and enjoy the drive. In smaller towns, following signs to *Centro Ciudad* will get you to the heart of things.

Freeways and Tolls: Spain's freeways come with tolls, but save huge amounts of time. Each toll road *(autopista de peaje)* has its own pricing structure, so tolls vary. Near some major cities, you must prepay for each stretch of road you drive; on other routes, you take a ticket where you enter the freeway, and pay when you exit. Payment can be made in cash or by credit or debit card (credit-card-only lanes are labeled *"vias automáticas"*; cash lanes are *"vias manuales"*).

Because road numbers can be puzzling and inconsistent, be ready to navigate by city and town names. Memorize some key road words: *salida* (exit), *de sentido único* (one way), *despacio* (slow), and *adelantamiento prohibido* (no passing). Mileage signs are in kilometers (see the appendix for a conversion formula into miles).

Road Rules: Seatbelts are required by law. Children under 12 must ride in the back seat, and children up to age 3 must have a child seat. You must put on a reflective safety vest any time you get out of your car on the side of a highway or unlit road (most rental-car companies provide one—check when you pick up the car). Those who use eyeglasses are required by law to have a spare pair in the car.

Be aware of typical European road rules; for example, many countries require headlights to be turned on at all times, and nearly all forbid handheld mobile-phone use. In Europe, you're not allowed to turn right on a red light unless a sign or signal specifically authorizes it, and

AND LEARN THESE ROAD SIGNS

Speed Limit (km/hr)	Yield	No Passing	End of No Passing Zone
One Way	Intersection	Main Road	Expressway
Danger	No Entry	Cars Prohibited	All Vehicles Prohibited
No Through Road	Restrictions No Longer Apply	Yield to Oncoming Traffic	No Stopping
Parking	No Parking	Customs or Toll Road	Peace

on expressways it's illegal to pass drivers on the right. You should also stay in the right lane unless you are passing. Ask your car-rental company about these rules, or check the "International Travel" section of the US State Department website (www.travel.state.gov, search for your country in the "Country Information" box, then click "Travel and Transportation").

Traffic Cops: Watch for traffic radars and expect to be stopped for a routine check by the police (be sure your car-insurance form is up to date). Small towns come with speed traps and corruption. Tickets, especially for foreigners, are issued and paid for on the spot. Insist on a receipt *(recibo)*, so the money is less likely to end up in the cop's pocket.

Fuel: Gas and diesel prices are controlled and the same everywhere—about $6 a gallon for gas and $5.50 a gallon for diesel. Unleaded gas *(gasolina sin plomo)* is either *normal* or *super*. Note that diesel is called *diesel* or *gasóleo*—pay attention when filling your tank.

Theft: Choose parking places carefully. Stow valuables in the trunk during the day and leave nothing worth stealing in the car overnight. While you should avoid parking lots with twinkly asphalt, thieves break car windows anywhere. If your car's a hatchback, take the trunk cover off at night so thieves can look in without breaking in. Try to make your car look locally owned by hiding the "tourist-owned" rental-company decals and putting a local newspaper in your front or back window. Parking attendants all over Spain holler, *"Nada en el coche"* ("Nothing in the car"). And they mean it. Ask your hotelier for advice on parking. In cities you can park safely but expensively in guarded lots.

FLIGHTS

To compare flight costs and times, begin with a travel search engine: Kayak.com is the top site for flights to and within Europe, easy-to-use Google Flights has price alerts, and Skyscanner.com includes many inexpensive flights within Europe.

Flights to Europe: Start looking for international flights about four to six months before your trip, especially for peak-season travel. Depending on your itinerary, it can be efficient and no more expensive to fly into one city and out of another. If your flight requires a connection in Europe, see our hints on navigating Europe's top hub airports at www.ricksteves.com/hub-airports.

Flights Within Europe: Flying between European cities has become surprisingly affordable. Before buying a long-distance train or bus ticket, first check the cost of a flight on one of Europe's airlines, whether a major carrier or a no-frills outfit like EasyJet and Ryanair. Be aware of the potential drawbacks of flying with a discount airline: nonrefundable and nonchangeable tickets, mini-

PRACTICALITIES

mal customer service, time-consuming treks to secondary airports, and stingy baggage allowances. To avoid unpleasant surprises, read the small print about the costs for "extras" such as reserving a seat, checking a bag, or checking in and printing a boarding pass.

Flying to the US and Canada: Because security is extra tight for flights to the US, be sure to give yourself plenty of time at the airport. It's also important to charge your electronic devices before you board because security checks may require you to turn them on (see www.tsa.gov for the latest rules).

Resources from Rick Steves

Begin Your Trip at RickSteves.com

My mobile-friendly **website** is *the* place to explore Europe in preparation for your trip. You'll find thousands of fun articles, videos, and radio interviews; a wealth of money-saving tips for planning your dream trip; travel news dispatches; a video library of my travel talks; my travel blog; my latest guidebook updates (www.ricksteves. com/update); and my free Rick Steves Audio Europe app. You can also follow me on Facebook and Twitter.

Our **Travel Forum** is a well-groomed collection of message boards, where our travel-savvy community answers questions and shares their personal travel experiences—and our well-traveled staff chimes in when they can be helpful (www.ricksteves.com/ forums).

Our **online Travel Store** offers bags and accessories that I've designed to help you travel smarter and lighter. These include my popular carry-on bags (which I live out of four months a year), money belts, totes, toiletries kits, adapters, guidebooks, and planning maps (www.ricksteves.com/shop).

Our website can also help you find the perfect **rail pass** for your itinerary and your budget, with easy, one-stop shopping for rail passes, seat reservations, and point-to-point tickets (www. ricksteves.com/rail).

Rick Steves' Tours, Guidebooks, TV Shows, and More

Small Group Tours: Want to travel with greater efficiency and less stress? We offer more than 40 itineraries reaching the best destinations in this book...and beyond. Each year about 25,000 travelers join us on about 1,000 Rick Steves bus tours. You'll enjoy great guides and a fun bunch of travel partners (with small groups of 24 to 28 travelers). You'll find European adventures to fit every vacation length. For all the details, and to get our tour catalog, visit www.ricksteves.com/tours or call us at 425/608-4217.

Books: *Rick Steves Barcelona* is just one of many books in my series on European travel, which includes country and city guidebooks, Snapshots (excerpted chapters from bigger guides), Pocket guides (full-color little books on big cities), "Best Of" guidebooks (condensed, full-color country guides), and my budget-travel skills handbook, *Rick Steves Europe Through the Back Door*. A more complete list of my titles—including phrase books, cruising guides, and more—appears near the end of this book.

TV Shows and Travel Talks: My public television series, *Rick Steves' Europe*, covers Europe from top to bottom with over 100 half-hour episodes—and we're working on new shows every year (watch full episodes at my website for free). Or, to raise your travel I.Q., check out the video versions of our popular classes (covering most European countries as well as travel skills, packing smart, cruising, tech for travelers, European art, and travel as a political act—www.ricksteves.com/travel-talks).

Radio: My weekly public radio show, *Travel with Rick Steves*, features interviews with travel experts from around the world. It airs on 400 public radio stations across the US, or you can hear it as a podcast. A complete archive of programs is available at www.ricksteves.com/radio.

Audio Tours on My Free App: I've produced dozens of free, self-guided audio tours of the top sights in Europe. For those tours and other audio content, get my free **Rick Steves Audio Europe app,** an extensive online library organized by destination. For more on my app, see page 6.

APPENDIX

Holidays and Festivals

This list includes selected festivals in Barcelona, plus national holidays observed throughout Spain. Many sights and banks close on  national holidays—keep this in mind when planning your itinerary. Before planning a trip around a festival, verify the dates with the festival website, the Spanish national tourist office (www.spain.info), or my "Upcoming Holidays and Festivals in Spain" web page (www.ricksteves.com/europe/spain/festivals). Also see the "City of Festivals" sidebar on page 26.

Be prepared for big crowds during these holiday periods: Holy Week (Semana Santa) and Easter weekend, Labor Day, Ascension, Pentecost weekend, Assumption weekend, Spanish National Day, Constitution Day, followed closely by the Feast of the Immaculate Conception—both the previous and following weekends may be busy, and Christmas and New Year's Day. Look out for any local holiday that falls on a Tuesday or Thursday—the Spanish will often take Monday or Friday off as well to have a four-day weekend.

Jan 1	New Year's Day
Jan 6	Epiphany (Día de los Reyes Magos)
Mid-Feb	Les Festes de Santa Eulàlia (parades, kid-friendly activities)
March/April	Holy Week: April 14-20, 2019; April 5-11, 2020
April	Easter and Easter Monday: April 21-22, 2019; April 12-13, 2020
April 23	El Día de Sant Jordi (St. George's Day, Barcelona's version of Valentine's Day)
May 1	Labor Day (closures)
May	Ascension: May 30, 2019; May 21, 2020
May	Pentecost and Whit Monday: May 9-10, 2019; May 31-June 1, 2020
May-Sept (Saturdays)	La Festa Catalana (local folk traditions)
June	Corpus Christi: June 20, 2019; June 11, 2020
June 23	Festival of St. John the Baptist (bonfires, fireworks)
June-Aug	Música als Parcs (jazz, classical music)
July	Grec Festival (dance, theater, and music)
Mid-Aug	Festes de Sant Roc (Barri Gòtic street festival)
Mid-Aug	Festa Major de Gràcia (music, dancing, food, and drink)
Aug 15	Assumption of Mary (religious festival)
Late Aug	St. Bartholomew Festival, Sitges (carnival, traditional Catalan entertainments)
Sept 23	St. Tecla Festival, Sitges (fireworks, castellers)
Late Sept	La Mercè Festival (fireworks, parades, music)
Oct 12	Spanish National Day
Nov 1	All Saints' Day
Dec 6	Constitution Day
Dec 8	Feast of the Immaculate Conception
Dec 13	Feast of Santa Lucía
Dec 25	Christmas
Dec 31	New Year's Eve

Books and Films

To learn more about Barcelona's past and present, check out a few of these books and films.

NONFICTION

Barcelona (Robert Hughes, 1992). This is an opinionated journey through the city's tumultuous history, with a focus on art and architecture. *Barcelona: The Great Enchantress* (2004) is a condensed version of Hughes' love song to his favorite city.

Barcelona: A Thousand Years of the City's Past (Felipe Fernandez-Armesto, 1992). A historical and artistic perspective on Barcelona, this book also details the tensions between the city and the rest of Spain.

The Battle for Spain (Antony Beevor, 2006). A prize-winning account of the disintegration of Spain in the 1930s, Beevor's work is the best overall history of the bloody civil war.

Discovering Spain: An Uncommon Guide (Penelope Casas, 1992). Casas, a well-known Spanish cookbook author, insightfully blends history, culture, and food in this personal guide.

Homage to Barcelona (Colm Toíbín, 1990). This rich history of Barcelona includes anecdotes from the author's time in the city.

Homage to Catalonia (George Orwell, 1938). Orwell writes a gripping account of his experiences in the Spanish Civil War fighting Franco's fascists.

Hotel Florida: Truth, Love, and Death in the Spanish Civil War (Amanda Vaill, 2014). In this popular history, Vaill reconstructs events of the Spanish Civil War through the letters, diaries, and photographs of the war correspondents who covered it.

Iberia (James Michener, 1968). Michener's tribute to Spain explores how the country's dark history created a contradictory and passionately beautiful land.

The New Spaniards (John Hooper, 2006). Hooper surveys all aspects of modern Spain, including its transition from dictatorship to democracy, its cultural traditions, and its changing society.

Travelers' Tales: Spain (Lucy McCauley, 1995). This collection of essays from numerous authors creates an appealing overview of Spain and its people.

FICTION

The Carpenter's Pencil (Manuel Rivas, 2001). The psychological cost of Spain's Civil War is at the heart of this unsentimental tale of a revolutionary haunted by his past.

Cathedral of the Sea (Ildefonso Falcones, 2006). A humble medieval *bastaixo* who toils to build the Church of Santa Maria del Mar gradually climbs the social ladder of medieval Barcelona.

The City of Marvels (Eduardo Mendoza, 1986). A young man rises from poverty to wealth and power in 1890s Barcelona.

For Whom the Bell Tolls (Ernest Hemingway, 1940). After covering the Spanish Civil War from Madrid, Hemingway wrote his iconic novel about an American volunteer fighting Franco's fascist forces.

Nada (Carmen Laforet, 1943). This semiautobiographical novel details the experiences of an orphaned university student in post-civil-war Barcelona.

The Queen's Vow (C. W. Gortner, 2012). The life and times of Queen Isabel are vividly re-created in this historical novel.

The Shadow of the Wind (Carlos Ruiz Zafón, 2005). This best-selling thriller is set in 1950s Barcelona; sequels include *The Angel's Game* and *The Prisoner of Heaven*.

Stories from Spain (Genevieve Barlow and William Stivers, 1999). Readers follow nearly 1,000 years of Spanish history in brief short stories printed in Spanish and English.

FILMS

Barcelona (1994). Two Americans try to navigate the Spanish singles scene and the ensuing culture clash.

Biutiful (2010). A black-market figure and father of two learns he has a terminal illness; this film follows him (Javier Bardem) to Barcelona's underground where he must tie up loose ends before his time runs out.

L'Auberge Espagnole (2002). This comedy-drama chronicles the loves and lives of European students sharing an apartment in Barcelona.

Manuale d'Amore (2005). The four episodes of this film follow the love stories of four couples, with Barcelona and Rome as backdrops.

The Mystery of Picasso (1956). Picasso is filmed painting from behind a transparent canvas, allowing a unique look at his creative process.

Salvador (2006). Barcelona is the backdrop in this story about the life of Salvador Puig Antich, an anarchist and bank robber executed by Franco in the 1970s.

Vicky Cristina Barcelona (2008). In this Woody Allen film, a macho Spanish artist (Javier Bardem) tries to seduce two American women when his stormy ex-wife (Penélope Cruz) suddenly re-enters his life.

Women on the Verge of a Nervous Breakdown (1988). This film, about a woman's downward spiral after a breakup, is one of several piquant Pedro Almodóvar movies about relationships in the post-Franco era. Others include *All About My Mother* (1999), *Talk to Her* (2002), *Volver* (2006), and *Broken Embraces* (2009).

Conversions and Climate

Numbers and Stumblers

- Europeans write a few of their numbers differently than we do. 1 = 1̸, 4 = 4̸, 7 = 7̸.
- In Europe, dates appear as day/month/year, so Christmas 2020 is 25/12/20.
- Commas are decimal points and decimals are commas. A dollar and a half is $1,50, one thousand is 1.000, and there are 5.280 feet in a mile.
- When counting with fingers, start with your thumb. If you hold up your first finger to request one item, you'll probably get two.
- What Americans call the second floor of a building is the first floor in Europe.
- On escalators and moving sidewalks, Europeans keep the left "lane" open for passing. Keep to the right.

Metric Conversions

A **kilogram** equals 1,000 grams (about 2.2 pounds). One hundred **grams** (a common unit at markets) is about a quarter-pound. One **liter** is about a quart, or almost four to a gallon.

A **kilometer** is six-tenths of a mile. To convert kilometers to miles, cut the kilometers in half and add back 10 percent of the original (120 km: 60 + 12 = 72 miles). One **meter** is 39 inches—just over a yard.

1 foot = 0.3 meter	1 square yard = 0.8 square meter
1 yard = 0.9 meter	1 square mile = 2.6 square kilometers
1 mile = 1.6 kilometers	1 ounce = 28 grams
1 centimeter = 0.4 inch	1 quart = 0.95 liter
1 meter = 39.4 inches	1 kilogram = 2.2 pounds
1 kilometer = 0.62 mile	32°F = 0°C

Clothing Sizes

When shopping for clothing, use these US-to-European comparisons as general guidelines (but note that no conversion is perfect).

Women: For pants and dresses, add 32 in Spain (US 10 = Spanish 42). For blouses and sweaters, add 8 for most of Europe (US 32 = European 40). For shoes, add 30-31 (US 7 = European 37/38).

Men: For shirts, multiply by 2 and add about 8 (US size 15 = European size 38). For jackets and suits, add 10. For shoes, add 32-34.

Children: Clothing is sized by height—in centimeters (2.5 inches = 1 cm), so a US size 8 roughly equates to 132-140. For shoes up to size 13, add 16-18, and for sizes 1 and up, add 30-32.

Barcelona's Climate

First line, average daily high; second line, average daily low; third line, average days without rain. For more detailed weather statistics for destinations in this book (as well as the rest of the world), check www.wunderground.com.

J	F	M	A	M	J	J	A	S	O	N	D
55°	57°	60°	65°	71°	78°	82°	82°	77°	69°	62°	56°
43°	45°	48°	52°	57°	65°	69°	69°	66°	58°	51°	46°
26	23	23	21	23	24	27	25	23	22	24	25

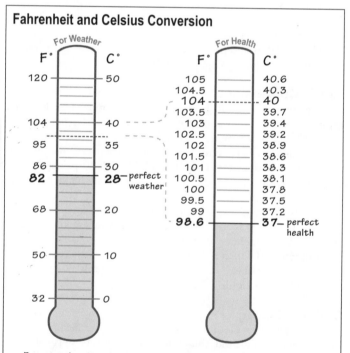

Fahrenheit and Celsius Conversion

Europe takes its temperature using the Celsius scale, while we opt for Fahrenheit. For a rough conversion from Celsius to Fahrenheit, double the number and add 30. For weather, remember that 28°C is 82°F—perfect. For health, 37°C is just right. At a launderette, 30°C is cold, 40°C is warm (usually the default setting), 60°C is hot, and 95°C is boiling. Your air-conditioner should be set at about 20°C.

Packing Checklist

Whether you're traveling for five days or five weeks, you won't need more than this. Pack light to enjoy the sweet freedom of true mobility.

Clothing

- ❏ 5 shirts: long- & short-sleeve
- ❏ 2 pairs pants (or skirts/capris)
- ❏ 1 pair shorts
- ❏ 5 pairs underwear & socks
- ❏ 1 pair walking shoes
- ❏ Sweater or warm layer
- ❏ Rainproof jacket with hood
- ❏ Tie, scarf, belt, and/or hat
- ❏ Swimsuit
- ❏ Sleepwear/loungewear

Money

- ❏ Debit card(s)
- ❏ Credit card(s)
- ❏ Hard cash (US $100-200)
- ❏ Money belt

Documents

- ❏ Passport
- ❏ Tickets & confirmations: flights, hotels, trains, rail pass, car rental, sight entries
- ❏ Driver's license
- ❏ Student ID, hostel card, etc.
- ❏ Photocopies of important documents
- ❏ Insurance details
- ❏ Guidebooks & maps

Toiletries Kit

- ❏ Basics: soap, shampoo, toothbrush, toothpaste, floss, deodorant, sunscreen, brush/comb, etc.
- ❏ Medicines & vitamins
- ❏ First-aid kit
- ❏ Glasses/contacts/sunglasses
- ❏ Sewing kit
- ❏ Packet of tissues (for WC)
- ❏ Earplugs

Electronics

- ❏ Mobile phone
- ❏ Camera & related gear
- ❏ Tablet/ebook reader/laptop
- ❏ Headphones/earbuds
- ❏ Chargers & batteries
- ❏ Phone car charger & mount (or GPS device)
- ❏ Plug adapters

Miscellaneous

- ❏ Daypack
- ❏ Sealable plastic baggies
- ❏ Laundry supplies: soap, laundry bag, clothesline, spot remover
- ❏ Small umbrella
- ❏ Travel alarm/watch
- ❏ Notepad & pen
- ❏ Journal

Optional Extras

- ❏ Second pair of shoes (flip-flops, sandals, tennis shoes, boots)
- ❏ Travel hairdryer
- ❏ Picnic supplies
- ❏ Water bottle
- ❏ Fold-up tote bag
- ❏ Small flashlight
- ❏ Mini binoculars
- ❏ Small towel or washcloth
- ❏ Inflatable pillow/neck rest
- ❏ Tiny lock
- ❏ Address list (to mail postcards)
- ❏ Extra passport photos

Spanish Survival Phrases

Spanish has a guttural sound pronounced like the J in Baja California. In the phonetics, the symbol for this clearing-your-throat sound is the italicized *h*.

English	Spanish	Pronunciation
Good day.	*Buenos días.*	**bweh**-nohs **dee**-ahs
Do you speak English?	*¿Habla Usted inglés?*	**ah**-blah oo-**stehd** een-**glays**
Yes. / No.	*Sí. / No.*	see / noh
I (don't) understand.	*(No) comprendo.*	(noh) kohm-**prehn**-doh
Please.	*Por favor.*	por fah-**bor**
Thank you.	*Gracias.*	**grah**-thee-ahs
I'm sorry.	*Lo siento.*	loh see-**ehn**-toh
Excuse me.	*Perdóne.*	pehr-**doh**-nay
(No) problem.	*(No) problema.*	(noh) proh-**bleh**-mah
Good.	*Bueno.*	**bweh**-noh
Goodbye.	*Adiós.*	ah-dee-**ohs**
OK.	*Vale.*	**bah**-lay
one / two	*uno / dos*	**oo**-noh / dohs
three / four	*tres / cuatro*	trehs / **kwah**-troh
five / six	*cinco / seis*	**theen**-koh / says
seven / eight	*siete / ocho*	see-**eh**-tay / **oh**-choh
nine / ten	*nueve / diez*	**nweh**-bay / dee-**ehth**
How much is it?	*¿Cuánto cuesta?*	**kwahn**-toh **kweh**-stah
Write it?	*¿Me lo escribe?*	may loh eh-**skree**-bay
Is it free?	*¿Es gratis?*	ehs **grah**-tees
Is it included?	*¿Está incluido?*	eh-**stah** een-kloo-**ee**-doh
Where can I buy / find...?	*¿Dónde puedo comprar / encontrar...?*	**dohn**-day **pweh**-doh kohm-**prar** / ehn-kohn-**trar**
I'd like / We'd like...	*Me gustaría / Nos gustaría...*	may goo-stah-**ree**-ah / nohs goo-stah-**ree**-ah
...a room.	*...una habitación.*	**oo**-nah ah-bee-tah-thee-**ohn**
...a ticket to ___.	*...un billete para ___.*	oon bee-**yeh**-tay **pah**-rah ___
Is it possible?	*¿Es posible?*	ehs poh-**see**-blay
Where is...?	*¿Dónde está...?*	**dohn**-day eh-**stah**
...the train station	*...la estación de trenes*	lah eh-stah-thee-**ohn** day **treh**-nehs
...the bus station	*...la estación de autobuses*	lah eh-stah-thee-**ohn** day ow-toh-**boo**-sehs
...the tourist information office	*...la oficina de turismo*	lah oh-fee-**thee**-nah day too-**rees**-moh
Where are the toilets?	*¿Dónde están los servicios?*	**dohn**-day eh-**stahn** lohs sehr-**bee**-thee-ohs
men	*hombres, caballeros*	**ohm**-brehs, kah-bah-**yeh**-rohs
women	*mujeres, damas*	moo-**heh**-rehs, **dah**-mahs
left / right	*izquierda / derecha*	eeth-kee-**ehr**-dah / deh-**reh**-chah
straight	*derecho*	deh-**reh**-choh
When do you open / close?	*¿A qué hora abren / cierran?*	ah kay **oh**-rah **ah**-brehn / thee-**ehr**-ahn
At what time?	*¿A qué hora?*	ah kay **oh**-rah
Just a moment.	*Un momento.*	oon moh-**mehn**-toh
now / soon / later	*ahora / pronto / más tarde*	ah-**oh**-rah / **prohn**-toh / mahs **tar**-day
today / tomorrow	*hoy / mañana*	oy / mahn-**yah**-nah

In a Spanish Restaurant

English	Spanish	Pronunciation
I'd like / We'd like...	Me gustaría / Nos gustaría...	may goo-stah-**ree**-ah / nohs goo-stah-**ree**-ah
...to reserve...	...reservar...	reh-sehr-**bar**
...a table for one / two.	...una mesa para uno / dos.	**oo**-nah **meh**-sah **pah**-rah **oo**-noh / dohs
Non-smoking.	No fumador.	noh foo-mah-**dohr**
Is this table free?	¿Está esta mesa libre?	eh-**stah** eh-stah **meh**-sah **lee**-bray
The menu (in English), please.	La carta (en inglés), por favor.	lah **kar**-tah (ehn een-**glays**) por fah-**bor**
service (not) included	servicio (no) incluido	sehr-**bee**-thee-oh (noh) een-kloo-**ee**-doh
cover charge	precio de entrada	**preh**-thee-oh day ehn-**trah**-dah
to go	para llevar	**pah**-rah yeh-**bar**
with / without	con / sin	kohn / seen
and / or	y / o	ee / oh
menu (of the day)	menú (del día)	meh-**noo** (dehl **dee**-ah)
specialty of the house	especialidad de la casa	eh-speh-thee-ah-lee-**dahd** day lah **kah**-sah
tourist menu	menú turístico	meh-**noo** too-**ree**-stee-koh
combination plate	plato combinado	**plah**-toh kohm-bee-**nah**-doh
appetizers	tapas	**tah**-pahs
bread	pan	pahn
cheese	queso	**keh**-soh
sandwich	bocadillo	boh-kah-**dee**-yoh
soup	sopa	**soh**-pah
salad	ensalada	ehn-sah-**lah**-dah
meat	carne	**kar**-nay
poultry	aves	**ah**-behs
fish	pescado	peh-**skah**-doh
seafood	marisco	mah-**ree**-skoh
fruit	fruta	**froo**-tah
vegetables	verduras	behr-**doo**-rahs
dessert	postre	**poh**-stray
tap water	agua del grifo	**ah**-gwah dehl **gree**-foh
mineral water	agua mineral	**ah**-gwah mee-neh-**rahl**
milk	leche	**leh**-chay
(orange) juice	zumo (de naranja)	**thoo**-moh (day nah-**rahn**-hah)
coffee	café	kah-**fay**
tea	té	tay
wine	vino	**bee**-noh
red / white	tinto / blanco	**teen**-toh / **blahn**-koh
glass / bottle	vaso / botella	**bah**-soh / boh-**teh**-yah
beer	cerveza	thehr-**beh**-thah
Cheers!	¡Salud!	sah-**lood**
More. / Another.	Más. / Otro.	mahs / **oh**-troh
The same.	El mismo.	ehl **mees**-moh
The bill, please.	La cuenta, por favor.	lah **kwehn**-tah por fah-**bor**
tip	propina	proh-**pee**-nah
Delicious!	¡Delicioso!	deh-lee-thee-**oh**-soh

For hundreds more pages of survival phrases for your trip to Spain, check out *Rick Steves' Spanish Phrase Book*.

Catalan Survival Phrases

Catalan may look similar to Spanish (*castellano*), but there are important variations in pronunciation. The letters **c** and **z** before vowels are pronounced as "s" (unlike the Spanish "th" sound). The letters **b**, **d**, **r**, or **t** at the end of a word are usually not pronounced (unless the final syllable is stressed). An **s** between two vowels sounds like a "z."

English	Catalan	Pronunciation
Hello.	*Hola.*	**oh**-lah
Do you speak English?	*¿Parles anglès?*	**par**-luhs ahn-**glays**
Yes. / No.	*Sí. / No.*	see / noh
I (don't) understand.	*(No) entenc.*	(noh) ahn-**tehnk**
Please.	*Si us plau.*	see oos plow
Thank you (very much).	*(Moltes) Gràcies.*	(**mohl**-tehs) **grah**-see-ehs
I'm sorry.	*Ho sento.*	oh **sehn**-too
Excuse me.	*Perdó.*	pehr-**doh**
(No) problem.	*(Cap) problema.*	(kahp) proh-**blay**-mah
Good.	*Bé.*	bay
Goodbye.	*Adéu.*	ah-**day**-oo
one / two / three	*uno / dos / tres*	**oo**-noo / dohs / trehs
four / five / six	*quatre / cinc / sis*	**kwah**-trah / seenk / sees
seven / eight	*set / vuit*	seht / **voo**-eet
nine / ten	*nou / deu*	**noh**-oo / **deh**-oo
How much?	*¿Quant és?*	kwahn ehs
Write it?	*¿M'ho escriu?*	moh ah-**skree**-oo
Is it free?	*¿És gratis?*	ehs **grah**-tees
Is it included?	*¿Està inclós?*	ah-**stah** in-**klohs**
Where can I find / buy...?	*¿On puc trobar / compar...?*	ohn pook troo-**bah** / koom-**prah**
I'd like / We'd like...	*Voldria / Voldríem...*	vool-**dree**-ah / vool-**dree**-ahm
...a room.	*...una habitació.*	**oo**-nah ah-bee-tah-see-**oh**
...a ticket to ___.	*...una entrada per___.*	**oo**-nah ahn-**trah**-dah pehr ___
Is it possible?	*¿És possible?*	ehs poh-**see**-blah
Where is...?	*¿On està...?*	ohn ah-**stah**
...the train station	*...l'estació del tren*	lah-stah-see-**oh** dahl trehn
...the bus station	*...l'estació d'autobuses*	lah-stah-see-**oh** dow-toh-**boo**-zehs
...the tourist information office	*...l'oficina de turisme*	loo-fee-**see**-nah deh too-**rees**-meh
Where are the toilets?	*¿On estan els serveis?*	ohn eh-**stahn** ehls sehr-**vays**
men / women	*homes / dones*	**oh**-mehs / **doh**-nehs
left / right	*esquerre / dreta*	ehs-**keh**-reh / **dreh**-tah
straight	*dret*	dreht
At what time does this open / close?	*¿A quina hora obre / tanca?*	ah **kwee**-nah **oh**-rah **oh**-brah / **tahn**-kah
Just a moment.	*Un moment.*	oon moo-**mehn**
now / soon / later	*ara / aviat / més tard*	**ah**-rah / ah-vee-**aht** / mehs tahr
today / tomorrow	*avui / demà*	ah-**voo**-ee / deh-**mah**
Long live Catalunya!	*¡Visca Catalunya!*	**vee**-skah kah-tah-**loon**-yah

In a Catalan Restaurant

English	Catalan	Pronunciation
I'd like / We'd like...	Voldria / Voldríem...	vool-**dree**-ah / vool-**dree**-ahm
...to reserve...	...reservar...	reh-zehr-**vah**
...a table for one / two.	...una taula per una / dues.	**oo**-nah **tow**-lah pehr **oo**-nah / doo-**ehs**
Is this table free?	¿Està lliure aquesta taula?	eh-**stah yoo**-rah ah-**kwehs**-tah **tow**-lah
The menu (in English), please.	La carta (en anglès), si us plau	lah **kar**-tah (ehn ahn-**glays**) see oos plow
service (not) included	servei (no) inclós	sehr-**vay**-ee (noh) in-**klohs**
cover charge	preu d'entrada	**preh**-oo dahn-**trah**-dah
to go	per emportar	pehr ehm-por-**tah**
with / without	amb / sense	ahm / **sehn**-seh
and / or	i / o	ee / oh
tapas (small plates)	tapes	**tah**-pahs
daily special	plat del dia	plah dahl **dee**-ah
tourist menu	menú turístic	mah-**noo** too-**ree**-steek
specialty of the house	especialitat de la casa	eh-spah-see-ah-lee-**tah** dah lah **kah**-zah
combination plate	plat combinat	plah koom-bee-**nah**
half portion	mitja porció	**meet**-yah poor-see-**oh**
appetizers	entrants	ehn-**trahns**
bread	pà	pah
cheese	formatge	foor-**mah**-jeh
sandwich	entrepà	ehn-trah-**pah**
soup	sopa	**soh**-pah
salad	amanida	ah-mah-**nee**-dah
meat	carn	karn
poultry	aviram	ah-vee-**rahm**
fish	peix	paysh
seafood	marisc	mah-**rees**
fruit	fruita	**froo**-ee-tah
vegetables	verdures	vehr-**doo**-rehs
dessert	postre	**poh**-streh
tap water	aigua (de l'aixeta)	**eye**-gwah (deh lah-**shay**-tah)
mineral water	aigua mineral	**eye**-gwah mee-nah-**rahl**
milk	llet	yeht
(orange) juice	suc (de taronja)	soo (dah tah-**rohn**-zhah)
coffee	cafè	kah-**feh**
tea	te	teh
wine	vi	vee
red / white	negre / blanc	**neh**-greh / blahnk
glass / bottle	copa / ampolla	**koh**-pah / ahm-**poy**-yah
beer	cervesa	sehr-**veh**-zah
Cheers!	¡Salut!	sah-**loo**
More. / Another.	Més. / Un altre.	mehs / oon **ahl**-treh
The same.	El mateix.	ahl mah-**taysh**
The bill, please.	El compte, si us plau.	ahl **kohmp**-teh see oos plow
tip	propina	proo-**pee**-nah
Delicious!	Boníssim!	boo-**nee**-zeem

INDEX

MAP INDEX

Start your trip at

Our website enhances this book and turns

Explore Europe

At ricksteves.com you can browse through thousands of articles, videos, photos and radio interviews, plus find a wealth of money-saving travel tips for planning your dream trip. And with our mobile-friendly website, you can easily access all this great travel information anywhere you go.

TV Shows

Preview the places you'll visit by watching entire half-hour episodes of Rick Steves' Europe (choose from all 100 shows) on-demand, for free.

your travel dreams into affordable reality

Radio Interviews

Enjoy ready access to Rick's vast library of radio interviews covering travel

tips and cultural insights that relate specifically to your Europe travel plans.

Travel Forums

Learn, ask, share! Our online community of savvy travelers is a great resource

for first-time travelers to Europe, as well as seasoned pros. You'll find forums on each country, plus travel tips and restaurant/hotel reviews. You can even ask one of our well-traveled staff to chime in with an opinion.

Travel News

Subscribe to our free Travel News e-newsletter, and get monthly updates from Rick on what's happening in Europe.

Audio Europe™

Rick's Free Travel App

Get your FREE **Rick Steves Audio Europe**™ app to enjoy…

- Dozens of self-guided tours of Europe's top museums, sights and historic walks
- Hundreds of tracks filled with cultural insights and sightseeing tips from Rick's radio interviews
- All organized into handy geographic playlists
- For Apple and Android

With Rick whispering in your ear, Europe gets even better.

Find out more at ricksteves.com

Pack Light and Right

Gear up for your next adventure at ricksteves.com

Light Luggage

Pack light and right with Rick Steves' affordable, custom-designed rolling carry-on bags, backpacks, day packs and shoulder bags.

Accessories

From packing cubes to moneybelts and beyond, Rick has personally selected the travel goodies that will help your trip go smoother.

Rick Steves has

Experience maximum Europe

Save time and energy

This guidebook is your independent-travel toolkit. But for all it delivers, it's still up to you to devote the time and energy it takes to manage the preparation and logistics that are essential for a happy trip. If that's a hassle, there's a solution.

Rick Steves Tours

A Rick Steves tour takes you to Europe's most interesting places with great

with minimum stress

guides and small groups of 28 or less. We follow Rick's favorite itineraries, ride in comfy buses, stay in family-run hotels, and bring you intimately

close to the Europe you've traveled so far to see. Most importantly, we take away the logistical headaches so you can focus on the fun.

Join the fun

This year we'll take thousands of free-spirited travelers—nearly half of them repeat customers— along with us on four dozen different itineraries, from Ireland to Italy to Athens. Is a Rick Steves tour the right fit for your travel dreams? Find out at ricksteves.com, where you can also request Rick's latest tour catalog. Europe is best experienced with happy travel partners. We hope you can join us.

See our itineraries at ricksteves.com

A Guide for Every Trip

BEST OF GUIDES

Full color easy-to-scan format, focusing on Europe's most popular destinations and sights.

Best of England
Best of Europe
Best of France
Best of Germany
Best of Ireland
Best of Italy
Best of Spain

COMPREHENSIVE GUIDES

City, country, and regional guides with detailed coverage for a multi-week trip exploring the most iconic sights and venturing off the beaten track.

Amsterdam & the Netherlands
Barcelona
Belgium: Bruges, Brussels,
  Antwerp & Ghent
Berlin
Budapest
Croatia & Slovenia
Eastern Europe
England
Florence & Tuscany
France
Germany
Great Britain
Greece: Athens & the Peloponnese
Iceland
Ireland
Istanbul
Italy
London
Paris
Portugal
Prague & the Czech Republic
Provence & the French Riviera
Rome
Scandinavia
Scotland
Spain
Switzerland
Venice
Vienna, Salzburg & Tirol

HE BEST OF ROME

e, Italy's capital, is studded with
an remnants and floodlit-fountain
es. From the Vatican to the Colos-
with crazy traffic in between, Rome
derful, huge, and exhausting. The
, the heat, and the weighty history

of the Eternal City where Caesars walked
can make tourists wilt. Recharge by taking siestas, gelato breaks, and after-dark
walks, strolling from one atmospheric
square to another in the refreshing evening air.

*Pantheon—which
dome until the
2,000 years old
over 1,500).*

*Athens in the Vat-
es the humanistic*

*diators fought
ther, entertaining*

*one ristorante.
at St. Peter's
riously.*

Rick Steves guidebooks are published by Avalon Travel,
an imprint of Perseus Books, a Hachette Book Group company.

POCKET GUIDES

Compact, full color city guides with the essentials for shorter trips.

Amsterdam
Athens
Barcelona
Florence
Italy's Cinque Terre
London
Munich & Salzburg

Paris
Prague
Rome
Venice
Vienna

SNAPSHOT GUIDES

Focused single-destination coverage.

Basque Country: Spain & France
Copenhagen & the Best of Denmark
Dublin
Dubrovnik
Edinburgh
Hill Towns of Central Italy
Krakow, Warsaw & Gdansk
Lisbon
Loire Valley
Madrid & Toledo
Milan & the Italian Lakes District
Naples & the Amalfi Coast
Normandy
Northern Ireland
Norway
Reykjavík
Sevilla, Granada & Southern Spain
St. Petersburg, Helsinki & Tallinn
Stockholm

CRUISE PORTS GUIDES

Reference for cruise ports of call.

Mediterranean Cruise Ports
Scandinavian & Northern European
Cruise Ports

Complete your library with...

TRAVEL SKILLS & CULTURE

Study up on travel skills and gain insight on history and culture.

Europe 101
Europe Through the Back Door
European Christmas
European Easter
European Festivals
Postcards from Europe
Travel as a Political Act

PHRASE BOOKS & DICTIONARIES

French
French, Italian & German
German
Italian
Portuguese
Spanish

PLANNING MAPS

Britain, Ireland & London
Europe
France & Paris
Germany, Austria & Switzerland
Ireland
Italy
Spain & Portugal

Credits

RESEARCHER

For help with this edition, Rick relied on...

Amanda Buttinger

Amanda came to Spain 20 years ago for what was to be a short adventure. But she's still there today, living with her husband and two energetic boys (the handsomest *chulapos* in Madrid). She maintains her American roots while enjoying *madrileño* and Spanish traditions, leading Rick Steves tours through Spain and the Basque Country, and researching guidebooks across Europe.

CONTRIBUTOR
Gene Openshaw

Gene has co-authored a dozen *Rick Steves* books, specializing in writing walks and tours of Europe's cities, museums, and cultural sights. He also contributes to Rick's public television series, produces tours for Rick Steves Audio Europe, and is a regular guest on Rick's public radio show. Outside of the travel world, Gene has co-authored *The Seattle Joke Book.* As a composer, Gene has written a full-length opera called *Matter*, a violin sonata, and dozens of songs. He lives near Seattle with his daughter, enjoys giving presentations on art and history, and roots for the Mariners in good times and bad.

Photo Credits

Avalon Travel
Hachette Book Group
1700 Fourth Street
Berkeley, CA 94710

Printed in Canada by Friesens.
First printing October 2018.

ISBN 978-1-63121-827-9
Fourth Edition

For the latest on Rick's talks, guidebooks, tours, public television series, and public radio
show, contact Rick Steves' Europe, 130 Fourth Avenue North, Edmonds, WA 98020,
425/771-8303, www.ricksteves.com, rick@ricksteves.com.

Rick Steves' Europe

Managing Editor: Jennifer Madison Davis
Assistant Managing Editor: Cathy Lu
Special Publications Manager: Risa Laib
Editors: Glenn Eriksen, Julie Fanselow, Tom Griffin, Katherine Gustafson, Suzanne Kotz,
    Rosie Leutzinger, Jessica Shaw, Carrie Shepherd
Editorial & Production Assistant: Megan Simms
Editorial Intern: Nola Peshkin
Researcher: Amanda Buttinger
Contributor: Gene Openshaw
Graphic Content Director: Sandra Hundacker
Maps & Graphics: David C. Hoerlein, Lauren Mills, Mary Rostad
Digital Asset Coordinator: Orin Dubrow

Avalon Travel

Senior Editor and Series Manager: Madhu Prasher
Editors: Jamie Andrade, Sierra Machado
Copy Editor: Patrick Collins
Proofreader: Jamie Real
Indexer: Claire Splan
Production & Typesetting: Krista Anderson, Lisi Baldwin, Rue Flaherty, Jane Musser
Cover Design: Kimberly Glyder Design
Maps & Graphics: Kat Bennett, Mike Morgenfeld

Let's Keep on Travelin'

Your trip doesn't need to end.

Follow Rick on social media!